GREAT AMERICAN

RAILROAD STORIES

75 YEARS OF *TRAINS* MAGAZINE

KALMBACH BOOKS

WAUKESHA, WISCONSIN

Editor's Note:
Over 75 years, the appearance of a magazine changes a great deal. You can see the evolution of TRAINS' magazine covers since 1940 as you travel through these pages. Accompanying each article is the cover of the issue in which it appeared.

While the articles in this collection have been reformatted, they are reprinted as they originally appeared. For easier reading, some elements of style, such as punctuation and spelling, have been made consistent. As the articles reflect the times they were written in, some language that now may be considered offensive was revised, but nothing was changed to alter any writer's intent.

Where possible, the stories are illustrated with their original photographs. When the artwork was not available, other representative photographs were substituted. To keep the focus on the writing (and to include more stories), fewer photos are featured.

Kalmbach Books
21027 Crossroads Circle
Waukesha, Wisconsin 53186
www.Kalmbach.com/Books

Published in 2014
18 17 16 15 14   1 2 3 4 5

Manufactured in China

Hardcover ISBN: 978-1-62700-184-7
Softcover ISBN: 978-1-62700-182-3
EISBN: 978-1-62700-183-0

Editors: Randy Rehberg, Jeff Wilson
Art Director: Tom Ford
Consulting Editors: Kevin P. Keefe, Robert S. McGonigal, Jim Wrinn

Cover photo: Sierra Railroad's Mikado 34 and Harriman cars are silhouetted east of Warnerville, California, on April 22, 1972. The photo was taken by Ted Benson, and it appeared in TRAINS June 1973.

Library of Congress Control Number: 2014942402

WAYBILLS

Preview isn't exactly the word for this issue of TRAINS. We can't hope in 8 pages and cover to give you a fair sample of anything but format. At any rate, you'll gain a little insight into this new monthly which starts in November.

TRAINS attempts to bring to the reporting of railroads and their ways the crisp journalistic technique of *Fortune*, the unending curiosity of the *National Geographic*. It never is dull with too much fact, always as live and nerve tingling as the sight of two Mikes cannonading up to the Moffat Tunnel with the *Exposition Flyer.*

Photographs are selected for suitability for reproduction as well as for interest to you. The halftone engravings are made by craftsmen who work not only with mechanical and chemical processes but with Art at their elbows. We pay more for this kind of plate, but the clarity of reproduction is worth it. Fine paper, high grade ink, and the best of presses enhance the printing of fine plates. TRAINS reproductions compare favorably with original photographic prints.

Articles in TRAINS are never too technical, always mindful of the fact that the average man who loves railroads is no trained mechanical or civil engineer, but too that he abhors unanswered questions. If you wonder what becomes of the ticket the conductor collects from you, about the development of particular locomotive types, how there are always cars enough on each passenger train even for seemingly unexpected stragglers, about hundreds of other angles of the railroad business from the intricacies of the timetable to the history and income and expenses of that one-Mogul branch that meanders off back of Red Oak Junction, then we've made TRAINS to order for you.

This column by Al Kalmbach appeared in a special preview issue prior to the publication of the magazine's first issue in November 1940. It featured several articles, photo essays, and the cover from the first issue.

CONTENTS

Selected Contributors

WALLACE W. ABBEY (1927-2014) studied journalism at the University of Kansas, served as TRAINS managing editor 1950-1954, and worked in railroad public relations at Soo Line, Milwaukee Road, and the Transportation Test Center.

WILLARD V. ANDERSON hired on with Al Kalmbach in 1936 and retired in 1979 as managing editor of *Model Railroader*. He served in several Kalmbach editorial positions, including a few years as editor of TRAINS. He died in 1989.

LUCIUS BEEBE (1902-1966), for 21 years the flamboyant *New York Herald Tribune* columnist, is credited with inventing the railroad book market in 1938 with his picture book *High Iron*. He went on to write 39 more books, 27 about railroads.

JIM BOYD (1941-2010) was born in Dixon, Ill., and worked briefly in television and as a field technician for GM's Electro-Motive Division before becoming the original editor of *Railfan* magazine in 1974. He served in the position until 1998.

JOHN R. CROSBY lived in Fort Wayne, Ind., and worked for three decades in engine service for the Pennsylvania Railroad, Penn Central, and Conrail. He has numerous first-person bylines in TRAINS and *Classic Trains*. He died in 1995.

GEORGE H. DRURY attended Bates College, went to work at Kalmbach Publishing Co. in 1972 as a copy editor, and retired in 1997 as librarian and senior editor for Kalmbach Books. He wrote numerous articles on rail travel in Europe. He died in 2013.

RON FLANARY, of Big Stone Gap, Va., is a prolific author, photographer, and railroad artist. He has numerous bylines in TRAINS, *Classic Trains*, and other enthusiast publications.

FRED W. FRAILEY is a columnist for TRAINS. A veteran journalist, he worked for the *Kansas City Star*, the *Chicago Sun-Times*, and *U.S. News & World Report* before completing his career as editor-in-chief of *Kiplinger's Personal Finance*.

MARK W. HEMPHILL was editor of TRAINS 2000-2004 and now is director of railroad consulting services for HDR Engineering. He is the author of *Union Pacific: Salt Lake Route* (Boston Mills Press, 1995).

DON L. HOFSOMMER is a retired professor of history at St. Cloud State University. He has written numerous books, including *The Southern Pacific 1901-1985* and *The Tootin' Louie: A History of the Minneapolis & St. Louis*.

J. DAVID INGLES is the senior editor of *Classic Trains* magazine. He came to TRAINS in 1971 from the sports desk of the *Illinois State Journal*. At TRAINS he held the positions of associate editor, managing editor, and editor 1987-1992.

JOEL JENSEN is a Nevada-based photographer whose work is represented in major galleries. His books include *Railroad Noir*, with Linda G. Neimann (Indiana University, 2010), and *Steam: An Enduring Legacy* (W. W. Norton, 2011).

A. C. KALMBACH (1910-1981) was born in Sturgeon Bay, Wis., and grew up in Milwaukee. A 1932 Marquette University graduate, he founded his company and *Model Railroader* magazine in 1934, followed by TRAINS in 1940.

KEVIN P. KEEFE is the vice president-editorial for Kalmbach Publishing Co. He was on the staff of TRAINS from 1987 to 2000, including eight years as editor. He studied journalism at Michigan State University.

E. W. KING JR. began his career on Norfolk & Western and later worked at Seaboard Coast Line, Rock Island, Chicago & North Western, and Canadian Pacific. He is the author of *The A: Norfolk & Western's Mercedes of Steam* (Pentrex, 1991).

DAVID P. MORGAN (1927-1990) was the editor of TRAINS magazine 1953-1987. A native of Georgia, he spent his teenage years in suburban Louisville, Ky., and began his journalism career in 1947 on a weekly newspaper in Taft, Texas.

DON PHILLIPS has been a Washington, D.C.-based columnist for TRAINS since 1977. He spent 19 years as a reporter for *The Washington Post*, mostly as a transportation writer, and later worked for the *International Herald Tribune*.

H. REID (1925-1992) was a Virginia native and a longtime newspaperman at the *Norfolk Virginian-Pilot*. He authored three books, including *The Virginian Railway* (Kalmbach Books, 1961).

PAUL D. SCHNEIDER is a writer and film producer in Los Angeles. He served on the staff of TRAINS 1990-1991 and later produced more than 25 On Location video documentaries for the magazine, many of them Telly Award winners.

WILLIAM BENNING STEWART is a veteran Indiana-based writer, especially on subjects related to Hoosier traction and the Monon Railroad. He is a retired corporate relations executive and speechwriter.

LINN H. WESTCOTT (1930-1980) was born in Los Angeles, attended Carleton College in Minnesota, and was one of A. C. Kalmbach's first employees. He served as editor of *Model Railroader* 1961-1977, and later was editor emeritus.

JOHN H. WHITE JR. is curator emeritus of transportation at the Smithsonian Institution. His *A History of the American Locomotive 1830-1880* (Johns Hopkins Press, 1968) is the definitive volume on 19th century steam.

JIM WRINN is the editor of TRAINS. A graduate of the University of North Carolina-Chapel Hill, he came to the magazine after a career in daily newspapers in his home state, including 18 years as a reporter and editor at the *Charlotte Observer*.

FOREWORD

From the moment he conceived of TRAINS magazine in 1940, founder and publisher A. C. Kalmbach put good writing at the forefront. He might have seemed an unlikely man of letters, given his background as a printer, model railroad publisher, and electrical engineering graduate (Marquette University, 1932). But Al Kalmbach had a passion for compelling journalism and good old-fashioned story-telling, especially about railroading, evident in the very first thing he wrote about his new magazine in a preview issue from October 1940 [and reprinted on page 3]: "Trains attempts to bring to the reporting of railroads and their ways the crisp journalistic technique of *Fortune*, the unending curiosity of the *National Geographic*. It never is dull with too much fact, always as live and nerve tingling as the sight of two Mikes cannonading up to the Moffat Tunnel with the *Exposition Flyer*."

As far as Al was concerned, the writing came first, ahead of the pictures, the maps, the statistics and all the other things that would distinguish the magazine in the decades to come. It was no small matter that the first feature in the first issue of TRAINS was by Lucius Beebe, the dean of New York high-society columnists. TRAINS would belong in the company of America's best magazines, Al figured, no matter what the circulation figures said.

That Al succeeded is evidenced by this wonderful anthology, marking the magazine's 75th anniversary even as it underscores the enduring appeal of railroading as grist for great writing. All the elements that Al intended to show-case in TRAINS are here: the passion for the subject displayed by professionals and enthusiasts alike, the independent journalism that has always set TRAINS apart among railroad periodicals, the gritty and gripping tales (some of them very tall!) of working railroaders, the often poetic evocations of a business rooted deeply in America's romantic past.

When it came to passion, and an ability to convey it, the publisher himself was among TRAINS' best writers. Self-taught as he might have been, Al Kalmbach could grab the reader with a direct, plain style. Consider this short excerpt from a story he wrote for the third issue, January 1941: "Under the vast dirtiness of the station shed there's a smoky, oily train smell. It's as distinctive—and to me, as pleasant—as the fresh smell of farmland in spring. Air pumps throb up ahead, men shout, mail and express trucks bump about, and steam traps hiss angrily. All about is an undercurrent of excitement, people saying good-bye, trainmen checking watches, enginemen eternally fondling their beasts."

With the establishment of TRAINS, Kalmbach was tapping into a long-established literary vein. In 1940, railroads were an overwhelming presence in American life, and had insinuated their way into the work of all sorts of writers. Trailblazing novelists of the early 20th century, notably Thomas Wolfe, often unspooled their plots against a backdrop of steam locomotives and passenger trains. Specialized writers such as Robert Self Henry, author of *This Fascinating Railroad Business*, established that there was a recognizable, enthusiastic market for good writing about the industry. So did Beebe, with his trailblazing and best-selling railroad picture books. With their short stories for *Railroad Magazine*, Harry L. Bedwell, E. S. Dellinger, and "Haywire Mac" represented the venerable tradition of old hands sitting around the caboose stove. Al Kalmbach had read and absorbed all this and more, feeding his ambition to have the new TRAINS provide a critical mass for the genre.

The writers in this book prove he was successful. They represent every strand of what has made TRAINS a great magazine. There is the vivid narrative journalism of seasoned reporters such as Fred W. Frailey and Wallace W. Abbey, the authoritative perspective of professional historians like Don L. Hofsommer and Smithsonian curator emeritus John H. White Jr., and the contributions of Ron Flanary and Jim Boyd, exhibiting the exuberance of the knowledgeable railfan. The pungent and often harrowing world of the working railroad man is brought to life by a number of contributors, ranging from the youthful perspective of Paul D. Schneider, an irreverent participant in the railroad game, to John R. Crosby, the literary star of locomotive engineers, to E. W. King Jr., chronicler of the Rock Island in chaos.

And all seven of the men who have led Trains as editor-in-chief have found their way into these pages.

Of course, there is one writer who stands above them all. When Al Kalmbach first hired David P. Morgan as an assistant editor in 1948, the publisher added "talent scout" to his long list of skill sets. Soon, in January 1953, Al showed he was a genius when Morgan took over as "The Editor." In the ensuing three decades-plus, Morgan, or "D. P. M." as his admirers would come to know and love him, nurtured a relationship between editor and reader that must stand as some sort of record in magazine publishing.

David mastered all the duties of a great editor, from rewrite to copy editor to picture editor to business manager. But it was as a writer that D. P. M. developed an everlasting bond with readers. Part hard-hitting reporter, part essayist, part pundit, even part poet, Morgan had a breathtaking mastery of his subject and the chops to convey it. None other than

Fred Frailey, a veteran of metro newspapers and national magazines, cites Morgan as his chief inspiration. Frailey proudly asserts, "I studied at the David P. Morgan School of Journalism." It's no surprise, then, that Morgan is an abiding presence in this book, with three pieces to showcase his astounding range, including his signature essay "Confessions of a Train-Watcher."

Morgan's influence on the writing in Trains went beyond the words themselves. Alone among railroad periodicals, the magazine treated its contributors as professionals—regardless of their backgrounds—and that served to cultivate their best work. Although the pay was modest, Trains authors were paid for their stories upon acceptance, via a standard writer's contract. Their work would be subjected to rigorous editing and fact-checking. Everyone was given a galley proof. Best of all, D. P. M. provided invaluable coaching. The entire experience often led the most accomplished

journalists to cite Morgan as a primary inspiration. "He influenced my writing style more than any other professional," says Don Phillips, longtime *Washington Post* reporter and Trains columnist.

As today's Trains celebrates its 75th anniversary, the magazine is as dedicated as ever to the proposition that the sprawling business of railroading merits great writing. The industry is more technical now, more impersonal, more remote, but over the past 20 years it has rebounded financially in spectacular fashion and continues to put an exciting imprint on the American landscape. By some measures, railroading is bigger than ever. All the more reason to keep alive Al Kalmbach's pledge of 1940, to offer Trains readers the "crisp journalistic technique" and the "unending curiosity" so splendidly displayed in these pages.

KEVIN P. KEEFE,
Vice President-Editorial
Kalmbach Publishing Co.

INTRODUCTION

I am about to usher you inside one of railroading's hallowed halls. On the following pages, you'll discover—or rediscover—some of the best stories to appear in Trains magazine.

It is like entering a giant roundhouse full of treasured locomotives. With anticipation, I unlock the door and motion for you to enter. Not only is the building itself impressive, but what you're about to find will thrill you as well. The atmosphere is different—the scent of valve oil

and the taste of coal soot linger in the air. Page by page, you'll find stories that are like locomotives—full of character and personality and each one unique.

Since 1940, Trains has printed thousands of outstanding stories that have transported many of us to railroads we'd never heard of and to places we thought we'd never venture. In my youth, Trains' authors took me on many such journeys and taught me so much about the exciting world of railroading. Through

them, I became interested in railroads that I had no business caring about. They allowed me to see a world of railroading beyond my own realm and made me curious to see what was around the next bend.

Enjoy your visit with the best writing from 75 years of Trains magazine.

JIM WRINN,
Editor
Trains magazine

Trains
NOVEMBER 25¢

November 1941

THE TRAVELING SALESMAN

Victor H. White

You've never heard of the Montana, Wyoming & Southern Railroad? You'll find it today in a Northern Pacific folder— 20 miles long, Bridger to Belfry and Belfry to Bear Creek.

Late one bright summer afternoon in 1923 I boarded at Bridger what was jokingly called a *Galloping Goose*, one of the earlier straight gasoline passenger cars and the most comfortable railroad coach I ever traveled in. I'm not poking any fun at the *Galloping Goose*. The back of it was rounded like the stern of a boat with a semicircular leather seat. This rear part was curtained. In good weather they rolled up the curtain and you rode in the open air. Sitting in the extreme rear when the car got going at a pretty good clip, the springs moved you up and down fully a foot. The rougher the roadbed, the more fun you had.

Twenty minutes after leaving Bridger we were in Belfry, mighty near the Wyoming line—as near, in fact, as the Montana, Wyoming & Southern ever came to using the Wyoming end of its name. It went, and I suppose still goes, into Belfry on a three-cornered track, like a huge wye about a half mile long on each of the three sides. You headed into Belfry station, then backed a half mile to the main line, then ahead again eight miles to Bear Creek.

Returning from Bear Creek, you are supposed to enter Belfry on the other side of the wye, stop at the station, back onto the main track, and go ahead 12 miles into Bridger. But that was not the way it was done.

A little shed at Bear Creek protected the *Galloping Goose* at night and served as repair shop when necessary. There was a small wye to turn the car around.

The first gasoline cars were ornery. If you got an engineer that could keep one percolating, you didn't argue with that rare mechanic. You let him run the railroad.

The Montana, Wyoming & Southern had such a man. I met him once—a young, slender, smiling fellow whom everyone instinctively liked. I forget his name, which, perhaps, is lucky, because he might not enjoy my squealing on him as I'm going to do.

The "Chief," as they called him, didn't see any sense in turning the *Galloping Goose* around twice. He ran it straight ahead into the shed at Bear Creek every night. In the morning he backed it down to the little passenger station with a

Montana, Wyoming & Southern Consolidation No. 12 joined the railroad's roster in 1924. The railroad's general manager at the time, William H. Bunney, took these photos, helping document the coal-hauling short line's equipment. *W. H. Bunney*

surprising disregard for the fine little wye that was made to turn things around.

You won't believe this, maybe, but the line is all down grade from Bear Creek to Belfry, and the engineer could lean out the window of his one-car train and see what was behind him about as well as what was ahead. He backed the train every day the full eight miles to Belfry and thus stood at the Belfry station ready to go straight ahead into Bridger. What was the use of turning around twice? The Chief said he had never been behind schedule one minute by doing it.

You say it's against rules. I mentioned that too. The Chief told me he had heard the same thing once or twice, and he grinned.

But that isn't all about this little railroad that I have such a friendly feeling for. Once in Belfry I decided suddenly to catch the one o'clock train for Bridger. I ran four blocks and found it already a block away, fast gathering speed. But the agent still stood on the platform. "Want to catch it?" he asked.

"I did want to," I admitted, a bit embarrassed.

Maybe you won't believe this either, but it happened. That agent jumped up and down on the platform, waved both hands and yelled at the top of his voice. A passenger on the open air veranda of the *Galloping Goose* saw him and yelled to someone farther ahead. Passenger passed the word forward to passenger until the news reached the engineer that someone was left behind.

If anyone connected with the Montana, Wyoming & Southern is listening, let me express my appreciation again. That train backed up and got me.

I met a shoe salesman in Butte who told me a story:

"Certain state laws," he said, "compel railroads to carry the weight of baggage allotted under a passenger's ticket on the same train he rides on himself.

"This happened in Illinois previous to 1920. I had five trunks of sample shoes and had to see one shoe dealer in a town halfway to Chicago. I purchased a ticket 20 minutes before a special-fare, all-Pullman flyer was due. This train carried no baggage, nothing larger than a suitcase which could be put in a rack or between the seats. I needed two of my trunks badly. They were within the weight limit on my ticket and I had a copy of the state law in my pocket. I sprung it on the station agent as soon as he had sold me the ticket.

" 'Sorry,' he said. 'There's no baggage car on No. __; there's no way we can take it.'

" 'You've got to take it!' I told him.

"He shook his head, but I could see he was worried. When the train came in, I refused to get on without my trunks. I defied them, good humoredly, but seriously enough, to leave me after selling me a ticket for first available transportation and at a premium rate. The *Limited* lost five minutes while we chewed the rag. The conductor looked at his watch, getting nervous. He was on the spot.

" 'Come on,' he said, 'let's get aboard.'

"The three of them—conductor, brakeman and station agent—heaved up my trunks of sample shoes, stood them on end in the vestibule of a Pullman. The train made up the 10 minutes lost, and the rest of my checked, prepaid baggage came through later on proper schedule. I had the two trunks I needed, took a nice order in the little town, and saved a day's time for my company."

On the Union Pacific one time I stopped the *Portland Limited* on the sage-brushed plains of Eastern Oregon. I got on at Baker with a ticket for Arlington, which is halfway down the Columbia

The early McKeen gasoline car was called the *Galloping Goose* and, along with the Consolidation, was in use on the MW&S about 1924. *W. H. Bunney*

River toward Portland. It was early September, end of the summer season, and the train was loaded with schoolteachers and tourists finishing vacations. The *Limited*, heavy with three extra Pullmans, lost time climbing the Blue Mountain grade east of Pendleton and came into that Western city of roundup fame two hours late.

This was one time I knew too much about railroads. From Pendleton to Arlington is only 80 miles. A train can't make up two hours in a two-hour run. It just so happens, however, that the Columbia River runs down hill and the Union Pacific runs beside it on a strip of perfect roadbed if there ever was such a thing. We couldn't possibly reach Arlington before 3 p.m.—but we did, at 2:23 to be exact, and, because this was impossible, I never thought of getting off until I saw *Arlington* on the west end of a station we were just leaving.

The *Portland Limited* sped two or three miles while I was thinking what to do and before I found the Pullman conductor catching 10 winks with his feet stretched comfortably across two seats in an adjoining sleeper.

There was no use to wake him. Three cars ahead I found the train conductor, showed him my ticket stub. "You carried me past my station," I told him.

"Sorry," he said sympathetically. "Best I can do is take you to The Dalles and provide passage back on No. 2 this evening."

"No," I insisted, "that won't do. I must catch No. 2 at Arlington for Baker this evening, else I'll lose a day's time."

"That's the only thing we can do. We can't back this train up." He looked at me incredulously, as if I expected him to.

"You can stop and let me off," I suggested. By then we were five or six miles from Arlington. "I can bum a ride on the highway, see my man in Arlington, and still make connections."

"But we'd be responsible for your safety," he objected.

I grinned. I was just a kid of 23 then and had a lot of confidence. "I know this country," I told him. "You're better off taking a chance on my safety than on my expenses for 24 hours. If you take me on I'll want a written statement so I can see that my company doesn't lose any money." I told him not to blame the Pullman conductor, that he likely was up most of the night considering the crowd on the train and needed a nap. "It was my own fault," I admitted. "All I want now is a little cooperation. Just let me off," I pleaded, "and don't worry about me."

That conductor, like every one I ever met, was a real fellow. He reached for the signal cord, walked back to where I had my suitcase, and spoke to the porter. The *Portland Limited* was slowing. They opened a vestibule door; the porter got off and put down the little square step very firmly amid the eastern Oregon sagebrush. "Watch your step," he cautioned me and reached back for my suitcase.

I departed from the *Limited* with as much pomp and ceremony as if this were Grand Central Station. "You take good care of yourself, sir," the porter advised. He picked up his box, climbed back aboard, the big engine shot up its black plumes of smoke, and the train moved off, leaving me in a vast lonely silence broken only by the gurgling of the mighty Columbia River that flowed beside me.

I likely was standing at that moment on soil that Lewis and Clark passed over in 1805.

But I was in no mood to appreciate historical drama. I ducked between the strands of a barbed-wire fence, walked about a hundred feet to the Columbia River Highway, stopped the first car, and 20 minutes later I was calling on the merchant I had come to see.

⚒ ⚒

There are more pages in my diary. When you keep traveling on railroads, exciting things happen every day, but there's never any danger about the excitement. In 12 years of continuous travel, I was never in a wreck, never saw one, was never even close enough to hear any details of one. I am never more courteously treated, nor do I feel more comfortably relaxed, than when I'm on a train.

[The Montana, Wyoming & Southern Railroad does not go to Wyoming, let alone points south of there. The 20-mile independent short line was constructed to serve the Bear Creek coalfield in south-central Montana, and delivers trains of as much as 100 cars of coal to the Northern Pacific at Bridger. From Bridger to Belfry the MW&S follows the Clark Fork River in a fertile, well-irrigated valley which has never known a crop failure and which ships more than 200 cars of sugar beets a year over the railroad.]
(editor note from original story)

FORGOTTEN RAILROAD

July 1942

Linn H. Westcott

Imagine yourself magically transported back to early summer in 1902.

You live in a gingerbread house on Elm Street, the white one with the cast-iron elk on the front lawn. There's a hitching post and stepping stone out in front by the gravel street, and four times an hour the new electric streetcar grinds its way around the corner and disappears between rows of willow trees.

But you're at the office now, feet up on the rolltop desk in a stuffy store window across the way from the courthouse. After the usual morning routine the daily paper gets its turn. Headline: Bret Harte Dead. ... He wrote "The Luck of Roaring Camp," one of the first documents of the human side of mankind, and was an authority on Western frontier life. Wouldn't it be something to see the mining camps in action! You glance into the paper. There's an ad for the new *20th Century Limited* making its first run June 15. But look at this down here:

"Visit beautiful Colorado Springs, see fascinating Cripple Creek Mining District, gorgeous Pikes Peak, famous Manitou Springs and the Garden of the Gods, Cave of ____ " and so on, "via the Rock Island Railroad, the quick way to the Rockies."

It isn't long before the family is riding across the plains, little Mary pushing her nose against the glass, and Johnny quite disappointed because there are no Indians galloping along with the train. As the porter lights the gas lamps in the car he tells how unfortunate it is that it will be dark when the train approaches the

mountains. "They rise up from the distance like storm clouds back in Virginny—man, they is a pretty sight! When you get to the Springs, go to the hotel jus' one block north of the depot: that's a fine place to stay."

After two days of visiting all the common sights at the Springs—two days you'll never forget—you happen to get talking to a portly gentleman in the purple-carpeted lobby of the hotel. It turns out he's a mining engineer who made his stakes at Cripple Creek, and he is already thinking about retiring.

"When I came to Cripple Creek—that was only 10 years ago, but seems like 20—the camps had been active scarcely a year, and the best of the mines had not yet been located. It all happened for me by accident. You see, I was an oil-claim specialist back in Titusville, Pa., got mad at the fellows I was working with, and headed for Canon City, southwest of here, where there was quite an oil field a few miles north, in Oil Creek. Somehow I got to talking to an old prospector here in the Springs on the last day of my trip, and I decided to go to Canon City by way of the mining camp.

"There was a dirt road into Cripple Creek from the Florissant station of the old Colorado Midland in those days. Ordinarily you could ride the wagons returning to the camp, but the previous week had been so wet that I had to walk the 16 miles in mud. I tell you I was tuckered out when I reached the mines. Sort of liked the setup, though; a lot of tents and a few log buildings stood where the town was built the following year. On the east was a steep ravine called Poverty Gulch. That's where a fellow named Womack found some rich dirt in 1890 and located the Gold King Mine across the Midland Terminal wye. The Midland Terminal—in fact, any railroad—wasn't there yet, and travel into Cripple Creek was a matter of days if you weren't real lucky."

This new friend goes on to tell you how he was over at the foot of Mount Pisgah, scarcely two miles west of Cripple Creek, to look at the old diggings of 1874 that disappointed so many prospectors. After that and a similar rush in '84 people didn't expect much to come from these mountains—that is, except for this fellow Womack, who was a sort of cowhand. "Womack kept diggin' holes here and there and gettin' his boss mad by doing it, but when he found the Gold King claim the story was different. Just the same, he sold it soon for $300, and in the next 10 years, the new owners took $250,000 out of that hole.

"Well, while I was over at Pisgah, as I was saying, I sort of got the prospecting bug myself, and I never did get down to Oil Creek. There were prospectors already diggin' holes all over Gold Hill, Mineral Hill, and in the valley to the south, but even if I was an oilman, it seemed to me that, the way the land lay, there should be better findings on the other side of Gold Hill. Before my trunk arrived I was out there with a mule and a brand new diggin' outfit, trying samples in the gulches first, later on the sides of the hill.

"It was while I was diggin' up on the sides of Battle Mount and Ball Cliff that I had my luck. My claim became part of the Portland Mine, one of the best in the district."

I   I

Well, the conversation goes on to the trials and tribulations of mining partnerships, the fluctuating costs of supplies, assaying frauds, and—oh, yes—the transportation problems.

"Glad you mentioned it, partner; railroading has become quite a fad with me of late. The fellows that own our mine had a lot of trouble with the Midland Terminal and the Florence & Cripple Creek, and last year we built our own railroad to Cripple Creek—the finest little railroad in Colorado, we think.

"The Midland Terminal built down from the Colorado Midland at Divide in '93 and barely beat the Florence & Cripple Creek narrow gauge from the south, both lines reaching Victor and Cripple Creek in '94. Everything was fine until the two companies got together on their rates and held us miners up for a good share of our profit, sometimes all of it. A New York outfit known as the Denver Southwestern Railway Company bought both companies in 1899 together with the Golden Circle Railroad, a narrow gauge feeder that tied a bow knot on top of the hill. They also got thick with the mills that reduced the ores here in the Springs and at Florence, so they had us from every direction.

"But we weren't caught sleeping. Five years ago we built a 6.2-mile electric interurban line up Poverty Gulch, swinging around the top of the hill to an elevation of 10,560 feet, the highest interurban in the U.S. It connected Cripple Creek and Victor by way of the upper summits, and the experience we had in building the line came in mighty handy when we decided to build all the way to Colorado Springs. The original company was the Cripple Creek District Railway Company, but we changed the name to Colorado Springs & Cripple District Railway even before the electric was completed.

"The new steam line starts about a mile from here and works right up the side of the mountains, then turns west to the mines. It is 45.82 miles long, 10 miles shorter than the Midland route. We named it the Cripple Creek Short Line. It has a beautiful roadbed, nine tunnels, and a number of curved timber trestles. The last spike was driven last year, and in the meantime, branches were built in the district, and a new low-level interurban line was built to Victor, so the electric now forms a circle route.

"The railroad was not intended as a passenger line, but the success this season has been very gratifying. In fact, we received, in the first six months, $300,000, including the freight revenue, and it cost only $186,000 to operate the line. Of course we've got $2 million of bonds to pay off sooner or later, and interest and taxes must come out of that apparent profit. In all, we have 84 miles of track, 12 miles electrified. And with the increasing loadings at the mines the prospects look good.

"Ride up on that line; you'll never forget it."

And so you do.

I   I

The train, four open-end coaches behind a huge (for 1902) Consolidation, pulls out of the station on a sunny afternoon. All the car windows are open, and the sun-warmed air breezes through. Mother is very perturbed because Johnny leans so far out the car windows and Mary insists upon playing with the ostrich plume upon her straw hat.

After crossing the almost-dry bed of Fountain Creek, as the conductor punches tickets, the train turns directly toward the mountains as though to attack them. Over to the left is the Portland Mill, where the railroad's loads of ore are reduced; on the right, as you climb a ridge, is a wye connecting with the Standard, Golden Cycle, and other mills. The great bluff of mountains, now only a mile in front of the train, is a fault or block that was pushed far above the plains in ages past. The train enters Bear Creek Canyon and the rock cropping out on the far side echoes the puffing while everybody leans out the left-hand windows to see the beautiful timber trestle ahead. This bridge swings the train around to the east. But not for long, for the train immediately starts climbing right up the side of the bluff. At milepost 5 it has risen 1,000 feet above the city, scarcely two miles away as the crow flies.

Rounding Point Sublime the train swings into the upper extremities of the bluff. Out on the point is a wooden sign freshly painted to name the rock that

A 2-8-0 steam locomotive and its four trailing passenger cars are almost lost in the scenery as they traverse hairpin curves on the line looking north from Tunnel No. 8. *L. C. McClure*

forms a steeple between the track and the plains. Far below is the Broadview Hotel and Resort, and beyond, just miles and miles of what now by comparison looks like flat land. But three days ago you traveled that stretch on the Rock Island and you know it is anything but flat.

Around the curve is Tunnel No. 1, perfectly straight, and cut through reddish volcanic rock. A little spring trickles out of the side of the cut and a gang of trackmen sits in the shade while the excursion train clicks by. Steadily the engine pulls its gliding train through more tunnels, into deep canyons, across them by curved trestles, and back to the face of the bluffs for another breathtaking view.

From the north side of North Cheyenne Canyon one can see, across the chasm, a tunnel through a solid dome of granite, leading directly onto a sturdy trestle. Below, Silver Cascade Falls glistens in the sunlight. In a moment the

train pierces that same tunnel and argues with the trestle.

In South Cheyenne Canyon, St. Peter's Dome dominates the scenery up ahead, and while all the passengers are exclaiming *oh!* and *ah!* you have a good chance to inspect the right-of-way from the rear platform. The track is, of course, standard gauge, made up of 75-pound rails, 60-pound on sidings. It is ballasted with decomposed rock and is well ditched to catch the runoff from upper slopes. According to the brakeman the railroad cost nearly $4 million, including cars, locomotives, and the electric lines in the district. The track is a steady climb of 4 percent for 20 miles out of Colorado Springs. The curves are sort of tough, too, being as sharp as 16 degrees.

A forest fire some years before cleared much of the sloping ridges of the larger trees. The loops, an engineering feature of the railroad, come soon after the train rounds St. Peter's Dome. These are not real loops of the spiral kind, but a sort of

doubling back, passing through three tunnels and hairpinning again in the process.

While the engine takes a long drink at Duffields the passengers get out and stretch. Duffields is a shelter stop 3,000 feet above the plains, which are here seen for the last time. Directly below is the line the train passed over scarcely a few minutes before. To the east is Cheyenne Mountain, impressive, yet you can see right over it, and just north is the steep path to St. Peter's Dome.

Resuming its journey, the train meets an eastbound ore train at the Summit siding. Unlike most railroads the summit on the Shore Line is a misnomer, for the elevation is 9,913 feet, yet Cripple Creek is nearly as high, and three passes on the Short Line are even higher than Summit. While the steady climbing stops here, the railroad does not descend the other side but overcomes a series of minor ridges from this stop onward.

Bear Creek Trestle once hosted trains; by the 1940s, the right-of-way had been converted to a road. *Linn H. Westcott*

The rock formations in Cathedral Park, some miles beyond, are gorgeous, and here is the ninth and last tunnel. The line swings across a beautiful alpine meadow on a small trestle, and the best view is from the rear platform.

Just before Cameron the Midland Terminal's track swings along from the north; both lines enter a shallow valley and then double back the other side, crossing each other as they round the curve. The ME goes on to Victor Pass, as does a branch of the Short Line, but the CS&CCD main line makes another double loop and climbs to the true summit at Hoosier Pass, 10,315 feet above sea level.

Far off to the southwest are the snow-capped Sangre de Cristo Mountains, and nearer is the blue-tinged peneplain through which the Arkansas River cut a way for the Denver & Rio Grande's Royal Gorge Route. Nearly a thousand feet below lies the town of Cripple Creek, treeless since the great fire that swept the town a few years after its incorporation.

The railroad descends the hillside quickly around more hairpin loops. Below on the left, as the train comes to a stop at the depot, is the narrow gauge Florence & Cripple Creek, and above is its brother, the Midland Terminal, which ends upon a peculiar wye, two legs of which are on trestles over Poverty Gulch. Even more

unusual is the Short Line's terminal, for here engines and whole trains are turned on a balloon (Colorado name for a return loop). This particular loop has its neck at the terminal end.

Cripple Creek is connected with Victor, where the biggest mines are located, by five railroad routes: the Florence & Cripple Creek (narrow gauge), the Midland Terminal's main line, the two electric lines of the Short Line (one of which serves as an alternate steam route), and via Cameron over a branch of the Short Line. Besides these there are numerous branches and spur connections and the Golden Circle Rail road mentioned before. The trolley routes are favored for views and seeing mining operations close at hand, and are especially interesting since it is not necessary to return the same way.

The big mines are located near Victor and, had they been discovered first, Victor would have been the largest of the towns in the district. Here also is the messiest tangle of railroads short of Pittsburgh.

While back at Cripple Creek waiting for the returning train, you look over a couple of the locomotives. After all, it's 1902, and everyone, not just the railfan, is interested in locomotives. The railroad owns 12 in all, most of them Consolidations built by Schenectady in 1900. These engines have 22" x 26" cylinders, 51" drivers, 180 pounds steam pressure, 37,750 pounds tractive force, and 168,500 pounds on the drivers. Total weight with tender is 277,600 pounds. Four locomotives are 2-6-2 Prairie switchers, purchased to help in the construction of the road. They have 22" x 24" cylinders, 51" drivers; total weight with tender is 217,760 pounds. Besides these there are eight 57-hp electric coaches, three trailers, and 12 steam passenger cars.

$$\mathbf{I} \quad \mathbf{I}$$

It is summer of 1942. The right-of-way of the Cripple Creek Short Line was opened to the public as a highway two years ago. The trees along the way are now much recovered from the ancient fire, and this route is one of the most scenic roads in all the Rockies. You can drive past the

Consolidation No. 8 leads train 93 toward the summit, at an elevation of 10,000 feet. The locomotive was retired in 1922 (as were the railroad's other 2-8-0s). *L. C. McClure*

long-deserted Portland Mill, where the remaining locomotives stood knee-deep in mud for 20 years. You see the old weathered sign on Point Sublime. The great timber trestles are now gone, but the spring still trickles near Tunnel No. 1. Miners dig for their fortunes on Gold Hill, but the ties of the interurban line are chipped and railless. Many of the old mines are deserted too; one bears on its plank side a theater poster reading *Gone With the Wind*.

But the mines are producing plenty today. Since water was the miner's worst enemy, tunnels were cut to drain the mines at ever-lower levels, and last year the greatest draining project of all was completed, drying out many of the richest veins.

What happened to the railroads? The Midland Terminal is now the sole survivor. Since the peak of mining operations was in 1900, the Short Line got in on a good thing rather late. It did pay two dividends on its stock and a few years of interest on the bonds, but was not profitable for any of the later owners.

About 1910 business declined, and three roads just couldn't all be profitable. The Colorado Springs & Cripple Creek was acquired by Colorado & Southern but operated separately by that Burlington subsidiary. Later it was leased by Florence & Cripple Creek, and all three lines were for a while under a related control. The F&CC was the first to go, probably because it was narrow gauge and the mill at Florence had no other important customers. Then, after some years of profitless operation, the Short Line entered receivership under the hand of the manager of the Portland Mill.

Operation was discontinued in 1918, resumed again for a while, and permanently abandoned in 1920. A fellow named Corley scrapped the line two years later, and for a long time, it was a toll road known as the Corley Highway.

Today you can drive the Corley Highway through the nine tunnels, and you can ride the Midland Terminal in a sort of doodlebug to Cripple Creek, both rides being even more interesting for knowing the Cripple Creek story.

[Material was supplied by John C. Carter, Mac Poor, Jack Thode, T. G. Wurm, and H. A. Stanley.]

December 1942

THE JARRETT & PALMER SPECIAL

TRAINS staff

First Wire between Brooklyn Towers Fastened!

Rutherford B. Hayes Elected 19th United States President!

Paris-London Companies Plan Long Railroad Tunnel under Channel!

General Custer and Entire Command Obliterated by Sioux in Wyoming!

The Great Train Arrived at San Francisco Sunday, June 4 at 9:43 a.m.!

These are some of the U.S. newspaper headlines for the year 1876. However, *The Great Train* not only made the front pages of the papers of this country, but the story was printed in papers of nearly every country in the world. And with good reason.

The *Jarrett & Palmer Special* was the most famous train of the 19th century. It was the first through transcontinental train, as far as is known, and it was the first train in the history of railroading to operate over such a distance on such a fast schedule.

Jarrett & Palmer, managers of the Booth Theater, New York, arranged for the train to carry Lawrence Barrett, the internationally known actor, and Frederick Thorne and C. B. Bishop to San Francisco. All three were scheduled to appear in Shakespeare's *Henry V* at McCullough's California Theater, San Francisco, on June 5.

The fastest regularly scheduled train between the two cities required seven full days to complete the trip. When Henry C. Jarrett proposed to the railroads that they arrange for a train to make the trip in just half that time to carry the illustrious Barrett and anyone else who wanted to go, the railroads jumped at the opportunity. Here, they speculated, was a chance to show the world what could be done on the already world-famous American railroad systems. The enthusiasm felt by officials of the lines that were to participate spread rapidly.

The *New York Herald*, leading paper of the country, picked up the story, giving the enterprise full support. In an editorial, "From Ocean to Ocean," appearing in the May 26 issue of the *Herald*, it was stated:

Our friend Jules Verne, whose imagination of American railroads was so excitable that he made trains on the Union Pacific line leap over chasms and bridges, undertook to depict an extraordinary journey of his hero across the continent in his novel Around the World in Eighty Days. *But his*

A total of 20 locomotives shared duties on the transcontinental run. No. 77, a 4-4-0, was one of eight locomotives on the Union Pacific to handle the train. *Union Pacific*

imagination fell short of the reality which Messrs. Jarrett & Palmer propose to perform with their lightning train, which leaves New York for San Francisco on the first of June ... which will, be remarkable, not merely as a feat of daring and energy, but as an illustration of what resources in swift travel our railroads are yet to display.

Because the train was to start from New York, all arrangements for its journey were handled by the Pennsylvania Railroad. The train was first made up in Pittsburgh and ran as a special on May 31 to Jersey City to test the equipment, which consisted of locomotive No. 573, a baggage car, a combined commissary and smoking car, and a Pullman Palace Hotel car, *Marlborough*. The baggage car was painted red with gold lettering on both sides as were the other two cars behind it: Jarrett & Palmer's Special Transcontinental Express.

Built into the baggage car was a wooden reserve water tank of about 1,800 gallons capacity. A small donkey-engine was used to pump the water from the tank to the tender. Four thousand pounds of extra coal was also carried in the baggage car and was shoveled through the end door and into the tender en route. The next car, a 12-wheel coach, carried commissary supplies and also served as a smoking car.

The *Marlborough* was an elaborately ornamented Pullman having carved hardwood trimming throughout its interior. The forward part contained the kitchen, with an ice box, stores of meat and game, the dinner service, shifting tables, and the dormitory of the conductor and steward and his assistants. The main compartment was furnished in the lavish purple, red, and gold style of the time, and accommodated 36 passengers, computed on the basis of two passengers to a berth.

The test run from Pittsburgh to Jersey City being nonstop, special arrangements were made for lubricating the locomotive. The eccentrics were oiled through a rubber tube and, the drivers by means of copper pipes. No trouble was encountered, and when No. 337 reached Jersey, it

was placed under guard as a protection against any possible tampering with the mechanism.

The round-trip fare, including a week's stay at the Grand Palace Hotel in San Francisco and privilege of return in six months, was $500. The tickets were in book form, five inches by four. The covers of the book were solid silver, burnished in the center. Making up the ticket and its various coupons were 10 leaves, all engraved from steel plates. Each ticket book was enclosed in a white satin-covered case which cost $40.

The transcontinental party consisted of about 40 members, among them Jarrett and Palmer, and the three actors: Barrett, Thorne, and Bishop. Other famous figures of the time who made the trip were a Mr. Weede of the *New Orleans Times*; Gen. Horace Porter, vice-president of the Pullman Car Company; a Mr. Roman, correspondent of the *New York Herald*, the *London Times,* and the *Illustrated London News*; M. Morrier, correspondent of the *Paris Presse*; S. S. Moon of the *Railway*

Central Pacific 4-4-0 No. 149, also known as the *Black Fox*, pulled the *Jarrett & Palmer Special* on the final leg of its journey, from Ogden, Utah, to Oakland Pier. Its crew members stand proudly by the locomotive. *Southern Pacific*

World; Col. Alberg of the English Army; A. J. Cassatt, third vice-president of the Pennsylvania Railroad (later that road's great president who built the New York terminal); and Frank Thomson, general manager of the Pennsy. Some of the passengers rode *The Great Train* to Pittsburgh. Others only went as far as Chicago, and about half the original party stayed aboard until San Francisco was reached.

Not only did the newspapers of the country sponsor the idea, the New York post office endorsed the project and made arrangements for forwarding mail to the Pacific Coast and many other points on the route of the train. New York Postmaster James gave notice that mail for Pittsburgh, Chicago, Omaha, Sacramento, and San Francisco would be forwarded on the *Jarrett & Palmer Special*. Typical of the mailpouch tags was the one carrying the mail for Pittsburgh:

Pittsburgh
from
New York

Mail dispatched by Jarrett & Palmer's special fast transcontinental train through to San Francisco in 3 days, 12 hours, closing at the New York post office June 1, 1876, at 12.10 a.m.

If the Pullman *Marlborough* seemed lavishly adorned, so were some of the articles describing events concerning the affair: This is a bit of lavender and old lace from the pen of one *Herald* reporter, which appeared in a late extra on May 31, the night of departure of *The Great Train*:

As the ferry boat left the Cortlandt Street slip after midnight with the adventurous travelers, their miscellaneous baggage, their sorrowful friends, their band of music, their stock of fireworks, and numerous appendages, there was quite an ovation. Roman candles and other pyrotechnic inventions lighted up the boat on its way across the Hudson.

Wherever the train appeared along the route it was met by huge crowds which, having word of its being on the way an hour beforehand, lighted bonfires, played brass bands, and fired cannons. When the *Special* passed the centennial grounds at West Philadelphia at 2:40 a.m., all the buildings were lighted in honor of the speeding train. Between New York and Pittsburgh public schools in the vicinity of the Pennsylvania trackage were closed, and factories emptied of workers that they might pay tribute to those aboard the train. The arrival at Harrisburg was cause for an ovation in which more than 3,000 people participated.

At Altoona, D. M. Boyd Jr., general passenger agent of the Pennsylvania Railroad, also a member of the party, sent this telegram to the New York office of the railroad:

Special Transcontinental Express,
Pennsylvania Railroad.
Altoona, June 1

We have made an even run of 327 miles without stopping, and have at no time, while slowing up through towns and for crossings, run slower than 25 miles an hour. The rate of speed has only been thus reduced at three or four points. The speed during the rest of the run has averaged 48 to 50 miles an hour. The train has been on time at all stations, frequently from one to two minutes ahead. The perfect condition of the track and uniformity of the speed that has been maintained gives a feeling to the passengers of a moderate schedule.

D. M. Boyd Jr.

The arrival at Pittsburgh was the occasion for wild celebration. The *Pittsburgh Post*, issue of June 1, published an article, part of which was:

This morning at 10:39, two minutes ahead of schedule time, the Transcontinental Express from New York to San Francisco in 84 hours, arrived at the Union Depot over the Pennsylvania Railroad, a large crowd of persons being present to witness its arrival. ... The car inspectors, after concluding the inspection of the rolling stock at the Union Depot, were interviewed by our reporter, and they stated there was not a journal or pin on the engine in a hot condition. "She was perfectly cool," said one of the engineers.

The train made no stop between Jersey and Pittsburgh, covering the 438½ miles in 10 hours and 5 minutes. Locomotive 573 was cut off and one belonging to the Pittsburgh, Ft. Wayne & Chicago Railway (now Pennsylvania main line), over which line the train traveled to Chicago, pulled the train out of Pittsburgh. Twenty-five stops were made before Chicago was reached, and four different engines were used. In spite of the stops and engine changes, the 468.3 miles of the second leg were covered in 11 hours 6 minutes. The Chicago & North Western Railway took the train over between Chicago and the transfer grounds at Omaha. From Omaha to Ogden the journey was over the line of the Union Pacific, and from Ogden to San Francisco the Central Pacific did the honors. The farther the train progressed westward the more excitement it created. On June 3 the *New York Herald* carried this story:

The Great Run
While the citizens of New York are quietly pursuing their daily avocations, retiring to rest at their regular hours and rising betimes in the morning; while the **Herald** *is gathering up the news from all quarters of the globe and setting the enormous machinery to work to lay it before the people with the rising sun,* **The Great Train,** *which is to show us how near we are in point of time to the Pacific Coast, is speeding on night and day, never pausing and never tiring, on its way across the continent to San Francisco. Our advices today are from Cheyenne, and we learn from them that the lightning train is ahead of time; that it is flying through the valley of the Platte at the rate of 50 and sometimes even 60 miles an hour; and that the voyagers confidently count on taking their Sunday dinner in the California city. Halfway across the continent—1,650 miles— in 39 hours is no child's play, even for the iron*

horse. But we must not forget that the best part of the journey is passed, that the worst has yet to come. Nevertheless, we wish the train Godspeed and its living freight such a Sunday dinner as San Francisco so well knows how to furnish.

On June 4 this editorial appeared in the *Herald*:

The Fast Train
Still the Transcontinental Express thunders on, making a uniformly rapid progress, which will be judged by the fact that first "slowing up" experienced by the voyagers on the journey from New York was in Weber Canyon, where a party of Chinese were repairing the washed-out track. The train was at Winnemucca at 20 minutes past 8 p.m., and expected to land the passengers in San Francisco in time for breakfast. The most trying portion of the journey before the train was the ascent and descent of the Sierra Nevada, a task requiring caution going down as well as patience going up, the grades being over 100 feet to the mile. ... The scene at Cheyenne, with Mr. Jarrett firing Roman candles and one of the party, whose name is modestly concealed, telling the excited throng what time was made on the run from Gotham, is worthy of the artist's brush, and must take its place in history when someone qualified for the task undertakes to describe the material progress of the United States for the next centennial.

A dispatch from the *Herald* correspondent in San Francisco, dated June 4, stated, in part:

The Jarrett & Palmer transcontinental train arrived here at 9:39 a.m., local time. ... The trip across the continent was made in 80 hours 20 minutes, calendar time. The trip, since leaving Elko Station ... was wonderful for swiftness over mountain range and through deep valleys. As each station was passed the excitement grew apace and the party was received with that enthusiasm and hospitality peculiar to the Pacific Coast.

The success of the trip has caused great satisfaction this side of the Sierras and, though the people are accustomed to great efforts, our journey across the continent elicits wonder and astonishment here in California. Everybody seems surprised that the party is not fatigued to a degree of exhaustion, and the ovation we

received was only to be expected on this side of the Sierra Nevada. Indeed, the closing scenes of our journey were more exciting than any that had preceded, for we were treated more like heroes from a battlefield than as men who had peaceably sat in a railroad car to be whirled across the continent in half time. None of the passengers, sensible as they were that the achievement was wonderful, ever dreamed that the people of a whole city would turn out en mass on a bright Sabbath morning to welcome 18 or 20 gentlemen who would rather slip out of sight than face a multitude of excited citizens. But so it is. Ever since we set foot on the pavements of San Francisco we have been surrounded by throngs of people who, if anyone opened his lips to a personal friend, clustered about him eagerly catching the few disjointed sentences dropped by a speaker who had crossed the American continent from the Atlantic to the Pacific in less than three days and a half.

It is quite evident that the correspondent had trouble figuring the running time. Other newspaper comments throughout the country were varied and vague concerning the actual running time. No one seemed able to calculate it with any degree of accuracy from the reports given them. However, G. Davidson, United States service chief, Pacific Coast Area, cleared the issue up with fair accuracy in a statement from his headquarters:

Between Jersey City and Oakland Point: Lightning train left Jersey City Pier June 1, 1 h. 3m.; arrived Oakland Point June 4, 9 h. 22m.; apparent running time 80 h. 13 m. 7 s.; actual time occupied in running between Jersey City and Oakland Point 83 h. 32 m. 7 s. ... From Jersey City to Market Street Ferry slip, San Francisco ... apparent time 80 h. 40 m. 18 s.; actual time 83 h. 53 m. 45 s.

Davidson based his calculations on the time of departure from Jersey City as being 1:03 a.m. Actually the train left at 12:53 a.m. The discrepancies in figuring elapsed time are easily understood, for this was a number of years before the adoption of standard time. The schedule of the entire run as it appeared in the *Official Railway Guide* was:

Schedule of Jarrett & Palmer Transcontinental Special ——— New York to San Francisco ——— June 1 to 4, 1876

— THURSDAY, JUNE 1 —

Pennsylvania Railroad

Miles				Actual Time
0.	Left	New York	Philadelphia Time	12.40 a.m.
1.0	"	Jersey City	"	12.53 a.m.
56.8	"	Trenton	"	2.00 a.m.
88.2	"	Mantua	"	2.39 a.m.
154.4	"	Lancaster	"	4.26 a.m.
191.2	"	Harrisburg	"	5.18 a.m.
322.8	"	Altoona	"	8.12 a.m.
439.5	Arr.	Pittsburgh	"	10.58 a.m.

438.5 miles in 10 hours 5 minutes. Average speed, 43.50 miles an hour. Entire run made without a stop.

Pittsburgh, Ft. Wayne & Chicago Railway

Miles				Actual Time
	Left	Pittsburgh	Philadelphia Time	11.05 a.m.
0.	"	Pittsburgh	Columbus Time	10.34 a.m.
1.0	"	Allegheny	"	10.50 a.m.
34.7	"	Homewood	"	11.49 a.m.
101.4	"	Canton	"	1.30 p.m.
188.8	Arr.	Crestline	"	3:55 p.m.
188.8	Left	Crestline	"	4:00 p.m.
260.6	"	Lima	"	5:39 p.m.
320.0	"	Fort Wayne	"	7:05 p.m.
424.4	"	Valparaiso	"	9:20 p.m.
468.3	Arr.	Chicago	"	10:19 p.m.

468.3 miles in 11 hours 6 minutes. Average speed 42.1 miles an hour. Stopped 25 times. Changed engines 4 times.

Chicago & North Western Railway

Miles				Actual Time
	Left	Chicago	Columbus Time	10:50 p.m.
0.	"	Chicago	Chicago Time	10:30 p.m.
74.8	"	Rochelle	"	11.59 p.m.

— FRIDAY, JUNE 2 —

Miles				Actual Time
138.1	Left	Clinton	Chicago Time	1:15 a.m.
177.8	Arr.	Loudon	"	2:03 a.m.
177.8	Left	Loudon	"	2:20 a.m.
219.4	"	Cedar Rapids	"	3:26 a.m.
340.4	"	Boone	"	6:31 a.m.
441.4	"	Dunlap	"	8:57 a.m.
488.5	Arr.	Council Bluffs	"	9:58 a.m.
491.0	"	Transfer Grounds	"	10:00 a.m.

491.0 miles in 11 hours 30 minutes. Average speed, Chicago to Council Bluffs, 42.60 miles an hour. Fastest speed made, 62.2 miles an hour. Stopped 9 times. Changed engines four times.

Union Pacific Railroad

Miles				Actual Time
	Left	Omaha	Chicago Time	10:43 a.m.
0.	"	Omaha	Omaha Time	10:10 a.m.
91.7	"	Columbus	"	12:22 p.m.
153.8	"	Grand Island	"	1.48 p.m.
291.0	"	North Platte	"	5:18 p.m.
414.2	"	Sidney	"	8:06 p.m.
516.4	"	Cheyenne	"	10:41 p.m.

— SATURDAY, JUNE 3 —

Miles				Actual Time
572.8	Arr.	Laramie	"	12:33 a.m.
710.0	Left	Rawlings	Laramie Time	3:09 a.m.
846.6	"	Green River	"	6:20 a.m.
957.0	"	Evanston	"	9:10 a.m.
1032.8	Arr.	Ogden	"	10:57 a.m.

Average speed, 41 miles an hour; maximum, 72 miles an hour. Stopped 22 times. Changed engines 7 times. 10 hours 21 minutes ahead of schedule time.

Central Pacific Railroad

Miles				Actual Time
0.	Left	Ogden	Laramie Time	11:01 a.m.
0.	"	Ogden	San Francisco Time	9:44 a.m.
91.7	"	Kelton	"	11:46 a.m.
182.8	"	Toano	"	2:07 p.m.
218.4	"	Wells	"	3:00 p.m.
275.2	"	Elko	"	4:22 p.m.
358.9	"	Battle Mountain	"	6:48 p.m.
419.2	"	Winnemucca	"	8:20 p.m.

— SUNDAY, JUNE 4 —

Miles				Actual Time
588.8	Left	Reno	San Francisco Time	12:25 a.m.
623.7	"	Truckee	"	1:56 a.m.
689.1	"	Colfax	"	4:30 a.m.
743.2	"	Sacramento	"	6:09 a.m.
791.2	"	Stockton	"	7:13 a.m.
852.7	"	Niles	"	8:52 a.m.
879.2	Arr.	Oakland Wharf	"	9:29 a.m.
882.9	"	San Francisco	"	9:43 a.m.
882.9	"	San Francisco	New York Time	12:57 p.m.

(The parties on the train were to arrive in San Francisco in time to dine there on June 4.)

879 miles in 23 hours 45 minutes. Average speed, 31 miles an hour. 16 stops. The entire run made with one engine. The brake shoes on the cars were badly worn on arrival at Ogden, and not having any of the same pattern to replace them the train was run by "hand brakes" (only) from Ogden to Truckee, and the speed was materially lessened on the heavy descending grade, as the men were fearful of losing control of the train.

Grand total of distance, 3,313.5 miles. Actual time of transit, 84 hours 17 minutes. Average speed for entire distance, 40 miles an hour. Stopped 72 times. Engines used, 20.

Newspapers in the United States and abroad carried daily updates of the special train's progress, including woodcuts illustrating events along the way. *London Illustrated News, courtesy Union Pacific*

From New York to San Francisco today, on regularly scheduled trains of the Pennsylvania and Union Pacific railroads, is 61 hours 10 minutes. At New York the *Golden Arrow*, No. 79, which is a daily train, leaves at 11:40 p.m. and arrives in Chicago at 4:40 p.m. Elapsed time, 18 hours. After an hour and 20 minutes layover in Chicago the Union Pacific streamliner *City of San Francisco*, leaves at 6 p.m., arriving at San Francisco at 9:50 a.m. on the second day. Elapsed time, 43 hours 10 minutes. The

City of San Francisco leaves Chicago on the second day of the month and every third day thereafter. It is quite probable that if a special transcontinental train were to attempt a record run from New York for San Francisco today, as did the *Jarrett & Palmer Special* in 1876, the elapsed time would be under 50 hours.

⚓ ⚓

A 13-gun salute was fired as Lawrence Barrrett stepped from the first of the carriages bringing the party to the Palace Hotel on the morning of June 4. The hotel manager acted as host to the entire

party at a breakfast which was an elaborate affair. Mayor Bryon and leading citizens were present and many speeches were made. On June 5 Mr. Barrett appeared at McCullough's California Theater. He played to a very, very large audience.

[Information courtesy of Mutual Magazine, *Pennsylvania Railroad]*

Pullman Company

TROOP-TRAIN RIDER

William Forsythe

Everyone knows there are many troop trains moving these days, but few people know there is a civilian, a key man, on every train.

His presence is demanded by the government. Even without the demand, it would be most wise to have him on every train. He is the escort, or train rider, representing the railroad.

He has few specified duties, but his life is so arduous that many men simply can't stand it. Great physical strength is not needed, but nerve control is everything. Breakdowns have occurred; near-breakdowns have been numerous. The escort can't tell anyone what to do, but he is responsible for every detail of the train's operation. He never knows when he will go to work, and once on the job, he never knows when or where he'll get a bath and a bed. He must have full information about the train movement, but is forbidden to disclose the least bit of it. During recent months, he has also been escorting trains filled with German and Italian prisoners.

Where did this escort come from, and what kind of chap is he?

Obviously he must know at least a little about the railroad he's representing, and he's got to mix with all peoples in all circumstances. Some railroads have created the position of train rider on a temporary or duration basis, and found a few

A Southern Railway Mountain type (4-8-2) leads a troop train near Craggy, N.C., in August 1944. The train is en route from Knoxville, Tenn., to Asheville, N.C. *Frank Clodfelter*

individuals able and willing to accept the job. Occasionally, operating department officers and employees serve as train escorts. But the chief source of supply is the traffic department. Solicitation of the traditional type is out, now. The men are already trained in meeting the public. Payroll disturbance is avoided, essential duties provided for the men, and they become better educated about their railroad.

I   I

To illustrate the work of a train rider, let's suppose you, a traveling freight agent for the XY&Z Railroad, are assigned to this duty for a one-month period. After straightening up the desk, you set aside a supply of matches, scratch pads, and other advertising novelties your company may have available. You stop at the bank for a hundred dollars in cash and a couple of blank checks, then you pack up the following:

• A shoe-shining outfit.

• Knife, fork and spoon. Most eating en route is from paper plates and cups;

borrowing personal effects, except in emergency, is bad form.

• A pair of Pullman slippers for relief on the long runs.

• An extra pair of shoes.

• All the socks and underwear you possess.

• A small glass jar of powdered or flaked laundry soap. If you reach a small junction town in late evening with all clothing dirty, for only a 12-hour stay, you'll simply have to do your own washing.

You stop at the office, pick up the advertising. You buy a carton of cigarettes for the mess sergeant and others.

You go out on line and make two or three trips that aren't so bad. Then you get a stinger. The train has 11 sleepers and 30 flats of automotive equipment; you travel in mountain territory over a clogged railroad. Fifty-one hours you ride, with little sleep, and finally, at 11 a.m. one day, you deliver your train to a connecting line at Replogle Yard, six miles from Centerville.

Half dead, you use the roundhouse phone to check in with the passenger office downtown and then canvass all hotels for a room. None is available. You leave your name and this telephone number. You take a bath in the roundhouse shower, dropping three pieces of clothing and soiling them unspeakably. You lie on a bench for troubled sleep; the bench is hard, and engineers are boisterous fellows.

The clerk arouses you; one of the hotels is calling. They have had a checkout and are holding a room for you. Fuzzy in the head, you say only "Thank you very much" and hang up. It is 4:30 p.m.

The telephone rings immediately, and you get out of the clerk's way. He answers, but motions you to the instrument. It is the passenger office downtown. The man reads from an order of the Military Bureau:

"Main 12345, with [he reads the consist], en route from Someplace to Camp Anywhere, and routed via AB&C Railroad to Centerville, thence XY&Z System to destination, will be delivered Replogle Yard at 2:30 a.m. tomorrow. You will escort the train. Nice ride to you. See you next trip."

A fireman drives you downtown to the hotel and you leave a call for 1 a.m. You're too tired to eat, but boy, do you sleep! You are awakened in time, order a cab, and depart for Replogle Yard. En route, you treat the cab driver to a full meal; he's entitled to it for finding you a good place to eat at such an hour. The train is reported two hours late. You sit down. You smoke cigarettes. You explore the car shop, roundhouse, yard. Time passes. The train is delivered at 9:30 a.m.

The first thing to do is get your suitcase aboard. If you see the Pullman conductor, he will tell you where your assignment is, and the suitcase can be left there; if you don't see him, put the suitcase anywhere but *in* the train. And don't sit down; you have work to do. Look up the train commander, introduce yourself, and offer assistance. If he wants anything, write it down, else you'll forget it. He may be indefinite about food requirements, which means you must see the mess sergeant very quickly. You ascertain where the commander is riding, and write that down; his berth or room is train headquarters. The car men are out with ice and are sticking hose into the car tanks. You leave the commander.

Patrol every faucet and toilet in the train to see there is plenty of ice and water. This trip will take you through the kitchen car, where you meet the mess sergeant. He is grateful for a package of cigarettes, says he will need food for evening dinner. You suggest he make a food order and bring it to headquarters as soon as the train is moving. There is a slight bump; the new engine is hooked on. Finish your patrol and get on the ground to meet your train crew. The crew is ready to leave but awaits your okay. Going to headquarters, you learn the commander is ready. No soldiers are wandering about, so you give the word, and at 10:10 a.m., the train moves.

The train conductor is a freight man who says food can be obtained at a city you are due to reach about 4 p.m. He can order it by wire, to be filed some 60 miles out. With him and your Pullman conductor you now visit headquarters. Lift the tickets and pass them to the conductor. The commander signs the form acknowledging his transportation has been furnished. You make out the train conductor's report. The mess sergeant appears with a list of food. Approved by the commander, it is handed to you, and on to the conductor. The Pullman conductor has personally counted the men and vouches for correctness of their number. Otherwise, you'd have to do it yourself. Your routine work is done.

⊥ ⊥

If the commander seems to want it, you stay with him for conversation. If he has work of his own, you leave him. With your conductors you move to the rear of the train where, with the flagman now included, you settle down to the serious business of this trip, which is Running the War, and Running the Railroad. The conductor tells you of his early days as a boomer, points up your rudimentary knowledge of the rule book. Thereafter, you'll never forget the meaning of the whistle signal, one long and two short; hearing it, you'll always listen for the "toot-toot" answer from the other engine. The Pullman conductor moves over all railroads, and tells of recent trips from coast to coast and from the Gulf to Canada.

About noon a soldier backs down the aisle passing paper plates and cups from big boxes held by a following soldier. Right behind them is another man with thick slices of bread and hunks of butter. The passengers reach for their eating tools. Another pair of soldiers carry between them a huge tub about 30 inches deep filled with succulent beef pot roast, potatoes, carrots. They ladle it out and they don't stint. They're halfway through the car when the first men of the kitchen detail, having finished their distribution, struggle to pass; finally they make it. When the boys reach your end of the car the conductor and flagman really turn on the personality. Are they hungry! And they are fed along with you and the soldiers. Most of the time, they'll eat with their fingers and like it. Fruit is distributed later and everyone is lazy.

The men are forbidden to pass from car to car, cannot ride on platforms. There is no liquor. They may smoke, gamble, sleep, mend clothing, buy candy or ice cream at station stops if they can get the windows opened. They may write letters, postal cards, or telegrams. All such messages are gathered by noncommissioned officers and delivered to the train commander for censoring.

At a stop of 30 minutes or more the train commander may order the men exercised. It is quite a picture to see 300 boot-camp graduates, shirts off, performing snappy calisthenics in a railroad yard, led by a lieutenant atop a flatcar the yardmaster had obligingly spotted for him. That's one car movement that will never be recorded!

To a good citizen, it is almost inconceivable that there are in America those who would aid the enemy. But all those posters aren't put out for nothing: Loose talk is sabotage, and you must not discuss your train's movement with the enlisted men; you must not tell *anyone* where you're going, how many men you have, what the outfit is—or anything else. This is most serious. And curiously enough, it is the only thing that may cause friction between you and the men. They know you are fully informed, and don't like to be brushed off. You soon learn the best way is to explain frankly that you have your orders, just as they have their orders, and you must keep still.

Actually, the boys do pretty well. They can read names lettered on station buildings and locomotives. Out of all aboard there will surely be at least a few who've been here before. Gossip spreads from car to car in some way. The men put two and two together, and are rarely surprised to learn, on reaching their destination, where they are.

At 4 mph, the train rolls into the camp that is to be home for your soldiers for six days or six months. You look through the car, and see only the stern ends of soldiers; they're all looking out the window in concentrated inspection. You go to the platform for a look yourself. No matter what the hour, many mournful inmates stand near the track to help initiate these newcomers. They moan "You'll be sorry." They droop theatrically and shake their heads. "Oh, this is a hell of a place. I wish I'd never come here." Nothing like making the younger fry feel right at home!

You bid good-bye and good luck to the train commander and other friends made en route. A cab is available, and you go into town, to the hotel where

It's less than two weeks after the attack on Pearl Harbor, and soldiers of the 35th Infantry Division have boarded their cars and stowed their gear as they leave Camp Robinson, Ark. The date: December 18, 1941. *U.S. Army Signal Corps*

your company keeps a room for train riders, and phone the office. There'll be nothing moving for 36 hours, so you check into the room. The bellboy who takes you up goes away with dirty clothes for laundering, your suit for pressing. You shine shoes, bathe, shave, make out overdue reports for mailing to headquarters. The suit is returned. You dress, drift down to the lobby, and buy a paper. You enjoy a leisurely dinner of your own selection at a table with a cloth. Later there'll be a movie. Next day you sleep until ten o'clock.

At times, incidents en route and bad luck with schedules can make it a pretty hard life. Several nights in a row of sleeping on trains, sometimes on coach seats, will tucker you out. Something goes wrong with nearly every move. Lights in one coach may go out, and the carmen

pass you along from division to division with nothing but excuses until the commander finally refuses to turn a wheel until they're fixed. You can see his viewpoint. Uncle Sam is paying heavy money for this transportation and should have the best there is. On the other hand, the railroad is short-handed in every department. Many materials, on priority lists, are hard to get. The cars are being run almost 24 hours a day every day.

A careless soldier may not notice that the toilet valve sticks, and in 30 minutes the car tanks are drained. Your train may be pulled by a freight engine that can't make the scheduled time. Minor illnesses are handled by the medical officer always aboard, but in case of serious ailment, you must find the nearest army hospital and means of getting the man to it. It may be the commander's first train, and he feels it his duty to inspect the conductor's train orders, ask mileages, running time, and similar weighty questions. Most of them are A-1 swell fellows.

Stops out on line can complicate things. Say you have a string of flats behind your passenger cars. On every flat is a guard of two soldiers. The guard is changed every 12 hours or so. Some soldier may get down on the wrong side and endanger his life by walking down the main line. Reaching the passenger cars, he finds all doors closed. The escort must be alert to every happening.

En route at night you may be aroused at any time, and for any reason. Whether it's serious or not, you've lost sleep. This is not your regular territory where you have friends, and in strange towns between trips, you are the lonesomest man on earth. You write long, long letters to your wife, your office, friends at home. Sometimes you visit a railroad office and ask for work, just to have something to do. You're too old to be in the army yourself. This is your essential-duty way of helping your country. One good thing about it, there's little monotony!

April 1944

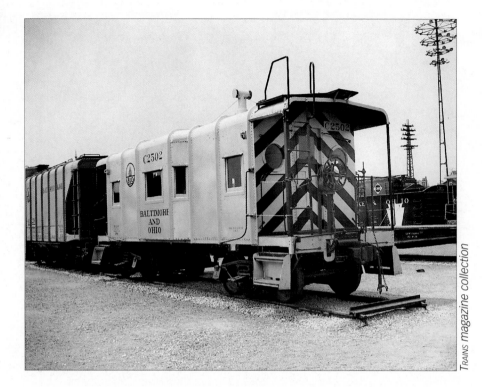

THE CABOOSE

H. Reid

Railfans from far and near gather around "Old-Timer" Echolls to hear his tales of the iron pike.

He knows them all, and it is no difficult job to get him started. One day when I met up with him, he greeted me with a cheery "Hi ya, young feller," and as he laid down a popular railroad publication, he continued, "I s'pose you came to listen to one o' my yarns … what'll it be?"

Before I could answer, he'd already begun talking. "Did you see this article about cabooses in this here magazine?" he asked. Again he gave me no chance to say a word, but began his story. …

"Now I wonder why this feller didn't say any thing about our Norfolk Southern silver crummies? I guess he couldn't take 'em all in just one article, eh? Yep, we're awful proud o' them cabooses. They found out that silver paint stands up better than the usual red. Have you seen the insides o' them? Why, gosh all hemlock, they're regular hotels in themselves! … Not like them we had to ride in a long time ago.

"In the old days the trainmen had to ride in the open, until somebody got the idea o' nailin' some boards up on flatcars or boxcars, which ever ones the railroad wasn't usin' at the time. Those flimsy con- traptions sheltered the crews from the weather, though. Then came the problem of heating. I've been told that they threw some sand on the floor, and built a fire on top this to keep themselves warm. Then, when they actually built cabooses … which were flimsy little things, but I'll get to that later … anyway, unreliable pot-bellied stoves were added, and the crews not only kept themselves warm, but they could cook their meals at the same time. Boy, I've eaten my best meals over those stoves! You've probably read about caboose chefs … well, it's all true, every word of it. These fellers can cook better than any them classy society Frenchies.

"Well, pretty soon the conductors wanted to see what was going on around the front part the train, so a small hole was sawed in the top of the rolling palace, and then the conductor poked his head out o' the opening and saw all he wanted to. Some o' them even put up benches on the roof so's they could be comfortable. I reckon it got pretty cold up there, and eventually the cupola that you know of today came into use by many roads, and the others were quick to follow the practice of placing a permanent enclosure on top o' the crummy.

J. L. Austin, a flagman on the Winston-Salem Southbound, prepares breakfast in his caboose between runs at Wadesboro, N.C. *Philip R. Hastings*

⌶ ⌶

"I was going to tell you about the first real cabooses, wasn't I? Some o' them were remodeled boxcars, and some were dinky four-wheelers. The little four-wheelers were dangerous at first. The designers hadn't figgered on pusher-engines … and they made the cabooses entirely out o' wood. When a pusher-engine coupled up to the end o' the train and began to put pressure on the crummy, well … things were liable to happen … and they often did! Naturally, with an all-wood underframe that wasn't reinforced with steel, the cabooses were likely to telescope. Many's the hapless feller who was crushed to death in such an accident. Gradually, steel underframes found their way beneath the caboose, and they're just as safe, nowadays, as any other rolling stock.

"Cabooses have even been used for passenger cars; did you know that? I remember a railroad out West … it seems to me it was called the Camino, Placerville & Lake Tahoe. …

Anyhow, they used a caboose to carry passengers for about 30 years. There's a road up in Canada, the Dominion

Atlantic, that still uses a crummy for a varnish baggage-coach. The Canadians call cabooses *vans*.

"Yep, they collect nicknames just like everything else. I s'pose you could make a great big collection o' names that have been slapped on the poor caboose. *Monkey buggy, jailhouse, rest room, brain box, hash hut, shack, zoo, go-cart, chariot, cabin car, den, baby's wagon, way-car, glory buggy*, and *doghouse* are just a few o' the monickers. In fact, you can call 'em any thing that you can think of and most o' the time trainmen will know what you're talking about.

"There've been some tall tales circulating around concerning cabooses. It's hard to believe the one I heard about the mountain-climbing Norfolk & Portsmouth Belt Line hack. One day, so the story goes, a runaway caboose slid down a slight grade to where a bridge was located. The bridge must have been up to let a ship through, but this car had no regard for the boat whatsoever, and kept right on going. When it reached the bridge, it still showed no signs of stopping, and actually began climbing up the diagonal supports of the bridge! It probably liked it way up in the air, because it just sat there on top o' that bridge and didn't even make an attempt to come

back down to earth, either. This line always did have trouble with that bridge."

⌶ ⌶

The Old-Timer's story was interrupted momentarily when a whistle shrieked out. … "Say, there goes one o' our standard cabooses behind that extra freight over there. They paint them the regular tuscan-red color."

As I watched the crummy slowly fade from view, and the trim N. S. initials vanish into nothingness, the old man filled his pipe and again glanced at his magazine. It wasn't long before he began to speak again. "Now let me see, where was I?" … Reminded that he was telling me about the early stages of the caboose era, he started talking in earnest. …

"There isn't any set rule regarding the placement of the cupola … this is left entirely up to the railroad itself. I s'pose you've seen some in the middle, some on the side, and others on top way in the back. The Lehigh Valley even has some cars in use today without any cupola at all! And the insides are always handsomely furnished … especially out West, where the crew has to live in the hack for such long periods o' time. Closets and lockers are to be found in each and every

Crew members stand by a Union Pacific wood caboose in Grand Island, Neb., in 1898. *Union Pacific*

caboose in operation today. … And the things that are put in them!

"Gosh a-mighty, what the different railroads haven't done to their shacks! … You see, they hardly ever send their cabooses on to any neighboring roads, so the home road doesn't have to build its crummies in accordance with the other roads' requirements. That's why you see so many goofy-looking experiments. The Southern is working on some new bay-window cabooses, and the Reading Company, so I'm told, has just completed something like 50 new all-steel crummies that are modern masterpieces of railroad craftsmanship. The Milwaukee Road, as you know, pioneered the bay-window cabooses, and it's working on about 100 new ones of this description. … And the Baltimore & Ohio has some weird glory wagons with side cupolas.

"There are long cabooses, and short ones; high ones, low ones; some with eight wheels, and others with but four. I think the Association of American Railroads said that there are over 21,000 cabooses in operation on American rails today. A large portion of these are of entirely different construction. I can remember some super-long ones in Vermont; they belonged to the St. Johnsbury & Lake Champlain. … Then the Reading Company, one of the

few remaining roads still using four-wheelers, has some mighty nice little hacks, and the St. Louis Terminal Railroad has some unusual ones that it calls *shelter cars* which give the appearance of a flatcar with a small hut attached on the top. … And the Lehigh & New England also uses some distinctive four-wheelers. The Southern Pacific simply letters its cabooses with the road's initials, while the narrow gauge teenie-weenies of the Denver & Rio Grande Western are burdened with lettering.

"Many cabooses are equipped with high-speed passenger trucks. I remember that the Lackawanna has some of these, and so does the Boston & Maine. I think you'll find a lot of archbar trucks still being used on the American cabooses just about as frequently as any other type. Four-wheelers seem to be outmoded … like the narrow gauge! There's a soft spot in my heart for the little fellers, though. Almost all railroads at one time or another have had some on their roster. They are popular with the fading slim-gauge pikes. Have you seen pictures of those miniatures of the abandoned Uintah Railroad? You couldn't even cuss a cat in them, they're so small. I recollect a four-wheeler in Pennsylvania, belonging to the Coudersport & Port Allegany … a typical

jerkwater outfit, anyway. … It had one o' its glory wagons rigged up with a Railway Enthusiasts electric sign. The Enthusiasts fixed it up to suit their needs, and the C&PA was kind enough to install this contraption on the end of the caboose!

"Yep, young feller, the caboose has played an important part in the history of American railroads … and don't let anybody tell you different. Why, when the Pennsylvania wanted to perfect its automatic rear-end release and quick rechargin' valve, it installed one in a caboose in Scully, Pa. In fact, just about all o' the new fangled safety devices find their way to the caboose before they've finished testing 'em."

⌶ ⌶

The old gentleman's train was pulling out in a short while, or I suppose he would have kept on talking until all hours of the night. He excused himself and made his way to a long wooden caboose. Agilely hopping up to the deck, he waved a cheery farewell as the train slowly began to roll. Somehow his words lingered in my mind, repeating themselves over and over again. … "The caboose has played an important part in the history of American railroads." … Nobody will ever tell me differently, either.

June 1944

New York Central

HAUNTED ROUNDHOUSE

W. T. Coniff

There is a haunted house at the foot of West 72nd Street in New York.

Well, it is not exactly 72nd Street, for since the completion of the Express Highway, the bridge high above the maze of tracks that the railroaders call "The Farm" is at the foot of 71st Street. There, crouched under the towering structure of the elevated highway, is the old Hudson River roundhouse, and it is haunted by the wraiths of the iron horse of steel and steam that vanished from New York's West Side with the electrification of the

New York Central's freight and terminal operations in the city.

It is a far cry since the boom days of the '20s, when the 72nd Street Yards hummed with business and half a hundred steam yard-engines called it home. Now, spluttering diesel-electrics that look like misshapen black beetles haunt the crumbling stalls where only a few years ago the last of that sturdy stable of steam yard-goats and powerful, businesslike freight-haulers were quartered. A gap in the circular walls separates the old roundhouse into two segments facing each other across the turntable pit. The old tracks extend out into the vacant space, and open pits yawn like uncovered tiger traps beneath the massive columns that straddle the huddle of old buildings and shelter it in part from the rains and snows of the changing seasons. Only a few of the stalls are utilized now; diesels spend little time in the roundhouse. A relief crew brings them in, two by two, like animals into the ark, across the bridge-like turntable for the brief inspection and servicing that they receive each 24 hours.

⚒ ⚒

Gone is the cinder pit with half-naked fire-cleaners shaking cascades of glowing coals down through the pans of incoming engines. No whistles moan at the coal chute where impatient hostlers jockeyed steam engines back and forth for "smokeless coal" and the "sneezo" that was regular fare for the road engines. The coal chute has vanished with the water plug in the wholesale renovation that accompanied the change in motive power.

Of the once sizable shop force, few remain. About five men on each shift inspect and service the diesel-electric yard engines and the straight electrics that haul freight trains into the city from Harmon, northern terminus of the electrified section, 33 miles away. You can hear the shop force about its work when engine bells ring without apparent reason and air brakes apply and release, as engines are tested on the storage tracks in the Basin Yard under the echoing vault of the great girders that carry the landscaped park area and highway above the railroad tracks for several miles north of 72nd Street.

At the southern end of the semicircular house is the engine dispatcher's office and foreman's headquarters. On the callboard that covers most of one wall in the dispatcher's office are the designations of all engine crews working in freight or yard service between New York and Harmon, and the through trains that are manned from this terminal. Tags bearing the names of each engineer and fireman are hung on their various assignments.

The initiated can spot vacancies and predict, with some degree of accuracy, the number of men that will be used as long as 12 hours in advance. Down the center of the board is the Extra List, the men on which are subject to call at any time. They are the shock troops of the railroad and give the service elasticity to absorb the unexpected influxes of traffic, floods, wrecks, or any other contingency that may arise.

Twenty-four hours a day the two telephones keep up an incessant and insistent clamor. The dispatcher, sometimes talking into the two instruments and carrying on a conversation with someone in the outer office at the same time, jots down notes of projected movements, calls men for various assignments for points as far north as Hudson and Poughkeepsie and from all the towns along the division. He notes the arrival and departure of engine crews and makes corresponding changes on the board. Men call in to "mark off" or "mark up," and supervisory officials make brusque requests for information on train delays.

Engineers and firemen are continually coming and going through the narrow doorway of the outer office, exchanging rough jibes with the harassed dispatcher, glancing through the sheaf of ever-changing bulletins and notices that must be acknowledged before each trip. A yellow register slip must be signed when going on or off duty, and departing engine crews must compare their watches with a standard clock. Notices of brotherhood meetings and obituary announcements are tacked near the bulletin board. Through the foggy glass of the windows one can see the full flow of America's war effort bound for the far-flung battlefronts of the world.

The float job, with its string of battered old flatcars that enables it to reach across the float or pontoon to the busy float bridges without putting the locomotive's weight on the pile-supported approaches of those structures, unloads the tethered car-floats which perform so much of the interchange work for railroads in the metropolitan area. The slow, careful diesel worries the cars off, first on one side and then on the other, trimming the weight carefully before doubling onto the center track of the clumsy, cranky, blunt-bowed craft and pulling the 24-car draft up into the yard where it is swiftly

batted out or shoved onto the hat track for the hump engine's attention. Another engine grinds by with a long string of flatcars loaded with army-colored tanks, squat and grim; crated Spitfires are bound for the open pier where floating cranes transfer the tanks and trucks and planes to lighters that will carry them to shipside. The running gear of an electric locomotive of meter gauge is bound for South America, and here, on an inbound draft, is a drop-end gondola with huge mahogany logs, hewed square as they hew them only in British Honduras.

⚒ ⚒

"A great gang used to work here in the old days," said one of the laborers in the roundhouse. "I've seen 20 engines lined up at the cinder pit waiting to have their fires cleaned. When times were good they couldn't get enough men. There were all kinds of emigrants in here at different times—Irish and Italians and Poles and Finns, right off the boat, willing enough but gullible and green. I remember one big Italian fire-cleaner, an enormous fellow, strong as a bull.

"They used to send yard engines in then to have their fires cleaned while the crews went to supper. One of the firemen had an idea that by a little strategy he could stretch their 20-minute lunch period to a longer period!" The old fellow chuckled to himself and continued. "Well, just before they brought the engine in the fireman shook his fire down until the grates were barely covered. He had noticed that the big Italian was in the habit of shaking the fire thoroughly before looking into the firebox. They put the engine on the pit and scrambled off as the fire-cleaner climbed on and pulled the shaker bar off the tank. 'Give 'im a shake, Tony,' the fire boy said on his way out the gangway. Already the big fellow had the shaker bar on the grate levers and was swaying back and forth for dear life. He went across the row, front section, middle and back, and then he stepped back, pressed the door pedal, and bent down to look in at the empty firebox.

"Well, sir," the old fellow went on, "the fireman had his long supper hour. They had to build up a fire with wood, and it took almost an hour to get the engine ready to go out again, but the big

New York Central's 72nd Street roundhouse bustled with activity in 1916. *New York Central*

fire-cleaner never heard the last of that 'Give 'im a shake, Tony' as long as he was here!'

Outside on the ready track two R engines, coupled in multiple with heavy cables looped between them, awaited a crew. "Look at 'em now," an old-timer in the shop force said.

"There is no difference in any of them. They will pull so much, not a pound more; they will run so fast, not a mile faster if you were falling down a well with them. Perhaps they are an improvement over the steam engines here in the city, but they have their shortcomings too. For one thing, they are dirty; the old steam engines were scalded and scoured and wiped and polished once in a while anyway; but these things aren't even swept out except once in a blue moon. You can't wet them down or wash them, for they have no water, and if you did, you'd be apt to get electrocuted. Those big traction blowers that keep the motors cool blow a fine grit into everything and through everything. In the winter that dry, searing heat will burn your legs off while your back is freezing and the frost is forming on the rivet heads of the cab, and you have to keep the window open a little no matter how cold it is, or you are apt to drowse for a minute and miss a signal or wake up with somebody's caboose in your lap." He shook his head and wandered off toward the locker room.

Behind the office, in a long, bare room, the stationary engine runs almost without noise. A muffled exhaust beside the flaring mouth of the black stack trails a ribbon of steam high in the gloomy recesses where birds seek shelter from the cool breezes off the river. Next, the long sand track leads directly through the roundhouse to the racks where the sand boxes of the diesels are refilled each time they come in for servicing.

Outside, under the arch of the viaduct, a heater car or *kitchenette* is spotted at the hoses to receive fuel and water. In each of these units, of which there are five, a vertical, oil-burning boiler carrying a steam pressure of 200 pounds per square inch is used to supply heat on mail and express merchandise trains hauled by R type locomotives. These engines, designed for freight service, are not equipped with heating boilers, as are the S and T types of passenger locomotives. Even in the summer, kitchenettes are used when shipments of live fish consigned to the New York market require that the water be heated for their finny passengers.

It is gloomy under the shadow of the Express Highway. Water drips monotonously down from the clammy condensation on the towering girders. A little to the north the general yard office is the pulsating heart of the battle to keep them rolling—the office that integrates the ebb and flow of wartime traffic into an orderly pattern and translates it into terms of trains and men. Behind it, toward the river, is the Railroad YMCA, or as it is more commonly called "The Lord's Barn," where men eat and sleep between trips.

Across the shallow turntable pit in one of the dingy stalls of the old roundhouse is a test rack for the diesels. Heavy cables snake across the floor and an imposing array of gauges and meters are banked above the elevated platform that runs for an engine-length beside the old pit. Here, under the searching eyes of vigilant inspectors, the ills and ailments of the new motive power are diagnosed and corrected. A monthly report, sworn to before a notary public and similar in many respects to that required by the Interstate Commerce Commission for steam locomotives, is encased in glass in each cab, as symbolic of virtue and integrity as a framed marriage license in a New England home.

Diesel-electrics and other types of electric motive power now in use on the New York Central's Electric Division require no turntable. Equipped to operate from either end, they run in either direction by changing the controls. The slow attrition of the years made little impression on the stoutly built old roundhouse, but one by one, the changes in motive power have stripped it of its functions until it has been virtually eliminated as a factor in the maintenance and repair of the present equipment. The long, cavernous tunnel under the highway and park area may well turn out to be the successor to the picturesque old ruin of the once-busy engine terminal, but whatever happens to the old Hudson River roundhouse, the gallant ghosts of the vanished steam engines will haunt the spot forever and a day.

December 1945

THE LOCOMOTIVE FIREMAN

G. W. O'Connor

It has been said that at some time in the life of every boy there is a period—long or short—when he feels that the only life worth living is that of the man who sits with his hand on the throttle and his eye on the gleaming rails ahead.

Some of us never get over this feeling, and the locomotive engineer remains, and always will remain, the hero of the railroad. We are proud to know him and are perhaps even a little bit envious of him. We like to learn as much as we can about his work.

Many have learned a lot about the engineer's work, but few (other than those in the business) have learned much about the work of the fireman. Yet every engineer, when he started out in the engine service, had to begin as a "smoke agent." Perhaps the fireman is not so glamorous but his work is nevertheless very important and interesting.

Personally I have never had the pleasure of firing, or even riding on, a stoker-fired engine, so I shall confine myself mostly to describing the fireman's work on hand-fired engines.

Obviously, the first requirement for a fireman is that he must know how to fire. Anyone can shovel coal but not everyone can keep an engine hot. It requires a little knowledge and skill. I had a chat with a traveling engineer one day about instructing firemen, and he told me that he preferred to have his student firemen come from working on a farm.

"Then," said he, "I can tell him to load the firebox like a hay wagon, around the edges first."

Particular attention is also paid to keeping the corners well filled, and after that, the coal is placed wherever the fire looks brightest. Some firemen bang the heel of the shovel on the door opening as they throw the coal in, which scatters the coal more evenly over the top of the fire instead of heaping it all in one place.

Modern power is equipped with air-operated firedoors. There is a little pedal below each door, and when the fireman steps on it, the door opens. It stays open as long as the pedal is held down, and as soon as the fireman removes his foot from the pedal, the door closes. Before the days of air-operated doors the fireman had to swing open the firedoor by means of a chain strung between the handle of the door and the roof of the cab. After putting in his scoop of coal he had to swing the door shut.

The matter of closing the door between each scoop of coal is really very important, as a moment's reflection will show. If the door is left open great quantities of cold air will be drawn into the firebox, not only diminishing the heat from the fire but also (which may be even more important) striking the boiler and chilling it in certain spots, resulting in uneven contraction from the cold. Uneven contraction, in turn, causes leaks—perhaps around the tubes, perhaps elsewhere—but still leaks.

An example of this condition occurred on the transport *President Grant* in World War I when it sailed for France with an inexperienced crew of stokers who left the firedoors open much of the time. Soon the boilers were leaking so badly that it was thought the ship would have to return to Hoboken without completing the trip. Now, it so happened that a railway regiment, the 21st Engineers, containing many experienced railway firemen, was on board. Volunteers were called for to fire the ship's boilers, and the railway firemen took over. They knew enough to keep their doors closed as much as possible, and here is the interesting point: The leaks in the boilers not only got no worse but they even made up a little and the trip was successfully completed.

It can easily be seen that if open firedoors had such bad effects on a steamship's boilers, where the draft is comparatively mild, a locomotive boiler with its violent draft would suffer much worse. Keeping the doors closed, by the way, is one of the advantages of stoker-fired engines, as they do not have to open up for every scoop of coal.

Keeping the tender full of water was among the many jobs of a fireman in the steam era. *Dave Bunge*

⊥   ⊥

"Little and often" is a good motto to follow in the hand-firing of soft coal-burning engines, though the hard coal-burners do not require such frequent attention, just as we find it in our domestic furnaces. Of course, in any type of engine, the heavier the load, the more fuel will be consumed.

A traveling engineer told me he had a young chap come to him for instruction one time, and it was found that he was loading the fire much too heavily. On this particular road they had a system whereby a student would make a run, or perhaps several runs, with an engineer, and when the engineer felt that the student had progressed satisfactorily, he would sign a card to that effect and the student would move on to another engineer. When three engineers had signed the card the student was qualified as a fireman.

This particular young man was just about sunk, as be had his heart set on becoming a fireman and two engineers had already turned him down. This was his last chance.

My friend told him about liking men from the farm and found that this chap had come from a farm. Perhaps this gave him a little confidence, but still he over-fired his engine so that it commenced to lose steam. The regular fireman raked over the fire and got it going again.

"Now some more?" asked the student, taking up the scoop again.

"No, take a rest," said my friend, and the student uneasily got up on the seat box. They started up a grade.

"Now shall I?"

The engineer waved him back on the seat. "No, you're too anxious," said he. "I'll tell you when."

Then, a little later, the steam began to drop. "Now, put on a little," said the engineer. The young chap went to work and was surprised when the engineer stopped him after only a few scoops of coal had been thrown on the fire. He watched the steam gauge, no doubt expecting to see it go way, way down, but instead it climbed! He learned something, and from then on, he started to improve. By the end of the day he was firing without any further advice from the engineer. They had a freight train going 50 miles an hour, and he was able to make the steam gauge climb when he wanted to.

A happy young man went home that night instead of the down-hearted one who had come to work in the morning. He had mastered the art of stoking an engine, he had one signature on his card, and he now knew he could get the others. He was on his way to being a fireman.

So you see the necessity for knowing not only where to place the coal but how much to put in at a time. Not too much and not too little. Some firemen like a heavier fire than others, believing that a thick bed of coals is not torn up so easily, especially if the engine slips in starting. They have a little more reserve or leeway. Others believe that a thin fire uses less coal, and I think they are right, as I notice that thinner fires are claimed as an advantage of certain grate bars. It may take a little more skill to run a thin fire successfully, but I believe, with the advocates of a thin fire, that it will save fuel.

I I

Besides the actual stoking, an important duty usually left to the fireman, although really the engineer's responsibility, is the keeping up of the water level in the boiler. If the water is allowed to get too low there is great danger of burning the boiler, and in extreme cases, the boiler may be so weakened by the burning that it will explode. On the other hand, the water level must not be allowed to get too high, or wet steam will get into the cylinders and the engine will lose power, to say nothing about washing the oil out of the cylinders. Some years ago when I was working for the Bell Locomotive Works (makers of oil-burning steam dinkies), we had an engineer call in from a nearby job saying that his engine hardly had enough power to move itself let alone do any work. The answer was high water. He had allowed it to rise so high that he was getting nearly all water down to the cylinders.

The gauge glass is the ordinary means of reading the water level although it is not supposed to be used except as a checkup or super precaution. Enginemen are supposed to use the gauge cocks arranged at three different levels on the back of the boiler. The top one, when opened, should blow steam, the middle one a mixture of steam and water, and the bottom one water only. I say the gauge glass is not *supposed* to be used except as a checkup and that the gauge cocks are *supposed* to be the real water level indicators, but the fact is that the reverse is usually the actual case. The glass is the principal indicator used, and the gauge cocks are the checkup.

I remember that it struck me as something odd the first time I heard an engineer say that there was "half a glass of water" in the boiler. Of course he meant that the gauge glass was half full, but it sounded as though he meant that half a drinking glass of water was all the boiler had in it.

Anyone can look at a gauge glass and tell where the water level is, but only the experienced can tell whether a gauge cock is blowing steam or water. To the uninitiated it all looks like steam but there are ways of telling which is which. Many enginemen rely solely on the sound. Water will make more of a roaring noise while steam will make a hissing sound. If the nozzle of the gauge cock can be seen it will be found that the white cloud from a jet of water will be white right up into the nozzle while if the jet is blowing steam there will be a space of half an inch or so before the white cloud forms, making it possible to see up into the nozzle while the steam is blowing.

Those who have had experience in operating a steam boiler, even a domestic steam furnace, know that the introduction of cold water will pull down the steam pressure, and the student fireman on a locomotive learns this very, very early in his career. The experienced fireman must therefore know not only *how* to put water into the boiler but *when* is the most advantageous time to do it. As to what is the proper water level, this varies very considerably with conditions, including the judgment of the engineer.

When putting water into the boiler it is often possible on local passenger runs to start the pump or injector whenever the throttle is closed so as to pull down the steam only when it is not being used by the engine. This may also prevent the safety valve from blowing and thus save fuel and firing effort. I have seen a skillful fireman on such a run keep his steam gauge at the same pressure throughout the trip, hardly varying it a pound either way.

On longer runs it is necessary to put water into the boiler while the engine is working steam—but then the rate at which it is pumped or injected can be cut down so as not to affect the steam pressure too much.

In addition to putting on the pump or injector whenever the throttle is closed the fireman usually opens the blower in order to keep the fire from slumping too much. The blower is a steam jet located in the smokebox and used for producing a forced draft when the engine is drifting and therefore not producing draft by means of the exhaust. The term *forced draft*, by the way, is not technically correct in connection with a locomotive. When air is sucked through the fire and the boiler tubes, as in the locomotive, it is properly called an *induced draft*. A forced draft forces the air from below the fire. The term *forced draft* is usually used in locomotive work in spite of not being technically correct.

A point often overlooked by those without experience is that an engine is usually fired left-handed, with the left hand held down near the scoop and the right hand out at the end of the handle.

Most people naturally shovel right-handed but it is not hard to change. The fireman—in this country, at least—is on the left side of the engine, and it is easier for him to stay there than to be crossing over and back all the time, as he would have to do whenever he started or finished putting in coal if he were to fire right-handed. It is better to have him on the left side in any case, as he can then take signals from the left side of the train and relay them on to the engineer.

In keeping up steam the engineer can often help or hinder the fireman. If he opens up and uses unnecessarily large amounts of steam in getting his train under way he will pull down the steam pressure, and the heavy exhaust may also tear up the fire, especially if the engine should slip. The proper way to run the engine is to use only as much steam as it will take without pulling the pressure down, except that, if the run is short, as mentioned earlier, the pressure may be pulled down in making a snappy get away and recovered later when the engine is not working steam. The proper use of the cutoff by the engineer will also greatly help the fireman, as the steam will then all be used to the best advantage.

In addition to knowing how to fire, the fireman must also know the Book of Rules, including the meanings of the hand and wayside signals. He must qualify the same as the engineer on the division where he is to work and must pass an examination as to his knowledge of the locations of all signals, switches, stations, and other characteristics of the line.

On some roads the engineer and fireman call all the signal aspects to each other. On others they call only those which are not indicating clear with no restrictions. The usual way of calling them is, for example: "Yellow over green" or "double yellow," or perhaps "red."

As soon as possible the student fireman learns to stop his train in case the engineer should be come incapacitated from any cause.

After the student fireman has qualified to work alone (that is, without having a qualified fireman with him) there will still

Being able to keep the fire at just the right intensity was a fireman's most important task. *Don Wood*

be much to learn and also ample opportunity to acquire knowledge of the ways of the railroad as well as further details of the locomotive. A man aspiring to become an engineer will find the air brakes a most fascinating study. It is the subject for many a roundhouse discussion, as is also the Book of Rules—especially that part relating to train orders and operation in other than automatic signal territory.

Like many other jobs on the railroad, the firemen's runs are put up for bids and the award goes to the man with the most seniority. Until a man is old enough on the railroad to "own" a run he works on

the extra list, covering any run where he is needed. Day or night, he is always on call.

The work is hard, and the hours are often long and inconvenient. A new fireman should realize that on the railroad someone has to work nights and Sundays, not to mention Saturday afternoons and holidays. Aside from any special interest he may have in locomotives he can look forward, as a compensation for the disadvantages of his work, to the size of his pay check, and he has the additional satisfaction of knowing he is part of one of the most vital industries of our nation.

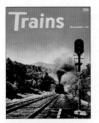

November 1946

TRAINS *magazine collection*

THE LAST OF THE WOODBURNERS

Lucius Beebe

Out behind the shops and enginehouses and in the shadow of the four towering chimneys of the vast Brooks-Scanlon Corporation lumber mills at Foley, Fla., is a pile of rusted and disintegrating cabbagehead smokestacks, souvenirs of the days, not so many years ago, when all the motive power of the Live Oak, Perry & Gulf Railroad as well as that of its parent corporation, Brooks-Scanlon, was woodburning, as befitted one of the biggest lumber mills in the South.

Today Brooks-Scanlon's private road engines are still woodburners, both in the deep yellow pine forest of the interior and in the yards at Foley, but in 1943, the last of the company's Live Oak, Perry & Gulf's locomotives was converted to coal burning operation.

"In three years the price of coal has been hiked on us three times, and I'm thinking about changing the whole setup to diesel," M. J. Foley, president of the concern, told us. "But I don't think we could get along without No. 5. That's the pride and joy of the mill, and I think our men would walk out on us if we didn't keep it in commission just as it is."

Outside in the bright Florida noontide, No. 5 rolled slowly by with a cut of timber cars, a proud aristocrat among locomotives and obviously a member of the old order. From the sparkling brass candlesticks on either side of its headlight and the deer horns mounted in the oldest of railroading traditions, to its tender filled with sawmill scraps, No. 5 bespoke long hours of affectionate labor by its crew. The smokebox and boiler lagging shone blue and glistening under the tropic sun, the tires of its drivers were scrupulously rimmed with silver paint, and off the backhead of the boiler, with its gleaming brass pipes and feedlines, one could eat dinner without hesitation.

"Once in a while we run her out on the main line as far as Perry," Mr. Foley said. "That's five miles, and there's no reason why she should not go on to the other end of the run to Live Oak. That's 40 miles. Only we have no fueling platforms for her to wood up at anywhere along the line, so she sticks pretty much to the yards nowadays. We load her from a chute, just the same as we would from a coal tipple, only it's filled with scrap and trim from the planing mill."

No. 5, a Baldwin-built Prairie type engine, was the only one in running order at Foley at the moment, although a somewhat less elegantly maintained sister woodburner was over the pit in the shops nearby having its grates overhauled. In the woods to the south were several other woodburners, we were told, none of them so splendid as No. 5 and none of them boasting a true

Crewmen toss pine knots into the tender of Mississippi & Alabama 2-6-2 No. 4 at the wood (or wooding-up) rack in Leakesville, Miss., in September 1948. *C. W. Witbeck*

cabbagehead stack. Their stacks are conventional capped chimneys with a spark arrester in the smokebox.

The Live Oak, Perry & Gulf was one of the last railroads serving as a common carrier and with regular passenger service to use woodburning motive power, and even today its converted Ten-Wheelers with soft coal in their grates are as wonderfully maintained as they were in the old days. A round trip the entire length of the line, 44 miles, is scheduled every day, and a daily mixed consist also makes a round trip by way of Mayo on a branch connecting with the main line at Mayo Junction, 20 miles west of Live Oak. The mixed trains carry either a combine or an antiquated coach, and during the war passenger revenue was not inconsiderable.

This railroad, originally chartered as the Live Oak & Perry Railroad Company, has been a going concern since 1903, when its original segment of track from Live Oak to milepost 31 was built by Thomas and R. L. Dowling, owners of the Dowling Lumber & Naval Stores Company. It was extended through to Hampton Springs, a resort town 15 miles west of Foley, in 1906, and during the Florida boom of the middle '20s it did a handsome passenger business on this branch, its passenger revenue sometimes running to $60,000 and $70,000 a year. Up till 1915 its engines carried tall balloon stacks

rather than the round cabbagehead chimneys of a later era. The Hampton Springs branch was torn up after the hotel there closed in 1944, and today the railroad passenger revenue doesn't run to much more than $3,000 to $4,000 annually.

The LOP&G connects at Perry with the South Georgia Railway and the Atlantic Coast Line, and at Live Oak with the ACL and the Seaboard Railway. Its greatest traffic, naturally enough, is in lumber, both rough and finished, and more than half of its mixed and freight trains are cars loaded with Brooks-Scanlon's products.

The talk in Perry's various lumber workers' saloons had it that other woodburning private railroads are scattered around Florida, notably those of P. B. Wilson Company at Holopaw in Osceola County about halfway down the peninsula of Florida, and in the yards of the Putnam Lumber Company at Cross City a few miles south of the LOP&G. There was also talk of a common carrier some 80 or 90 miles to the west of Perry, the Marianna & Blountstown, that still maintained woodburning power. Investigation proved, however, that even the Marianna & Blountstown burned its last cordwood fuel back in 1944, although its engines,

The Mississippi & Alabama's only steam locomotive, Prairie (2-6-2) No. 4, puts out a cloud of wood smoke near Vinegar Bend, Ala., in August 1948. An internal (in the smokebox) spark arrestor takes the place of the large balloon stack. *Thomas Lawson Jr.*

never possessed of the cabbage stacks of the Live Oak, Perry & Gulf, are identical in appearance with what they previously were. Photographically it might still be functioning on turpentine knots in all its original glory.

The M&B is not without its interesting aspects, however, according to O. O. Miller, its general manager. It is owned by Alfred F. du Pont of Wilmington, Del., who came by it quite incidentally to the purchase of a large tract of timberland during the Florida boom of 1926. Out of 1,200 shares of the railroad outstanding, 1,197 had been held by the original lumber company, and Mr. du Pont was surprised when, one fine morning, he woke up to find himself owner of an up-and-going little railroad 29 miles long. A parallel incident is recorded by Petronius in his *Satyricon*, wherein Trimalchio, the Roman millionaire capitalist, once discovered the island of Sicily casually included in a list of recently acquired real estate. Mr. Miller had not heard about Petronius but recalls that Mr. du Pont has never ridden on his own railroad. There are no passenger accommodations on the trains, anyway.

⚋ ⚋

Elsewhere the legend of the woodburners persisted. The 76-mile-long South Georgia Railway, running northward from its connection with the Live Oak, Perry & Gulf at Perry to Adel in Georgia, was variously reported still to have a

couple of woodburners and to have scrapped them. Investigation at Quitman, where the South Georgia's shops are located, disclosed that neither of these is, in fact, the case. In 1943 it converted its three woodburners to coal, and their cabbage stacks, mournful reminders of brave yesterdays, are rusting beside the roundhouse where J. J. Davis, the road's master mechanic, showed them to us.

"We ran shy of yellow pine three or four years ago, but I hated to see the old times go," he remarked. "We'd been trailing turpentine smoke through the woods since 1897, yes sir. A long time, and when you get as old as I am you don't like change. It ain't always progress."

A shrieking Ten-Wheeler with the insigne of the Georgia & Florida on its tender boiled past on the main line and Mr. Davis allowed that business was so brisk they had to lease an extra engine to help out the three on their own power roster. From 1906 through 1926 the South Georgia had paid fabulous dividends, sometimes as high as $60 on a $100 par share, but of late its operating profits have been far more modest. Railroad connoisseurs know the South Georgia as the present possessor of a singularly well proportioned Ten-Wheeler, No. 6 of the now abandoned Kishacoquillas Valley Railroad, purchased from that road after its tracks were torn up a few years since.

Up in Louisiana the Red River & Gulf, owned and operated by a lumber industry, also once was woodburning, but its two remaining locomotives today burn

more conventional fuel, and a great part of its trackage is being torn up. The RR&G's No. 200, a noble cabbage stack Prairie type engine, is still in good operating condition in the company yards at Long Leaf, La., where the line exchanges freight with the Missouri Pacific, but it hasn't been fired up in several years. On an adjacent rip track are three or four even older engines with huge balloon stacks waiting to be broken up for scrap.

Aside from being distinguished by the presence of four members of the Crowell family among its executives, the Red River made the public prints during the war years when it resisted pressure for its sale to the army to be used as a full-size working experiment in demolition. Army engineers were anxious to dynamite its trestles and tie knots in its rails for practice purposes, but the owners resisted all bids. Today most of its track except the 12 miles between Long Leaf and LeCompte by way of Holdup is being torn up by a junk concern.

⚋ ⚋

Like fossilized relics of the era of crawling animal things in the shallow waters of inland seas, there seemed to be traces of the evidence of woodburners all around us. Their discarded shells were everywhere at hand; their tracks ran endlessly, like those of forgotten swamp monsters across the Mississippian soil, and might eventually form deposits of shale for future excavators to ponder over. But the living crustacean himself seemed to have perished from the changing face of the earth, and we mourned for the little Ponchartrain Railroad running out of New Orleans in the '80s and over piles and trestles to happy picnickings at Bayou St. John; we mourned the *Nancy Hanks*, crack varnish train of the Central of Georgia in the '90s, celebrated for its wood smoke trailing for miles behind its daily going through the astonished countryside. It was named by William Wadley, builder of the Central of Georgia, not for Abe Lincoln's mother, but for a racehorse of the identical name. Colonel Wadley, an admirer of horseflesh in the old southern tradition, caused a likeness of his favorite mare to be etched in the stained glass windows of the parlor cars and otherwise insinuated into the decorative scheme.

The ghosts of the cabbage stacks were at every turn, as was the legend of their brave flowering, but the only authentic woodburners we had actually encountered were those in the yards of lumber companies, like gentle dinosaurs in well-upholstered zoos. We wanted them untamed and running free.

⊥ ⊥

It was a cool spring morning in Alabama, 75 miles north of Mobile, the day we discovered what, so far as can be established, is the last woodburning common carrier anywhere in the United States. Mobile, the night before, had been celebrating Mardi Gras in a sort of miniature imitation of New Orleans, which was currently doing the same thing on an epic scale of uproar and hooray, and we had absorbed a preposterous quantity of whisky which was certainly not the kind Kentucky colonels are forever hoisting through their imperials in the distillers' advertisements.

When, beside the improbable iron of the Mississippi & Alabama Railroad a few miles outside of Vinegar Bend, Ala., we discovered what was to all appearances a wooding-up platform liberally stocked with turpentine knots cut of a length for locomotive boilers, we inclined to credit the illusion to the evening previous, which had been devoted to ill-advised enterprise in the Battle House taproom. It would go away later.

But when the up-train from Leaksville, 27 miles down the line from Vinegar Bend, came into view under a creditable facsimile of a forest fire combined with a Paine's Fireworks representation of the Burning of Chicago, we knew that nothing but fat pine on the grates could ever produce such a traveling conflagration, and, moments later, the contents of the tender justified us.

The Mississippi & Alabama's only locomotive, a tolerably well preserved 2-6-2, lamentably lacks a cabbagehead stack in the great tradition; a spark arrester inside the smokebox prevents it from putting the adjacent landscape to the torch. Three or four wooding-up platforms along the right-of-way between Vinegar Bend and Leaksville provide fueling facilities at convenient intervals, but as the major portion of the road's

The engineer oils the valve gear of Brooks-Scanlon No. 5, a cabbage-stacked, woodburning 2-6-2. *Frank Clodfelter*

revenue derives from turpentine logs bound for the trying furnaces of Mobile, it might quite well consume part of its own freight in an emergency. There are occasional high cars of finished woods from the mills at Leaksville, and the day we discovered the M&A, it was hauling out two carloads of mine props bound for the coal pits of Belgium aboard a vessel then loading in Mobile. The Gulf, Mobile & Ohio's daily drag freight would pick them up that afternoon from the Vinegar Bend exchange track.

Passengers and the mails on the M&A may ride aboard its caboose, a jaunty vehicle devoid of sashes in its windows or doors in the door frames, or in a gasoline motor wagon bearing a strong resemblance to the closed vans favored by Little Sisters of the Poor and other charitable orders in large cities.

This particular day the GM&O's *Rebel* was two hours off schedule, and both the steam train and the motor van were on hand when it drew into Vinegar Bend and started unloading mail sacks. It is doubtful if, except in railroad pageants and similar inspired groupings, such dramatic contrasts were ever spotted on adjacent tracks as were represented by the crimson-painted diesel-electric streamliner and the last woodburner, panting under a cloud of undulant soot in a brake in the Alabama woodlands.

Vinegar Bend itself is a communal last chapter. Once, a local ancient told us, it

was a hustling township boasting a huge planing mill, numerous stores and residences, and a 42-room hotel. The railroad owned half a dozen engines, each one smokier and more pyrotechnical than the next, and life went on at a giddy pace. But the family that lived in semi-feudal magnificence amidst the conveyor belts and circular saws and fresh wood smells had fallen on evil days. The nearby timber had been exhausted, the mills had shut down, the workers had moved away. Today no trace of the teeming years remain except a boarded-up 17-room house, in which live two senescent and declining descendants of the Turner family, and the stucco station of the Gulf, Mobile & Ohio Railroad. The Mississippi & Alabama is only a vestigial trace of the railroad it once was, and it and the Mississippi Export Railroad, a number of miles to the south and completely dieselized, are now the two ends of the same 80-mile-long parent railroad with the center section abandoned. For its 17 miles of track the M&A now pays $5,000 a year rental. Vinegar Bend was, in a land of trees and a world of lumber, the precise ghost-town counterpart of scores of vanished towns that once flourished and were populous in the mining regions of Colorado. The last woodburning locomotive was head-end power on what was literally a ghost train to yesterday.

June 1948

MAKE MINE AN UPPER

Cornelius Vanderbilt IV

I'm an upper-berth addict—and I admit it.

You see, I'm always on the go. When it isn't transcontinentaling under the Stars and Stripes, it's transsiberianing under the Hammer and Sickle. When it isn't flying down to Rio, it's caravaning up to Tronjem. When it isn't sailing over the deep blue sea, it's junketing through the Indian Ocean. Such, to me, is life. For 30 years now I have been "roving correspondent" for any number of national magazines and newspaper syndicates.

Ashore or afloat, up in the air or down beneath, these itching feet seldom stay put. I've been doing it so long I can scarcely count the times or occasions. My daily travel column becomes dull when I stay put.

I   I

This I do acknowledge: My native land I've crisscrossed many hundreds of times, so that I know practically every employee on every railroad, half of the camp attendants on the national highways, and more stewardesses and pilots than I ought to. Grand folk, most of them, more interested in you and me than nine-tenths of us are in any of them.

And every one of them knows just what to expect when he spies me coming along: "There's that upper-berth guy again" they say to themselves. Sometimes they pass this information along, so that by the time I reach my location in the vehicle I'm about to clamber into, it has become a veritable chant.

I'm so inured to the uppers that I'm sure that the day my wandering hours are through, I'll have an upper constructed in a corner of my home, with all the noises, whistles, bumps, and other gadgets that go with it! Charlie Driscoll, who writes the late O. O. McIntyre's column, says that when they lay me down to sleep they'll have to put me on the upper level, underground, or I may get up and come to life again!

Twenty-odd years ago the president of an eastern railroad confided to me that there's no place as homelike as an upper berth. His information went right home and stayed there. Ever since then, I've been the greatest living example and exponent of the Pullman Company's most unsalable space.

Ten years ago I made a mail-order survey of the more prominent railroad presidents in this land. Seventeen out of 23 of them said they preferred uppers. This gave my ego a great mental lift. It sent me sailing through space, and only once or twice since then have I deigned to lay my 180 pounds on such an inelegant thing as the lower, on steel or sea.

I've just finished my more than 300th trip from the Atlantic to the Pacific behind the iron horse. I spent four nights on two different trains, in two separate compartments. Every one of those nights I slept in the upper, and left my bags, typewriters, cameras, spats, and skis down below.

In defense of my favorite means of voyaging-slumber, let me go on record here and now as being unalterably opposed to the new-fangled cars which some of the railroads in this country and abroad are now introducing to try to make the upper berth more sleepable.

Some American lines are taking much advertising space to shriek out to prospective customers that their "20th century improved type of uppers" are equipped with windows, air-conditioning, and dressing rooms! That's the very thing I've been trying all these years to get away from!

One of the chief charms of the upper heretofore has been that there was no window, through the cracks of which the bitter night air could creep. If there is ever such a thing as to give me a sore throat, flu, or a touch of pneumonia, it is the window beside the lower berth, which spans the entire length of the body when the sleeper is the most exposed. Just to think that any railroad should have the nerve to install such an instrument of bacterial terror is enough to turn me into an aviation enthusiast, even though I detest air travel.

Who would ever think of moving his bed beside the longest window in the house and going to sleep beside it, just as if Emily Post had said it was the thing to do?

Now that applies to the air-conditioning racket too. Some sleepers today are equipped with them, and life is not as simple as it used to be. In fact, it's positively drafty.

The other evening I spent a good half hour pulling levers above my head, trying to turn the noisy, windy gadget off. I had asked the porter in my most polite tone to do so earlier, but he was a shifty fellow, and he muttered something about its being against regulations to monkey with the Pullman car machinery. He added, *sotto voce*, that he would turn on some heat instead. But I didn't want heat, nor did I want the cold. I like to leave the car ventilator open at night. It usually gives me sufficient air, and out there on the New Mexican desert with the thermometer in the zeros, it was quite cold enough to suit me.

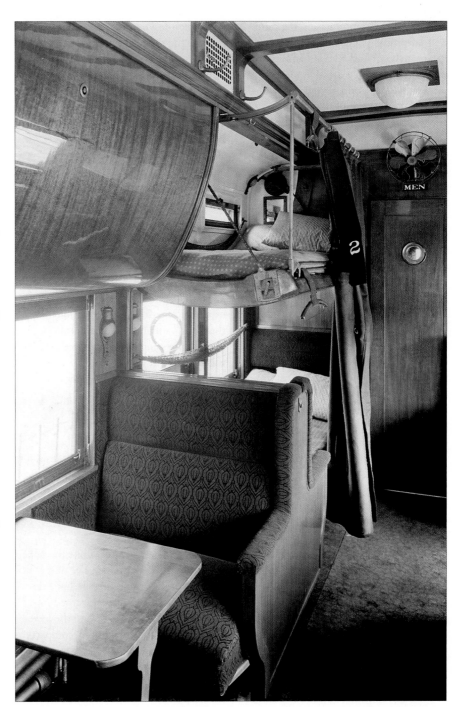

A Pullman section in the daytime (left) provided facing seats and an optional table. At night (right), the upper berth folded down and the seats converted to form a lower bed. Curtains provided privacy. *American Car & Foundry*

Well, of course, no heat came on. The porter failed to answer the bell. Guess he was out in the baggage car playing craps with the rest of the train crew. And I was up on my hind legs on all kinds of doo-dads without effect.

"Just think," I was saying to myself, "of your ignominy, should you catch cold in the upper tonight. Why, you couldn't face the world for days. You'd be the laughing stock of all Wilshire Boulevard, from Perino's to Mike Romanoff's, and back again."

Yes, it was true. I couldn't face my friends in the great Southwest for eons if I should get the sniffles from all of this, because for decades I had been preaching the Theory of the Upper Berth.

And as for dressing rooms, the third well-advertised point, well, what did that mean, anyway? And who is Houdini enough to contrive a dressing room up there above the world so high! Impossible. A Catch-penny Phrase. Something new to fool the uninitiated. And yet—

Wasn't there such a thing as the Federal Trade Commission, or whatever that government agency was called, which prohibited companies and individuals from advertising untruths?

Well, give them their darned old dressing rooms, providing it was just what it said; as for me, I'd take the old-style upper just the same.

As if he anticipated my thought, the gentleman with the underslung Gen. Dawes pipe and the oversized O. O. McIntyre cane came to give me the once-over. Said he, in a drawl that couldn't be mistaken for anything save Mississippi:

"Suh, dis is ma furst trip a-crost dis country. My friends toll ma ter take a lower bert. Well, suh, I dun sleep verra bad last night. De porter, he tell ma, yo crost all de time, an always in uppers. Well suh now, will ya tell ma why?"

If this was English, ex-King Edward VIII was a pretty good American. But as it wasn't rhetoric my informant was after, I put my best foot forward and told him some of the reasons why I preferred the upper berth. First of all, it is the only berth equipped with a constantly-in-place box spring. Over this goes the usual train mattress, with which the lower is also equipped. When occupying a section, compartment or drawing room, two train mattresses go on top of the box spring. All the time you occupy the berth, then, there is a resiliency, a give, to the motion that takes place beneath you. Never does the upper give in, when the roadbed is bad or the going tough.

Then there is the little matter of no window, which we have just discussed at greater length. No drafts, temperature constantly the same, yet—in the open Pullman sleeper—considerably more air. You see, the lower gets no air at all on a warm night, except through opening the window, which brings in cinders and dust,

or through leaving the curtain up, which exposes the sleeper to all the goings and comings in the car at night. And when I retire for the night, I like to think I'm going to be left alone to my own discretions. Furthermore, I can sleep as long as I like in the mornings, for I neither hear nor feel the swish of other passengers in the aisle as they pass my bedside. I've worked so long on morning newspapers that I do like to sleep late. This is seldom possible in a lower, for when you haven't got children who play tag in the aisles, you have got their parents who peel oranges. Or when the porter isn't rustling bags, he's making up the other berths.

As for the dressing and undressing angle that so many of my compatriots express, to me it is more of a molehill than it is a mountain. Usually I do as much undressing as possible in the men's washroom, and I dress there leisurely as well. I go to and from my upper in my dressing gown and pajamas.

And last but not least, when the pocketbook is low, I know of no cheaper way of traveling in comfort. It beats tourist class on an ocean liner hollow, for you have your privacy all the time, and need never share your hideaway with another living soul.

I I

But genuinely, you see, I like the upper. I don't do it to save money. I've never been accused of being miserly, but I do travel heavy, and I've never learned to economize on baggage, so into the lower berth of the section, bedroom, compartment or drawing room goes all my heavy duffle, while I ride the rods up top.

One winter when I was on a lecture tour I spent 48 nights out of 52 in upper berths. I delivered 121 lectures in 39 states and traveled 14,000 miles. I was never the worse for wear, from beginning to end. The test came when the lecture bureau signed me up for another season!

On the other hand, I'm certain I lost one of my charming wives to the wiles and guiles of the upper-berth mode of travel. Ladies are not accustomed to the strange idiosyncrasies of men, especially not to men who move often and fast, and who love it.

Uppers in foreign lands have more or less the same advantages they have in America. One summer I crossed from China to Europe in an upper berth in a compartment shared with one other adventurer. We were nine days together, without end. Into my little place in the clouds I fitted my portable noiseless typewriter. I even cooked my breakfast coffee up there on a Sterno stove. For four days on end I never emerged from my hiding place, and I saw the panorama of Asia and Siberia, Soviet Russia, and Europe pass me by.

Time and again I've traveled from Paris to Constantinople, from Bombay to Calcutta, from Shanghai to Harbin, in the upper berth, and I have yet to show scars. It has been a grand, carefree existence, watching the world go by below me.

On ships all over the seven seas, I've chosen the upper berth just as regularly. On the Gota Canal trip in Sweden, or the Nile trip in Egypt, you'll find me up there if you look hard enough.

In fact, it was on a ship that I first got acquainted with and acclimated to this mode of life. I was a private in the AEF in World War I. Assigned to a transport which put out of Hoboken, N.J., one stormy night, I found my berth at the very bottom of a tier of five, in the forward hold of the transport. The other men aboard were from a National Guard outfit in Oklahoma. They had never seen the sea. I had already crossed it 44 times. So I knew something of the way it could kick up.

I glanced around me. My compatriots were all peeking through anything they could, to see the Statue of Liberty and the skyline of New York fade away. Hurriedly I shifted my duffle bag, overcoat and blanket to the topmost rung. Then I went on deck.

Later I learned there was a hullabaloo about it. But when I blew in and went to bed, all I had to do was to shinny my way up five tiers, and that was nothing in those days, for I only weighed 100. It was a rough trip, all right, and if I had stayed down there, five tiers below, I'd have had "everything" coming my way. As it was, all I got was a good case of homesickness and an experience which pointed the way to future occupancy of upper berths wherever I roam.

May 1950

Henry R. Griffiths Jr.

EXTRA 1555 WEST

Willard V. Anderson

Two caboose hops west of Pocatello, Idaho, you climb into the cab of Extra 1555 West, a Union Pacific time freight which is now waiting for a clear signal to pull out on the main line from the yards at Huntington, Ore.

You have ridden this train all the way from Pocatello, but up till now it has been known as No. 257. It will run as Extra 1555 West from here to Pendleton and Rieth, Ore., and then become known once again as No. 257 when it leaves CTC territory and proceeds on to Portland.

You don't recall much about those two caboose hops which brought you here from Pocatello. You boarded the first caboose at Pocatello after leaving the comforts of the *City of Portland* and after a quick look-see at the yard installation there under the guidance of terminal trainmaster M. Thomas. You remember meeting conductor A. A. Schuster, and you know you'll never forget how engineer Ivan Matson spotted the caboose steps right in front of you as he braked the train from his cab 117 cars ahead—a courtesy he performed just for you, since conductor Schuster normally boards the caboose as the train proceeds at walking speed through the yard. But last night Schuster was not alone, and trainmaster Thomas had arranged with the man in the control tower to keep in touch with Matson by means of the yard's communication system. That's why Matson was able to spot the rear steps of the crummy smack over the crosswalk where you and the conductor were standing.

It was late when you boarded No. 257—something after 10 p.m. Mountain time, and you were still accustomed to Central. Too, the walking around the yard had done you in; you were not accustomed to the 4,463-foot elevation of Pocatello. Accordingly, you hit the leather-padded bench right after shaking hands with flagman H. E. Donaldson, who thoughtfully dimmed the oil lamp so you could go to sleep.

And somehow you managed to sleep, fitfully, despite the run-ins and run-outs of slack between the 117 cars ahead. You remember wondering dully how the man in the zulu was faring up there only a few cars back of the locomotive, and you wondered, too, where the railroad men got that name of *zulu* to describe a boxcar transporting one head of cattle and one man. Outside of that, you don't remember a thing until you were aroused in the middle of the night and were told it was time to get off the caboose and grab a bite to eat before returning to the train for the second installment of your rough ride to Huntington.

Somehow, at 3 a.m. in Glenns Ferry, it seemed too late for a hamburger sandwich and too early for ham and eggs, so you ate breakfast cereal and drank a cup of coffee and were ready to go back to the hack. You met a new rear-end crew, but you can't recall the men's names; all you can remember is that you had just dropped off to sleep again when you were awakened as the caboose was removed only 9 miles out of Glenns Ferry. Through your sleep-muted ears you heard the flagman tell you that two Mallet pushers were being coupled on ahead of the caboose for the 11-mile climb from Hammett to Reverse. And then you closed your eyes again and didn't awake until the conductor shook you and announced that

you were nearing Huntington. You ate at a railroad men's restaurant across the square from the Huntington station—this time it was ham and eggs, plus fried potatoes, toast and coffee, 80 cents—and decided you didn't have time to get a shave in the barber shop next door because there were several customers ahead of you.

I   I

But now you're in the cab of diesel No. 1555, and fireman C. C. Jones has taken you under his wing. He explains why the identification boards now read X-1555 instead of 257—it's because all freight trains run as extras in the CTC territory between Huntington and Pendleton—and comments that while westbound passenger trains are running pretty well on schedule, the eastbounds have been coming through rather late for the past couple of days. The West Coast area has been having a severe winter, he says, and trains have been losing time between Portland and here.

Engineer Murray H. Arms and brakeman M. R. Thielen arrive, and Thielen motions you to his padded seat alongside the fireman's position. "I'll be in and out for a while anyway," he says. "You might just as well make yourself comfortable."

Soon he's out in front of the diesel, lining switches through the yard tracks so Arms can go pick up his train. A yard switcher with a cut of cars idles past on the adjacent track as Arms eases his three F3 units back on to some stock cars which you recognize as the same ones you saw last night as No. 257 crawled through Pocatello Yard. Farther back in the train, however, the consist has changed somewhat, and Extra 1555 West is carrying 99 loads and one empty. The zulu is still with you.

Now your train is intact, from the OWR&N caboose to diesel 1555. Back in 1936 Union Pacific acquired a lease of the Oregon-Washington Railroad & Navigation Company along with the Oregon Short Line, whose rails you rode last night. Both the OSL and the OWR&N are now integral parts of the Union Pacific, and for many years prior to the acquisition they had been operated as a part of the system.

The dwarf signal in the yard throat winks from red to yellow, and engineer

Arms eases his 4,500 hp forward—gently, so as to take up all slack before picking up speed. Starting a diesel-powered freight train requires restraint on the part of the engineer. On a steam train, you start the drag one car at a time, making use of the slack to help you get started. With diesel power, you must be sure your slack is out and that all brakes are released at the rear of the train before you pick up speed. If you don't you're likely to snap a drawbar.

I   I

Now you're out on the single-track main line, running entirely by signal indication. You don't stay on the main for long; the dispatcher shunts you into the passing siding at Lime, only 5 miles west of Huntington, to get out of the way of No. 18, an eastbound passenger train which should have been at Huntington long before you left. Like other eastbound trains, 18 has been delayed by weather. If it weren't for centralized traffic control, you would still be sitting at Huntington, awaiting the arrival of 18. But CTC enables the dispatcher to get Extra 1555 West on her way with a minimum of delay.

With a full night and a morning of riding behind you, you have a feeling you've come a long, long way from Pocatello by the time you stop at Durkee, 20 miles west of Huntington, to pick up two Mallet pushers for the 13 miles of 2.2 percent grade that lies ahead. Actually, you've come only 350-odd miles, and had you stayed on the *City of Portland* you would have been here only six hours after leaving Pocatello. But you're riding a freight train, remember, and you've made two division-point stops which have cut into your running time.

There is another delay now at Durkee. The helpers are on the rear end, ready to go, but the red CTC signal holds you. No. 26, the mail and express train which left Portland last night, is coming down the hill; you can see the smoke of her steam locomotive up on the mountainside. The dispatcher has lined the turnout so 26 will take the siding while Extra 1555 West holds the main.

No. 26 slides past, and the signal changes to green. Your engineer whistles off, and you feel a slight bump as the

The hump yard at Pocatello, Ida., receives cars from various branch lines, sorts them by destination, and forwards them east or west over the Oregon Short Line, which Union Pacific leased in 1936. *Union Pacific*

Mallets begin pushing at the rear. Normally, you would have diesel helpers instead of steam, but the coal strike has caused a shift in power as a means of moving the mostest with the leastest amount of solid fuel.

X-1555 moves slowly up the hill and around a horseshoe curve which gives you a good view of the two helpers; you don't have to lean out the cab window at all but just look straight to your left. One helper is cut in directly ahead of the caboose; the other, several car-lengths ahead. This way, if the drivers of one engine begin to slip, the engineer has a chance to stop them from spinning before the effect is felt by the other engine—slack sees to that. If both helpers were coupled just ahead of the caboose, one slipping engine might cause the other to slip too.

The speedometer needle hovers around the 15-mile mark as 1555 and her two sisters drag the front of the train up the mountain, their engines roaring in unison. After topping the worst of the grade at Pleasant Valley you pass Extra 1455 East, which has just come up the 1.3 percent grade west of the summit. At Encina, you see X-1455's helper, a single-unit diesel which precedes you down the slope to Baker. Your Mallets cut off at Encina and run back to Durkee to await another assignment.

Engineer Arms uses dynamic braking to hold his train to 25 miles an hour down the hill. The traction motors hum like streetcars as they build up the electrical current which holds the train back as the current is dissipated in the grids on the roof. Occasionally Arms uses his air brakes to keep within the 25-mile mark without overloading the motors and grids. A load of more than 600 amperes will damage the grids, and Arms keeps an eye on the ammeter needle and applies locomotive air when the needle swings close to the deadline. He doesn't use the train air; he wants to keep the cars all bunched up on the locomotive and thus avoid a run-out of slack.

Fireman Jones (whom you're calling Casey now) gives you a briefing on the country through which you're passing. These are the Blue Mountains, he tells you, and the crest you just topped at Encina is the lower of two summits crossed by this UP line in this same mountain range. Encina is 3,968 feet above sea level; Kamela, the other summit, beyond La Grande, is 4,205 feet above the sea. Baker, through which you're now passing, is not only a helper station on the railroad but is also the center of a beef cattle country which contributes traffic to the railroad.

The train is drifting easily now; engineer Arms uses his dynamic brakes only occasionally and calls on the diesel power plants even less frequently. It's downhill all the way to Union Junction, with the exception of one short grade which crests at Telocaset, a 1 percent rise which the diesels handle with ease. From Telocaset to Union Junction you make a 1½ percent drop into the Grande Ronde Valley, and on the way down, Casey calls your attention to "Wind Holler" on the slopes of Craig Mountain.

"There's always a wind blowing here," he says, "and sometimes it gets so strong it blows slack coal out of the hopper cars on passing freights. It's even been known to blow cars off the passing track!"

It's beginning to snow as you pass Extra 1445 East at Union Junction, where UP connects with the Union Railroad of Oregon. This 2½-mile line's sole reason for existence is to handle freight into and out of Union, Ore. X-1445 is on the passing track and has a three-unit diesel on the head end and Mallet No. 3539 on the rear to help it up the grade to Telocaset.

Now you're on the wide floor of the Grande Ronde Valley; mountains can be seen, dimly through the snow, in all directions. You pass Hot Lake, where Nature has provided an open-air, year-round bath tub for the patrons of Hot Lake Sanitarium. Not far from the sanitarium is a hot spring where natives scald hogs without having to heat the water. A little farther on you come to Lone Tree, a passing siding named for one lone pine which stood until some youthful pranksters cut it down. Local authorities fit the youths' punishment to their crime, and made them water other trees which were planted in the valley.

You're glad, now, that you left the *City of Portland* back there at Pocatello nearly 24 hours ago. If you hadn't, you would have passed through the Grande Ronde Valley in the small hours of this morning and would have missed Casey's personalized travelogue, from which you have learned that deer and elk abound in the valley and that the farmers raise grass seed, wheat, and cattle. "It's Paradise," says Casey. As X-1555 comes to a halt in the yards at La Grande, Casey swings down to the ground and helps you with your luggage; you hand it down to him and clamber after it and follow Casey through the deepening snow toward the station and another meal.

It's dark outside when you've finished your dinner, and you wonder whether you ought to seek out the caboose and get some sleep or whether you should ride one more subdivision in the cab. You decide on the cab, for, after all, the diesel has a brilliant headlight, and you'll be able to see the 2.2 percent grade which lies ahead. The snow is getting deeper, and you anticipate a grueling fight against gravity on slippery rails.

Herbert Davies is holding down the engineer's seat and A. J. Singleton occupies the fireman's side of the cab. The brakeman's surname is Taylor, but that lethargy which stole upon you in the caboose last night is beginning to come on again, and you forget his first name or initials. The cab is warm, and you find yourself dozing off as the diesel stands in the yard, waiting for the return of several cars of hogs which were removed from the train so the animals could be watered and fed. At last they're back, and engineer Davies backs the locomotive into position, then revs up the motors for the eight-mile run to Hilgard. Here two 3500-series Mallets are cut in at the rear and the climb to Kamela begins.

You're wide awake now. The diesels are roaring as you've never heard them roar before, and you get a sort of surging motion as the wheel-slip indicator flashes on and then goes out as Davies feeds sand to the rails. The lead truck—the one right beneath you—emits a gritty, grinding sound as it breaks a path through the ever-deepening snow. The speedometer registers 8 miles an hour as the climb begins in earnest, and the wheels below you send constant flashes of light from the slip indicator on the instrument board.

Davies turns to Taylor. "Get me a Dixie cup," he requests, and the brakeman fetches the paper cup. Davies takes out his pocket knife and cuts a portion off the top of the cup. The diameter of the remaining part just matches the diameter of the wheel-slip indicator. The engineer fits this improvised dimmer over the slip indicator and the flashes become less annoying. They're still visible through the bottom of the waxed paper cup, but now the spinning wheels whisper instead of shouting for help. Davies continues his sanding.

It's a long 11 miles to the top of the grade, and fireman Singleton lets you use his seat as he makes a constant tour of the engine rooms, answering alarm bells as the laboring diesels protest their load. You roll down the fireman's window, and by the light of the underbody floodlight, you can see that the pilot is plowing snow. Alongside the tracks, a huge white levee marks the work of a wing plow after a previous storm.

⚏   ⚏

At last, you reach Kamela. The diesels settle down to a contented purr as the rear-end crew uncouples the helpers and reassembles the train. Switch maintainers have been at work with shovel and broom, and the flares of the oil switch heaters are welcome dots of yellow in a world of white surmounted by a black sky. Snow swirls in the glare of the headlight. Inside the cab, it's warm. You find yourself dozing again and wondering between catnaps where you got that huge oil stain on the cuff of your trousers. It must have been back there at La Grande when you walked past the diesel fueling station with your trousers outside your galoshes instead of tucked in, as they should have been.

There's double track at Kamela. It extends, in fact, from Nordeen on the east to Ross on the west, some 7½ miles. X-1555 is on the right-hand track. You proceed, after dropping your helpers, only to be stopped by a red light at Ross. You wait, and pretty soon a headlight comes down the other track from behind you. It's No. 17, and as the passenger train glides past, you can see its diesel is plowing snow. The steam hose and air line dangling between cars leave a mark of their own in the snow, and after the train has passed, you look at the track and are reminded of your son's toy railroad with a third rail down the middle.

The CTC signal beckons you on, and X-1555 enters single track to follow No. 17. You doze in your chair and miss the passage of the eastbound *City of Portland* somewhere between Ross and Pendleton. Somewhere, too, in this 53-mile stretch, the dispatcher puts your train in the hole and holds it there for an hour or so to await some other eastbound passenger

No. 257 begins the 11-mile, nearly 2 percent climb to Reverse. Diesel No. 1444 is leading the parade along with B units 1412 and 1402; 107 cars to the rear, two 2-8-8-0s are pushing beneath a double-barreled canopy of smoke. *Henry R. Griffiths Jr.*

train whose number you fail to get. During the wait, engineer Davies has to break the train to allow a motorist to cross on a highway crossing. When the long wait is finally over and Davies opens the throttle, the diesel makes a valiant effort but doesn't budge the train. The flagman, a rookie, made a poor connection of the air line when he recoupled the train after letting the motorist through, and the back end is without air. It takes a few minutes to remedy this situation. Meanwhile, the dispatcher has begun to wonder what the trouble is, and he turns on the light above the telephone shanty to show he wants to make conversation. Brakeman Taylor answers the call, and the train is ready to go by the time he returns.

You pass through Pendleton and proceed to Rieth Yard, 3½ miles beyond the Pendleton station. One of the crew helps you with your luggage and takes you to the yard office, where you learn that X-1555, which has now lost this identity to become No. 257 again, won't leave Rieth for three hours or more—the longest breathing spell you've had since leaving Pocatello. You ask a clerk where you can find something to eat at this early hour of 2 a.m.; he recommends the hotel at Reith. Another man says he'll be glad to drive you to the hotel if you wait a few minutes. You're thankful for the lift, and your driver turns out to be the postmaster, cattle broker, bus-line operator, etc., of Reith. He stops his pickup truck in front of the hotel.

"When you're ready to go back," he says, "just take one of my buses. It won't cost you a cent."

The breakfast matches the one you had at Huntington, both in consist and in price. You wish your schedule allowed time to rent a room for a little shut-eye, but you know you'd never be able to get out of bed after only a couple of hours of sleep, so you catch the bus—a converted sedan with a home-made section added amidships—and take your free ride to the yard office. The driver explains that the bus runs from Reith to Pendleton for revenue passengers, but railroad men going to the yard office are always transported for free.

Back at the yard office, you sit in a chair and feel the stubble on your chin. You haven't shaved since just before leaving the *City of Portland* Sunday evening; now it's early Tuesday morning. With the yardmaster's consent, you shave in his office—in cold water and without a mirror—and wish you had a chance to change your clothes. You perform a few other personal chores you haven't had a chance to attend to for nearly 36 hours, and then you sit and wait and wait and wait. Then the yardmaster tells you the caboose has been coupled to 257, and if you wish, he'll drive you down there in his personal car. You take him up, but quick. You're asleep long before 257 leaves Reith. You don't wake up until a conductor you've never seen before tells you you're nearing The Dalles, and it's time to change cabooses. You'll have to ride the rear end from here on into Portland, he says, because your permit gives you access to cabooses and diesel cabs but not steam locomotive cabs. And steam will be the power out of The Dalles.

⚏   ⚏

You stay with this caboose until it's taken off, and you climb into the "new" one when it's coupled on the rear. You haven't had a chance to eat at The Dalles, as you did at other stops, but somehow your stomach doesn't mind. You don't feel hungry at all, and the coffee flagman J. W. Keeney offers you before the train gets moving is ample to appease the inner man. Later, when swingman R. J. Condon cooks bacon and eggs, he offers to deal you in, but you decline. You're satisfied with coffee.

As you sit in the cupola while 257 runs along the edge of the broad Columbia River, you get to thinking that it's strange, but this is the first caboose crew you've seen on the Union Pacific which has offered you even as much as a cup of

A 126-car westbound extra behind an A-B-A set of EMD F3s winds along the Snake River 4 miles west of Glenns Ferry, Ida., not far from the bottom of Medbury Hill at Hammett. *Henry R. Griffiths Jr.*

coffee. All the other crews didn't even brew coffee, and this is the first railroad you've seen where there wasn't a pot of coffee on the caboose stove. "Caboose coffee" is a tradition on most railroads—and the stronger it is, the better.

At any rate, the coffee aboard OWR&N caboose No. 3554 is of sufficient quantity and sufficient strength to bring UP back into the tradition of railroading. Its aroma wafts to the cupola as a constant reminder that you're among real railroad men. And conductor Cross's beautifully accented anecdotes about his Swedish acquaintances (occasioned, no doubt, by the presence of a man named Anderson) while away the time between points of interest on this line along the south bank of the Columbia.

As a matter of fact, there are plenty of points of interest along the Columbia, especially today, not quite two weeks after the West Coast's worst weather for years in 1950: highway crews still at work clearing U.S. 30, plowing and bulldozing and even drilling through huge drifts of "tapioca" which froze into a solid mass after rain fell on the pellet-like snow; portions of the old Columbia River Highway

which the highway crews haven't even attempted to clear. UP's passenger trains made a lot of unscheduled stops along here immediately after the storm, dropping off provisions for residents and rescuing motorists stranded in the snow. There's a new Buick convertible now, still standing where it bogged down almost two weeks ago. And there are some freight cars, imprisoned on a UP siding at Oneonta by a slide which kept snowplow crews busy for hours.

There's Tooth Rock Tunnel at Bonneville, built in 1935 as part of a line relocation occasioned by the building of Bonneville Dam. And there's the dam itself—of special interest to you because you met a man on the *City of Portland* who introduced himself as the controller of the Reynolds Aluminum Company and said his company had built an aluminum ingot plant at Troutdale because of the abundant cheap electricity made available by the dam. In order to make ingots at Troutdale, he said, his company had to ship millions of pounds of alumina—partly processed bauxite—from reduction plants in Arkansas, and in spite of the freight charges involved, could do it more cheaply at Troutdale than if the whole process were done in Arkansas.

Time passes swiftly until you reach Troutdale. There, No. 257 is broken into two parts, one to be forwarded to Seattle in Washington, the other to go on with you the few remaining miles to Portland. You sit a long time at Troutdale, watching a man with a huge snow shovel cleaning the snow out of a gondola on a siding. Then, at last, the Seattle block is taken off the head end, 2-10-2 No. 5407 is restored to the front, and you're off on the last lap of your ride to Portland.

Flagman Keeney swings across the space between the two seats in the cupola and closes your windows tightly. "Long tunnel coming up," he says, and soon you're in the void of a mile-long bore beneath the city of Portland. "The engine men wear gas masks in this one," says Keeney. Long after you emerge, you can look back and see smoke still pouring from the tunnel. And then your train stops in Albina Yard. You pick up your bag and follow Cross and Keeney (the swing man left the caboose at Troutdale) to the yard office, where Keeney telephones for a cab for you. A swift ride to the Heathman Hotel, a hot bath, then dinner. You hang out the sign DO NOT DISTURB, and retire for a night and a day.

Illinois Central

MEMO TO THE PUBLISHER

David P. Morgan

You know me, Al: a traffic-minded soul forever risking the epitaph of hypocrite by citing the airlines as Exhibit A for that sphere of railroad management worried by The Passenger Problem.

My brief for this approach is two-fold:

1. The airlines are steadily eating into long-haul, first-class railroad passenger traffic and are seriously threatening coach, mail, express, and l.c.l. revenues as well.

2. If the railroads would recover lost traffic and take the offensive, then they must adopt the airlines' superbly personal promotion and service tactics.

In my book at least, the contemporary hoopla about The Passenger Problem is entirely too self-contained. We are experimenting with single-entree meals to cut dining car deficits; we have jacked up fares to cover boosted operating costs; we are petitioning state public service commissions to discontinue branch-line locals. Much of the program is weeding out the garden so that productive plants may have room to grow.

In 1950 the railroads are looking into the mirror and the reflection they see is often negative. This year more and more railroaders are asking *What's wrong with railroad passenger service?*

Very good. But what about asking this one: *What's right with the airlines?*

When railroad management does look over the enemy's front lines, it is to attack federal help and handouts. Now I find a parallel to this phase of the question in an international situation known as Korea. Our infantrymen are holding the line there not because the United States delegate to the United Nations has protested the Red invasion, but because of a wonderful new 3.5-inch bazooka that stops Russian T-34 tanks. Translated into the nonpolitical climate of domestic transportation, the rails should hit airmail pay padding and other facets of government aid to the airlines at every opportunity— but they must meantime fight competition with a 3.5-inch bazooka. Pleasing people is the key; it always has been, and it always will be. And the airlines are pretty good at it.

Here in Milwaukee the number to dial for a demonstration is MArquette 8-6320. It's the information-reservation desk of Northwest Airlines, whose swank street-corner office at North Water and East Wisconsin is the most impressive location of any airline or railroad ticket office in the city. Late in June my curiosity got the best of me; I phoned Northwest for a reservation on another airline out of Chicago to Texas. I wanted to spend a July 4th weekend at home. The obvious opportunity to examine airline service firsthand was intriguing.

The fact I was riding Milwaukee Road's *Hiawatha* to Chicago instead of Northwest's 9:11 p.m. flight had no effect upon the pleasant feminine voice that answered MArquette 8-6320. The girl seemed charmed to accept a reservation

---

Milwaukee to Corpus Christi

A saving in time…

Air . . . . 14 hours one way
Rail. . . . . .30⅓ hours one way

…is costly in dollars

Air round-trip fare plus tax $170.39
Rail coach round-trip fare plus tax $74.23
*Rail coach-sleeper round-trip fare plus tax .$113.85

*Roomette between St. Louis-Houston, otherwise coach all the way

All fares and times shown here include time and coach fare of CMStP&P trains from Milwaukee to Chicago. Rail route in both fares and time is CMStP&P-GM&O-MP; airline is exclusively Braniff International Airways.

---

request, to ask for my phone number, and to promise to call as soon as Braniff International Airways had confirmed my space. The attached cost-and-time schedule [below] explains why I was flying into the Southwest. The airline tariff set me into debt $20 (there is no aircoach service from Chicago to Texas—yet), but speed was imperative if I wished to have a reasonable layover at home.

I   I

Early a.m. July 1, therefore, found me drinking coffee in the Marshall Field restaurant at the Chicago Midway Airport, holding in my pocket $166.06 worth of tax-paid Braniff tickets (actually a 6¼" x 3¼" slip in an outer jacket marked with my name, flight, and destination) and awaiting the 2:30 a.m. departure of BNF Flight No. 25.

The terminal struck me as being typical of current commercial aviation: modern, cramped, staffed by young and friendly personnel, busy. For 10 cents visitors could climb to the roof of the crescent-shaped building and inspect the field they had helped pay for; Chicago & North Western *400*s draw a similar gallery any noon or evening in Milwaukee, but in Chicago, airport sightseers are encouraged to see the works.

The four-engined Douglas DC-6 assigned to my schedule had arrived in Chicago at 10:05 p.m. as the nonstop *Texanaire* from Dallas, had been serviced, then spotted at the Braniff gate for passengers and mail since midnight. It was difficult to realize that this 300-mile-an-hour ship currently sells for roughly $1.1 million— approximately the cost of two 6,000-hp diesel freight locomotives or nearly the price tag of Great Northern's twin *Internationals*, diesels included. It also was difficult to believe that this silver DC-6, striped in red and blue, was carded to be in Houston by 9 a.m.

I checked my single bag through to Corpus Christi, then walked out to the plane and up to its door on a mobile staircase. Seats were not individually reserved, so the purser extended me the choice of a seat facing backward or a seat overlooking the wing. I explained that visibility was highly desired and he consulted his space chart again with the look of a man who wants to please. In a moment a seat behind the door was mine.

I declined an offered pillow (minus any 25-cent charge) and buckled up the safety belt.

A few minutes after 2:30 refueling had been completed, the door locked, and the steps rolled away. One by one, each of the four Pratt & Whitney 18-cylinder radial air-cooled engines was fired up. Landing lights splashed the loading ramp, brakes were released, and the DC-6 taxied across to its appointed runway. I switched off the spot reading light and drew back the curtain. Up front a captain, co-pilot, and flight engineer ran through a methodical preflight check; back in the cabin a hostess and purser asked passengers to tighten seat belts. The plane tugged vainly against its disc wheel brakes as each engine was run up in test.

Suddenly she was moving. Four engines, capable of a combined 8,400 hp, wound up triple-bladed 15-foot 1-inch props to a brilliant silver sheen. The marvelous acceleration pushed me back in the seat as the circus colors of ticket offices and tower and parked planes swept past. At 100 miles an hour Flight 25 left the concrete and roared into the night, climbing at 1,100 feet a minute. Almost instantly all sensation of speed melted as Chicagoland suburbs and Illinois prairies flattened out below under a dazzling July moon. Each medium of transportation lends its own unique thrill simply because it involves movement—in aviation I think the takeoff is the chocolate-sundae feature of the business.

But no passenger seemed excited. Maybe they were Texans. A few were sleeping in upper berths ($5 extra); others were reading pocket books or *Chicago Tribs*. One or two were dozing in their seats, oblivious of it all (possibly the same breed of traveler who slumbers through the Royal Gorge on Rio Grande No. 2).

I looked out, studied the dimension of the wing like all flight novices, then looked down. But the landscape from the air, at first so tremendously fascinating because of the perspective, soon grew dull. I drew the curtain, smoked awhile, then tried to sleep. The cushioned chair was comfortable enough, but I subconsciously sensed an increasing bumpiness. Not rough but annoying. At length, unable to sleep, I felt for the window and pulled back the curtain. …

In 1950, this four-engine, propeller-powered Braniff International Airways Douglas DC-6 represented the latest in heavy-duty, modern airline passenger travel. *Braniff*

Swoosh! A glare of high-powered lights, the thud of rubber on concrete, the weird whine from a gimmick titled *reverse pitch* (e.g., hydraulically twisting the propeller blades so that they act as brakes): Flight 25 was on the ground at Kansas City at what I recall as 4:30 a.m. The DC-6 rolled up to an administration building that virtually fronts on industrial KC. Engines were cut off; crew and a few passengers mingled below the ship's wings during a 20-minute stop. Across the Missouri River lay terminal tracks I had ridden over less than 90 days before as a passenger on Wabash Railroad's *City of Kansas City*.

ɪ   ɪ

Perhaps, Al, I've dwelt too long on the sheer aesthetic end of flying. What I want to get across is that this airline game offers a glamorous, exhilarating world all its own—and a lot of customers are willing to overlook long taxi rides, Dixie cups beneath their seats, frightening fares, and what-have-you for a box seat in the big top. And maybe that's worth dwelling on because the railroads have as much to offer; vista dome equipment is incontestable proof of that. But even domes must be merchandised.

Here are a few more check points for any railroader's competition notebook:

✓ I suspect the main reason why airline meals are free is because they couldn't charge much for them anyway. Too light,

too obviously prepared in an off-plane kitchen. Nice, but way down the ladder from dining car fare.

✓ Braniff personnel impressed me as being capable and full of enthusiasm. For instance, on arrival at Corpus Christi, I asked if I could change my return reservations to allow for a longer Dallas layover. Within three minutes my request had been granted and my ticket rewritten accordingly. A similar request in Dallas received the identical courteous attention.

✓ Any airline's big, booming advantage is *speed*, of course. It can and is being met by the railroads in *convenience*. I refer to dawn-to-dusk coach streamliners, overnight hauls, etc. But airlines have made the public time conscious, and the roads must spell out their convenience sales promotion in terms of time.

✓ Even a DC-6 seems cramped to me. Braniff's model seats 54, and a super version due soon may carry double that number on aircoach flights. But thus far railroad-like lounge and dining and recreation space is prohibitive on any airline. More than once on my Texas round trip I had the urge to stroll into an observation-lounge for a tall, cool drink and a windowful of what Pullman-Standard justly plays up as "eye-level scenery."

✓ I was academically aware while flying Braniff (which has flown 23 years with but one fatal accident) that the railroads are 16 times safer than scheduled commercial airlines but the safety made absolutely no difference to me at the ticket

counter. I'd feel downright foolish refusing air transportation on such grounds when I daily assume an immeasurably greater risk every time I ease my Ford into a city street. Summing up, there is no cause for playing down our safety record—the railroads have earned it the hard way—at great cost in equipment and training and have a right to be proud of it. But the 16:1 ratio is not holding airline traffic trends down; in 1945 scheduled airlines handled 3.3 million revenue passenger miles and in 1949 6.6 million (year ending September 30, 1949).

✓ Back in 1945 (and earlier) I chided friends in the aviation game like this: "Your ultra-personal approach to carrying passengers indicates you're not in *mass* transportation. A load of 21 reserved-seaters on a DC-3 with a hostess at their beck and call—that just ain't the masses. If the postwar world boosts your traffic, free meals and complimentary pillows and public address systems maintained so one can understand the announcement will go out the window." Five years later I find very little has gone out the window, but airline traffic has been doubled. And the new passengers are not all businessmen or next-of-kin rushing to dying relatives. One pilot told me of a rustic patron aboard a coach flight who asked the hostess for his bag en route. Informed that his luggage was in a separate compartment beyond reach, he frowned and explained, "I've got my lunch in there."

This ACF-built Missouri Pacific lounge diner on the *South Texas Eagle* offers a quality of food and expanse of lounge that airlines can't match. *American Car & Foundry*

Adding it all up, I must thank Braniff for once again making me acutely aware of our competition. Subsidies aside for the moment, Braniff is fighting a good fight for traffic in the face of odds like costly equipment, wishy-washy CAB rulings, weather, railroads, and other airlines. I admire Braniff.

But neither Braniff nor Northwest nor any other airline has the present or foreseeable potential to shove the railroads out of the passenger business—if the railroads gear their sales and services up to the fever pitch of their rivals. The single statistic that 17 percent of *Shasta Daylight* passengers would have traveled by air if the Espee streamliner had not been in operation indicates that there is no static defense line. If much traffic has been lost, then much traffic lies open to recapture by *Shasta*-like service.

In the few days and weeks after my trip, I've been researching through TRAINS mail for the October issue's "News and Editorial Comment" department. Two items, one fresh and another in file, caught my eye. First, ICC has approved a ticket redemption plan under which nine Eastern roads are allowed to charge from 10 cents to a quarter for cashing unused fares. Second, 1947 statistics (latest I have) indicate that *16 scheduled airlines spent 12 times as much for advertising as all 131 class 1 railroads*. Call me dense, but I simply cannot reconcile this data in the competitive year of 1950.

Regarding item No. 1, I bought an Eastern Air Lines ticket from Northwest's Milwaukee office for a Houston-Corpus Christi flight last Christmas; the train was late, however, and I missed the EAL plane. A week or so later I presented the unused ticket to Northwest, which promptly and politely cashed it on the spot without question. Which explains why I call MArquette 8-6320 when I wish to fly. As to item No. 2, I am reminded of the famous Southern Pacific ad entitled "A short course in railroading … for airline executives." Written as a friendly censure of misleading airline blurbs, the full-pager was also a beautiful piece of railroad travel promotion. It was widely quoted, railroad officialdom applauded, the trade journals played it up. But instead of becoming a mold and an example for other roads, Espee's ad was soon a shrine. Many admired, but the industry's lamentable lack of public relations nerve held them back. So the airlines once again enjoyed the last laugh.

Maybe this brief and impartial examination of two 1949 annual reports in the industry will clarify my argument [shown at bottom of the page]:

I think a wartime experience of Bill Akin's spells out a lot. Following combat as a B-25 pilot, Bill was assigned to Air Force statistical control in General MacArthur's Tokyo headquarters. The job covered the movement of personnel, he tells me, and the arrival of 80 men as replacement troops was referred to as "80 bodies." Now I wonder if this economical but impersonal term, necessary to the military, doesn't have its counterpart in railroading. Are we selling passenger transportation as statistics, as "bodies," as so many revenue miles? Are we punching tickets and checking baggage and proffering menus just because passengers show up to ride?

It was not pessimism that produced enough grass roots traffic to support Central of Georgia's *Man o' War* and *Nancy Hanks II* streamliner success. But birthday parties for grade-school kids and radio plugs paid for by enthusiastic shop employees helped out no end. Nor was it optimism that made Chicago & Eastern Illinois a railroad voice in the dark when it resisted an Eastern fare increase and protested aircoach rates as uneconomic. But either inertia or ignorance held other railroads back from whole-heartedly endorsing C&EI's actions.

You and I and perhaps a million other Americans familiar with railroading know that the machine and men capable of stemming the airline tide are available. What worries me is whether or not the railroads—not just CofG or Espee or New Haven, but all of them—will see fit to throw this organization into action, to please the passenger, to make him wonder what was once so wonderful about the airlines.

Carrier	Total Revenues	Net Income	Advertising Budget
Braniff	$18.4 million	$221,595	$581,322
MKT Railroad	$75.1 million	$4.8 million	$259,420

TRAVEL VIGNETTES

A. C. Kalmbach

It takes far less than the whistle of No. 57 on the night air to make me want to go train riding—not even one of those tantalizing pages in the *Official Guide*. All that's needed is memory.

Memories of little open-platform coaches winding through the woods and under the granite cliffs of the northern Michigan Peninsula on the Copper Range; memories of a succulent slice of roast beef in the *Century* diner with Count Felix von Luckner across the aisle doing sleight-of-hand for the late dining passengers and the crew; memories of the snow-frosted peaks of Glacier National Park as seen across Whitefish Lake in the setting sun from the lounge car of the *Empire Builder*.

Waving fields of wheat and then cactus and desolate miles of black volcanic rock, all in the same day of riding the Santa Fe.

Mississippi River steamboats whipping a spray with their stern wheels, seen from a grandstand seat in a Burlington vista dome.

The white-hot billets of steel that warm even the air-conditioned interior of a B&O car as it runs right through a steel mill in Pittsburgh.

Mile after mile (113, count 'em) of Pacific Coast sparkling in the afternoon sun alongside SP's *Daylight*.

The unbelievably far-up and spidery-thin web of the Royal Gorge bridge seen from the bottom of the canyon during the stopover of Rio Grande's Royal Gorge.

The other trains always in fascinatingly close view as we swing 'round Pennsylvania's Horseshoe Curve.

Bannerman's fantastic rock castle, a piece of the Old World transplanted into the Hudson River alongside the route of the *Empire State Express*.

Merchandise Mart, world's largest commercial building, spreading its thousands of window lights onto the Chicago River as the *Arrow* slides out of Union Station on the Milwaukee Road.

A Katy steam locomotive, yellow oil flame spurting from its firebox, streaking across the Texas prairie, seen from a bounding Texas Electric interurban with the breeze whipping through the open windows.

The Front Range of the Rockies coming into view disguised as a far-off bank of clouds while the UP's *City of Denver* approaches the city of Denver.

The endless parade of ships through the Detroit River viewed from seats on the 50-yard line, a Grand Trunk car ferry taking us on the last lap of a journey from Canada into Detroit.

The huge electrically lighted figure 1 on the First National Bank signaling St. Paul as the *Hiawatha* rounds a curve of the Mississippi.

Lake Michigan, foaming white and dull gray under storm clouds, seen from the warm comfort of a *400* coach.

The soft green beauty of New England hills and white church spires in the valleys below the Rutland.

The wildness of the Adirondacks where the New York Central runs along a forest trail through the evergreens with glimpses of green water beyond the tree trunks.

Bag in hand, Al Kalmbach pauses on the platform at the union station in Albany, N.Y., while on a business trip in 1940. TRAINS magazine collection

The wild flowers beneath the windows of Maryland & Pennsylvania's doodlebug, remindful of childhood walks through the woods in May.

Whirlpool Rapids, wild and gray and almost unreal, directly below the Lehigh Valley-Grand Trunk sleeper as it crosses the Niagara River at dawn.

French-speaking, French-looking local passengers in the coach out of Montreal.

Important-looking characters, maybe politicians, maybe 5-percenters, in the lounge of the *Congressional*.

School teachers, no doubt about it, on the *Grand Canyon*.

Blasé, sleepy produce buyers on the 4:35 a.m. Milwaukee Road train to Chicago.

Endless miles of Nevada desert, with the inevitable mountains in the distance, and dry washes along the UP tracks.

The raw, primeval rock of the Feather River Canyon viewed from a balcony seat atop the *California Zephyr*.

The majesty of the College Peaks rising above the Rio Grande tracks in the Arkansas Valley south of Tennessee Pass.

The tall tales of blizzards and washouts in years gone by, contributed by dead-heading crewmen in the smoking car of the night local *Mail*.

The green of Potomac Valley foliage outside the dining car windows of the *Capitol Limited*.

The white round moon shining coldly on snow-covered Allegheny slopes seen from a darkened bedroom of that same *Capitol Limited*.

Ice, spray-piled into weird shapes as NYC's *Prairie State Express* buzzes onto the long trestle across Sandusky Bay.

Spanish moss and 18th century balconied houses beside the *Sunset Limited* west of New Orleans, and the first incredible view of the Crescent City itself, golden in the afternoon sun, as the *Sunset* crosses the heights of the Huey Long Bridge.

And history rides the rails, side by side with Loewy-modern creations from the shops of Pullman-Standard, ACF, and Budd.

The C&O Canal that George Washington surveyed, now still and vegetating in the shadow of the B&O's Potomac River embankments.

The Abraham Lincoln country around the Alton north of Springfield.

The little markers along the NC&StL recalling the *General* and *Texas* of Civil War fame.

The gold rush country of the 49ers and tragic Donner Lake, viewed from the heights of SP's scenic line over the Sierras.

The route of Lewis and Clark, almost as wild now as when these explorers made their 4,000-mile journey to the coast nearly 150 years ago, but vastly more comfortable in Northern Pacific or Milwaukee air-conditioned cars.

Yes, only memories are needed to make me restless to board the nearest train—memories and the dreams of yet unexplored thousands of rail miles.

Southern's Saluda grade outside Asheville.

The car ferry across the fabulous tides of Bay of Fundy to ride the Dominion Atlantic.

The Mopac through sleeper to eternal spring (so the Chamber of Commerce tells me) in Mexico City.

Even during as long a lifetime as the insurance company wishes me, there'll always be new railroad routes to see, new trains to ride … and memories of many past rides I'd like to take again and again.

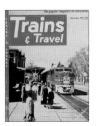

Howard Bull

BIG ONE AT SHED 27!

Howard Bull

There is a definite link between yesterday and today when the Norden fire train, the last of a long line of such firefighters-on-rails that once served the Southern Pacific, blows its wheezy, high-pitched whistle and rolls off down the Hill.

The Hill is the crest of the High Sierras on SP's famous Overland Route, and Norden, with its train-order office and interlocking plant hidden under heavy timber snowsheds 7,000 feet above sea level, is just a mile west of the old Summit station on the westbound main.

Not too many years ago a half dozen or more fire trains protected the Sierra country of middle California between Colfax and Truckee, a 65-mile segment of crooked, steep mountain railroading where the tracks snake through mile after mile of tall timber. In those days there probably were more miles of railroad under snowsheds than there were miles out from under them, but today it's the other way around. Modern rotary snowplows and line relocations have combined to remove the need for miles of sheds. In the old days the fire trains which protected the sheds could be found softly steaming and purring, awaiting a call at any hour of the 24, at Blue Canon, at Emigrant Gap, at Cisco—this one was taken away in 1928—and at the old

The extra machinery and piping on the fire train's 4-6-0 give it a sort of Rube Goldberg appearance. Much of it is for the steam pump, which is on the boiler. Here, the train unlimbers its forward "guns." *Southern Pacific*

Summit itself. And down on the eastern slope they were at Andover and Truckee. But as the need for them vanished, the fire trains passed into the limbo of history with the Donners and the wagons that were hoisted up over the rocky precipices of Emigrant Gap when settlers moved westward, until today only the Norden fire train remains.

I   I

You are the fireman on the Norden fire train. Your deep slumber is shattered at 12:50 a.m. by the wail of the siren atop the Norden interlocker and the din of the big electric bells in the hall outside your room. They are designed to get the fire train's four-man crew up and out in record time. The night watchman has the air compressor on the engine throbbing, filling the main reservoirs. He blows six blasts on the shrill English-type peanut whistle, a type of whistle that distinguishes fire-train locomotives by their sound alone.

You shake off the sleep and clamber aboard the engine, 4-6-0 No. 2252. The

brakeman releases the hand brakes on the two water cars while the engineer, Johnny Luker, makes a standing brake test. Then the brakeman gives him the "plug"—a few pounds more of brake application from the rear of the train. You drag the chains from under the 2252's 63-inch drivers and climb up on the tender and throw out the water hose that continually supplies the engine while she is waiting under steam on the spur. The conductor has his orders and clearance now, and is lining the switch to let the fire train out onto the main line.

"Big one at Shed 27! Transformer blew—all circuits out. You've got no signals but the operator says go!" The conductor shouts the brief description of the situation ahead as he hands up the orders to Luker in the cab. You pull past the crossover, back upgrade through it, and move backwards east through the cavernous snowsheds without benefit of automatic block signals. Soon auxiliary batteries will have them going again, as they now are supplying power for the Norden interlocker, but for the time

being, your sole authority is the sheaf of train orders and the clearance you got from the dispatcher through the operator.

The SP through here is protected by automatic train control as well as by block signals and remote-controlled interlockings. Backing up as you are—the fire train always faces west—Luker has to forestall an automatic brake application as he passes each signal even though the signal is out. Your two water cars, since they are preceding you down the track, enter the next track circuit before the engine does. The inductor the engine passes over just before it reaches a signal can't tell that it's a train backing up, and registers a train in the block ahead. Luker forestalls the brake application by shoving a brass handle on a brass box in the cab.

It's a thrilling sensation to ride a galloping old-timer such as the 2252 as she works upgrade through the sheds. Luker eases off on the throttle as you reach the summit, and your 25- or 30-mile-an-hour speed downhill seems like twice that. The conductor and brakeman and the section

The fire train always faces west, and consequently must back up to reach points where its services are required east of its Norden home. The fire train's cars are rolling platforms from which powerful streams can be played in any direction. *Howard Bull*

boss and his gang—who were likewise aroused by the emergency siren and bells—are riding the tops of the swaying water cars. Presently the communicating whistle in the cab beep-beeps—the stop signal. You are at the fire.

Yes, a transformer has blown—to bits! These big transformers have moving parts that are lubricated with heavy grease, and that flaming grease has shot in a thousand directions, covering the top of one shed. She's a goner, you can see immediately. Your job is to protect the other sheds.

The fireman and engineer on the fire train handle the steam-operated water pump which is mounted atop the boiler of the 2252 and supplies water at high pressure to the hoses. Your controls are four valves—two for the nozzles which protrude hornlike from the engine's smokebox, two for the hoses which extend from the water cars. You have, too, the valve which regulates the flow of steam to the two-cylinder pumping engine, a small hydrostatic lubricator, and a pressure gauge. It's old equipment, true, but plenty powerful and trustworthy.

The section men unreel the hoses and begin spraying the sheds to ward off the crimson inferno that has doomed the shed the exploding transformer sprayed with flame. You look back at the fire as

the spindly framework crashes down on the roadbed, covering the rails and warping them to uselessness.

You and Luker tend the pump, turning it on, then off, increasing the flow, decreasing the flow, filling the lubricator, until nearly dawn. There is nothing remaining of the burned shed except smouldering embers, twisted rails, and concrete stumps of foundations. You have kept the fire under control and saved the adjacent sheds. As you pack up to return to Norden a track gang is already laying new steel on the eastbound main. Signal maintainers, telephone and telegraph linemen, are stringing new wires.

⊥ ⊥

The Norden fire train is, as I have said, a link with the past. Its two cars are ancient red water tanks with platforms on top. Its rear end has an electric headlight and a pilot, for it leads off much of the time. Its engines are 54- and 55-year-old Cooke Ten-Wheelers, one month the 2252, the next month the 2248 as they take turns going to the shops. There is a touch of the past in the knob on the sand dome cap and in the lever which once operated the sanders manually and still protrudes from the base of the dome. There are some old-timers around the SP who can remember seeing these little teapots

double-head passenger trains up the Hill or roll them across the Valley. Certainly the 2252 and the 2248 are among the oldest engines still in use.

What now? Even when the fire train is chained in the siding back at Norden you've got work to do. Most of the time there's no draft in the little engine's boiler, so each morning you must blow out the netting in the firebox to keep it clean. Each evening Luker does the same thing.

And there's family life, too, if you're married. The engineer of the fire train lives in a separate house, while the others— you, the conductor, the brakeman, and the engine watchman and your families—live in a two-story edifice you call the Woolworth Building. Pressure cookers are handy here some 7,000 feet up. Or you can walk up through the sheds to the "car," a beanery built into the protective planking, and eat a good meal served by Lee and Jimmie, Chinese cooks, who know how to satisfy the hungry crews of the freights that stop at Norden, as all westbounds do.

And, to fill in those long moments that fire-train crews and their red-trucked brethren alike must fill, there is an occasional spirited canasta contest among the crew members and their wives. But you've got to be prepared—more than likely the women will win.

March 1952

OUR TRAIN WAS SNOWBOUND—AND HOW WE ENJOYED IT!

by W. S. Dulmage as told to Victor H. White

I was interested to read of the *City of San Francisco*'s plight in snowbound Donner Pass, high in the Sierra Nevada Mountains of California, for there is in my 80-plus years of existence a similar and exciting experience.

On a regular run in January 1891 we were pounding along the new Great Northern cutoff from Havre toward Great Falls, Mont. It was a murky afternoon, and the temperature was falling. There was enough snow on the ground to make the prairie blend with the sky, and there wasn't any break in the expanse save for a few protruding bluffs along the edge of the "Little Rockies."

Then the snow began and the thermometer plummeted past zero. The engineer knew that standing still more than a minute would freeze our train to the tracks. The snow wasn't deep, but the wind that came with it piled it up a foot thick with a surface so hard that a herd of buffalo could have passed without leaving a mark.

About 25 miles north of Fort Benton, we headed into a shallow cut and suddenly bore down on a herd of beef cattle, tails to the wind, seeking shelter from the bitter cold. Our engineer, knowing that he didn't dare stop, highballed into them with the throttle wide. Cattle piled up on the track like boulders before a bulldozer. We came to a stuttering standstill.

The bark of the baggageman's rifle and the mail clerk's .45 brought a lot of questions a few minutes later from the customers in the dining car, where I was performing my duty as head steward. "We wouldn't be attacked by Indians in this kind of weather," I assured a nervous Easterner.

A tall cowboy at another table rubbed his chin and grinned. "Nice weather for cattle-huntin', eh, steward?" He'd guessed what had happened and knew that the wounded critters were being put out of their misery. I'd guessed it too, but my business was to reassure my guests—and to start immediate conservation of food supplies.

      ⊥   ⊥

That was the beginning of a sitting spell on the plains of Montana that lasted just two days short of two weeks. The train froze to the track immediately. The temperature went down to somewhat between 30 and 40 below. We began to have fun.

Fortunately, we were not handicapped in those days with all the modern equipment that must have worked such a hardship on the *City of San Francisco.* When night came, we lit only alternate lamps to conserve oil. Our fireman banked his fire to save coal, and the steam pressure was allowed to fall to only what was needed to heat the train. A little coal goes a long way for that purpose. With the train warm, we could shovel snow into water tanks and coolers and it would melt.

The passengers were well and in high spirits the entire 12 days. There were no complaints that I can remember. There was plenty of good whiskey and fine brandy in the shiny mahogany buffet car, and a plentiful supply of the world's best beef lay in handy cold storage around our engine. By the third day, we were serving directly from a storage box almost as big as all outdoors. I've often suspected that those choice steaks served without charge had something to do with the Great Northern's enviable reputation for fine dining service ever since.

The first gray morning dawned with saltlike snow still falling. We could have walked away easily enough if there had been any place to walk to, or any way to keep from freezing. But nobody tried it.

A telegrapher from the baggage car had gone up a pole with climbers, rigged a portable key and detailed our plight to the dispatcher, and in the morning, he began transmitting private messages, charging a rate left to the conscience and financial ability of the sender. A New York broker gave him a tip of $25 to send 10 words to his wife. He sent over a hundred words to the husband of a mother and small daughter and refused 50 cents.

We rationed our food (we likely carried considerably more than did the *City of San Francisco*), and thanks to the supply of fresh meat and to a little milk from a shivering cow that had dropped a late fall calf, we suffered no serious food shortage.

Maybe you think we didn't have fun? Our evening routine was something like this:

From 5 to 7:30 we served dinner to our passengers. At 7:45 we stacked the tables in one end of the car, arranged the chairs in rows, and a vaudeville troupe en route to San Francisco gave a show—with a full

The westbound *City of San Francisco* became snowbound in the Sierras in January 1952, recalling the author's experience on the Great Northern in 1891. *San Francisco Examiner*

change of program each evening—to the most appreciative audience I've ever seen. The show broke up about 11; we piled the chairs with the tables and danced to the accompaniment of the same generous entertainers. We served well-aged liquor that would be the envy of any railroad today, and there was no cover charge.

When warming weather and a wrecker finally broke us into motion again, we had perfected plans to burn suet and gristle from the dead cattle along with ties chopped from the roadbed. But we could have gone a few more days without that. Remember the axe and shovel kit that we used to carry in each car? We were certainly glad we had them!

In the time we were marooned, we were never without plentiful water, light, and heat. That's how modern and safe railroading was 60 years ago—and you must forgive me for boasting like this—but every member of our crew did feel a justifiable pride in the way we were able to care for everybody. And it still sort of indicates that railroads are sacrificing something besides the whistle when they give up steam.

There is one big advantage nowadays, though, in the matter of the steward keeping his suit in good condition, what with cash drawers and folding money. The gold coins of those days were always so heavy in my coat pockets that I never really could keep my regulation blue uniform in proper shape.

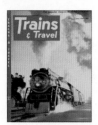

June 1952

THE PRESS PREVIEWS THE CONGRESSIONAL

Wallace W. Abbey

"Man, will you look at that bar car!"

Across the platform of Pennsylvania Station in New York, a train is arriving, and the exclamation of a banjo-eyed porter as he looks from the vestibule of his standard coach into the lounge car of the new *Congressional* is a perfect vocal description of why you are deep in the catacombs of this terminal, far from your typewriter. In fact, the whole idea is for you to look not only at the *Congressional*'s lounge but at its coaches and diners and parlor cars as well. You are going along on the Pennsylvania Railroad's press demonstration run of its new train, its big show for the fourth estate, which—the railroad hopes—will circulate descriptive adjectives far and wide among customers regular and prospective.

The presentation of a new train by a railroad to its patrons is often comparable to the launching of a ship or the introduction of a new automobile model. There is much shouting in the public prints. There are visiting dignitaries and champagne-bottle breakings. Cars of the new streamliners are parked in strategic cities for all to ogle. And there is the press run, where you give your name and title to the lady at the gate, a boutonniered member of the public relations staff hands you your press kit of publicity releases, and nobody says anything about who's paying for all this.

The day, of course, is representative of the kind that the weatherman saves for outdoor affairs of state, ball games, and press trips. It is raining buckets. But that doesn't matter down in the depths of the depot, where you wander up and down the platform, mentally noting the makeup of this, the newest of the Pennsy's trains: a tuscan-red GG-1 electric locomotive, four coaches, a coffee shop-lounge car, four more coaches, a full-length dining car, a kitchen and lounge car, an all-room parlor car, five conventional parlor cars, and a parlor-observation car. Eighteen in all, their stainless steel exteriors set off by tuscan-red letterboards and belt rails, name and number panels, and little keystones near the ends of each car. Names and numbers are in gold.

❧ ❧

You nod to a member of the Pennsy's uniformed, white-gloved policemen and board one of the parlor cars. An organized riot of reds, whites, and blues greets you. They aren't the overpowering shades of the patriotic trio, but they are beautiful and they beat anything you've seen in the way of interior decoration aboard a train. You walk through the cars. The colors are basic in all of them, but within the continuity there is no monotony. You'd always visioned the

The rainstorm that dampened the New York Division of the Pennsylvania while the southbound press run was under way has just stopped, and here the train, with its sides sparkling, swings into the lower level of Philadelphia's 30th Street Station. *Wallace W. Abbey*

Pennsy as a rather conservative road behind its tuscan-red tradition, and you're rather pleased with the freshness of this new equipment.

The colors, in fact, sort of remind you of the way you'd paint a youngster's playroom. The entire train, even behind the newness of it all, is light and airy and quite a departure from anything you've seen. You recall that as you came down the stairway a few minutes ago the *Broadway Limited* was being pulled from the depot to its servicing track over on Long Island, and you realize that the *Congressional*, a newcomer to the Pennsy's fleet, outshines its standard-bearer.

The interior embellishments are obviously the result of considerable expenditure of time and money. Etched glass panels are profuse, dividing the smoking compartments from the rest of the coaches and the observation section from the lounge in the last car. You peek into a couple of drawing rooms and find carved linoleum panels above the sofas. Oil paintings of an Early American theme are practically everywhere.

You commandeer a parlor chair and inspect the contents of the press kit.

There's a pink press release that tells the story of the new *Congressionals* and *Senators*—for actually, the Pennsy is putting into service four new trains next Monday, March 17. There'll be two *Congressionals*, each making a round trip a day between Washington and New York, and two *Senators*, each plying one way between Washington and Boston over the Pennsy and the New Haven. The handout tells you that the 64 cars built by the Budd Company for the new trains cost almost $11 million. And it describes the equipment—the all-electric kitchens, electronic ovens in the coffee-shop cars, the way that pairs of rooms in the all-room parlor car can be joined and used as conference rooms by traveling bigwigs, and all the rest.

There's another pink sheet in the kit detailing the four days of special events preceding the inaugural runs of the new trains. There's another, more complete, car-by-car description of the equipment. There's a short one telling that the new trains cost about three times as much as the ones they're replacing. There's a story on their rolling eateries, complete with menus and recipes. And, thankfully, since

you're a little vague on the background of these trains, there's a concise history.

You find that the *Congressional Limited* was first operated in 1885 to carry members of Congress between Washington and New York after the close of the legislative day. It was an extra-fare, all-parlor car train, painted black until Frank Thomson, then president of the Pennsy, saw the cream-and-green private train of the president of Mexico and ordered the *Congressional Limited* painted likewise. But later it was given a tuscan-red livery when that color was made standard. The extra fare was discontinued and coaches were added in 1931. The *Congressional* has traveled some 11 million miles in the three generations that it has been in business. The *Senator* can lay claim to no such ancestry. It came to life in 1929.

☤   ☤

"Hello there, Tom!" Among the reporters, railroad writers and manufacturers' representatives filing through the train you finally spot one you know— Tom Shedd Jr., eastern editor of *Modern Railroads*. The two of you wander back to

The observation lounges are similar in contour to postwar cars used on other Pennsy streamliners. *Wallace W. Abbey*

the observation lounge, so that you can use what little visibility there is out of the rear end to look over the railroad. A technician is fiddling with the public address system.

"How's this now—can you hear me?"

A voice comes back from someplace: "Yeah, that's swell. But when you throw the switch it cuts everything out." The bugs are ironed out by the time you begin to roll—on time, naturally.

The invitation which rests in your inside coat pocket offered you two methods of inspecting the *Congressional*: riding from New York to Washington on this set of equipment, or from New York to Philadelphia on this train and back on its twin. You chose the latter. And now, as you flash across the Jersey Meadows, pause for a Newark platform that is too short, and get under way again over the Pennsy's fabulous electrified New York Division, the trimmings that help make the trip a success begin to appear, properly cooled with tinkling ice cubes. You estimate privately that about three-fourths of the effort and expense that a railroad goes to put on a shindig such as this must be to little avail. But you also decide that what is spent in the cork-popping department is decidedly not wasted by anyone concerned.

Suddenly, you are in the movies. Somebody is shining a hot floodlight in your face, and somebody else is pointing a buzzing camera at you. "For the railroad," the first somebody says. They move a couple of ash trays and shoot some footage of the scrumptious brunette who has been sitting across the aisle. The guy next to her drools over her properly when the camera is going, but he doesn't stop when the camera stops. Then he decides he'll be cute and hikes up his pants to show a leg. There is no comparison.

A cultured voice in the ceiling announces that luncheon is being served in the dining and coffee-shop cars, and that if you are detraining at Philadelphia perhaps you'd like to eat now. The idea is acceptable to some, but you still feel comfortable from a late breakfast, and decide that you'll eat on the return trip or just skip lunch altogether. But you are tempted when you remember how the diner had been strategically spotted at the foot of the stairs in Pennsylvania Station, and how you had been frankly astonished how anything in those subwaylike depths could be so inviting.

Tom spots someone he knows and introduces you. It's Eugene DuBois of the Pennsylvania's public relations gang, the fellow who sent you your invitation. Gene in turn introduces J. P. Newell, operating vice-president of the road, who sits and

chats a while. As you talk, a team of photographers dragging a blonde and a redhead begin popping flashbulbs furiously in the forward end of the lounge. They achieve the desired spontaneous result by rearranging the customers, moving the furniture, and pleading for silly grins.

The big fellow with the little camera asks you to turn your chair toward Tom's. Then he looks around and spots Newell, grabs him, and places him on the right arm. On the left arm, between you and Tom, he perches the redhead. His assistant points the flashgun at the ceiling so that its light will bounce and look natural. You ask him, "Who are these for?"

"*Look* magazine."

The cameraman instructs the girl, "Now, make like you're telling them a story—with gestures!" Which she does. You make weak jokes with Tom that if this picture appears in *Look* you'll really have to have a story to tell when your wife sees it.

Then all is serene again. The photographers and their redhead disappear, and Newell wanders forward through the car, greeting his guests. A waiter pauses to offer an extemporaneous remark on the *Congressional*'s riding quality. The smoothest train he's seen, he says, and do you know how he can prove it? You don't. He takes a plastic ash tray that has a nonskid surface on the bottom, the kind standard in Pullman lounges, and turns it over on the end table. Nothing happens. You give him the fish eye, so he explains.

"See, it doesn't move! You can't do that on any other train I've been on."

The voice in the ceiling announces that you are about 15 minutes from 30th Street Station in Philadelphia, and reminds, "To those of you who are detraining at Philadelphia, remember that you may be some distance from where you placed your coats." Yours is conveniently crumpled in the baggage rack of the car you're in, so you stay put until the *Congressional* swings around the curve into the depot. Across the platform you see that your twin train, the one you're going back on, has already arrived from Washington with its contingent of visiting firemen.

The platform between the two glistening trains is aswarm with photographers. Some are shooting pictures of the railroad's president Walter S. Franklin, who is standing, wreathed in a smile, in the glare of newsreel floodlights. Others are focusing on a pair of costumed twins who represent the twin *Congressionals* in the manner that mass journalism requires such things as trains, which do not wear nylons, be represented. First the girls pose, waving, in the rear door of one train; then they cross the platform and wave from the pilot of the red GG-1 of the other train.

You find the observation lounge of the New York-bound press train vacant. In fact, neither train has been anywhere near full to its capacity of 703 revenue seats. Some of the photographers are kneeling in the ballast outside the station, popping away on low-angle shots, as you pull out for Manhattan. The rain has stopped and has left everything sparkling as the sun bounces off little drops of moisture.

"Did you order this, sir?" A waiter places a glass before you. No, you didn't, you say, but since he's brought it, you'll not make him carry it back. You hand him a coin, which he accepts with thanks, and then, as if in afterthought, he says, "Oh—there's no charge for the drink, sir."

"I know." He gets the idea immediately and thanks you kindly. Miles of meditation later, after you've sipped it all and unceremoniously sucked on the ice cubes, Clyde Leech, a special representative of the Pennsy's publicity department and host on this side of the press trip, introduces himself. He sees that your glass is empty, and demands that you have another. How can you refuse?

The trip back is pretty quiet. A movie cameraman invades the observation lounge for a while to shoot your departure from Newark, and somewhere along the line, you overtake a tremendously long train of refrigerator cars pulled by two GG-1s—with the old color scheme of green, however. Then you are in the tunnel under the Hudson River, and back at track 11 in the station, from where you started. The guests disperse, returning to their desks and advertising agencies and workaday worlds. The Pennsylvania Railroad has shown its new *Congressional* to the press.

The southbound press train pauses at Philadelphia while some of its guests transfer across the platform to the section returning to New York. *Wallace W. Abbey*

Later in the afternoon, when you are idly thumbing through a magazine while waiting for the *Broadway Limited* to be readied, the public-address announcer says something that strikes a familiar note in your mind: The *Congressional* is now ready at gate such-and-such for Washington. You assume the role of a promising, but tired, young businessman and stroll through the gate and down the stairs to see the old-style *Congressional*. The new trains won't be in revenue service until another six days have passed.

Frankly, you tell yourself, you've seen better-looking commuter trains on a couple of railroads back home. What greets you is an endless string of monitor-roofed red coaches and parlor cars and a pair of quite conventional diners. You wander along the platform, looking through the windows at plush seats in faded shades of red and green. But at the end of the platform, you come upon a modern touch: the old *Congressional* has a tuscan-red locomotive!

Then you watch the people streaming down to the train. To you, a good many of them appear to be the kind that are required to commute, maybe once a week, maybe more often, between New York and Washington. Then you look at their conveyance. Brother, what a surprise is in store for them next week!

February 1953

THE WILD RIDE OF DEATH VALLEY SCOTTY

Wallace W. Abbey

Young man, the Santa Fe will put you into Chicago in 46 hours if steam and steel will hold together.

We've got the roadbed, the equipment and the men—don't forget that. But let me tell you that you'll be riding faster than a white man ever rode before!"

John J. Byrne, general passenger agent of the Santa Fe, looked at the roughly clad man who had come into his Los Angeles office, had displayed a roll of bills and had said, "Mr. Byrne, I've been thinking some of taking a train over your road to Chicago. I want you to put me there in 46 hours. Kin you do it?"

Byrne fingered the $5,500 the man had paid unhesitatingly for the special train, glanced again at the figures he had penciled hurriedly, and commanded, "You be at the depot at 12:30 tomorrow afternoon. We'll start at one!"

Exactly at 1 p.m. on Sunday, July 9, 1905, a three-car train nicknamed the *Coyote Special* started in Los Angeles' old La Grande Station with a blast of impatient exhaust, picked up speed, and disappeared down a track lined with thousands of cheering Angelenos. Death Valley Scotty was on his way.

Walter Scott came from Kentucky to the endless wastes of Nevada as a boy. He knocked around quite a bit—through Death Valley as water boy for a Government surveying party, around the country and the world as a rider for Buffalo Bill Cody, and finally back to Death Valley, the vast sink-hole of undeserved fame that gave him his nickname. He wasn't exactly one to avoid publicity, and was, in fact, known as a colorful character out of the wilderness, a man obsessed with the idea of speed, even before he startled John Byrne and the Santa Fe with his proposition of a speed run to climax all speed runs.

For Death Valley Scotty wasn't the first to utilize the fast track of the Santa Fe as a means of racing time or tradition. Nellie Bly, a girl reporter on the *New York World*, started it with a publicity stunt in 1890. On a final lap of a 72-day race around the world, Nellie went from Los Angeles to Chicago in 69 hours. Then in 1900 A. R. Peacock, vice-president of Carnegie Steel & Iron Company,

Engine 1010, a Prairie type 2-6-2, completed the Needles-Seligman segment of the *Coyote Special*'s journey from Los Angeles to Chicago. Shown here in 1955, 50 years later, the 1010 was used to reenact the run on TV's *Death Valley Days*. *Santa Fe*

chartered a two-car special which was in Chicago 57 hours 56 minutes after it left Los Angeles. H. P. Lowe of the Engineering Company of America raced from New York to Los Angeles in 1903 to be at the bedside of a sick relative, setting a new record of 52 hours 49 minutes over the Santa Fe.

Walter Scott arrived at La Grande Station minus only the fanfare to make the occasion complete; he spoke briefly to the assembled crowd and climbed aboard the Pullman *Muskegon*. The Santa Fe was ready to shatter all these running records with the *Coyote Special*. Forty-six hours in 1905 was good time considering that when the Santa Fe put on its weekly transcontinental *De Luxe* at $25-a-person extra fare in 1911 it established its running time as 63 hours.

Scotty was accompanied by his attractive wife [Ella]; Frank Newton Holman, a Santa Fe man sent along to chronicle the event for all time; and Charles E. Van Loon, a press association correspondent. His train was three cars—a baggage car, a diner, and the *Muskegon*. Ahead of him lay a Santa Fe Railway primed as it had never been primed before to speed him on his way. There was hardly a man who would ride the train, prepare its engines, or watch it storm past from inside some desert telegraph office who hadn't heard of Scotty's coming and was not ready for it. Assigned to handle the throttles of the special's engines were the "Nervy Nineteen," the road's best engineers who, as Holman wrote, had been picked because they thought there were no curves in the Santa Fe!

Out of Los Angeles it was John Finlay on the seat box of the 442, a big Ten-Wheeler, a good engine to maintain the

special's killing schedule over the hills between Los Angeles and the desert. Finlay loosed the reins and let his steed run. The *Coyote Special* left Los Angeles and sped through the cluster of little towns along the right-of-way with Finlay whistling constantly at the cheering, waving throngs which lined the track.

Hardly had the trip got under way when Scott, his companions, and conductor George Simpson felt the urgent grab of the air brakes under the sleeper. Simpson rushed to the vestibule and peered ahead toward the engine. He saw the fireman clinging to the rushing engine.

"A tank box has gone hot on us," the conductor told Scotty. "The fireman's playing the hose on it!" Soon the hotbox cooled, and Finlay pulled back on his throttle, determined to regain the precious moments the bad journal had cost. He trimmed 10 minutes off the running time to San Bernardino, where a helper engine clamped its coupler to the 442's to help lift the train to the top of Cajon Pass.

Higher and higher, with the pair of stacks rending the sky, the *Coyote Special* climbed through the eroded formations of California's big hill. A mile from Summit the helper uncoupled and sprinted ahead through a switch. A switchman flung the lever around and Scott's train rocketed past with never a hesitation. The boys at La Junta had switched engines on the Nellie Bly special in 42 seconds, but nobody had ever before cut one off on the fly!

Finlay brought the special into Barstow at 3:55 p.m., 26 minutes ahead of time. His best speed had been 96 miles an hour. Quickly his engine was uncoupled, and T. E. Gallagher backed the 1005, a fleet-footed Prairie type, down to be coupled on. Scott hardly had time to wave to the crowd before his train was gathering speed for the next lap to Needles. The evening was warm on the desert, and the cab of the 1005 was searing. Gallagher braked the train to a stop at Needles at 7:17 p.m., and the 1005 yielded to a like engine, the 1010, impatient for the touch of Fred W. Jackson's gloved hand on its throttle. While Jackson sped them out of Needles, the Scott party sat down to a late dinner.

Fred Harvey, of the culinary Harveys, had been apprised of the flamboyant desires of Walter Scott, and he'd assigned an excellent chef named Geyer to the *Coyote Special*. On hearing of her husband's assignment, Geyer's wife had protested that some other man perhaps should break his neck for such a fool stunt. But Geyer replied in his thick accent, "If dot man in der enchine can stand it to pull der train, I can stand it to ride behind him yet!" The menu he served was typical of Fred Harvey, with entrees designed to please the outdoorsman guest of honor:

Caviare Sandwich a la Death Valley
Iced Consomme
Porterhouse Steak a la Coyote,
    two inches thick and a Marvel of Tenderness
Broiled Squab on Toast,
    with Strips of Bacon au Scotty
Stuffed Tomatoes
Iced Cream with Colored Trimmings
Cheese   Coffee   Cigars

But eating such succulent dishes aboard a hurtling diner was next to impossible. Three miles out of Needles

Walter Scott, *Santa Fe*

the train whiplashed on a curve and Geyer's splendid supper crashed to the floor.

Up front, the engine crew had both injectors going to feed water to the boiler, although their train was light and would have been easy to pull at normal speeds. Jackson rolled her along at a mile a minute or more. And he was going nearly that fast—a fantastic thought—when the *Coyote Special* boomed across the high, spindly Colorado River bridge and into Arizona.

And so the *Coyote Special* ran on winged wheels through the night beneath the boundless depth and beauty of the Arizona sky. Jackson took water at McConnico, and ran Kingman, the regular water stop, to avoid stopping amid the crowd that he knew would be waiting. A third Prairie engine took the train at Seligman and started the first round of the battle against the joined forces of time and the three rocky barriers—the Arizona Divide, Glorieta Pass, and Raton Pass—that lay ahead.

There was little desire for, or likelihood of, sleep back in the *Muskegon* that night, as Walter Scott, the cowboy from Nevada, and his companions listened to the exultant song of the racing engines, consulted their watches—and hung on.

The special thundered into Williams at 1:28 a.m., and another powerful Ten-Wheeler took over. There was another Prairie waiting at Winslow and still another Ten-Wheeler at Gallup. All along the railroad the Santa Fe had its best engines ready to wheel Death Valley Scotty to Chicago faster than any man had ever gone. Aboard each engine and back in the cars were competent, confident railroaders—quiet, sincere men who brought the *Coyote Special* into each division point well ahead of its incredible schedule and saw it on its way again in scant seconds. As the train passed over the turnout to the yard at Albuquerque with the briefest shudder, Division Superintendent Gibson pocketed his watch and smiled for the first time since he'd climbed aboard at Seligman.

"Mr. Scott," he said, "I've brought you over the Albuquerque Division 34 minutes faster than any train went over it before." The *Coyote Special* had erased the record of the Lowe special and bettered Gibson's own estimated running time by four minutes!

The big engines took over at Albuquerque—a relay of three 1200-class

Pacifics, massive two-year-olds with 69-inch driving wheels and power to flatten the mountains of New Mexico. It was well into the morning when the 1211 highballed out of Albuquerque with Scotty's three cars and began to climb through Apache Canyon toward Glorieta Pass. Once the train was over the top, the pace down the mountain precluded all movement back in the Pullman. With the mileposts zipping past one a minute and the train whipping around reverse curves, it was fruitless to get out of the seat. One passenger got up, and as the train lurched, his shoulder crashed through the window.

A banjo-eyed, thoroughly frightened dining car waiter expressed his concern: "I've seen a lot of railroading first and last, but running like this is plumb ridiculous—just plumb ridiculous!" But Scotty had said Chicago in 46 hours, and Chicago in 46 hours—or better—it was going to be. Shortly before 3 p.m. the special pounded through the defile in Raton Mountain and started downgrade toward La Junta, Colo. The worst was over.

I I

It was easier after that, and faster. At La Junta the mountains were behind. Ahead were the long, straight, flat stretches of railroad across which the *Coyote Special* could ramble at 85 and 90. For 300 miles Death Valley Scotty raced across the high plains at an average of better than 70 miles an hour.

East of La Junta, too, the Santa Fe assigned its real speedmakers, balanced-compound Atlantics with 79- and 73-inch drivers—engines that had seen only a year of service on the fastest trains of a fast railroad. There was one waiting for the *Coyote Special* at every stop—Syracuse, Dodge City, Newton, Emporia, Argentine, Marceline, Shopton, Chillicothe.

Scott clambered into the cab of one of these high-wheelers and bailed coal into its flaming innards with the fireman. He was obviously having the time of his rather singular life laying waste to records made in his favorite medium—speed. He saw to it that crew members received $20 gold pieces. And on the second evening out of Los Angeles as his special paused in Dodge City, Scott dispatched this telegram to President Theodore Roosevelt:

Ella Scott, *Santa Fe*

An American cowboy is coming east on a special train faster than any cowpuncher ever rode before. How much shall I break transcontinental record?

Teddy did not reply.

Josiah Gossard set a new record for the fastest time over the 124 miles between Emporia and Argentine—130 minutes. He did it with four slow orders out against him. The special hurried across Missouri in the early hours of Tuesday, July 11. At Shopton, Iowa, where the Mississippi River crowds the yard and shops against the pleasant green bluffs,

engineer Charles Losee eased the 510, another of the new Atlantics, to a coupling with the *Coyote Special* and set off to dissolve all previous speed records in the overwhelming glory of a greater one set on the beautiful speedway that is the Santa Fe's right of way across western Illinois.

Cameron and Surrey, two hamlets just west of Galesburg, are 2.8 miles apart. Losee covered that distance with the 510 and the *Coyote Special* in 95 seconds—106 miles an hour! He rewarded the cheering crowds along the Santa Fe—and speed-demon Walter Scott back in the Pullman—with a new world's record!

The special dropped five minutes at Chillicothe while Losee exchanged the 510 for the 517. And at South Joliet, 40 miles from its goal, Scott's train lost another four. But its schedule was far from threatened, and it still did the 239 miles across Illinois in as many minutes.

Losee hurried the *Coyote Special* down those last 40 miles through the outskirts of Chicago, and stopped under the high trainshed of Dearborn Station at 11:54 a.m. to the accolade of an exuberant Chicago. Death Valley Scotty stepped from his train 44 hours 54 minutes after it had begun to move out of Los Angeles. A wild speed dash had more than granted him his wish to cover the 2,265 miles of the Santa Fe's main line faster than any man had.

I I

How good was Scotty's record? As the *Coyote Special* ate up the miles, Walter Scott obviously was getting the speed he'd paid for. The running time of his special was so good, in fact, that a better regular schedule wasn't established for some 30 years. In 1936, using its new 3,600-hp diesel No. 1, the Santa Fe lopped 20 hours off previous running times and inaugurated the new 39¾-hour *Super Chief.*

March 1953

Library of Congress

THE BLACK WALL

Helen Thomson

Every spring when the rains came, the people of Conemaugh Valley in the 1880s were concerned about the dam at South Fork, Pa.

Many of them felt that sooner or later there would be trouble, but it never occurred to anybody that a break-through would mean any more than the flooding of the flats between South Fork and Johnstown, 12 miles down the river. Nobody believed that the old reservoir behind the dam was capable of sending 5 million gallons of water pounding down the valley.

The reservoir was built in 1852 as a feeder for the Pennsylvania Canal, a mode of transportation made obsolete by the advent of the railroads. It had been leased by the Pennsylvania Railroad to the South Fork Hunting and Fishing Club, most of whose members were iron and steel company executives from around Pittsburgh. The club had heightened the dam until the lake behind it was 3 miles long, more than a mile wide, and at least 70 feet deep at the breast. Rumor had it that because the lake had been stocked with trout and bass the flood gates were never opened to release the pressure of surplus water. However, the club's engineers had adjudged the dam safe, and the club members had such faith in that

After the dam at South Fork gave way, the resulting wall of water left a path of devastation down the Conemaugh River Valley. Rails, houses, trees, and railroad cars and locomotives were crushed together in a tangled web. *Library of Congress*

opinion that they used the top of the dam, which was 35 feet wide, as a driveway.

ɪ   ɪ

The Johnstown of 1889 was a railroad town, as it is in 1953. In 1871 the Cambria Iron & Steel Company of Johnstown offered the first American-made steel rails for sale, and even before the flood, Johnstown's tonnage was more than three times that of most cities its size. Because of its importance as a railroad center the Baltimore & Ohio ran a branch from Rockwood, on its main line from Pittsburgh, up to Johnstown.

By noon on Friday, May 31, it had been raining hard in Johnstown for 16 hours. On their way to work that morning the men going into the Cambria Steel works noticed that the Conemaugh was within six inches of its banks. During the morning many of them went back home to move their furniture up to the second floor, a chore they did every spring. About

eleven o'clock Herbert Webber, an employee of the Hunting and Fishing Club, was a mile back from the dam attending to a camp when he noticed that the surface of the old reservoir seemed to be lowering. When a mark made on the bank convinced him he was right, he ran to a point from which he could see the front of the dam. It looked like a huge watering pot; jets of water squirted through the masonry for a distance of 30 feet, so great was the pressure behind them. Mr. Webber commandeered all the help he could get hold of, and for three hours, frantic efforts were made to save the dam. But it was too late. At three o'clock the center gave way, and a few minutes later, the side sections opened like gates and 700 acres of water crashed down the valley. Incredible as it seems, observers at the dam reported that the level of water in the lake fell 50 feet in five minutes.

All morning messages about the dam's condition were sent into Johnstown, but flood warnings were an old story there, and the first sign anybody in the valley

paid serious attention to was the insistent shrieking of a locomotive whistle from the direction of South Fork. Since the main yards of the Pennsylvania Railroad at Johnstown parallel the Conemaugh River, they were right in the path of the flood. The men in the yards, alerted by the whistle, saw an engine tearing down the valley and heard a roaring, grinding noise made by something they could not see. Within a span of seconds the thing that caused the rumbling burst into view—a black wall of seething water carrying trees, livestock, wrecked houses, and all kinds of miscellaneous debris to which clung screaming human beings; in one hour it took over 2,000 lives and did $12 million worth of damage. So great was its force that it tossed blooms around as though they were straws. (A bloom is a piece of pig iron weighing 15 tons.)

Men who got to the hills report that in 10 seconds—just 10 seconds—the flood took the roundhouse, including 18 locomotives inside it, and 15 others in the repair shops and the yards. They saw those mighty engines weighing from 70 to 100 tons each tossed and turned like so many packing boxes. Most of those engines ended up buried in the 60 acres of debris that the flood left in Johnstown. Three of them were found in the bed of the Conemaugh and one was discovered in a graveyard. W. A. Smith, general manager of the Associated Press, was among those watching from the hillside above the railroad yards. In his description of the flood he said:

During the height of the flood, the spectators were startled by the sound of two locomotive whistles from the very midst of the disaster. Two engineers, with characteristic courage, had remained at their posts and while there was destruction on every hand, and apparently no escape for them, they sounded their whistles. This they repeated at intervals, the last time with triumphant vigor as the waters by some miracle receded from the sides of their locomotives.

At the Cambria works the water covered the track in the yards with a layer of stones 10 feet deep. Near the plant there was what appeared to be a freight-car wheel lying on the ground. However, the wheel was still attached to its car which was buried under a mass of gravel and debris. After the flood several lanes were dug through the wreckage down to the tracks and three of the little yard engines were resurrected with only slight damage. Within a week they were puffing around the part of the yard that had been cleared, their smokestacks barely visible above the level of the ground.

A freight was lying at South Fork when the dam broke. A noise like thunder made the engineer and the conductor look out of the caboose—and into the approaching flood. They cut the engine loose, and with the throttle wide open made a frantic dash for a bridge they knew would take them to high ground. They streaked down the valley with a 40-foot wall of water 20 yards to the rear of the engine. They arrived at the curve that led to the bridge only to find the far end of the bridge blocked by a freight train. Engineer Bennett then reversed the

lever and succeeded in checking the engine as it slid across the bridge. Then the men jumped and ran for their lives. When they reached the hillside they looked back and saw the bridge and their engine and freight train swept away like a bundle of matches.

At Conomaugh above Johnstown the flood picked up a four-track railroad crowded with trains, and twisted and turned the heavy steel tracks as though they were so many willow wands. One of the curious facts about the flood was that many times rails were broken within a few feet of the fishplates coupling them to the next rail when every natural law would seem to dictate that they should have broken at the plate.

And the flood played other tricks. At Conemaugh, for example, out of all the locomotives that had been in the yards one lone engine stood comparatively undamaged in the middle of the wreckage, debris heaped to its headlight. The engine was Pennsylvania No. 1309, a 54-ton class R Consolidation. George Hudson was its engineer and conductor Sheeley had charge of its train. Fortunately all of its crew escaped to the hills. Two days after the flood, No. 1309 had smoke curling from its stacks and steam issuing from its safety valves. It was all ready to go. All it needed was a track to run on!

As the flood reached Johnstown, it slowed down to an estimated speed of 24 miles an hour, mainly because the Pennsylvania Railroad bridge held and the debris jammed against it served as a dam. Johnstown lies at the foot of a narrow V-shaped valley where the Conemaugh and Stony Creeks join to form the Conemaugh River which flows into the Ohio. When the bridge dammed the flood, the water surged back up both creeks and then came back into Johnstown. The waves from the two creeks went round and round in slowly diminishing circles until most of the buildings they carried were ground to pieces. Men, women and children circled in those terrifying vortices for hours.

Some escaped drowning only to suffer a worse fate. The first wave of flood water had destroyed freight cars carrying petroleum, and by nightfall the wreckage at the bridge, soaked with oil, was afire.

Eyewitnesses report that as darkness came on, the night was made horrible by the smell of burning flesh and the screams of people begging to die as they drifted helplessly toward the fire at the bridge. The conductor of a passenger train safe on the hillside tells how the men from the train took the bell cord and threw it to people floating by. He reports that they saved seven and could have saved more if so many had not been too terrified to risk letting go of their precarious holds on the wreckage they clung to in order to grab at the rope. Others were too badly wounded to make the effort. Some were so absorbed in prayer and hymn singing that they neither saw nor heard those attempting to rescue them.

⚒   ⚒

The day after the flood the busiest "street" in Johnstown was the Pennsylvania track. The Pennsylvania trains had to stop at the eastern end of the bridge and the hundreds of people they were already bringing to Johnstown got into town by walking across the railroad's bridge to the Pennsylvania depot. By the morning after the flood, the water had receded enough to allow the wreckage-clearing squads to begin work. The worst heap of debris in the city was a huge tangle of barbed wire and railroad track so knotted together that it took 200 men a week to remove it. And then its removal was achieved only with the help of locomotives and cranes mounted on flatcars. Temporary tracks were built to the mass of wreckage, and the workmen managed to get big chains through parts of the heap to an engine—sometimes two of them—and the huge tangle was pulled apart.

Near the mass of track and barbed wire was a stack of the roofs of 40 frame houses packed together as one might stack 40 bent cards on top of one another. Beside the pile of roofs was the pantry of a house with the plates and saucers still on the shelves but with no sign of woodwork or any other recognizable outline of a house. Close to the pantry was a human foot and the crumbling remains of a shoe, a half-burned hat, and a knitting bag with part of a hand clinging to it.

Very often the workmen stopped digging and hauling and gathered quietly at

The stone-arch Pennsylvania Railroad bridge held against the flood, leaving huge piles of debris. The railroads were responsible for ferrying people and bringing in supplies after the flood. *Library of Congress*

a spot in the ruins. Presently the group would stir and out of it would come six men bearing a covered form on an improvised stretcher. Those little groups of men were seen frequently during the first days after the flood. There was usually a line of them waiting at the morgues. On the fences near the morgues—both the Pennsylvania and the Baltimore & Ohio depots were used for that purpose—and on the walls of the buildings themselves were several hundred notices of unclaimed bodies:

A boy about 10 found with a little girl about the same age. Both light haired and fair complexioned. Girl has long curls.

A young woman in early 20s. Dark hair and blue eyes. Clothing of fine quality. Single bracelet on the left arm.

A man about 35. Dark complexion, brown mustache, light clothes, left leg a little short.

At seven o'clock on Sunday morning the first relief train arrived in Johnstown—and none too soon, for food was already in short supply, with bread selling for 50 cents a loaf. By Tuesday the railroads were bringing food and other goods to the sufferers at a rate of between 8,000 and 9,000 packages a day. The full story of what had happened at Johnstown, the story that brought such generous response from all corners of the nation, was given to the public by a handful of reporters from the *New York Sun* and the artist of *Harper's Weekly*. This service was made possible by the engineer and the conductor of a Baltimore & Ohio train that took the two men to the scene of the disaster.

By the Monday after the flood the Pennsylvania was running from one to three trains a day on the old schedule, but there were few cars on each train, and 10 minutes after the gates were opened the trains were crowded with people who for the most part had come hundreds of

miles in search of friends and relatives. The *Sun*'s men arrived in Pittsburgh too late that morning to make the Pennsylvania train. At that time no passenger trains were being run into Johnstown by the Baltimore & Ohio. The branch from Rockwood was put at the service of wild-cat trains running on special orders with the object of getting relief to Johnstown as quickly as possible. However, when the *Sun* reporter talked to acting superintendent McIlvaine, he immediately got across to him the importance of getting the Johnstown story to the country if the flood victims were to get needed help.

Within 15 minutes after superintendent McIlvaine had made his decision, one of the Baltimore & Ohio light passenger engines was hitched to a single coach out in the yard. The engineer was W. E. Scott and fireman Charles Hood was his assistant. Conductor W. B. Clancy was in charge of the expedition and

The Johnstown flood claimed more than 2,200 lives and caused $12 million (in 1889 dollars) in damage. The high, steep walls of the river valley exacerbated the effects of the water as it rushed downriver from the broken dam. *Library of Congress*

brakeman Dan Lynn agreed to be a member of the crew even though he had already been without sleep for more than 24 hours.

At 9; 15 a.m. the train was ready.

"How long will it take us to make it, would you say?" the reporters asked McIlvaine.

"It's about 146 miles and all kinds of road," he answered. "There's an accommodation train you'll have to look out for and that will delay you."

"Can we get there in five hours?" the reporters persisted.

"I'd say five hours would be a good guess," McIlvaine told them.

The special ran fast from Pittsburgh to McKeesport. At McKeesport the regular train was overtaken, and from there on the special had a clear track. It is 19 miles from McKeesport to West Newton; the special made the distance in 20 minutes, which meant running considerably more than a mile a minute when the curves are

taken into consideration. And the curves on that stretch of the road are something to take into consideration. At times the single car which composed the train was almost swung off the track. The cover of the water tank flew open on the tender and lumps of coal dashed against the car.

At Connellsville the train stopped five minutes and underwent an inspection. From there on, the road is uphill at a grade of 65 feet to the mile, and the curves are worse than they are in the McKeesport area, if that is possible. However, there was no appreciable letup in the special's speed, and at 12:05 p.m., it arrived in Rockwood. At 12:20 the special left Rockwood in charge of engineer Oliver. All along the route up the valley there were crowds of people staring in silence as the train swept by. The roads leading in from the country to the stations were full of farmers' wagons laden with provisions for the flood victims.

The road from Rockwood to Johnstown lies in a deep gully; at the bottom of the gully flows Stony Creek, ordinarily a quiet little stream. On the day the *Sun*

reporters made their trip the creek was a torrent and there were frequent washouts, particularly in the 10 miles just south of Johnstown. Despite those difficulties the special completed its mission and delivered its grateful passengers at Johnstown at 2 p.m. that Monday.

Eyewitnesses report that the night after the flood the only light in Johnstown emanated from the Pennsylvania Railroad station. They said that the light from a single bulb on that building was a beacon in the midst of chaos and despair. That light was indeed symbolic of the part the railroads were to play in the rescue and rehabilitation of the people at Johnstown. For there is no question but what the combined resources and efforts of the railroads enabled the flood victims to take the first steps toward rebuilding their city so that today Johnstown has more than twice the population and many, many times the industrial capacity that it had on that fateful afternoon in May 1889.

September 1956

Wing Studios

I Came Out of This Alive!

by Hunter M. Picken as told to Phil Vander Horck

On the morning of September 20, 1954, an 83-car hotshot headed by a 6,000-hp diesel locomotive plowed head-on into a steam engine on a lonely main line in Montana.

At 3:45 a.m. I was awakened by the insistent ringing of the telephone in the living room. I made my way down the corridor from the bedroom and lifted the receiver. The callboy at the other end informed me that I was called for an extra west to Glendive at 5:35 that morning and that I should report to the roundhouse by 4:50. My long service as an engineer on the Yellowstone Division of the Northern Pacific, handling both steam locomotives and later the more comfortable diesels, had conditioned me to being roused at any hour of the day or night to report for duty.

Although the necessity for layovers required me to keep a sleeping room in Glendive, I was at my own apartment in Dickinson, N.D., when I was called that September morning. As I prepared a quick breakfast and rounded up the few things I usually carried with me to the roundhouse, I was thinking of my wife, who had gone to Mobile, Ala., to be with our son and his wife at the birth of their second child—a new grandchild for us.

There was nothing sinister in the ringing of the telephone, the creak of the stairs, or the sound of the brisk northwest wind as I walked the few blocks to the round-house to warn me that this was to be a red-letter day in my life—that before the next few hours had passed I would be pronounced dead by three different people and by some miracle live to tell this story!

I   I

At the roundhouse I met Arnold Wanner, who was to be my fireman on this run. I learned that we would be in the cab of No. 6011D, the lead unit of a four-unit General Motors diesel-electric locomotive rated at 6,000 hp, with 83 cars of high priority merchandise behind us: train No. 603. This particular train number identified the most expeditious shipping facility on the Northern Pacific and usually held priority over all opposing trains except first class, and we saw just another day's work ahead of us. Already we were mentally climbing down from the cab at the far end of the line. Looking over our orders, I saw that they gave us rights and waits over all but first-class trains, including a local eastbound freight, engine No. 1917 running as an extra.

I stowed my old black grip back in the engineroom, where the thunder of 16 idling cylinders told me that those 6,000 horses were ready to coax that mile-long string of wood and metal into motion. Anyone who has had occasion to visit the engineroom of a modern diesel locomotive as it is being revved up knows what a deafening roar can be created by those giant engines. In spite of my years of working around them I have never quite got used to the noise, and I soon returned to the cab and closed the communicating door. After completing my preliminary

checks and making the required air test of the brakes, I slowly advanced the throttle and watched the ammeter needle climb to indicate hundreds of amperes being delivered to the wheel motors. Slowly we began to accelerate and about 6 a.m., 25 minutes after sunrise, we were on our way to Glendive, 106 miles to the west.

It was a fine, clear fall morning with good visibility along the track ahead. We were protected by our cab enclosure from the chilly winds, and my fireman and I congratulated each other on having drawn a diesel run that morning rather than one of those occasional steamers that must be taken over this route. Everything was going smoothly as we rolled past Dickinson Dam, South Heart, and Belfield, over rolling hills striped with their alternate bands of brown and green formed by the strip-farming methods of this area. Past Fryburg and about 25 miles out of Dickinson the track drops downgrade into the southern rim of the North Dakota Badlands—the Little Grand Canyon, as it is often referred to—a region of picturesque domes, peaks and multicolored spires carved out through the ages by the wanderings of the Little Missouri River and eroded by wind and rain into fantastic shapes.

In due course we passed the little town of Medora on the southwestern edge of the Badlands, the area where Theodore Roosevelt once ranched and cavorted around on horseback, and where Roosevelt Park is now open and dedicated in his honor. Here we crossed the Little Missouri River and began a 20-mile upgrade. By this time it was clear that the strong northwest wind was exerting considerable drag on the long string of freight cars, and we were not making the time we normally would have been making. The cab was equipped with two-way radio which enabled me to maintain contact with the conductor and the other two brakemen in the caboose as well as with our division dispatchers. As we

approached a small station by the name of Sully Springs, about 30 miles out, I heard the voice of the dispatcher above the crackling of the loud speaker, asking where we thought we might take siding for train No. 2, the eastbound first-class passenger train which was headed our way somewhere up ahead. I weighed the various factors in my mind, then picked up the handset and replied that although the headwind had prevented me from making the time I had hoped for I expected to be at Beaver Hill, about 48 miles ahead, to take siding for No. 2, if nothing slowed us up further.

From the point where we then were to the end of our run the terrain becomes increasingly rough with many upgrades, downgrades, and curves which all combine to restrict visibility ahead and require us to depend more on block signals, radio communications, and train orders to ensure safety. It was about eight o'clock in the morning, and we were approaching the distant block signal east of Wibaux, Mont. It read clear, and my main concern was to reach Beaver Hill, 4 miles beyond Wibaux, and enter the siding there as quickly as possible for the eastbound passenger. We were rolling along about 50 miles an hour, and although the Wibaux tracks were hidden from view by a combination of rising terrain and a curve to the left we could see the smoke from the local extra freight, No. 1917, rising beyond the hill. I commented to the fireman. "Well, the local is there anyway"—assuming of course that it had been on the siding for 35 minutes or so waiting for us to pass. It was a matter of only about a minute until we reached the east switch of the Wibaux siding and noted that the block was also clear at this point.

The front end of Mikado No. 1917 is sheared completely off as it rests on its left side. *Wing Studios*

Every railroader knows that the time when everything is apparently going smoothly and "right on the advertised" is the time to be alert for something to go wrong—something that may call for instantaneous reaction on his part. An example: Many years ago I was engineering a big steam locomotive on the same line when the water gauge burst without warning, filling the cab with scalding vapor. I automatically grabbed the shutoff valve, my reflexes guiding my hand through the blinding steam so that I was able to shut it off in one quick motion, saving both my fireman and myself from possible severe burns. At such times there is no margin for reflection or deliberation, and whether a man lives or dies may depend on the rapidity and correctness of his involuntary reactions.

As we rounded the curve and came into sight of the tangent track, still high-balling at 50 miles an hour, the fireman and I were astounded to see No. 1917 with an extra water tender—not on the siding but directly ahead and facing us on the main line!

It is not my purpose in relating the story of this crash to condemn any of the opposing train's crew but merely to relate the incidents leading up to the wreck as they happened to me. As far as responsibility is concerned, all the salient factors have been investigated and are now a matter of record. Suffice it to say that due to human error, which creeps into the best-regulated schedules to throw the proverbial monkey wrench into the machinery, the steam locomotive had been run off the stock track and onto the main line—apparently just after we had passed the block at the east switch, since

the brakes of the steamer were set and the crew had not even had time to throw the switch behind them. A contributing factor no doubt was the fact that although we could see 1917's smoke, even before we saw the engine itself, the crew did not seem to be aware of the fact that we were approaching—not until we had actually rounded the curve.

As I grasped the situation and saw the probability of immediate death for all concerned—the fireman and myself in the cab of the diesel, the brakeman in the rear diesel unit, the three men in the caboose, and the crew of the other train—I immediately applied the brakes in full emergency position, at the same time operating the sander valve, and yelled to my fireman to lie down on the floor of the cab, knowing he would not have enough time to get back into the engine-room. I grabbed the horn in my left hand and held on, in the hope that the men in engine No. 1917 would be warned and escape death. I later found out that my warning had been heeded and that they all had jumped to safety. The engineer jumped at the last possible instant. I held the horn open during the next few seconds until we hit at just under 50 miles an hour. From that point on, my story must be reconstructed from what was told me after the crash.

I   I

At the instant of impact, the din of rending steel and shattering glass filled the air. The head diesel unit came to an abrupt halt, derailed and leaning some-what to the right although still upright, with her front end and cab smashed accordion-fashion back into the rear wall of the cab. The opposing steam locomotive was knocked 341 feet backward down the track and came to rest on her left side with the front torn off, leaving its jagged imprint clearly defined on the crumpled face of the diesel. The next 15 cars behind the diesel units, obeying the law of momentum, kept coming, piling up side-ways, on top of, and through each other, until the inertia of the following cars had been absorbed, and then lay still like a heap of building blocks on the line. Many feet of track, both on the main line and on the stock track, were torn up and twisted, but fortunately no steam explosion or fire accompanied the crash.

My fireman had not lost consciousness, and his first thought was for his engineer. Groping through the wreckage, he managed to locate me where I was

pinned under the crumpled metal and discovered that I was as still as death, with my head badly injured. He could detect no sign of breathing and reached for my right wrist in an attempt to take my pulse. He felt none so became resigned to the apparent fact that I was dead and managed to crawl out of the cab through a small opening.

At this point he met the brakeman who had been riding in the rear unit of the diesel. This had suffered little damage since it was the freight cars immediately behind it which had absorbed most of the momentum of the crash. The brakeman asked where I was, and Wanner informed him that I had been killed and was pinned in the wreckage of the cab.

However, in order to make sure, the brakeman himself climbed up into the wreckage, felt my right wrist, and climbed down again, convinced of the truth of Warmer's statement.

About this time a brakeman from the local arrived on the scene, asked the same question, received the same answer, and also climbed up into the cab to verify my demise. He also was forced to agree that I had succumbed. Whether or not my heartbeat could have been detected had they managed to reach the left wrist is a question which never will be answered, but what these three men, who were all convinced that I was no longer among the living, could not know was that my pulse has never been as discernible in the right wrist as in the left!

I have always been of slight build, and the officials and railroadmen who later examined what was left of the cab of No. 6011 stated that I was to their knowl-edge the first engineer in history to remain in the cab and survive such a head-on crash, that had I weighed about five more pounds I would almost surely have been crushed to death—so small was the space remaining in the smashed cab.

At this point the three men around the cab awoke to the fact that the diesel motors were still running and the fuel oil was spilling in all directions. The thought of fire galvanized them into action. They

at once went back and shut down all four engines. Upon returning to the front end they stood near the cab, examining the damage. Then one of them said, "Listen! I hear a noise in the cab. It sounds like Hunter moaning." Immediately they investigated and were amazed to find me moving.

By this time the telephone and tele-graph had done its work, and ambulances had been dispatched to the scene of the wreck. Doctors from Wibaux, Glendive, and Beach had also arrived. I am told that it was a very difficult task to get me out of the cab, but shortly I was in an ambu-lance and on the way to the Northern Pacific Beneficial Association Hospital in Glendive, 32 miles away. There I began to regain consciousness about 5:30 that after-noon. My fireman, by the way, after assisting in removing me from the wreck age had collapsed, and it was later discov-ered that he had suffered a cracked pelvis. Although he is not yet fully recovered he has returned to work firing a diesel switch engine.

I   I

Those 9½ hours after the two trains hit are a blank in my memory, but I am confi-dent that the first aid I received at the scene of the accident and on the way to Glendive plus the marvelous subsequent medical attention by my doctors and care by the nurses in the NPBA hospital were responsible for my being alive today to tell this story.

Since the day of the wreck the lead unit of the diesel has had a face-lifting and is now back in service, and the steam locomotive was cut up for scrap and will never again ride the iron. Like old No. 6011, I too have taken quite a beating but I have been nearly rehabilitated and am confident that I shall resume my occupation as a locomotive engineer in the not-too-distant future. I am most grateful to God for allowing me to continue to live, that I might have the privilege of further enjoying my family, my work, and my country.

CONFESSIONS OF A TRAIN-WATCHER

David P. Morgan

May 1957

This much is personal but pertinent. Ten years ago I had a choice to make about this lonely, frustrating, misunderstood, and immensely satisfying matter of train-watching.*

Either I had to sharply curtail my interest in railroading in order to seek and hold employment in some unrelated field like insurance or education or I could try to get my paycheck as well as my kicks out of locomotives and such. I was reluctant to cast my lot with any one particular railroad (After all, aren't they almost as intriguing for their differences as for their similarities?), and besides, I didn't have an engineering degree, which comes in handy if one wants upstairs eventually.

No, the gamble was more complex than that. I not only wanted to stick with railroading round-the-clock, but I wanted, as much as my one-fingered typing talent would permit, to explain and to share this preoccupation with others. Which provoked questions: Was railroading just an adolescent whim? Was it worth investing a life in? And who else really cared anyway?

Deliberate train-watching, on either an amateur basis or professional, is a sometimes thankless pastime, of course. Unlike stamp collecting or golf, it has never received Presidential endorsement. The urge is not easily explained, either, as is the love of flight, nor is it a fashionable lunacy like indulging in hi-fi or sport cars or a figure 8 on ice. People in the mass think of trains as things to ride on or things that carry coal and scrap iron and oranges, never as art and fun, drama and tragedy. Well, almost never, because I seem to recall a musical score on "Pacific 2-3-1," and Christopher Morley has written verse on the subject for *Atlantic Monthly*. As a rule, though, friends, family, and the general John Q. do not comprehend. It is even better for the train-watcher when they ignore him altogether. Otherwise he is the butt of ridicule ("Come again … you went a thousand miles to see a *steam* engine?") or the object of well-meaning sympathy ("This is a beautiful photo, honey—just look at all the trains in the roundhouse!").

As for the object of love, the railroads themselves, why, they now have what might be described as a controlled puzzlement about train-watchers. At first, way back in the early 1930s, most roads made the understandable but colossal blunder of rejecting their only genuine suitor: the man who liked them, not for what they could do for him, but just for being railroads. Then, gradually, the industry realized that here was something unique, a ready-made ambassador to

---

Train-watcher has an English flavor to it; *railfan* is the stock American equivalent. But you can use *enthusiast, student, historian, aficionado,* even *ferroequinologist,* and get the idea across. Anything, indeed, but *hobbyist*—which is a bit weak in view of railroading's appeal.

whom pay would have been an insult and removal of a treasured amateur standing. So railroading accepted the fan, scheduled excursions for him, sold him engine bells, told him how much a 2-10-4 weighed. I do not think that railroading understands him, though, that it has really convinced itself that the business might just be so engrossing that normal people would pay good money just to ride, and hang the destination.

ɪ   ɪ

By its very nature, railroading does not lend itself to armchair enjoyment. Somebody has called it the industry without a roof. Certainly anybody who has seriously watched trains has also made himself cold, dirty, tired, and miserable on their account. Enjoying a cocktail under the tinted glass of a dome is the exception; more typical is listening to the profanity of a switch crew which has just put a gondola on the ground in knee-deep snow, or contemplating one's trousers after open cylinder cocks unexpectedly scoured the top layer of cinders off the station platform. I recall the very day that this aspect of the game was impressed upon me. It was a bleak, wintry afternoon in Louisville & Nashville's South Louisville Yard, and I was watching an 0-8-0 kicking cars. I remember thinking that this was a rough, cold, dirty business, and not one for flower pickers. Not being the outdoor type by nature, I reluctantly concluded that my enthusiasm for engines and such, if continued, might lead into paths not all hearts and flowers. Once, at least, I was wise beyond my years.

It follows that the more difficult railroading is to behold and admire, the more of a public curiosity is the train-watcher. And it burns us up to receive the label *crank* (Of course a minority of fans are nuts; what assembly of human beings ever lacked 'em?), even in its more subtle forms, such as the arched eyebrow and the bemused expression. It is natural for anyone obsessed with the drama of an avocation to want to share his love or, at the least, to have both it and him treated with dignity. Thank God, I say, that

Lucius Beebe caught the disease so that at least the book trade could get a few $10 volumes of erudite prose as evidence that, to some people at least, railroading is art and that one need not be odd as a prerequisite to sense same.

I do not mean to stress this persecution complex business too much because, in his turn, the true train-watcher regards The Great Unwashed with that most cruel of human emotions … pity. Pity for a soul so drugged with the conventional that it does not respond to the sigh of air brake cylinders or the wallop of a crossing taken at 85. Pity for eyes that see not the beauty of a smoke plume, ears that hear noise instead of stack music, hands that grip Pullman handrails without touching magic.

ɪ   ɪ

So I had a choice to make 10 years ago, and in another sense the choice had already been made. I think it was made when I saw my first steam locomotive, that most awesome of all man's creations. The love of steam is something akin to the love for a woman: No explanation is really necessary, it is just there. And it can be carried to great extremes. Years after the graveside funeral service for steam has been completed and the body is all but in the ground, this magazine continues to receive an occasional letter from some suitor who deems the diesel a farce, who tells me that the railroads are variously wasting precious oil resources, shamefully scrapping good engines, indebting themselves to the bankers for generations, throwing honest men out of work, and losing their grip on the public consciousness—all because of dieseldom. What he argues on factual ground, though, is nothing more or less than his expression of horror and helplessness at the prospect of losing his love. And I sympathize. It is cruel to see steam go, and even the sure knowledge that its passage is a great economic blessing does not ease the pain.

Oh, yes, we train-watchers can be extremists about steam. Without apology, too. I recall forgetting play as a boy in Louisville and running to the end of the street at the first sound of slogging exhaust, and there standing enthralled as a heavy 2-8-2 came fighting up the

1 percent to Cincinnati with too much tonnage, the whole engine thrusting from side to side with the beat of the pistons, black smoke boiling skyward, and the stack deafening the ears with the old, old, ever-new talk of "I think I can, think I can." Yes, and the goggled, overalled engineer raising his right arm to me as if to say, "It's all right, son; we've got her by the tail." Hard, mean, tough work, and steam let you know about it, let you know all about the job at hand, let you know she had the tonnage in her teeth and was writing home about it.

Glory! … and yet, the urge for me was more than steam, else I should have turned down TRAINS because 10 years ago the handwriting was on the wall. Back then you could (and I did) allay your fears all you wanted with endless discussion of Norfolk & Western and poppet valves and Lima advertising, but the plain fact of the impending funeral was uncomfortably apparent. So the other virtues of the industry, some aesthetic and some not, made it seem inviting, steam or no.

Like what? Well, like the inherent nature, flexibility, and productivity of the railroad, particularly on this continent. For example, the Milwaukee Road has a freighthouse only a few hundred feet from the back door of my apartment. It looks local, suburban, small time; to most people it is local. Yet Milwaukee Road could spot virtually any one of the nation's 1,700,000 freight cars at that house, it could be loaded with virtually any material or product known, and that car could move without restriction to virtually any of 56,700 freight stations strung out along 222,000 route-miles of railroad in the U.S. as well as thousands of other sidings in Canada, Mexico, and Cuba. The railroads have a very mild word for this transport phenomenon; they call it simply *interchange*. It means a common 4-foot 8½-inch gauge and standardized dimensions, air brakes, safety appliances, couplers, etc., not to mention rules and regulations covering all the paperwork involved—the waybill, per diem, switch lists, etc.

In a sense, all of the physical plant of railroading is connected to and at the disposal of the shipper who uses that freighthouse behind my apartment. Cascade Tunnel, Conway Yard, Dotsero Cutoff, the energy of 26,000 diesel units, the talents and muscle of more than a million men and women all right there in my backyard, as near as my phone. And I find this interesting and vital and praiseworthy. The other night as I was driving out to that apartment, I paced a westbound Milwaukee Road time freight—three F7s leading 70 or more cars along at a sprightly 35 mph. Naturally the raw, bold drama was present, the chanting V-16s, the solid roll and sway of train tonnage following obediently along—coupler locked in coupler, flanges held in check by rail width of precise dimension. Yet there was more. The big mechanical reefer of Northern Pacific—heading back empty to home rails at St. Paul? And the vivid blue Boston & Maine box on roller bearings—cloth from a New England mill for Seattle or Harlowton or Superior?

Skip the importance for the moment; what is essential need not be exciting. And yet I do find this exciting, far more thrilling in fact than the Braves in the ninth or Mr. Greco's dancers or even—no, no, not music, for it has too much in common with the logic and harmony of railroading to bear comparison.

I find the railroad stimulating to watch even when action is absent, before and after the trains have rolled. Its buildings and men and geography and history are worthwhile cause for study.

Stations alone have recently been the sole subject of a scholarly, book-length examination (*The Railroad Station*, Yale University Press, $7.50), and well they might be. I like to poke around the big, rambling wooden junction depots where the crowds of drummers and picnickers of yesteryear have diminished in sound to the lonely clatter of a veteran L. C. Smith as the agent bills a car of feed from B. J. Jones & Sons. And Union Station, Chicago, at 1:30 a.m., when a handful of weary stragglers and deadheads go through the gate for Milwaukee Road No. 55. when the bar and newsstands are

TRAINS editor David P. Morgan pauses on a station platform at Joliet, Ill., to watch trains—in this case a Santa Fe streamliner behind EMD F7 diesels. *TRAINS magazine collection*

locked up and the last train out doesn't even rate a call on the loudspeakers. Plant City, Sioux City, San Rafael, 30th Street, Englewood, Taft … each a building, each an experience, each a few bricks and boards in the vast structure of railroading.

Or the men. Because of the moving about, either aboard train or from one office to another, most railroaders bear a certain stamp that identifies them in their walk and look and dry, caustic, well-intentioned humor. Because railroading is big, so it produces big men, men who can speak of the almost incredible fact of moving 14,000 tons in a single train with the ease of selling a shirt in Sears Roebuck. Also it produced the steward, say,

on the *St. Louisan* who seated and fed a dinerful of giggling but prim coeds, saw to it that the expense-account man's steak was medium-rare, mixed a pair of highballs for the coach passengers not allowed in the Pullman lounge, and still found time to smile at and cajole a mentally retarded little girl traveling to a special school. I watched him, and I was proud that he was a railroader and not (as he easily could have been) a bank clerk or a librarian.

I suppose, on balance, a railroad man is no better or no worse than any other. Certainly I have encountered my quota of crass, conceited individuals, one or two in the president's chair and, by the mathematical odds, a great many more behind the ticket counter and in the caboose. I recall an agent in LA who not only refused to switch my return ticket from one transcontinental to another but took positive delight in impugning my motives, at least until I threatened to dial either Mr. Gurley or Mr. Stoddard (I knew neither gentleman at the time) for satisfaction. Such events are reasonably rare, though, and even then I have at least been on home ground—talking to a railroader about a railroad. Anyway, I must equate such experiences with the countless officials who have trusted my editorial intelligence, with the North Western brakeman who patiently and perchance too simply explained to a lady that the train was delayed picking up mail because "You might say, we're Santa Claus's helpers," and with the Western Maryland fireman who let me run the stoker on his Pacific clear into Elkins.

The geography is good too. The layman thinks of the Canadian Rockies; I muse over the Spiral Tunnels. He waxes eloquent over the fishing in the Atlantic surf; I recollect Florida East Coast's 800s on the night perishable through Boca Raton. Man can build a highway across any manner of terrain because the automobile is—let's face it—an almost inexcusably inefficient, grossly overpowered thing that eats up grades and curves like an elephant steps on anthills. Yet where the highway can go, so can the railroad—and usually it got there first. I find it marvelous to look from the cupola of a caboose trailing tonnage over Tehachapi—to look up and discover one's road locomotive immediately overhead and at right angles. It is similarly remarkable to witness, say, Chesapeake & Ohio lift 8,000 tons of coal 700 feet up and 50 miles forward in just 2½ hours and with only 4,500 horses with which to work. Rio Grande Southern's Ophir Trestles, Horseshoe Curve, those tunnels under the Hudson—all fine and wondrous, and my only regret to date is that time and finance have not yet allowed railroading down the Riviera and up the Andes.

History, too, is within the realm of railroading. It is dramatic history, full of Casey Joneses and Stampede Passes and *Pioneer Zephyrs* (Hollywood, where art thou?), and it is also good. It is an exclusive story, for what other industry has used so little of our resources and produced so much in return for our economy? Did the steel barons anticipate demand, as Jim Hill did when he threw Great Northern across a wilderness that couldn't support a wagon, much less an iron horse? And how many men of history, no matter what their trade, possessed the corporate courage of Harriman as he gazed across Salt Lake, spurned his engineers' dubiousness, and ordered them to lay a railroad over the waters whether it was possible or not?

Oh, yes, this history has its scalawags, its Daniel Drews and Jay Goulds, but then so has the White House. Moreover, railroading's rogues have generally been aboveboard about it. When they fleeced the suckers they didn't write it off as social progress or as a defense of free enterprise. All of which brings up the basic railroad position of 1957 and a fundamental reason why I, for one, stay close to the rails and have faith in them.

Railroading remains one of the few institutions of the once-popular do-it-yourself school. Railroads ask no federal or state handout; they get none. For the railroad there are no rivers and harbors bills, no soil banks, no Washington-sponsored public relations agencies of the stripe of the CAB, no depletion tax allowances, no round-trip gasoline taxes, no nothing that doesn't come out of what the ticket or the cargo calls for. This is unusual. It is *so* unusual that people flatly refuse to believe it. Those of my acquaintance mutter something about that most ancient of debates, the land grants, and even when I have convinced them that these were loans, not gifts, they still manage to resolve their thinking with some meaningless platitudes about government and its obligation to help pay parity crop prices, drill oil, dredge the Missouri, widen highways, to do virtually anything for anybody. Excluding railroads. Me? I'm no Old Guard Republican. I just like people and industry to mean what they say, and when railroading says it's self-supporting, you can believe it.

So my acquaintances tell me that a brakeman was surly or No. 23 came in late or they paid $1.25 for a ham sandwich and potato chips, and I think, "Yeah, the railroads do a lot of things wrong—but every last tie and wheel and gallon of diesel oil they own is what they paid for, not you or I or us." And I admire this old-fashioned way of doing business. For one thing, it makes the life of an editorial writer easier and his conscience cleaner.

⚊ I ⚊

So I took railroading round the clock, as vocation as well as avocation, first as a freelancer, then for TRAINS. Ten years later I'm here to say the choice was correct. Just the travel would have been worth it—making 2,224 miles on an *Aerotrain* … accompanying a pair of hoppers from West Virginia to seaboard … riding a Camelback (and a turbine and a narrow gauge 2-8-0) … seeing the speedometer of a Hudson on 94 and of a diesel on 98 … yes, and lying in the upper berth in a Pacific Great Eastern drawing room high above the Fraser River Canyon, oddly thinking that my fall would be a bit more than most if a wheel got on the ground and we went down the slope.

Also the sights: a big cab-forward 4-8-8-2 standing in the rain at night in Reno, waiting to be off with a Sacramento local—a mountain battler sniffing through her compound air pumps … four Pennsy 2-10-0s attempting to restart 90 cars of ore on the steepest part of the grade also in the rain … Electro-Motive's production line … Cincinnati Union Terminal's vast arch … Tower A down in the third-railed blackness beyond the ends of the platforms in Grand Central Terminal. And the experiences! *Drinking* maple syrup at the skipper's urging on a Central Vermont caboose. Riding boxcar tops through a mild sandstorm on Espee's narrow gauge. Watching the railroad flow through the hands of countless dispatchers and ops and towermen (always finding it difficult to believe that those pen scratches and buttons and push-pull levers actually put trains in the hole, around each other, safely through interlockings). Talking to the brass, thereby getting a fresh perspective on a business, discovering why it frowns upon

"The most beautiful thing in steam," to author Morgan, was Southern Railway's Ps-4 Pacific. *Walt Thrall*

doubleheaders (labor costs), how long it takes to pick up a typical wreck (30 minutes per car), where it disagrees ("UP may cut the helpers off on the fly, but *we* don't!"). Talking to the worthy Brothers—listening to what it was to buck an extra board in 1934, survive aboard a 2-8-8-2 inside Moffat Tunnel, and find one's job of boilermaker had suddenly been eliminated by an engine that didn't have any staybolts or crown sheet.

I   I

You could call me a professional train-watcher, someone paid to do it—otherwise no different from thousands of other enthusiasts, like my dad, like you. It's like one of the automobile makers blurbed last fall: "No one can enjoy a new Ford more than you can." So it is with this wonderful world of trains.

The particular payoff of the work I do is that it allows me to see more of

railroading than some and to explain and/or share the experience. This can be a rewarding thing, too, this conversing each month in print with 37,000 other train-watchers. It is fine to get a kick out of railroading; it is better to know that you're not the only one. Just the other issue I threw caution to the wind and exclaimed out loud that the most beautiful thing in steam was a Southern Railway Ps-4, and soon a kindred soul in Mississippi—an engineer, in fact—replied amen to that. And now and then some couple stores the sedan, takes me at my word, and domes westward on *California Zephyr*, and the result is invariably the same, "You're right, it is a resort on wheels." The critics are stimulating too—the firemen who tell me diesels do need firemen and if I'd get out from behind a desk I'd find out why … the readers who declare the passenger business is going to pot because the rails don't give a damn and the readers who say I've got on rose-colored glasses if I think passenger

trains aren't losing a small fortune … and those who tell me I'm losing my touch if a Geep sounds enchanting (or displaying signs of hardening arteries because of certain nostalgic copy on steam).

The disturbing question a few of them ask is this: "Look, Dave, you're closer to the business than I am. Is it really on the rocks? How much longer can an impoverished industry like that stand the gaff?"

A solemn, serious query, that is. And even if I possessed a dogmatic, conclusive answer (which I do not), this would not be the place to print it. It is the place, though, to advance this thought. Even if railroading ended tonight at 11:59, you and I would have been the fortunate ones—those who experienced the great drama, who were close by during one of those rare seasons when man's genius produced something at once useful and beautiful.

Me? I'll remain a train-watcher.

SECOND TRICK AT BE TOWER

Richard J. Cook

It's 2:45 in the afternoon in the early part of May.

The sky is clear, but there is a sharp wind blowing from the southwest. It's a windy day but not very cold. You get out of your car, pick up your lunch, and slowly walk up the iron steps.

This is Berea Tower at Berea, Ohio. You have spent the better part of two weeks breaking in at this tower—the toughest on the division—learning the work on all tricks. You passed the examination on your knowledge of the signals and switches given by the signal maintainer and were reported to the chief dispatcher as "OK" for the job. Now your big chance has come. The chief called you last night to work second trick at BE for the regular man who is off sick. You have had experience working other towers on the Cleveland Division of the New York Central, and you have confidence in your ability to handle this one, even though it is the busiest.

Finally you've reached the No. 1 tower on the division, the one many men shy away from because of the responsibility, the sound judgment involved in making split-second decisions necessary to keep the trains running. You pause a moment to reflect that the second trick, which you are about to take over, is the busiest, and that this time you will be doing it all alone. There will be no one to turn to for advice as there was when you were breaking in. Then you continue on up the steps and walk in the door.

Inside, the first-trick operator greets you by wishing you luck that this first day of yours will be an easy one. You thank him, look over the train sheet for any special instructions, and sit down in the warm revolving chair at the long dark-green desk. You check to see that there are no overdue trains and wave good-bye to the first-trick man as he goes down the steps to his car. You're all alone now; it's your baby.

You get out your pens, sign your name and hours on duty—3 to 11 p.m.—at the top of the trainsheet, then lean back in your chair and survey the scene about you. Facing you are two telephone circuit boxes—one large one, one small one, each with a number of holes into which you can plug to close a telephone circuit. By plugging into these holes you will be able to talk to one of five dispatchers, one of three operators, or anyone who calls you on one of three message lines or three yard lines. You feel like a telephone operator with all of that equipment in front of you. To the left of the larger of these boxes is the loudspeaker which amplifies voices coming in over the telephone lines. This is a great help when one or more trains are rumbling by the tower.

The bell that you have been expecting rings twice. You plug into the lower right-hand hole and say, "Berea!"

"426 by at 2:54," says the voice of the operator at Grafton, 12 miles to the west.

New York Central's Advance LS-7, with 91 cars trailing F7 1678, heads west on track No. 1 at BE Tower. *Richard J. Cook*

"All right," you say. Now you place your plug in an upper hole where the Cleveland Terminal dispatcher's line is. You wait until the talking stops, then say "426 out of Grafton 2:54. Berea."

"Come on!" is the reply.

Now No. 426 is about 10 miles to the west of you, coming at 70 miles an hour. Time to act. You swing out of your chair, walk across the newly rubber-tiled floor to the large screen interlocking machine that fills nearly the entire length of the two-story building. You squeeze the handle of one of the 111 levers that protrude from the machine in a long line like so many outstretched hands, pull it toward you, wait for a click, then pull it again. Out there on the plant, some 500 feet to the east of you, a switch machine will respond to the electrical impulses set up when you reversed the lever. A series of interlocking bars inside the cabinet of the machine in front of you slide past each other and lock into place while the energized circuit quickly carries impulses downstairs to the instrument-filled relay room and then moves out across the plant to the switch machine, energizes the

motor which spins gears that, by means of levers and rods, moves switch points. You have "opened" one end of a crossover.

You do the same with the lever next to it, pull two more levers straight out without waiting for them to click, then walk back to your desk. You have just made the lineup for No. 426: a pair of switches for a crossover and two signals. The switches always come first, then the appropriate signals. This is one of the safety features built into your interlocking machine. You cannot get a signal for a lineup until a route is properly aligned. You keep in mind too that the only proper way to make a lineup is toward the approaching train—switches first, then the signals. A minute later you hear a short buzz and a little red light sparkles on a box on the desk just to your right. No. 426 is on the annunciator circuit and has the signal; if it didn't have the signal to proceed, the buzzer would keep sounding. Now that you have made your lineup there is nothing you can do but wait for the train to come.

As you sit there in your chair you look through the outward-swinging windows which are on all four sides of the tower and study the tracks below you. The

trackage, roughly in the form of a big X, is a maze of switches and crossovers. To the east run two lines; to the west run two lines. The four tracks which stretch eastward to the left behind you go into Cleveland, 12 miles away. The two outside tracks, Nos. 3 (westbound) and 4 (eastbound or westbound) swing off into Rockport Yard 3 miles away and go around the southern edge of the city to form what is called the Belt Line. The two inside tracks, 1 and 2, become the Lakefront Line and descend to the lake level in downtown Cleveland, continuing along the lake to Collinwood.

In front of you and to your left, those three tracks are known as the Big Four tracks. The high-speed Nos. 1 and 2 tracks go right down through tiny Linndale into the Cleveland Union Terminal, destination of all passenger trains stopping at Cleveland. The outside track, No. 4, goes as far as Short Line junction, 4 miles away, where it joins the Belt Line.

To the west, the continuation of the Lakefront behind the tower becomes the

Toledo Division—four tracks to Toledo and west. Again in front of the tower, two tracks leave the Big Four from Cleveland and join the Toledo Division. Two tracks continue in a southwesterly direction to become the double-tracked Ohio Division of the old CCC&StL (Big Four) to Columbus and Cincinnati, Indianapolis, and St. Louis.

A small amber light appears on the large track chart high on the wall behind the interlocking machine. 426 is now on the first circuit of your interlocking plant. Another light comes on; 426 is by your distant signal and is now just a hundred feet down the track. You rise from your seat at the desk, go to the machine, restore to normal (that is, push in the lever that controls the distant signal), turn to the window and watch the *Cleveland Special*, the morning train from Cincinnati, go by. You look her over carefully to make sure that all is well. After waving a highball to the rear end, you go back to the desk, note on the sheet in front of you the time 426 passed. Then you report this fact to the terminal dispatcher in Springfield, saying, "426, 3:06. Berea."

Your first train has passed. So far so good—although you forgot to ring the operator at Short Line to let him know ahead of time about 426. You know, however, that he has been expecting it. Still, you resolve not to forget it the next time.

After you return from putting the other three levers normal, you sit back in your chair to relax. But Grafton is ringing you again. 472 is out of Grafton at 3:10. This time you tell the Lakefront dispatcher. He says okay, and you go to the machine and start yanking out levers. The lineup is from the Big Four to No. 2 Lakefront. You pull, wait for a click, pull two more, wait for more clicks as you follow the correct sequence for this lineup. The signal is given; now all you have to do is watch the train go by.

I I

So far it's been easy, but you know that the busy part of the day is yet to come. You know that here at Berea, where all the NYC lines west of Cleveland briefly meet, it is possible to have as many as four westbound freights coming at you at the same time, that it is a common

occurrence to have three trains passing by the tower while others are following behind, that there are times when you have to leave the tower, go down on the ground and hand messages or orders to moving trains—oftentimes at night. You know because you yourself have seen it. You know how the trains bunch up and seem to come in herds, one right after the other, all trying to go via conflicting routes. You know how when the tiniest thing goes wrong all of the bells seem to start to ring, everybody on the railroad seems to focus his attention on Berea, and all want to know all at the same time what is going on. You know how nerve-racking it can be to have two or three telephone bells jangling your ears, to have the trains coming at you faster than you can handle them with more coming behind them. You shudder and hope that it doesn't happen to you—at least not on your first night.

A buzz interrupts your reverie. Something is "on the bell" on Lakefront track No. 1. You plug into the line of the Lakefront dispatcher at Cleveland, wait for a chance to talk, then say, "One. Berea."

"That's No. 3, Berea."

"All right!" You tell the dispatcher at Toledo and get his OK. Then you line up for No. 3 to the Toledo Division track 1, the high-speed line. No. 3 goes by the tower at 30 miles an hour, limited speed for a diverging movement. You restore your levers to normal and report the train by to the two dispatchers.

Another buzz and a red light. It's a freight coming out of Rockport Yard on track 4 against the current of traffic. The Cleveland Belt Line dispatcher, who handles all freight movements, says it's BF-9, engine 1818, a hotshot freight for the Big Four with 67 loads, 23 empties, all for Ballefontaine (and west). You give this information to the Big Four dispatcher at Springfield, Ohio. He groans appropriately at such a long, heavy train and then says, "All right."

Now you have to do some fast figuring. The time is 4:02 p.m.; No. 73, the westbound *Prairie State* for Detroit and Chicago, is due to go by you at 4:10. Quickly you ask Short Line where 73 is and find out that it is coming at his home signal, about 5 miles away from you. Can BP-9 with such a heavy train get started, come up the 3 miles from Belt Junction,

where it now is, and make it across the plant in time to clear No. 73? All of this must go on in your mind as quick as a flash. You decide to give the BF-9 only the first signal and wait for 73 to show up. Two minutes later 73 is on your bell. You call this in to Cleveland, report it to Toledo, pull two signal levers, and watch as 73 roars by you: two Geeps and 15 cars at 70 miles an hour.

On this lineup, in either direction, terminal to Toledo, trains can make full speed. 73 is by at 4:10, right on time. You quickly go to the machine, push and pull levers in a hurry as you make a new lineup. Your freight train, now slowing to a crawl, has the signal before he has to stop. At 4:19 BF-9's caboose follows a rumbling herd of freight cars through a puzzle switch and heads into the Big Four connection track. You ring Grafton and say, "1818 at 4:19." He acknowledges it. You write it on your sheet and report it to two dispatchers. It's 4:21, and something hits the bell on track 2 Toledo Division. Four minutes later No. 14, a Chicago-New York mail train, one of the fastest trains on the Central, streaks by bound for the terminal at 70 miles an hour. Right on time. You heave a sigh of relief. You'd forgotten all about 14, and if BF-9 had been any slower, you would have slowed up the fast mail, plenty! You resolve to be on your toes now.

Grafton calls again; the 1750 is by him. You call it in to the Belt Line dispatcher: "1750 out sf Grafton. Berea." A short pause. "That's a Big Four extra, Berea, Down 4 into Rockport."

"All right."

You mark the engine number down on the eastbound side sf the sheet, the time it passed Grafton, an E for eastward track, and 4L for the track he is to go to: 4 Lakefront. You get out of your chair, grab levers, and start pulling. Thia is the slowest lineup because more switches have to be reversed: 76, 75, 72, 71, 70, 69, 57, 38, 37, 36—and then the signal, 29. Always in that order. Your lineup is made from the Big Four to 4 Lakefront. That leaves you only the three Lakefront-to-Toledo Division tracks to run anything on because the extra is crossing over so many

The second-trick operator at Berea highballs FA-powered westbound fast freight NC-1 as it passes by the tower. *Richard J. Cook*

tracks. Therefore, you must be sure that there are no trains coming which would interfere. Actually, you hold off giving the signal (No. 29) to the 1750 until it hits your annunciator circuit. Six minutes later the red light for the Big Four eastbound track sparkles and the buzzer sounds. You push the small black button above the light on the box on the desk, and the buzzer stops. You reverse lever 29, and your extra has the signal to proceed.

Ten minutes later a chain of glowing amber lights starts to grow across your big track chart. That's the Big Four extra lighting up the track circuits on your plant. You get up leisurely, restore the signal lever, and watch the freight wind its way toward you. You wave to the engineer and check the engine number as the train starts by No. 80 signal just outside the tower. You didn't have to touch 80 or the other two levers which control the remote switch and signal at Belt Junction, 3 miles away, because they are always left reversed, lined for the normal eastbound movement on track 4. Only when you use the track in the opposite direction do you put these levers normal. This is a true extra; it has everything. Boxcars, hoppers mounded with graded black coal, gondola cars full

of scrap or steel bars, two flatcars loaded with poles—all go rumbling by you as you carefully look over the train, making sure that all is well. The caboose finally comes by below you. A highball, a brief tussle with clicking levers, a notation of the time on your sheet, a report to two dispatchers, and you have put another train by you.

⊥ ⊥

Business is slow, and as the shadows lengthen and the traffic on the highway increases, you lean back in your chair, plug into the Toledo dispatcher's line and listen to the progress of No. 46, the *Interstate Express*, as it comes toward you. It's only 5:10, but you start eating your lunch. You know you may not have another chance for a good while. Operators up and down the line kid each other and compare notes on their vacation times. 46 is reported by the tower at Elyria. It has yet to stop at the station there and won't be by you for another 25 minutes. Airplanes circling around the nearby Cleveland Airport fly over constantly, humming like diesels working on a grade. You ring Short Line to let him know where 46 is, then sit back again.

Track 2 buzzes. That's 46! You call it in to Toledo.

"Two, Berea!"
"46!"
"All right!"

You call it in to Cleveland, reverse one switch and two signals. Four minutes later 46 glides by at 65 per. Another one right on time.

Still things are quiet and you begin to get nervous. Things are *too* quiet for comfort. You finish eating your supper, check the temperature, note it, plus the condition of the sky on your sheet, then report to all five dispatchers, "Clear and 55. Berea!"

By the fifth time, you get tired of hearing yourself say it, yet you know that all five dispatchers have to write Berea's weather on their trainsheets because Berea is the meeting point of all three divisions and figures prominently too in all the passenger and fast freight reports which are sent daily to New York.

Another ritual to which you soon became accustomed when you started to work for the railroad is filling out your time slip. You tear one sheet from your book of time slips, date it, enter your name, number, station, and total hours worked: 8. Out of curiosity you again check in your ORT Agreement book for the rate paid at Berea. There it is: $2.003

per hour for first trick, $1.973 for second trick, and $1.967 for third trick—plus cost of living scale. You can't help thinking that the third-trick man, the one who has to work nights and sleep days, gets the short end of the deal. This book contains the written agreements between the Order of Railroad Telegraphers and the New York Central Railroad. It also lists all of the stations where operators work and the wages paid at those stations. Along with your rulebook it is your bible, one of the tools of your craft that you always have with you on the job. You joined the ORT shortly after you started to work because of the closed-shop rule and because you wanted to anyway. You may not know how to telegraph and you still may be only an extra operator, but you know that you belong to a brotherhood of sharp-witted railroadmen whose duty it is to smooth the flow of trains across the country. In all kinds of weather the operator is on the job telegraphing, telephoning, pulling levers, handing on orders, ready in case of emergency at his command post out on the line. You can't help feeling proud to be counted among these railroaders.

At 6:10 Grafton rings you. 1829 by him on the eastward.

"That's First NY-6, Berea. See if you can get him down the Lakefront!"

You switch over to the Lakefront side and report First NY-6, the 1829 out of Grafton.

"Down 2 Lakefront," says the dispatcher. Now you have a track for your train. You glance at your schedule of passenger trains and start to do some fast thinking. No 445, the *Capital City Special* for Columbus, is due to come by at 6:32, 20 minutes from now. Behind him will be No. 43 for Chicago, due by at 6:40. In the meantime, No. 6, the *Fifth Avenue Special* for New York, is scheduled for 6:38. First NY-6 is one of the most important freight trains on the Central and is closely watched by the freight traffic department to see that it loses no time either on the road or in the yards. To stop this train is almost as bad as stopping a passenger train. You don't do it if you can help it. To further complicate the problem, 445 has to cross over—which will conflict with

No. 6, since there is a difference of only 6 minutes in their schedules. Quickly you call Short Line to find out where 445 is. It is coming at his home signal, just getting up speed. Then the buzzer and light come on for the Big Four eastward track. First NY-6 is on it! You decide to take a chance, quickly line up for NY-6—Big Four to the Lakefront, tying up everything but your two westbound Lakefront tracks—give him the signal, and wait.

The minutes drag by. Short Line rings you; 445 is by him. No sign of First NY-6 yet. You check with Toledo. No. 6 is on time, probably leaving the station at Elyria, 15 minutes away. You get a tight feeling in your stomach. Maybe it won't work. Maybe you'll be stopping three passenger trains; 43 is on time too. Then NY-6 shows up, slows down for the crossover, and starts threading its way through the plant toward Lakefront No. 2. You watch with fascination as the string of lights eats its way across your track chart. You wave to the head end, give them a highball, and hope that they get the idea that you're in a pinch.

A loud buzz announces 445 on the circuit on track 1. NY-6 isn't even half way across yet. You start to think up excuses to tell the dispatchers when they ask why their trains were delayed. You do the best thing you can; you make the first part of the lineup for 445 and give him the first signal. Another buzz: track 4 Toledo Division. Almost in a frenzy now you write on your sheet on the eastbound side "1620, NYCX." You call it in to Cleveland. It's a Central extra for Collinwood.

"See if you can get him down the Big Four, Berea!"

445 is whistling for Front Street crossing. NY-6 still hasn't cleared. You call in the freight to the Big Four side. He tells you to put it down 4. You reverse traffic lever No. 125, but that's all you can line up right now. No. 6 hits the circuit. You watch your chart, tensely waiting for the caboose of NY-6 to clear the circuit. Your hands grip the levers, waiting … It's clear! You never shoved levers back more rapidly. The signal—a beautiful high green— shows up for 445, which is slowing just across the way from you. You wave to the caboose of NY-6 and the head end of 445 at the same time. More levers click into place. Six has the first signal. 445 is by. Six gets the second signal. 43 is on the bell.

You call him in, line him up, and let him go. Now you can line up for the extra down 4. Track 1 Lakefront! It's X43 to follow 43. Now there is no conflict. Six zooms by you at top speed; 43 is growling harshly up the grade toward you. You study the clock, start writing figures on your sheet. You have a lot to catch up with. 43 by, X43 tight behind him. The freight is rumbling by a few tracks over. You tell 50 people, it seems, the times that all of these trains are by you. And then, almost with no warning at all, it's quiet— as quiet as though there hadn't been a train along in hours and all you've had to do is sit back and take it easy. You collapse in your chair. You fingers are greasy with cold sweat.

A long jingle of a bell snaps the curtain of your mind, and you realize that the Big Four dispatcher is ringing you.

"Has the local shown up yet?" he asks you.

"No!" Immediately you know what is going to happen; you know that X448 is getting near Grafton.

"Copy 31 to the operator!"

You reach for the 31 order and say, "All right."

"31 No. 14 to all west and the operator at BE, period. X448—f-o-u-r, f-o-u-r, e-i-g-h-t—engine 5771—f-i-v-e, s-e-v-e-n, s-e-v-e-n, o-n-e—has right over opposing trains on westward— w-e-s-t-w-a-r-d—track crossover Grafton—G-r-a-f-t-o-n—to BE, period. Signed L. A. C."

You repeat the order just the way it is given you. Grafton repeats it next. The order is made complete and you write the time at the bottom of the order; also you write your name in the lower right-hand corner. Immediately then you go to the machine and put red "cans" over several levers that control signals and switches west to the Big Four as a reminder to yourself that no train must go west until X448 clears. Grafton calls you and asks for a block for X448. You check with him for the passing time of his last train west, and then give him a clear block. Now there are two trains coming east from Grafton.

You run another freight from Toledo No. 4 to No. 4 Big Four while you wait. It's the 5811 with 110 cars for Youngstown, and it will go over the single-track Lake

Second-trick operator Joe Machinski lines up the interlocked switches and signals (in that order), and then studies the freight's progress in lights on the track diagram. *Richard J. Cook*

Erie & Pittsburgh, south from Cleveland. The local shows up on your first circuit. You tell the Big Four dispatcher that the local has shown up so that he will know that his eastward track is free again. While X448 goes by you on the Big Four westward track, you run the local into the siding where the entire crew will leave their train to go to supper. The westward track is now clear, so the Big Four dispatcher annuls the order and normal operation is restored.

"That's Second NY-6, Berea," says the Cleveland dispatcher. "See if you can get him down the Lakefront."

Another train off the Big Four. Again you go through the routine of looking for a track; again you have to check to see if this move will clear a passenger train, this time No. 76, the *Mercury*. You have just a handful of minutes to spare, so you line up for the second NY-6 and let her go. The *Mercury* flashes by you minutes later. You have everything under control. Now the evening parade of eastbound trains starts, and you have to watch that you don't get any freights in the way. These are the blue-ribbon trains of the Central. The *Southwestern Limited*, the *Cincinnati*

Mercury, and the *Ohio State Limited* from the Big Four, the *New England States*, the *Pacemaker*, the *Commodore Vanderbilt*, and the *20th Century Limited* from Chicago all flash their marker lights at you as they head for the terminal or for the Lakefront. Flashes of brightly lighted coaches, people at ease in their roomettes, a few late diners in the sophisticated splendor of an elegant dining car, and a dreamy couple fingering their cocktail glasses in the nightclub setting of a lounge car—all roll below your windows like an illuminated tableau of the comfort and ease of modern transportation.

⊥　⊥

Your tower is in the block house on the frontier, the outpost in the forest of gleaming steel ribbons and black night. You are in command of the rolling trains, guardian of the command post of the railroad. Following the blue-lighted sign on the observation car of the *Century*, you send the Central's most important freight train, CB-4, one of the *Early Bird* fleet. The buzzes, the lights, the telephone rings, the rolling wheels become less frequent. Stillness descends more often around the four walls of your tower.

Mail and express No. 129; No. 427, the *Gateway*; and then 9 go west unchallenged by freight moves. The day is drawing to a close. Very soon another man will be sitting in the chair that you have been keeping warm; other hands will pull levers that will send a fleet of trains west to Chicago, Cincinnati, and St. Louis. Other voices will be heard over the telephone. But the trains will keep running past Berea; the trainsheets will keep filling up with numbers; tons of commodities will be rolled past the front door of Berea Tower in the ceaseless flow that is rail transportation.

Fifty-one trains have passed you since you came on duty; signal lights have blinked red, yellow, green; switches have been opened and closed under your guidance. You have been in command of an important post and have successfully completed your first tour of duty. You know that other days will not go as smoothly, trouble may occur, trains may bunch up even more. But you know too that you will be able to handle the situation when it comes.

You are an operator-leverman at BE Tower.

February 1959

I Rented a Railroad for $35

Robert B. Adams

The year was 1940. The country was worming its way out of the depths of the worst depression in its history, "My friends" was the byword on everyone's lips, and the storm clouds of World War II were gathering on the horizon.

Down east in the little New England town of Bridgton, Maine, a midget railroad was gurgling its death rattle. Improved highways were bringing with them the creeping paralysis of dwindling traffic; trucks were nibbling at the l.c.l. and freight car loadings; buses were providing faster and more convenient transport to the metropolises of Portland and Boston. Everywhere declining revenues were forcing curtailment of services to the public as well as postponement of greatly needed maintenance and repairs.

I I

Bridgton, Maine, at five o'clock on that warm summer afternoon in August 1940 had all the usual aspects of a sleepy New England town. There was no indication whatsoever that this was the terminus of what had once been the mighty Bridgton & Saco River Railroad, which in the year 1921 under Maine Central control had managed to net some $23,384 and pay a dividend of 20 percent from operations over its 21 miles of 2-foot-gauge, single-track road. The town of Bridgton now owned and operated as Bridgton & Harrison Railway the remaining 15.9 miles of

line, having acquired it in bankruptcy proceedings in 1930 for a mere $27,000. But even so, the first of the local citizenry of whom we inquired had no conception of the way to the depot. Railroading in Bridgton was emaciated and decadent.

Bridgton station was a little gem nestled in the center of the shallow valley just south and east of the business center. Its diminutive, aesthetic proportions seemed to snuggle right up to the dual station tracks of 50-pound rail laid to the 2-foot gauge. The miniature turntable onto which the tracks converged at the north end of the platform appeared too small to encompass the wheelbase of the ex-Sandy River & Rangeley Lakes gasoline cars for which it was designed. The enginehouse, shops, storage sheds, and master turntable adjacent on the southwest were incongruously small compared with normal facilities. I felt like a Gulliver in a Lilliputian fairyland.

"The train is down at the Junction—won't leave there till 6:18." The voice was full scale, as was the portly man behind the ticket window who answered my inquiry. I expressed my appreciation as I

No. 8 was moved out of the enginehouse into daylight for comprehensive oiling and inspection. The author's wife, Dottie, gets an up-close look inside the locomotive cab. *Robert B. Adams*

glanced at the full-size station clock. The time was 5:30 p.m.

Bridgton Junction lay isolated in a mass of field grass just south and east of the hamlet of Hiram. Obviously the founders of the Bridgton & Saco River had deemed it unwise to solicit either tourist or other traffic from such a small local town, for the tracks left the Junction station, swung in a gentle right-angle arc, and aimed due north on a tangent, bypassing Hiram about a half mile to the east.

A dirt road led to the Junction proper, rutted and full of chuckholes as a disused country road is apt to be. Our best time over this obstacle course without breaking any springs on the car proved to be insufficient, for just as we drove up the driveway to the station, the gas car, the B&H's only mode of transportation that evening, pulled out for its uncertain trek back to Bridgton. We watched it plow slowly through the weeds, conjuring up visions of the days when capacity trains made every connection with the Maine Central and the now idle, weed-choked yards

were worn bare with the traffickings of laborers breaking bulk freight for transshipment to narrow gauge boxes, flats, gondolas, and tankers to be hauled to the hinterlands behind midget Forneys. We drove slowly back to Bridgton in the gathering dusk.

⚒ ⚒

Dawn broke clear and warm the next day. The sun was a fireball on the eastern horizon. After a healthy New England breakfast we wandered back to the Bridgton yards, hoping that the normal exigencies of daytime operations would necessitate activation of one of the two locomotives we had observed in the enginehouse the day before. Spotted in front of the turntable was the gas car, hood raised, with a group of men prodding its vitals in a vain attempt to instill life into it. Their efforts proved more productive of expletives than of explosions, and eventually the need for the conveniences for heavy repairs caused the car to be ignominiously pushed into the enginehouse by hand.

M. E. Heath, treasurer and general manager, answered our inquiry at the

depot. He allowed as how the mail and express usually was routed by truck when anything happened to the gas car. Passengers could either fend for themselves or await repairs and an indeterminate future departure time. Neither appeared to be of any consequence. The locomotive would be ignited only for those rare occurrences of carload freight, camper's specials, or a private party.

Picture-taking was a disheartening experience that morning. Like a turtle that has been tapped on its back, the railroad had retired within its shell, and no amount of coaxing could induce it to return to motion. Lilliput was dead.

"Hey, there, are you the party that wanted to hire our locomotive?"

Flabbergasted at the unexpected thought and with contractions of the pocketbook brought on by an all-too meager vacation allowance, I turned to view my interrogator. A thin, wiry man of medium height introduced himself as C. L. Ames, president of the Bridgton & Harrison. With polite protestations I intimated that hiring locomotives was hardly indigenous to my occupation, but that I would like very much to have an opportunity to ride his railroad, particularly in view of the fact that I was right there on the premises and quite dubious of how long it might be before I would again be in the neighborhood.

"Well," he expostulated, "we frequently rent our train for fan trips and other outings for seventy-five dollars."

With the gentleness of a St. Bernard dog and the finesse of a prizefighter I attempted to reason that my wife and I, together with our wire-haired terrier, hardly constituted a crowd of such implementations as to necessitate a whole train for our conveyance.

"On occasions we have rented our train to private parties for fifty dollars," he countered.

It was becoming difficult to refuse, and the idea was beginning to germinate into a possibility. Then memory of my meager supply of cash caused constrictions, and I hastened to explain that such an undertaking was beyond my immediate means and that 10 a.m. of a summer weekday was an unlikely time for me to round up any acquaintances and have them appear immediately in Bridgton, Maine, to participate in such a venture.

"Once in a great while we do rent our locomotive at cost," he offered. "That's thirty-five dollars."

Wheels whirred in my brain, and faster than an electronic data-processing machine I came up with the answer. "I'll rent your train for thirty-five dollars now, if you will agree to allow me to send you a check for it when I return home in a week."

"Certainly," he said, "that will be fine." And without further ado or even waiting to obtain my name and references, he disappeared.

It seemed a matter of mere minutes before the doors to the end stall of the enginehouse were opened, and rattlings and bangings commenced emanating from within. Before I could walk from the yard throat to the turntable, smoke began curling from the smoke jack, and by the time I reached the locomotive, a roaring wood fire was blazing in the firebox and Everett L. Brown, the engineer-fireman, was starting to coal her up. Soon steam began to form, and with light pressure showing on the gauge, the engineer backed No. 8 out of the stall into the daylight for comprehensive oiling and inspection.

The 28-foot turntable was hand powered, but with the locomotive balanced in the middle like a ballet dancer, it took little effort to swing her around in line for the ready track. The engineer appeared eager, as though he was grateful for the opportunity to exercise his pet steed, and offered to make up a train of any consist desired from any or all of the available cars in the yard. Rather than risk the possibility of a high car derailing at an inopportune moment along the line, we settled for the lone coach on the station lead. A single white marker flag (only one could be located) was mounted in its bracket on the smokebox for official designation as an "extra" train. The dog was secured in the coach behind closed doors, and my wife and I joined the engineer in the cab.

"You take 'er," the engineer said before we left. "We have a speed restriction of 15 miles an hour on the locomotive because the track's not so good as it used to be. There are no other trains on the line, and the only thing you need to watch out for is the section crew. They're somewhere down near Hiram."

Although my locomotive driving experience had been the equivalent of that of millions of others of the populace never employed by a railroad, mere ignorance and unfamiliarity were to be no deterrents. Assimilation of matters railroading had been an osmotic habit from early childhood. Thus the physical manifestations of throttle, reverse, triple valve, and gauge cocks so unexpectedly placed within reach were not such as to create vertiginous reactions. Even the thought of the necessity for a traveling engineer as a guide to the intricacies of curves, grades, crossings, and other essentials lost its terrifying aspects in consideration of our speed restriction and the absence of traffic on the line. Softly we chuffed into motion, the single coach making no noticeable protest as the draft gear tightened. The throttle response was light, but the delayed reaction of the vacuum brakes seemed puzzling and uncertain. The kinked rails of the badly battered yard throat passed under our wheels with the smoothness of a knee-action Chevrolet; then we were steaming down the main with 16 miles of 50-pound rail ahead and only one indeterminate meet to be made with an itinerant section crew somewhere in the vicinity of a nebulous place called Hiram.

"Over there on the left is where the Harrison branch came in." Engineer Brown had his mouth to my ear so that his voice would carry above the reverberation of the steel wheels on the steel rails. The abandoned roadbed was obvious. Ten years previous we might have swung off on a leg of the wye at that point and covered the most scenic 5¼ miles of the railroad, for the tracks had traversed the shore of beautiful Long Lake the majority of the distance.

Sixty years ago when the railroad was a mere embryo in the mind of one A. G. Bradstreet, a civil engineer of no mean repute and Bridgton's exalted representative in the Maine legislature, it was proposed to carry the main line a full 38 miles southeastward at this point and construct through Naples, Raymond, Windham, and Westbrook, reaching Portland via a third rail laid in the tracks of the Portland & Rochester Railroad. This was the Bridgton & Presumpscot River Railroad, carrying an 1881 birth certificate from the legislature with a conditional clause that the road must attain its majority by being completed not later than November 1, 1884. In opposition to this were the proponents of the Hiram route led by George S. Farnsworth of Billerica & Bedford fame who wished for a shorter, less expensive line to connect but not compete with the standard gauge Portland & Ogdensburg to Portland.

Bridgton voters gave Bradstreet a running start, allowing him 90 days to raise sufficient funds to construct the line. The money was to come from the towns and people along the route. Should he fail in his efforts, the Mansfield followers would have equal opportunity to solicit

Author Adams was instructed that he could select the train's consist from any or all of the available cars in the Bridgton & Harrison yard.
Robert B. Adams

likewise along the Hiram route. Bradstreet's friends proved mercenary as well as verbose, and the bankers turned cold. Bradstreet himself, lacking personal wealth, accepted defeat early and left for Colorado and a more remunerative position as location engineer for the Denver & Rio Grande Railroad. The Hiram route became a fact.

I   I

"Whistle post!" The voice of engineer Brown startled me from my position of obliquity with head and shoulders protruding from the cab window. I had been contemplating the incessant rise and fall of the slender side rods on their rotating counterweights, envisioning the revolving miniature 35-inch drivers following their immutable path along the rails, and listening to the incantations of expanding exhaust steam erupting with magnified intonations from the stack. We had covered 2.2 miles from Bridgton by surveyor's measure and were rolling into Sandy Creek.

I blew for the crossing as only a confirmed neophyte could, querulously and with all the composure of a frightened schoolchild. It was an aimless gesture. The town was somnolent; the crossing deserted; even the picturesque mill pond didn't give a ripple. Yet this very same town, back on January 12, 1883, welcomed the arrival of the first construction train with all the aplomb of much flag-draping and bunting, a grand whistle salute, climaxed by a mighty discharge of small arms.

South Bridgton evidenced none of the reasons which, in 1886, justified the erection of a station building just three years after commencement of scheduled activities over the line. Historians have dubbed it a "soothing syrup" operation in appreciation of the moral and financial support rendered by the villagers in those uncertain days of individual stock pledges and town bond support. Maintenance of the edifice obviously had ceased for incalculable years, and the encroachments of crabgrass and weeds bore mute testimony that whatever traffic may have obtained in the past had long been dissipated. The rhythmic clack of our wheels on the rail joints was absorbed in the density of the vegetation. The gentle draft of our passing rippled the spires of the taller weeds, and our whistle echoed mournfully as it was refracted from the station walls.

We were rolling along as swiftly as our moderate speed limit would permit, chuffing lightly on the minor grades and drifting down the inclines as the narrow path of the rails adapted itself to the land contours of the forested hills and sandy plains of the region. Up ahead on the smokebox our single white extra flag fluttered lightly with the speed of our passing, while to the rear our canine passenger sat on the front seat of the coach, mutely gazing out of each of the numerous windows in turn, his forepaws uncertainly braced on the cane of the seat cover as the car rolled to the fluctuating elevations of the rails.

"We'll stop here for water!"

Brown's words were bewildering. From the pilot forward to the horizon atop a small rise, the rails stretched upgrade in a straight line, traversing a shallow fill in the foreground, trenching a hill in the background. There was not a habitation to be seen, nor was there physical evidence of watertank or spout.

"Spring water." Brown nodded authoritatively and winked.

Air hissed through pipes and valves as I made an application of the brakes. We slowed to a gentle stop on the grade midway between cut and fill.

"Come on," Brown exhorted over his shoulder as he slid down the handrails, feet never touching the steps. We followed in more awkward but more orthodox fashion, backward one step at a time while facing the locomotive. A small path led through the woods—worn bare by the countless treads of train crews. At the end was a crystal clear spring of pure mountain water emanating from the rock.

"Best damn water in these here hills," Brown vouchsafed as he dipped a container in the limpid pool and proffered it to us. The day was hot, and our enthusiasm for the excitement of the moment had caused us to forget mere physical inconveniences and desires. The water was cool and delightfully refreshing in the heat of the noonday sun. In startled bewilderment we suddenly realized that neither of us had thought to bring a lunch. It was too late to retrace our route. But then, what price food for a day on the narrow gauge?

"Berry picking's wonderful—that is if you like blueberries." Our engineer seemed telepathic. His nod led us to look down the bank where tramped grass and broken underbrush gave silent evidence of the numerous foraging parties which had preceded us that summer. We informed our guide that we had a penchant for blueberries, but that we would prefer to relegate blueberry picking to more leisurely times and confine the activities of the moment to matters railroading. The manner with which he promptly refilled the water jug and started for the idle train suggested that he was as anxious as we to resume operations.

The air pump was chanting a cordial welcome as we neared the track. Once back in the cab, Brown briefly explained the operations of the reverse quadrant and its enigmatical settings. As we got under way up the grade the stack talk was sharp and clear, gradually subsiding to a childlike prattle as we rounded the summit and started down the other side.

Ingalls Road and Perley's Mill appeared about to be reclaimed by the very wilderness from which they were so laboriously contrived in years gone by. One moment we were gliding through deep woods, the next, the station was upon us. And almost before the whistle could sound its imperious warning, we were past the crossing and rolling onward through the forest growth. The reasons for the very existence of full-fledged stations at these remote points were lost in the oblivion of dense undergrowth and unrecorded history.

Annals do reveal, however, that immediately to the south of Perley's Mill on May 22, 1911, with the official thermometer standing at 100 degrees, engineer Roland Woodbury attempted to pilot locomotive No. 5 through a stretch of kinked rails caused by the unseasonable heat and thereby instituted the first serious accident on the road. Woodbury suffered a pair of badly burned hands, and No. 5 needed to be coaxed back on the track but only after a full 6 inches had been cut from one rail to allow it to be forced into position. In 60 years of operation but four serious accidents occurred on the Bridgton & Harrison, each of which was caused by excessive heat or excessive cold and none of which bore any fatalities.

Innumerable rail joints later we topped the last ridge and started our descent to the shores of Hancock Pond. The panorama was striking. Before us the narrow-gauge tracks dipped through a lush green meadow that would have done justice to the Kentucky blue grass region. At the far end of the tangent an S curve swung gracefully to the right, crossed a county road, then bore left as it dipped to the lake shore. Two giant elms stood sentinel guard at the highway crossing as though to shield it from the mutations of the weather. We gathered speed on the downgrade. The whistle broke shrill and clear as we canted to the curve; the road flashed beneath our wheels; brakes grabbed as the pony truck led us into the reverse curvature. We slowed to a halt on the rocky ledge of the waterfront.

"Care to take time for a swim?" Brown inquired. The water looked tempting, but we declined. The weatherbeaten covered water tank at our left bespoke of cold north winds sweeping across icy waters in winter in contrast to the cool lapping of the waves this hot summer afternoon.

"The Notch" was interesting, but only mildly spectacular—a sharp curve beneath a projecting rock. The curve was the more forbidding, and we crept around it with caution. I had my hand on the brake, while the drivers slowly revolved at a mere 6 miles an hour. The precaution was wasted. There were no falling rocks, and the superelevation would have permitted a greatly increased speed. It was the preordination of a novice engineer.

Twin Lake was not even discernible in the wilderness. Somewhere on one side of the tracks or the other, vacationers were reveling in sparkling waters. A whistle blast for the country road crossing gave more confidence to the engineer than warning to motorists. The crossing was deserted.

"The Summit!" Brown shouted a short time later. "Better watch out for the track gang."

We crossed the dividing line of the watershed, although no apparent difference in altitude or in gradient was perceptible. Our meet with the section crew had been on my mind since leaving Hancock Pond. Now extra caution was enjoined. Our speed dwindled to a crawl as the watch continued. The blind side of the boiler to the left of my line of vision was vexatious. Left curves became occasions of great creepings with side rods gently rising and falling to the revolutions of the slowly rotating drivers and counterweights, brake shoes dragged, and an aura of pending danger permeated the cab. Suddenly there they were!

It was another left curve. I caught the glint of a white shirt sleeve as it moved in the sun behind some tree limbs. The brakes went into emergency spasmodically. My wife hit the boiler backhead with a jolt, and the dog in the coach was involuntarily jettisoned from his front railfan seat. The train came to a squealing halt.

"It's all right!" Brown was the first to recover his composure and reconnoiter. I looked. No rails had been removed from the roadbed; not a tie had been disturbed; even the ballast maintained its symmetrical weed-grown appearance. The rails curved left, and beyond the jutting smokebox I could see a small trestle over a stream. On the stringers, placed parallel to the rails at the edge of the bridge timbers, sat the three-man section crew—fly casting for trout!

I swallowed my heart, my stomach dropped back into place somewhere below my chest, and with a glance rearward into the cab to check the two members of the crew, I released brakes and reached for the whistle cord. A light toot warned the track gang of our intentions, and cracking the throttle slightly, I let No. 8 chug lightly by.

We rolled into Bridgton Junction with the imaginary pomp and ceremony of a limited completing a transcontinental passage. The ignominious oversight on the part of the Maine Central in failing to provide a standard gauge connecting train at that precise moment could not dampen the ardor of the occasion.

Brown ambled across the cab. "I'll turn her for you." His voice was authoritative, and since there were no visible physical properties for performing such an operation in that weed-grown jungle, I acquiesced most readily. We backed down the station lead on the descending fill to the level of the meadow and continued up the grade a short distance. Buried in the field grass on the left was an overgrown switch stand controlling the lead to the interchange yard tracks and the former enginehouse. Brown stopped, dismounted, and threw the switch. When he was in the cab once more, he reversed and pulled forward down the side track. Leaving the coach and its lonely occupant on the runaround track, he again pulled forward, then backed into the lead to a small turntable almost obscured by tall grasses. It took but a moment to find the exact point of balance, and together we spun the 38-ton midget on the rusty centerbearing. A short pull forward on the facing turntable lead, a backward movement to the coach, and our train was ready.

Highball!

I was back at the throttle again, feeling as though I were having a last reunion with a long lost friend. Mentally the route seemed easier now that I was partially familiar with the line, and the controls had lost some of their unnaturalness. The bark of the exhaust as we left the Junction sounded boisterous, and the surge of the train in response to the throttle felt urgent.

"The Notch" was a sharp curve beneath a projecting rock. The special train crept around it cautiously. *Robert B. Adams*

Slowing for the track gang at the trestle was a useless gesture since they had reeled in their tackle and had gone on to more promising pursuits. We did not see them the rest of the trip. The light climb to the summit assured a running commentary from the stack.

Once over the hill, it seemed but a moment before we were again awakening the echoes with our whistle as we blew for the Twin Lake crossing. A carful of happy vacationers stopped for the train and waved gleefully at our rolling equippage and the strange passenger in the coach.

The sharp curve at The Notch was taken at speed like a running dog banking into a hairpin turn, the drivers nudging the superelevation petulantly. A short dash through dense woodland and once more we were steaming majestically along the shore of Hancock Pond and braking for the stop at West Sebago.

"Line her up for the spout," Brown shouted as we approached the watertank. "We'll fill up here." Gingerly I managed to spot the tender almost directly in line. The cap clanked harshly as it was flipped open, and in a moment, fresh water was bubbling and gurgling around the steel

baffle plates within. We were just 7.2 miles from Bridgton Junction while 8.6 miles ahead lay the town of Bridgton.

It seemed perplexing that here, at the approximate geographical midpoint, we were obliged to take water while occupying the main line. There was no room for a siding. The roadbed along the lake originally had been contrived on wooden trestlework, and some seven years had elapsed after the opening of the line before sufficient earnings permitted substitution of substantial earthworks for creaking timbers at this location. As traffic increased the initial pair of 15-ton locomotives was supplemented by heavier ones—19 tons, 23½ tons, 25, 27¾, 33¼, and 38 tons. At the peak of operations some 50 employees were keeping five trains continuously hustling back and forth over this narrow single track hauling upward of 16,000 passengers and 15,500 tons of lumber, freight, and mixed goods, all without benefit of such modern contrivances as signaling or CTC. It was an impressive performance which kept the

The train rolled to a stop at Bridgton with a final sigh of vacuum brakes making their last gasp for air. *Robert B. Adams*

limited sidings utilized to capacity. Dividends flowed to stockholders ranging from the initial 2 percent declared in 1895, 1896, and 1897 to the maximum of 20 percent thrice declared by the Maine Central board to itself in the three years from 1921 to 1923 during the period of its control. In fact, late consternation was frequently expressed over the fact that during the 12 years of Maine Central ownership that road enjoined 85 percent of its original investment in dividends.

The clank of the tank cap signaled the end of watering operations, the dripping spout attesting to its utility. The cab resounded to the roar of the injector as the boiler was replenished. Adroit scoopfuls of coal were spotted over the brightest areas of the firebox, and as the stack erupted with visible manifestations of internal conflagrations, the brakes wheezed in release.

The upward grade from Hancock Pond seemed all too short. No. 8 talked and chatted all the way, her stack caressing the sentinel elms at the crossing with plumes of smoke while the whistle beckoned the echoes with its warning cry. For a moment

there was an impression of proudness as the midget drivers clawed at the narrow rails. The lead truck guided the inertia of 38 tons of clanking machinery through the alternate twistings of the reverse curve. The side rods chanted their cadence while the pistons whispered their approval with minute halos of steam around the cylinder heads. The locomotive seemed possessed, and I felt like letting her have her way.

Perley's Mill, Ingalls Road, South Bridgton passed in swift and desolate review. Even the location of our morning stop for spring water flashed past before recognition came. Fifteen miles an hour had never seemed so fast before. Sandy Creek appeared with its deep cut and high fill. The echoes rang to the shrill of the last crossing whistle.

We drifted into Bridgton yard limits with the muffled cadence of slowly rotating machinery, swayed to the uneven throat switches, and rolled to a stop just short of the picturesque station with a final sigh of vacuum brakes making their last gasp for air. There was no one to greet us from the station; no passengers to disembark except one lonely and bewildered dog.

Brown removed the extra flag from its holder, uncoupled the coach, and chuffed slowly through the maneuverings of runaround and lead tracks to the turntable. I helped him line her up for the enginehouse, and with a final plume of smoke and wisp of steam, No. 8 disappeared within, to be bedded down for an indeterminate number of days and nights. Quietness and inactivity prevailed. The Bridgton & Harrison had withdrawn into its turtle shell again. The time was 6 p.m.

Early the next morning we set forth on the balance of our interrupted vacation trip. There was no opportunity to thank Mr. Ames or Mr. Heath personally, but immediately upon our return home a check was posted to the Bridgton & Harrison Railroad for $35 representing rental of the remaining portions of that quaint little railroad.

[Note: The following year, in 1941, the B&H suffered the ignominies of perpetual abandonment, ultimately to be reincarnated in part as the Edaville Railroad in South Carver, Mass.]

Denver & Rio Grande Western

THIS IS IT!

David P. Morgan

This, for my money, is the most arresting single scenic site in all of American railroading: Hanging Bridge in the Royal Gorge of the Arkansas River on the Denver & Rio Grande Western.

The boiling waters crash through a canyon just 30 feet wide at the base and more than a thousand feet deep. Each day at 10:17 a.m. and 1:36 p.m. trains 2 and 1, the *Royal Gorge*, pause 10 minutes so that the passengers can absorb it all.

"Nowhere else does man come closer to realization of the Infinite," says the guidebook.

For a few moments one is suspended apart from the trappings of civilization, insulated against the works of man. Here is the culmination of uncounted centuries of the knifelike action of river on rock. Here the distractions of asphalt and neon and print are nonexistent.

Down here there is simply God … and the Rio Grande.

May 1965

3:52 A.M.
APRIL 30, 1900

Robert B. Shaw

Exactly what happened at the hamlet of Vaughan, Miss., an hour before dawn on April 30, 1900, when Illinois Central No. 1 slammed into the rear of a standing freight stalled on the main line by a burst air hose?

The first response to this question might be "Why does it matter?" The crash was certainly not one that was heard round the world but merely another in a dreary series of rear-end collisions all too typical of turn-of-the-century, manual-block railroading. To be sure, the accident was of some local interest. It was reported prominently by the Memphis press, and—in an era when the automobile was still only the toy of a few wealthy "scorchers" and the airplane no more than a gleam in the eyes of two bicycle mechanics—any engineer of a crack passenger train automatically rated as a popular hero. His violent death at the throttle of his locomotive evoked a dramatic image.

Only the engineer of No. 1, John Luther Jones, lost his life in this crash, and no one else was seriously injured. Damage barely exceeded $3,000. Jones was only one of more than 6,000 railroad employees killed in the line of duty that year. Such a minor incident rated no mention in the large metropolitan journals, and even in the *Railway Gazette*—the professional voice of the industry—it received only a curt four-line notice.

Yet, when far more serious disasters of the same era have been forgotten, this insignificant collision is remembered, if somewhat hazily, by millions around the world. The Illinois Central *Cannonball* has been transformed into a legendary essence that is reminiscent of the *Flying Dutchman*, and Casey Jones has become an American hero no less genuine than Johnny Appleseed, Kit Carson, or Buffalo Bill.

In fact, most people familiar with the famous ballad of Casey Jones are probably unaware that Casey is not exclusively a creation of folklore. Railroad hobbyists realize, however, that he was a definite historic figure, and that the event which catapulted him into immortality was a concrete if seemingly insignificant episode. Enough is known about the life of Jones that someone could write a book about him, and someone has: *Casey Jones* by Fred J. Lee, a former Illinois Central conductor and personal acquaintance of the engineer. Railroad fans who have *Tales of the Rails* or *Treasury of Railroad Folklore* in their libraries also know something of the process through which Casey Jones the man was elevated to Casey Jones the legend.

This is the only known photo of engineer Casey Jones at the throttle, in this case on the right-hand seat of Illinois Central 2-8-0 No. 638.
C. Bruce Gurner collection

So what really did happen there at Vaughan on the morning of April 30, 1900? Little aura of mystery persists over most railroad accidents; the essential facts are usually pretty obvious. But when Illinois Central No. 1 struck the rear of No. 83 the case was simply not important enough to warrant a searching probe by public authorities, and by the time the episode became famous, a thick overlay of romance and emotion hampered impartial analysis. Recently, however, certain official reports of the Illinois Central on the crash have come to light, and these offer some new information to the historian. The passage of time simultaneously provides him with a needed degree of protection.

Up to a certain point—in fact, to the instant before the collision—no significant dispute exists about the facts. Casey Jones, then 37 years old and an engineer for 10 years, was called at Memphis on the evening of April 29, 1900, to take an unexpected southbound run in the place of an engineer who was on the sick list. Jones had just brought the northbound Chicago express, No. 4, into Memphis at 9 p.m. and had been on duty approximately 7 hours. Assignment to him of the return run would mean 14 continuous hours on duty—if he were able to bring No. 1 into Canton on time. This was a double shift, certainly, but it did not constitute "excess time" in the strict sense of that phrase.*

Due out of Memphis at 11:15 p.m., No. 1 finally cleared the Poplar Street station with Casey at the throttle of his own favorite engine, No. 382, at 12:50 a.m. Scheduled time between Memphis and Canton, 190 miles, was 5½ hours, calling for an average speed of 35 mph. If Jones were to make up the entire 95 minutes, however, he would have to cover the division at an average speed of 49 mph, with four scheduled stops and numerous flag stops en route.

---

*According to an interview with fireman Simeon Webb for *Railroad Magazine* in 1936, he and Jones had come into Memphis on No. 2 at 6:25 that morning and were called to report for departure at 10 p.m., giving them the whole day off. Lee's version as reported here seems more reliable.

Between Memphis and Grenada, 102 miles, the track was uncongested, with only a single opposing freight train to pass, and Jones made up 60 of the 95 minutes. At the same rate he would be able to pull into Canton, 88 miles farther, on the advertised. It is appropriate to pause at this point and ask whether he wasn't a little too strongly imbued with the idea of "pulling her in on time." Of course the tradition of timekeeping was a respected one, but it should not have been allowed to take precedence over safety. The Illinois Central in those days was not in competition with any other form of transportation, or even with another railroad. At the turn of the century an average speed of 50 mph—involving top speeds well in excess of 70 mph—over a single-track Southern railroad innocent of block signals was probably excessive. Jones took No. 1 (the *Cannonball* was not an official name, and it is not clear whether this was actually used at the time or was merely assigned in retrospect) out of Memphis 95 minutes late. It might have sufficed for him to make up *half* the time to Canton, leaving the remainder of the task to the engineer who would complete the 200-mile run into New Orleans. Jones was undoubtedly an accomplished engineer, but wasn't he also a bit of a daredevil, a little too strongly aware of his own popular image? He had just had his own six-tone calliope whistle installed on No. 382 and hoped to impress his friends in Canton. This picturesque touch was actual and not merely part of the ballad.

After the accident General Superintendent A. W. Sullivan wrote in his report that Jones had been particularly cautioned by Superintendent King "not to attempt to do any reckless running with the view of establishing a record of making fast time, a better time than other men on the runs." This comment undoubtedly reflects an afterthought, but it does suggest that Jones had sometimes exhibited a certain spirit of bravado. His previous record as an engineer included nine suspensions for violations of the rules or minor collisions.

Simeon Webb, TRAINS *magazine collection*

As Jones and No. 1 were approaching the end of their famous run, conditions became more difficult. Jones was faced by a heavy concentration of traffic. Headed north toward him were four trains: freight No. 72, passenger No. 2, and passenger trains First and Second No. 26. Moving ahead of him in the same direction were freight No. 83 and passenger No. 25. At Durant he received orders to meet No. 2 northbound at Goodman and then to "saw" through a collection of passenger and freight trains at Vaughan. The first meet was made routinely, although the impatient Jones—practically on time at Goodman—was forced to take the siding there and wait 5 minutes for No. 2. As soon as the track was clear again, he opened his throttle and headed toward Vaughan, 13 miles farther south, at a speed officially estimated in excess of 75 mph.

Meanwhile, the first train to reach Vaughan was southbound double-headed freight No. 83. This pulled into the siding, but when northbound No. 72 arrived a few minutes later the discovery was made that the two freights had a combined length 10 cars too long to allow both trains to fit into the siding. Accordingly, they would have to saw south and north to let both No. 25 and No. 1 get by. Flagman J. M. Newberry of No. 83 was sent north to protect against both of these approaching trains. No. 25 approached

Vaughan cautiously, stopped while the two freights moved into a north-saw position, then was allowed to resume its run when the south switch was cleared. The two freights held their position until No. 2 approached from the south; then they moved south again to clear the north switch. No. 2 proceeded on for its meet with 1 at Goodman.

The two freights were now in a south-saw position and the north switch was clear—undoubtedly the situation which Jones was expecting. However, at this crucial point the two sections of No. 26 arrived at Vaughan, and the freights were obliged to move north once again to admit the passenger trains to the station, where they took shelter on the house track. All of these maneuvers had been accomplished with some dexterity, and now No. 83 began to pull south again. Right then an air hose burst near the end of No. 72, stalling the other train with four cars still out on the main, beyond the north switch.

At this moment the New Orleans express came racing down the long tangent toward the S curve leading into Vaughan. The night was apparently murky, so that one of the Memphis papers even proclaimed in a subheading that "Dense Fog Was the Direct Cause of the Accident." Nothing was said about fog in any of the official reports, however, and no defender of Jones has suggested that this was an exculpatory factor. The last leg of the curve was toward the fireman's side, which evidently interfered with the engineer's vision of the markers on the caboose, but Jones must have reduced his speed rapidly from the estimated 75 mph when the brakes were first applied, since damage was confined largely to the engine and mail car of No. 1 and the caboose and two boxcars of the freight. Jones's fireman saved himself by jumping, and the crew of No. 83 also got out of the way. The few injury claims by passengers and employees were later settled for insignificant amounts. The crash occurred at 3:52 a.m., only 2 minutes after No. 1's scheduled passing time at Vaughan.

The locomotive involved in the fatal crash was Ten-Wheeler (4-6-0) No. 382. It was built in 1898 by Rogers Locomotive and Machine Works. After the accident, it was rebuilt and remained in service until 1935. *C. Bruce Gurner collection*

The foregoing sequence of events is generally accepted, or at least it has not been seriously disputed.[†] There is no reason it should be, for it is not directly relevant to the crash. In fact, if any reader has found the description of the movements of the two freights to clear the main track at Vaughan a trifle tedious, he may dismiss it all as no more than an illustration of the difficulties of railroading 60 years ago. Only one point is germane: The rear end of freight No. 83 was occupying the main track beyond the north siding switch when No. 1 was due there.

No. 1 had the right of way by timetable at Vaughan, of course, but timetable authority is always subordinate to train orders. No record of the orders Jones received at Durant is extant, and whether he may have been ahead of his revised time is not certain. Probably he was not, for although his orders had instructed him to run 30 (or 35) minutes late to Grenada, he had made up 60 minutes of the total delay by the time he arrived there. The dispatchers—as well as Jones himself—apparently expected him to pull into Canton on time.

This question, too, is immaterial. Jones knew he had to come to a stop at Vaughan where the main track would be blocked. As engineer of the superior train, he was entitled to expect that the north switch would be clear, but he still should have approached the station cautiously. More than that, any train order, any expectation he may have had, would definitely have been superseded by a signal given by a properly posted flagman. Responsibility for the crash rests, therefore, on a single point: Was the freight train which protruded beyond the north

---

[†]Naturally, unimportant discrepancies as to details do exist. Fred J. Lee in his book says that No. 1 was 75 minutes late out of Memphis; other sources say 95 minutes. Botkin and Harlow's *Railroad Folklore* describes No. 1 as consisting of 6 cars; Lee says 12 cars. Lee infers that Jones met No. 2 at Durant, but the official report states clearly that the meet occurred at Goodman. None of these differences affect the responsibility for the accident.

switch *adequately protected* by a flagman? The official report‡ of the accident, which placed blame upon Jones, and Jones alone, necessarily answered Yes to this question; by the same logic his defenders answer No.

Superintendent Sullivan's final report on the accident definitely stated that "Flagman J. M. Newberry of No. 83, who was provided with necessary signals, had gone back a distance of 3,000 feet to protect while the movements above were being made." At this point he was around a curve from the rear of his own train, but clearly visible for 1½ miles from an approaching southbound train.

The justification for doubting this positive evidence rests on what has become in these days a rather delicate point. Jones—not as yet a folk hero—was dead, and his surviving fireman, Simeon Webb, was a Negro. Consequently, it has been suggested that the white crew members of No. 83 conspired to cover up their own neglect of flag protection, assuming that their concerted statements would be accepted over any denial that Webb might make. Unfortunately, this premise is not lacking in plausibility. It received support many years later when Webb participated in a recording of the incident in which he stated: "We saw no signals, we heard no torpedoes." But superintendent Sullivan's final report, within a month and a half of the accident, clearly quotes Webb as saying that he saw the flagman after hearing the explosion of a torpedo and "that had he or Engineer Jones looked ahead they could have seen the flagman in ample time to have stopped before striking No. 83." Furthermore, the torpedoes were heard by the postal clerk and baggagemen of No. 1, as well as by the other train crews at Vaughan station. Thus, if Webb's initial testimony were false, it is necessary to imagine that the white crew members not merely counted upon overwhelming his contrary evidence but actually intimidated him into backing

John Luther Jones, *Illinois Central Gulf*

them up. This is a little too much to believe. Certainly superintendent Sullivan would not have been entirely naive, and the crew of No. 83 were far from the only railroad employees at the scene. No. 72 and First and Second 26 were standing at Vaughan, so that any hastily concocted conspiracy to cast the blame upon the dead engineer would have had to be a very comprehensive affair. Finally, Jones— even before he assumed immortality— was not lacking for friends and supporters who would try to see that he received posthumous justice.

A supporting point is the fact that flagman Newberry went out to protect against not one but two trains. The crew of No. 25, also flagged down by him, testified that he was standing in the same position from which he claimed to have flagged No. 1 (and replaced the torpedoes). Having once gone out that distance, why would he have changed his position before his duty was completed and while the railroad's crack train was still expected? Another suggestive piece of corroborative evidence, supported by all witnesses at the scene, was Jones's failure to sound his whistle for the board at Vaughan—a significant omission in the

light of his obvious fondness for the whistle.

The evidence that No. 83 was properly protected by its flagman, that Jones was traveling at excess speed, and that somehow he failed to see the hand signals—in brief, that he was responsible for the crash—seems almost irrefutable. Webb's initial testimony surely deserves much more weight than his commentary many years later. His good faith on both occasions is not to be doubted, but is it not probable that—as the years passed by and memories became a trifle blurred—he too was captivated by the Casey Jones legend?

I   I

The monument erected to the memory of Casey Jones by his "admirers" at Cayce, Ky., in 1938 does assert that the crash occurred "by no fault of his own," but this is hardly an impartial opinion. Railroad historians have generally dodged a firm position on the question of responsibility. Fred J. Lee in his authoritative biography of the engineer renders no verdict of his own. Mrs. Jones, who was always vigorous in defending her husband's reputation, wrote a foreword to this book, and one suspects that Lee was simply too close to the situation to risk a judgment. Still, this former conductor's omission of any statement that would definitely have exonerated his hero would seem to be significant. Emotions will still run high over this crash, and some railroadmen may consider it insulting even to question Jones's innocence. They should remember, however, that unqualified defense of Jones is tantamount to declaring flagman Newberry guilty of inadequate protection. His memory is equally entitled to fair treatment by historians. So it seems, when all facts are considered, that the terse explanation of the accident in the original telegraphic report—Engr on No. 1 failed to see or answer flag of No. 83—was an essentially correct description of the event.

---

‡Immediate notification of the accident was sent from Vaughan by engineer James Gaffney of First No. 26, who was also a telegrapher. The station was closed and locked, and the men entered it forcibly to send this message. The official reports relied upon in this article consist of a "Telegraph Report of Accident" from Dispatcher W. O. Wood at Water Valley dated April 30 and letters dated May 10 and July 13 from general superintendent A. W. Sullivan. All were addressed to second vice-president James T. Harahan. Twelve years later Mr. Harahan—who had subsequently become president of the Illinois Central—was himself to perish in a rear-end collision.

SALUTE TO A DIFFERENT DIESEL

J. David Ingles

November 1966

A current television commercial centers its pitch on "striking off on your own," a course recommended for anyone with ambition and the desire for recognition.

The American Locomotive Company did just that in 1946, when, with General Electric, it brought out the PA-1 passenger diesel. Amid much fanfare Santa Fe No. 51, a cab-booster-cab set, debuted as Alco's 75,000th locomotive. The trio then went on tour as a showpiece for Alco's new line of passenger units introduced as competition mainly for Electro-Motive's E-unit series.

The PA's predecessor, the double-engined DL-109, was an attractive machine with a long, low-slanted nose and speedy body styling. But somehow it bore too much similarity to the chief competition.

Alco-GE struck off on its own with Santa Fe 51. Here was a diesel you could recognize instantly. There was no mistaking a PA's flat face, grilled headlight, long nose, and big feet. It looked large, powerful, brawny. Sleek it was not, but fast it was.

Inside the awkwardly graceful carbody was only one engine, not two as in most passenger units. In the original model, dubbed PA-1 (boosters were PB-1s), 16 cylinders' worth of Alco's 244-model diesel produced 2,000 hp. In later versions the rating was upped to 2,250 hp. A 2,400-hp version was offered, but after 1953 the passenger unit market was virtually gone and none was built.

Alco's PAs are usually termed *big* by any who come in contact with the beasts. Actually, their aesthetic qualities belie their true size. The proportions impress, not the dimensions. After all, a PA is more than 5 feet shorter than an E unit. Between those A1A 15½-foot-wheelbase trucks on a standard PA-1 is room for a fuel tank of only 1,200-gallon capacity. Flared-in skirts over the fuel and air tanks, long horizontal grillwork along the top of the carbody sides, and the famed long nose give the PA a kind of lumbering yet graceful appearance.

As diesels go, the PA was not altogether common. Fewer than 300 domestic PA cabs and PB boosters were built.* This is only about four times the number of predecessor DL-109 cabs and DL-110 boosters. But whereas the slant-nose DL cabs sold to only six roads, the PA series sold to 16 companies in all areas of the country except the Northwest. Production of the PA series lasted eight years and embodied three models which incorporated minor variations. The 2,000-hp version sold the best, accounting for 70 percent of total PA sales. Fifteen roads bought the PA-1s and five came back for later models.

In 1950 the 244-model V-16 engine horsepower rating was boosted to 2,250 hp, and the PA-1 model number was changed to PA-2. No reliable external body differences exist to detect the discrepancies, however. Some minor carbody variations became evident in the PA-3—the new designation in 1952. Although the horsepower rating remained at 2,250, some internal improvements were made, including a hardened crankshaft, a new water-cooled turbocharger, and an improved fuel injection process.

The most reliable carbody feature to look for on a PA-1 or PA-2 (and absent on the PA-3) is the stylish rain runoff trough to the rear of the cab door. It slants downward from the roof to the lower edge of the grillwork. This spotting feature is not totally reliable, though. Southern Pacific, for one, seems to have rebuilt the grillwork on all of its PAs and installed a different set of louvers.

Other roads added distinctive features to their PAs. Pennsy's famous inductive train-radio aerials found on most older PRR units were present on the PAs. They ran the length of the roof, one on each side. Nickel Plate hollowed out a notch in

the noses of its "Bluebird" PAs and inserted a bell. Normally a PA's bell is underneath the nose. Santa Fe has its radio aerials mounted on a small platform above the center of the cab. Among the many PA owners who installed large three-quarter-mounted number indicators on their units as replacements for the smaller number boxes built on the PA-1s and PA-2s were Katy, Mopac, Nickel Plate, Pennsy, Cotton Belt, Union Pacific, and Wabash.

The PA was essentially a passenger engine, as its model designation implies, but it was at home on tonnage as well as on varnish. The main reason for this dual capability was the PA's big GE traction motors, and many roads took advantage of this. Originally the DL-109 had been built as a dual-service unit for New Haven, but no other owner is known to have used them regularly on freights. On the other hand, nine roads can be counted as regular users of PAs on tonnage at one time or another. Some of these owners, such as Pennsy and Union Pacific, went through the formality of regearing the units for slower speeds and greater lugging ability, and theoretically banished their PAs from passenger service. Others, notably New Haven, Erie, Nickel Plate, Lehigh Valley, and New York Central, used PAs interchangeably on both freight and passenger trains. The PAs also saw occasional freight work on Cotton Belt, Gulf, Mobile & Ohio, probably Katy, and possibly other roads.

The continuing downward trend in passenger-train miles, plus the general standardization of the more numerous EMD products for passenger work, has all but extinguished the PA from the American railroad scene. By mid-1966 only about 70 of the nearly 300 units built were still around. A mere four railroads were operating PAs.

Last July the PA champ was Santa Fe, who was operating close to 40 units in passenger service. Espee, once owner of the largest PA fleet (66), still had 20 cabs and two boosters on the roster. But as Southern Pacific's PAs come due for repairs, they

are being retired, and it is doubtful that many will see 1967. Erie Lackawanna had its entire fleet in freight service, and Rio Grande's four cab units were still plugging along through the Rockies.

The PA era can be said to have covered two decades. Some of the first units, on Santa Fe, remain with us. The newest ones, on Southern, lasted barely eight years. Many persons fond of railroads and the machines that power the trains will miss the PAs. They often remind one of steam power—with their noise, smoke, and powerful look. Those who would like to see and hear the PAs had best hurry to their vanishing haunts.

ɪ   ɪ

Atchison, Topeka & Santa Fe, which followed up the prototype trio with 26 more cabs and 15 additional boosters for a grand total of 44 units, had the second largest fleet of Alco single-engine passenger units. They all carried the standard silver, red, and yellow Warbonnet dress of Uncle John's passenger units. In early 1960 PA-1 No. 53 was dressed temporarily in a blue-and-gold color scheme for a GE special. And of course, the first set of PAs, the famed No. 51 trio, suffered the ignominy of being repowered by Electro-Motive in an experiment not repeated by the builder. Reportedly, Santa Fe was not pleased by reduction in horsepower from 2,000 to 1,750 per unit.

The Alco fleet of AT&SF has always been in the role of understudy to the F units as far as mainline passenger work goes, but the big burblers do get a share of high iron assignments west of Kansas City. California and Texas traditionally have been PA stamping grounds on the Santa Fe. Most Barstow-Richmond runs have been entrusted to the Alcos, and this has made for grand shows over Tehachapi with both Southern Pacific and Santa Fe PAs. *San Diegans* have usually rated PAs too. Except for the *Texas Chief*, most Lone Star State passenger trains have the Alcos assigned. On Uncle John's main

---

*Units similar in appearance to American PAs have been built by Alco for export and by Alco's overseas licensee. These cabs are usually equipped with C-C trucks. They can be found in such countries as Australia, Greece, and India.

An Alco PA/PB/PB consist leads the Union Pacific's *Pony Express* across the desert near Victorville, Calif. The railroad's 14 PAs and PBs were assigned to passenger service in the West. *Donald Sims*

line, mail trains and the *San Francisco Chief* are the runs that usually have PAs. As late as summer 1966, one regular assignment brought a set of five PAs daily into Kansas City on No. 4; the return west was on No. 1.

As of July 1966, only a handful of Santa Fe's PAs were off the roster including one of the original set, No. 51-C. The Alcos are still receiving excellent maintenance and are among the smoothest-sounding Alco units running. Unless subsequent orders for dual-service U28Cs push the big Alcos off their current runs, it is feasible that Santa Fe's PAs will be around for a few more years.

Quite possibly the first owner of a PA will also be the last to operate one.

Ⅰ   Ⅰ

Denver & Rio Grande Western bought only two sets of A-B-A Alco passenger units—for use on the *California Zephyr*. They were the only A1A-A1A diesels D&RGW ever owned and were delivered in a silver paint scheme to match the stainless-steel streamliner. Later they carried the black-and-gold freight-unit scheme, and ultimately wore the final carbody-type-unit colors of silver and gold with black trim.

Around 1960 the PAs were bumped off the *Zephyr* by Fs and put into service on the Royal Gorge, usually in AB sets; the other two cabs were assigned to the *Yampa Valley* run to Craig. A couple of years ago one cab unit, 6001, was removed from service and placed in storage, and the future for the PAs looked dim. However, in 1965 the 6001 was restored to service with an engine from a booster, and the two B units were taken out of engine service and converted into steam generator cars, using the old carbodies and trucks with traction motors removed.

Thus, today D&RGW's PAs are still active—the cabs as power on the *Yampa Valley* and the Salida stub of the *Royal Gorge* and steam generator cars 251 and 252 usually helping out the F7s on the *Zephyr*.

Erie Lackawanna's fleet of 14 PA cabs were used in general passenger service throughout the system before declining patronage curtailed the number of trains. A special hangout for the PAs was the joint (with Pittsburgh & Lake Erie) Cleveland-Youngstown-Pittsburgh *Steel King* service. Each road used its PAs on its own end of the run. Erie's PAs also teamed up with E8s on mainline trains and were used alone on New Jersey locals and commuter trains.

When the Erie PAs were delivered they carried the old black-and-yellow winged paint scheme, and some later were dressed in the newer green-and-gray passenger garb. Since the merger with Delaware, Lackawanna & Western the Alcos have been getting the old universal Lackawanna gray, yellow, and maroon colors.

In the 1960s the EL PAs began to show up on freight trains, and in early 1965 the few units remaining in passenger service in the East were sent to Marion, Ohio, to join the others in the freight service pool. All are believed to be active hauling tonnage on the western lines of EL, making "The Friendly Service Route" one of but four current PA operators and the only one using them on tonnage.

Ⅰ   Ⅰ

Gulf, Mobile & Ohio was a significant Alco customer in the first round of dieselization, beginning with an impressive RS1 fleet and continuing with the first postwar FA-1 1,500-hp freight units purchased by any railroad, but its PA fleet numbered only three—all PA-1s. They were painted in the red-and-maroon Alton color scheme that survived the GM&O purchase.

For a time the PAs saw limited service on the Alton end of the road, but they soon found a home on the southern part of the system when the Alcos and EMDs were segregated by region. PAs teamed up with the three DL-109 cabs on the *Rebel* trains with conventional equipment until the demise of the service. They are believed to have been used then in freight service for a few years.

The first two of GM&O's PAs were bought new soon after the model was introduced on the Santa Fe. The third, GM&O No. 292, came from the *Freedom Train*. This unit was built for the train as No. 1776 by Alco-GE and painted in a scheme of white with red and blue trim. The *Freedom Train*, sponsored by the American Heritage Foundation, made a 33,000-mile tour in 1947-1948 that took it over 52 railroads in 48 states. It carried many of the nation's original historic documents in special exhibit cars and was escorted by two dozen armed U.S. Marines serving as guards. All the cars for the train except the power car, which came from the Santa Fe, were supplied by the Pennsylvania.

All three of GM&O's PA-1s had been removed from service by 1962, when they were sent to EMD as trade-in credit on the first order for GP30s. The commemorative plates from the flanks of the *Freedom Train* unit are displayed in Casey Jones Museum in the GM&O shop town of Jackson, Tenn.

Ⅰ   Ⅰ

Lehigh Valley passenger service during the diesel era was entirely in the hands of Alcos except for a lone RDC. The Valley's 14 PA-1s were the backbone of the fleet. They were the only regular A1A passenger cabs on the road, were used singly or in pairs, and carried the regular LV tuscan red colors.

After LV quit passenger service, the PAs were put into freight service. They were withdrawn slowly from the active roster to provide trade-in material on newer Alcos for LV and parent Pennsy. The last Lehigh Valley PA went to the torch in 1965.

In the days when Missouri-Kansas-Texas passenger trains were something to behold—after the 4-6-2s had

A lone Erie PA pauses with its train at Hoboken, N.J., in April 1959. Erie's 14 PAs, including No. 860, which was built in November 1949, all went to the Erie-Lackawanna upon the Erie's merger with the Delaware, Lackawanna & Western in 1960. *Louis A. Marre collection*

departed—like as not there was a pair of PAs up front. The *Texas Special* used E7s and later Katy had some E8s, but the polished group of 14 Alco cabs were prominent. They had the regular red-and-gray Katy color scheme for most of their lives, but a few received the solid red treatment just before their demise.

In the late 1950s, Katy's passenger runs had dwindled so that the Es and FP7s could handle them all, and the Alcos were stored. But not until John Barriger mercifully cleaned out the long junk lines of all makes and models of diesels at Parsons and Waco during the past year did the long-nosed PAs go to scrap.

Missouri Pacific owned 36 PA cab units, including some of each model, and used them in general passenger work throughout the system. All had the gray-and-blue eagle color scheme, although a few acquired the solid blue scheme in the early 1960s. The Alcos were used both singly and in pairs during the early years, and the nose m.u. connectors were applied later to most to enable three-unit operation.

There were more PAs than E units on the Mopac, but the Jenks era of standardization on EMD, coupled with reduced train-miles, spelled doom for the Alcos. From 1962 to 1964 all the PAs were removed from service and sent to scrap as trade-in credit on GP18s. Today the remaining Es and upgraded GPs handle Missouri Pacific-Texas & Pacific passenger trains.

New Haven's 27 PA-1s were simply a continuation of the dual-service program begun with the 60 DL-109 Alco cabs during World War II. When electrics still ruled exclusively west of New Haven the Alcos would double as passenger engines on the New Haven-Boston run and as freight power there and on other routes such as the bridge route between Maybrook, N.Y., and Cedar Hill, Conn.

The blunt-nosed PAs were delivered in the handsome green color scheme that the DL-109s inaugurated; many of the PA-1s later got versions of the McGinnis orange-and-black schemes.

Southern Pacific operated the largest fleet of PAs, with 66 A and B units (64 purchased new). Here a PA/PB/PA combo in *Daylight* red and orange lead the *City of San Francisco* in June 1951. *D. W. Johnson*

Despite the invasion of the dual-powered FL9s, some PA-1s lasted in secondary passenger service, including specials, until about 1963. Many were assigned to freights until the arrival of new GE U25Bs and Alco Centurys. Indeed, the last active New Haven PAs were in use on local freights as late as 1965. These were operated on runs west of New Haven that required service on non-electrified sidings on which the newly purchased ex-Virginian GE rectifier freight motors could not run for lack of catenary.

The **New York Central** itself had 14 Alco passenger units—nine cabs and five boosters. Subsidiary Pittsburgh & Lake Erie had six cab units which remained on the P&LE and handled all through trains on the Pittsburgh-Youngstown run. All 20 units carried the familiar two-tone gray-and-white NYC color scheme.

The NYC units were employed in general passenger work on most of the main lines, but originally were used for the most part on the Boston & Albany line. In later years they were utilized primarily as boosters behind E units on many trains, especially on the Chicago-Detroit-Buffalo route.

P&LE units stuck to their own track until about 1958 when passenger service was curtailed. Occasionally then they would slip out for freight and passenger work on the parent's lines. The six P&LE PAs were the first on the system to go to scrap; all had been sold to local dealers by 1961. The last NYC units were removed from service by 1964 and were scrapped soon after.

Two of the NYC units were purchased secondhand from General Electric. These had been built by GE for the *More Power to America* train which toured the country in 1950. NYC bought the cab and booster pair and numbered them 4212 and 4304.

Santa Fe No. 51 was the first PA built by Alco. The new locomotives pose with 10 lightweight cars on Cajon Pass in a classic Santa Fe publicity photo. The railroad eventually acquired 44 PA and PB diesel locomotives. *Santa Fe*

New York Central repowered a booster, 4302, with a 16-567C EMD diesel prior to 1961. Other than the Santa Fe No. 51 set, this is believed to be the only P-series Alco unit to be re-engined.

The postwar freight boom was responsible for steam-oriented **NKP**'s decision to dieselize its limited passenger services, since Berkshires were needed for freights and the little Hudsons couldn't cope with big trains and fast schedules. Eleven PA-1 cabs took care of NKP's needs; the Chicago-Buffalo trains rated a pair each and the St. Louis trains a single unit each, leaving one spare.

With the demise of the St. Louis passenger trains, the spare PAs went into freight service. Their train-control feature enabled them to be used as lead units on lashups of road-switchers between Bellevue and Chicago. In 1962 11 Alco DL-701 hoods were ordered, and the Bluebirds (Nickel Plate's PAs were dubbed *Bluebirds* in honor of their unique and attractive blue-and-gray paint scheme) were sold as trade-ins. Two of the new road-switchers came equipped for passenger service and joined the small group of GP9s that had been around as backup units for passenger trains in providing power for NKP trains in their last years.

Pennsylvania bought five A-B-A sets of Alco passenger units and used them in general service throughout the nonelectrified portions of the system. They had the pin-striped brunswick green color scheme when they were new but later carried tuscan red livery. Some were repainted into the black-green freight scheme when they went into that service.

In 1952 Pennsy began to standardize its diesel-powered passenger services by concentrating EMDs on the most important runs while other makes handled secondary trains. As a result, the PAs often showed up on such lines as Baltimore-Harrisburg and as backup power on the Pennsylvania-Reading Seashore Lines. Eventually most non-EMD passenger units were regeared by Altoona shops for freight service, and the PAs finished their days as dual-service units mostly engaged in hauling tonnage. During the shopping the gear ratio was changed from 60:23 to 64:19, and top speed was reduced from 100 to 80 mph. However, the units' original 2,000 hp rating was retained.

Toward the end the PAs could be found holding down such jobs as transfers around Philadelphia-Camden, pushers out of Williamsport, local freights out of Canton, and were available as passenger protection units. Components of the PAs were sold to Alco in 1962 when 15 new DL-640 freight hoods were purchased, and PRR cut up the PAs.

Ɪ   Ɪ

Cotton Belt's minimal passenger trains relied on two PA-1s as regular power, one unit per train; an FP7 and several Alco RS3s were available as alternates. The two Alco cabs carried the eye-catching red-and-orange color scheme of parent SP's *Daylight* trains and passenger units. After SSW ceased passenger operations altogether, the PAs worked in freight service for a short time before being sold to Espee for passenger work again.

Ɪ   Ɪ

Southern bought its six PA-3s in 1953 as replacements for its older DL-109s on the *Tennessean* runs between Bristol and Memphis. Two units were used on each train, while the spares usually held down the Chattanooga-Memphis local. Wearing the famed Southern green-and-white scheme, the PAs also saw occasional service on the *Royal Palm*.

By 1962 all six PAs were out of service and stored at Pegram Shops in Atlanta. They later went to Spencer (N.C.) shops to be cut up.

Southern Pacific was the proud owner of the largest fleet of Alco PAs and PBs: 64 units bought new plus two inherited from subsidiary Cotton Belt. They sported the grand red-and-orange *Daylight* scheme until the new red-nose-and-gray-flank garb became standard.

When steam still ruled a large portion of SP passenger trains, the small fleet of EMD E units were usually to be found on Golden Gate Route runs or between Los Angeles and San Francisco. The big Alcos ruled other long-distance passenger routes. Subsidiary Texas & New Orleans was assigned a dozen of the PAs which were bought for the Texas streamliner pool for the Dallas-Houston *Sunbeam* and *Hustler*, and the transcon *Sunset Limited*.

Espee owned only 28 E units; thus it was mainly F7s and FPs that took over in the 1960s as some of the Alcos began to disappear from the active roster. Lines out of the Bay Area—the Cascade Route and the Overland Route in particular—became the last bailiwick for the dwindling PA fleet.

By 1966 the question was beginning to be which would become extinct first—Southern Pacific's PAs or its passenger trains? As of July 1966 20 PA cabs and two boosters remained on the books, handling the *Cascade* and the *City of San Francisco*. Espee became one of the final four roads to run the PAs, but the curtain was closing fast on the three other operators of the big Alcos.

Ɪ   Ɪ

Union Pacific got the first of its 14 PA and PB units late in 1947. Wearing the usual UP yellow dress, all the Alcos were assigned to western district passenger service where they served until 1955. On occasion they were assisted over Cajon Pass by steam Alcos—UP 7000-series 4-8-2s. Thereafter UP converted them to freight engines by regearing them to a 74:18 ratio. They then served as freight haulers on the Kansas and Nebraska divisions until 1964, when the last units were stored. All went to

scrap as newer freight units were purchased by the system.

One of the PA carbodies is extant on the UP, however. The cab unit of the experimental coal-turbine No. 8080, formerly No. 80, utilized PA-1 cab No. 607. Another Union Pacific PA-1, No. 605, achieved some individuality when a big cast pilot was applied during the time the unit was in freight service. This was evidently an experiment performed by Omaha shops. No. 605 has since been scrapped.

Ɪ   Ɪ

Wabash bought two pairs of PA-1s in 1950 to power the overnight Detroit-St. Louis passenger trains *Detroit Limited* and *St. Louis Limited*. Until 1956 the Alcos served on these runs as pairs of twin units numbered 1020 and 1021 with the rear cabs carrying A suffixes. Subsequently they went into general passenger work, remaining in pairs. In 1961 the PAs were renumbered with individual numbers and split up. They could then be found on almost any of the Wabash passenger trains.

The 1051 was involved in a grade-crossing accident in 1962 and the original carbody was scrapped. Wabash bought the carbody of NKP No. 181 from Alco and had it shipped to Decatur shops, but the rebuilding was never completed. Meanwhile, the remaining three units had been repainted from the old Wabash blue, white, and gray colors to a solid blue scheme.

In 1964 the three PAs were removed from service and stored at Decatur. They were on hand at the time of the N&W merger and were to have become N&W 3850, 3852, and 3853. Alas, the sole opportunity to witness PAs lettered N&W was never realized because in early 1965 they were sold to local scrap dealers and cut up.

Jim Boyd

April 1969

When It's Short Line Time down South

Jim Boyd

When I was assigned by General Motors' Electro-Motive Division as field instructor for a shiny new SW1500 on the kaolin-hauling Sandersville Railroad at Sandersville, Ga., I packed among my possessions an *Official Guide*, a copy of Lucius Beebe's *Mixed Train Daily*, and a *Railroad Magazine* roster of Georgia short lines.

If the latter was correct, there existed in southwestern Georgia a collection of short lines and motive power that had no business still being around in 1968.

I recalled seeing in *Mixed Train Daily* something about the "Pidcock Kingdom,"

the minuscule rail empire of C. W. Pidcock, and a mention of Moultrie, Ga. A check of the book turned up pictures of a few smoking mixeds rambling through the weeds, a painting of the business car *Moultrie*, and a picture of a weatherbeaten enginehouse. Could any of this still exist in 1968? The *Official Guide* indicated that it did. The Georgia Northern, the Georgia, Ashburn, Sylvester & Camilla, and the Albany & Northern railroads were listed—under Southern Railway control. So much for that, I thought. I had seen what the SR could do to the likes of the Savannah & Atlanta, the Georgia & Florida, and even the Central of Georgia. When SR acquires a short line, everything is painted black and white; the interesting items, such as S&A's Baldwins and G&F's wild paint scheme, become lost in the pursuit of efficiency; and SR F units, Geeps, and switchers fill in the gaps. My roster showed the lines as having such gems as GE 70-tonners, an EMD SW8, a 660-hp Baldwin switcher, and—almost unbelievably—a pair of FTs. With Southern in control, however, this must surely be out of date. I dismissed the entire subject.

⊥   ⊥

Shortly after I arrived in Georgia I met some members of the Atlanta Chapter of the National Railway Historical Society who had a just-issued SR locomotive ownership list. There amid E8s and SD45s were those GN and GAS&C FTs. This called for action.

As soon as my work permitted, I packed maps, rosters, and camera gear into my Volkswagen and headed south. The January day was warm, and the sky was clear. Georgia grew greener as I headed south from Macon on the expressway. At the north edge of the business district of Cordele, Ga., the northernmost outpost of the Pidcock Kingdom, I found the sum total of the Albany & Northern. Beside a two-story brick office and freighthouse sat A&N engine No. 1 and a Southern steel bay-window caboose. A&N 1 was a GE 70-tonner with a pair of sealed-beam lights looking like frog eyes atop the nose, an impressive array of air horns on the cab, and a maroon, white, and gold paint job. A trace of SR influence could be detected, but she hadn't lost her character. That SR caboose wasn't the wooden hack or Jim Crow

combine for which I'd been hoping, but you can't have everything.

The *Official Guide* showed the A&N as extending from Cordele 36 miles southwest to Albany; the rails are there, but that isn't the whole story. From its connection with the Georgia, Southern & Florida (now just another SR main line) at Cordele, the A&N operates down as far as Warwick, 12.8 miles. The track still extends from Warwick to Albany, but a train would have rough going because of the high weeds, a few trees, and a number of unsafe bridges. When the A&N engine needs inspection or repair, it is run over the SR and the G&F to Moultrie.

The A&N train had already finished its work for the day when I arrived, so after taking a few pictures of No. 1 half in the shadow of the freighthouse, I headed south again for Albany.

⊥   ⊥

Did you know that the GN runs from Albany to Boston? You won't find any big-sky blue or a South Station here, however. The GN is the Georgia Northern, and Albany and Boston are 68 miles apart and both in Georgia. The GN is the backbone of the Pidcock lines. It is the longest (68 miles) and busiest (one train each way a day), and owns the most locomotives (three).

Two blocks north of the impressive Seaboard Coast Line/Central of Georgia passenger station in Albany, I found the GN engine terminal. This northern terminus consisted of a one-track wooden shop and a combination office and sandhouse. The business office is in a new air-conditioned building up near the CofG yard. In true short line logic, the first engine I encountered on the Georgia Northern was Georgia, Ashburn, Sylvester & Camilla No. 15, another frog-eyed 70-tonner. According to my roster, No. 15 was one half of the GAS&C's motive power.

The place looked uninhabited, but just as I was about to leave, an elderly man emerged from the shadows of the sandhouse. He told me that the southbound freight had left in midmorning and was probably in Moultrie by now. I departed Albany and got a good look at the GN's weed-grown but neat main line from an

overhead bridge south of town. A short drive south on Highway 133 and a right turn on Highway 112 led me to Bridgeboro, the junction of the GN and GAS&C. Bridgeboro consisted of a few homes, a combination gas station and general store, and a small trackside industry. The main lines—and I use the term loosely, since the only way to tell the main lines from the sidings was to see which ended and which kept on going—of GN and GAS&C crossed at a 60-degree angle with little formality. There was a wye in the southeast quadrant, as well as some yard tracks south on the GN main. An old farmhouse sat right in the middle of the whole affair.

While I was trying to make some sense of the tracks in the weeds, and feeling like a 1968 Lucius Beebe, a commotion on the west main of the "Camilla" (that's what local folks call the GAS&C) attracted my attention. From the west came a "train." A snorting old six-stack Baldwin DS-4-4-660 running cab-first had in tow a steel bay-window caboose, two boxcars, and an EMD SW8. The Baldwin was Georgia Northern No. 12. When the engine revved up you could watch the individual cylinders fire as smoke belched from each of the six stacks. The caboose, of obvious SR stock, was neatly lettered G.A.S.&C. RY. CO. 122 in yellow against its red sides. Despite its high number, 122 is the GAS&C's only caboose. The SW8 was GN No. 13, and true to her number was "broke down." Earlier in the day No. 13 had left for Camilla and had failed on the road. No. 12 had been sent up from Moultrie and had dragged the crippled train back to Bridgeboro, where No. 13 was set on the wye.

While I was talking with one of the crew members at the telephone box, I discovered that short line railroading in this part of Georgia is unlike anything I had encountered before. Since there are few operators on the line, and the status of the track is unpredictable at best, the conductor drives his own automobile and follows the train. This serves a number of purposes: The conductor can get his paperwork arranged in town before the

"The tall windblown grass was like golden wheat," recalls author Boyd, "and the train would appear over a hill and ramble down the slope dwarfed by the almost surrealistic scenery." *Jim Boyd*

train arrives, transportation and communication are provided in case of difficulty, and the crew can tie up anywhere on the road whenever their time is up and can drive home for the night. Sometimes the GAS&C train will make a round trip from Ashburn to Camilla and back in one day. More often it will go one way one day and return the next, and in case of problems, the train is left on the line and the crew comes back the next day and continues where they left off.

I asked when the northbound GN freight was expected. "Oh, he won't be here much before midnight. That southbound man is on the ground about a mile north of here." The GAS&C train was last seen preparing to leave for Camilla

with the Baldwin as I bounded up a gravel road to find the derailed train. The road crossed the GN about a quarter-mile from the engine, so I walked up the track to it. There it was—a real live FT. Its round snout was maroon with a white-and-gold band around the bottom a la Southern. A reflectorized number panel was affixed on the bottom of the nose door, and a bell hung straight out from the roof between the cab windows. GN No. 14, ex-Southern No. 4105, had no boxy dynamic brakes, but that overhung snout and the four portholes left little doubt that she was the real McCoy. She was posed grandly on a curve between a wooded hill and a thickly forested swamp that looked capable of producing every thing from cottonmouths to alligators. That swamp was so close to the track that

the classic three-quarter shot was a hazard I didn't care to risk. Back in the train, three boxcars were on the ground, and a crew from Moultrie was busy trying to return the situation to normal. They still had a long way to go before Extra 14 South would be producing ton-miles again, so I walked back to my car and started for the heart of the Pidcock Kingdom—Moultrie.

Moultrie is served by three railroads: a branch of the Georgia & Florida (SR), a branch of the old Atlanta, Birmingham & Coast (SCL), and the main line of the Georgia Northern. The AB&C train in the charge of an ACL Geep was just departing town as I arrived. No trace could be found of rolling stock in the G&F yard, but the GN produced another FT—GAS&C No. 16—switching the industrial tracks in the valley north of the yard. No. 16 was originally SR 4100, but now it had a distinctive appearance, with a steam locomotive bell in a vertical bracket hung jauntily on its left cheekbone. I'd never before heard a lone FT working, and it sounded unlike anything else La Grange has produced. The rumblings emitted from that original 567 engine resembled a combination of GP7, Alco switcher, and Ford tractor. The machine obviously was capable, but it lacked that sound of assured authority that typified the later EMDs.

No. 16 completed its chores by switching some covered hoppers at a fertilizer plant, put its train together, then chugged defiantly up the steep grade through town to the yard. While I stopped to admire a handsome 2-8-2 on open display at the north end of the yard, No. 16 pulled its cars into a siding, cut off, and pulled down to the shop. When I arrived there it was already in the shop, shut down, and the crew was going home. Nothing like quitting time to expedite matters. One of the crew explained that a freight made a round trip from Moultrie to Albany every day, and one job worked around Moultrie. I asked when the run was made to Boston, the south end of the line. "Only when we can't figure a way to get out of it," he said. He went on to explain that there was little business south of Moultrie, and that trains seldom ran there.

After the crew departed, I realized that I was standing in front of that very enginehouse pictured in *Mixed Train Daily*. It was little more than a roof hung over three tracks, with corrugated metal sides, and a wall only on the north end. The south end was open, with no doors to obstruct the view of the timber framework, the years' accumulation of parts and junk, and the lone FT it housed. A city street crossed the tracks at the edge of the open building, and there was little distinction between the pavement and the shop floor. Across the street to the south

was an impressive corrugated steel shed. By squinting through a crack in the doors I could make out the end of an open-platform office car—the new *Moultrie* in seemingly immaculate condition.

On the track that ran out of the south end of this shed was a creature that looked like the result of breeding a standard RPO car to the *Pioneer Zephyr*. GN railcar 2 was built by St. Louis Car Company for the Southern in 1939 and was powered by Fairbanks-Morse. That riveted steel construction looked strange on the shovel nose, and the A1A-3 wheel arrangement and fabricated power truck were fascinating, but the paint job was the eye-stopper. The car originally was painted the standard GN maroon with white bottom band and gold stripe. Although the white and gold were in fine condition, the maroon had turned completely to rust. I was told later that this railcar has been donated to the NRHS Atlanta Chapter museum and will soon be moved there.

By now light was fading fast, so I proceeded once more to Bridgeboro to see how No. 14 and her derailed boxcars were doing. The train was on the track again and had pulled into Bridgeboro. The engine had backed onto the wye, had coupled to three hoppers there, and had shoved back to pick up the disabled SW8 left by the Camilla job. The rail had spread, and two of the hoppers were on the ground. … This was one of those days. I decided to depart lest I catch the jinx, and as the VW rolled north I promised myself to return.

⟂ ⟂

That return took place two weeks later. Richard Dean, a steam fan from Atlanta, had become intrigued by my tales of the Pidcock Kingdom, and he drove down to Macon to meet me. We made our first stop at Cordele, where A&N No. 1 sat exactly as before. There was activity elsewhere in town, though, and we shot color slides of a Geep on a Seaboard local, a pair of Geeps on an ACL local, and a trio of ACL U25Cs that highballed south. All of these were lettered SCL, but they carried their old paint and stayed on home track. A Southern local was also working town with an F7 and a Geep. Everyone was busy but the A&N.

Richard and I took Highway 41 south to Ashburn, where we found neither train nor information on its whereabouts. We moved on to Sylvester, passing a trim GAS&C 2-8-2 on display at the edge of town, and caught the station agent as he was leaving for lunch. He told us that the train was working at Camilla and would probably leave there about 2 p.m. Since we had plenty of time, we cut over to Albany; 70-tonner No. 15 was there, just as before. The southbound GN freight was long gone, so we took Highway 19 south to Camilla. In Camilla we found SW8 No. 13 in much better health than she had been a fortnight earlier. She was finishing work at West Camilla and was preparing to head for Ashburn. *Preparing* meant going for beans, so while the crew ate lunch, Richard and I explored greater Camilla.

To our surprise we came upon a little 2-8-2 rusting away behind a warehouse. Short line logic again. This oil-burning Mike in the weeds at the west end of the GAS&C was Albany & Northern No. 9. As we contemplated the circumstances that might have brought this little jewel so far from home, an air horn announced that our crew had finished their lunch and were off for Ashburn. The train rattled across the SCL diamond on the east limits of town with two empty Southern boxcars, a gon loaded with poles, and a loaded Norfolk & Western box ahead of the caboose. The gon was set off east of town.

⟂ ⟂

The countryside between Camilla and Bridgeboro is rolling grassland, piney woods, and an occasional swamp in the lowlands. On this mild winter day the tall windblown grass was like golden wheat, and the dark green pines stood elegantly against the sky.

The track was seldom visible from the road, and the train would appear over a hill and ramble down the slope dwarfed by the almost surrealistic scenery. Someone once said that if the Lord were to build a railroad, it would look like the Camilla—no cuts or fills, the track simply rolling over and blending into the land. With the boxcars swaying from high

GAS&C No. 13, an EMD SW8, ambles across a clay road next to a shack with its short train in tow. *Jim Boyd*

center to low joint, the train passed almost noiselessly through this tranquil terrain. We followed it for miles past sun-bleached farm shacks, over red clay roads, through pine forests, and over swamps where the trees were delicately draped with Spanish moss.

Near Bridgeboro we left the train on its placid journey and drove on to Moultrie to catch the afternoon northbound freight on the Georgia Northern. As we approached Moultrie I spotted the train highballing out of town. I turned around and drove like a Messerschmitt pilot to get ahead of him. We pulled onto a dirt road and found ourselves at a crossing at the bottom of a hill. Moments later Extra 16 North growled over the crest and descended on us at a fearsome pace. The maroon FT boiled past making 35 mph with various freight cars, including a long string of tanks, rocking along behind. As the unit passed, the engineer came over to the left side and shouted at us. Neither of us understood what he said, and we didn't spend any time wondering as we sped north trying to catch the train again. At a spot outside Sigsbee the train came roller-coastering down a hill on tracks invisible in the weeds. This time as the unit went by the engineer was at the door yelling, and something whizzed through the air between Richard and me. … The hogger had thrown an apple at us!

The train stopped to switch at the next town, and we drove up beside the engine and called up to the hogger, "What's the problem?"

"Y'all do yer pitcher-takin' someplace else," he growled. "Ah don't like havin' my pitcher took!"

After the apple incident, the disgruntled hogger ignored us, but we continued shooting photos until the railroad left the highway and disappeared into the woods. As in a Western movie, the last look at Extra 16 North was as it swept grandly around a curve and into the woods.

We returned to Moultrie and had dinner while we waited for the night to get good and dark. When the last of the Southern fried chicken was down, and the last light had vanished from the sky, we got out our tripods and flashguns and went to photograph that fascinating enginehouse. GN FT No. 14 and Baldwin No. 12 both were facing the open end of the shop; the scene was reminiscent of the photograph in *Mixed Train Daily,* with diesels in place of the steamers. After we finished our lenswork on the GN, we stopped at the Georgia & Florida yard and were delighted to find Geep 701 and a caboose tied up there for the night. The two were in standard Southern paint, but were lettered for GEORGIA & FLORIDA in SR-style block letters. Not quite the quality of the GN, but satisfactory. We got a picture, packed our gear, and set our course for the return to reality.

If the down-home character of these lines seems too fragile to last, changes already are under way to modernize. Surprisingly, it was the run of a steam engine over the Georgia Northern that heralded the beginning of the end. Fresh from the shop and bearing the names of GEORGIA NORTHERN and C. W. PIDCOCK on her cab, SR 2-8-0 No. 630 made her maiden run on a three-day trip from Birmingham to Moultrie in February 1968 to celebrate the 75th anniversary of rail service into Moultrie. The Southern took this occasion to announce that the GN would be upgraded into a major freight route through southwestern Georgia. Richard visited the GN and the GAS&C in late summer of 1968. He reported that grading and ballasting were well under way, but that the motive power and operation were unchanged. The future of the roads is brighter than it has been in some time, but the unique character of the operation may be lost in the process. The story is not a new one. Some said that the FTs in which we took such delight had destroyed the rural charm of the Pidcock Kingdom when they bumped the 2-8-2s into city parks.

Each generation sets its own standards, and I doubt that even Lucius Beebe's beloved Virginia & Truckee haunted him more than the delightful railroads of Moultrie haunt me today. Along with the steamboat whistles of the Illinois Central 2100s, a Duluth & Northeastern 2-8-0 in the snow, PAs on the *Banner Blue* at Forrest, Ill., and E-5s on the *Morning Zephyr*, the maroon FTs of Georgia will be treasured in memory.

May 1969

Andrew Russell

FACING ON A SINGLE TRACK ...
JUPITER AND 119

John H. White Jr.

Standard illustrated histories of the U.S. rarely fail to show the time honored photograph of the golden spike ceremony.

The two locomotives present are thus among the most familiar to the American public. However, the great army of men around and upon the engines effectively hides them from view. Equally obscure is an exact record of the mechanical particulars of these historic machines. Both were scrapped over 60 years ago; builders' records and shop drawings have vanished during the intervening years so that today only a few photographs and a handful of conflicting general dimensions remain to tell their story. Whatever the engines said when they met head to head is forever lost.

We are able, however, to construct a general description from the fragmentary information available. That both machines were standard designs of major builders makes the task somewhat simpler. In fact, more representative American locomotives of the period would be difficult to find. Both were of the ubiquitous eight wheel or 4-4-0 wheel arrangement. This style of engine was so common in the United States that it was called the American type locomotive. Introduced in 1836, it was the standard form of locomotive by the early 1840s and maintained its leading position well into the 1880s.

The Central Pacific's *Jupiter* was one of four American types purchased from the Schenectady Locomotive Works in 1868. The *Jupiter*, assigned road number 60, was completed in July as the builder's 505th locomotive. She was shipped around the Horn to San Francisco and then up river by barge to the Central Pacific shops in Sacramento.

The *Jupiter* was built to a design perfected by Schenectady's celebrated superintendent Walter McQueen (1817-1893). McQueen emigrated from Scotland in 1830. He first worked as a machinist, locomotive engineer, and master mechanic on several New York State railroads. During these years he designed some high-speed locomotives for the Hudson River Railroad that gained national attention. When new proprietors, headed by John Ellis, took over the defunct Schenectady Locomotive Works from Edward S. Norris in 1851, McQueen was asked to head the mechanical department.

McQueen steadfastly advocated a simple, orthodox design free of experimental or patented gimcracks. His designs, dependable and well proportioned, if not innovative, made the Schenectady Works one of the foremost locomotive builders in this country. McQueen's overly conservative outlook eventually led to his unexpected retirement in 1876 as chief mechanical officer. The engines built by Schenectady to that date differed little from the *Jupiter*.

The *Jupiter* was built for dual service. Its 60-inch-diameter drivers and 16 x 24-inch cylinders assured ample traction for freight trains, yet permitted moderate speed for passenger runs of the day. Total engine weight was 65,400 pounds, about average for the time. Calculating the boiler pressure at 120 pounds per square inch, the rated tractive effort would have been 9,800 pounds. Horsepower at 20 mph would have been roughly 520. Top speed would have been anyone's guess but normal running speed would have been 35 mph. She was, of course, capable of much faster running over high-speed track.

The boiler was of the ordinary wag on-top, fire-tube style. The waist was about 48 inches in diameter. Later

With 60-inch-diameter drivers and 16 x 24-inch cylinders, the woodburning *Jupiter* was suitable for both freight and passenger service. *Trains magazine collection*

specifications, presumably after a new boiler was applied, show 179 tubes of 2-inch diameter by 11 feet long. From what we know of boiler practice of the 1860s, this also would be about right for the *Jupiter*'s original boiler. The cylinders were level but raised some three inches above the center of the driving-wheel axle to provide clearance for the leading truck wheels. No. 60 had an ordinary bar style frame; however, McQueen's characteristic flat, deep front rail was used. Most builders used a nearly square front rail but McQueen preferred the style he had used since the late 1840s.

Two crosshead-driven reciprocating pumps fed water to the boiler. Here again McQueen leaned to the conservative side; injectors had been introduced in this country eight years before. In fairness to McQueen, it must be stated that early injectors were not overly reliable and were not universally accepted until many years later. The leading truck was a conventional rigid, center-bearing, four-wheel carriage—no fancy centering devices for McQueen.

The steam dome cover was a distinctive feature of many early Schenectady engines, the *Jupiter* included. It was a plain ogee-shaped polished brass cover very European in feeling. It was first used by McQueen about 1855. The bonnet stack (insistently referred to in error as a balloon stack) acted as a spark arrestor for the woodburning *Jupiter*. The outer funnel-shaped casing served as a hopper to hold embers which were baffled down by the deflecting cone and wire screen over the

top of the stack. The wire screen, shaped like a lady's bonnet of the day, gave the stack its name. It was an antique device used on American locomotives since the 1830s. Few details are known of the *Jupiter*'s tender, but existing photographs indicate it was a standard 2,000-gallon U-shaped iron tank with a wooden frame. Two cords of wood could be carried. Simple arch bar trucks were used.

Little of the *Jupiter*'s service history is known, but as with any engine of the period operating 20,000 miles per year, repairs and rebuilding gradually eroded away the original locomotive. She is known to have been reframed and reboilered before being sold to the Gila Valley, Globe & Northern Railroad in 1893. By this time the feed pumps, diamond stack, and much of the original brasswork were undoubtedly gone. She surely was converted to coal burning. When the *Jupiter* was scrapped in about 1905 there was little of the original to weep over. At least the residual shell was permitted a graceful demise and was not resurrected like the curious parody of the *General* that represents the original in wheel arrangement only.

I   I

The other locomotive at the Golden Spike ceremony was the Union Pacific's 119. She was heavier and incorporated a few more modern components than the *Jupiter*, but like her counterpart, the 119 was a stock, rubber-stamp 4-4-0 of the period. The Rogers Locomotive and Machine Works of Paterson, N.J.,

*The actual Rogers construction number is uncertain, but according to chronological list, the 119 would have been the 1563.

Locomotive 119 is shown here at work on the Big Trestle near Promontory in May 1869.
Andrew Russell, courtesy Union Pacific Railroad Museum

completed the 119 and her four sisters several months after the *Jupiter*. The 119 was delivered in November 1868 as the builder's 1,563th locomotive.* A pioneer in the field, Rogers had been building locomotives for 15 years when William S. Hudson (1810-1881) was hired as its superintendent in 1852.

Hudson's career paralleled his rival builder Walter McQueen in nearly all respects. Both were natives of the British Isles and had apprenticed successively as machinist, locomotive engineer, and railroad master mechanic. During the years McQueen was at Albany, Hudson worked in nearby Auburn, N.Y. But here the similarities ended; Hudson was more given to innovation and experiment. While most of the engines produced by Rogers were on conventional patterns, Hudson managed to work in pet designs. He held numerous patents, and whenever possible, engines built under his direction were fitted with his innovations. The 119, for example, sported a leading truck built on the Hudson-Smith-Bissell patents. Swing hangers added a centering device to counteract the tilt of the locomotive on curves; a long radius bar moved the pivot of the truck six feet to the rear of the truck center.

Several other features distinguished the 119 from the *Jupiter*. The most obvious of these was the extended smokebox and the straight, or tubular, capped smokestack. The extended smokebox was introduced as a spark arrestor for coal-burning locomotives in 1860 by John Thompson. The 119's smokebox was a modification of Thompson's scheme patented in 1864 by Isaac H. Congdon

(1833-1899). Congdon became master mechanic of the Union Pacific Railroad in 1866. During his 20-year tenure with the Union Pacific, many of the road's locomotives were fitted with his several styles of spark arrestors. The 116 through 120 were equipped with Congdon's extended smokebox type—others may also have been so fitted. In theory the sparks would burn themselves out in the long smokebox chamber before being forced out of the stack; hence, no bonnet stack was required. A controversy over the merits of this form of spark arrestor raged throughout the 1880s. It was never universally adopted but it did lead the way toward the modern internal smokebox spark arrestor. A final point of distinction between the two locomotives was the injector mounted on the left side of the 119. Two cross-head pumps were used as well—the injector was used to feed the boiler water when the engine was stationary because the pumps worked only when the engine was in motion.

The boiler and cylinders were the same size and capacity as the *Jupiter*'s, yet the tractive effort was rated as 12,180 pounds. This would only be possible with a higher boiler pressure complemented by smaller driving wheels. Incidentally, the builder's list gives the drive wheels as 54 inches in diameter, while photographic evidence and later roster lists of the Union Pacific show the wheel size as 57 inches.

In certain superficial respects it might be argued that the 119 was more antique than *Jupiter*. The cylinders were on a slight incline—a holdover from the short wheelbase trucks of the 1840s. The

ornamentation—bell stand, dome cover, sandbox, and cab windows—is older in feeling than the smoother lines of McQueen's engines, but this involves minor, non-mechanical details.

We know little of the 119's service history. She was renumbered as 343 in 1882 and continued to work on the Union Pacific until dismantled in 1903.

⚒ ⚒

As representative locomotives of their age, the *Jupiter* and 119 would have the following cost and operating capabilities. First cost for a good quality American type engine was $8,000 to $10,000. The inflationary pressure of the Civil War more than doubled prices, but by 1868, prices had fallen nearly to the prewar level. Operating costs per mile during the 1860s were often 40 cents per mile, but this was an extremely variable figure governed by available fuel sources. The Union Pacific was well removed from wood or coal supply; thus fuel costs must have been high. The Central Pacific was favored with a good wood supply; however, labor costs were extremely high, as was the cost of importing locomotives by sea—often at twice the selling price.

Engines of this size generally pulled trains of 250 tons—say, 15 to 20 freight cars at speeds averaging 10 mph. A five- or six-car passenger train of 90 tons would have been typical for the period. Speeds rarely averaged more than 25 mph. Since operating and maintenance costs were directly related to speeds, railway managers constantly strove to hold speeds at the lowest acceptable rate. Increases were effected only when competing lines forced improvement in service.

The 119 and *Jupiter* were built toward the end of the era of highly decorated locomotives. Bright, gaudy colors, and elaborate lettering and striping were yet in evidence. But the bulk of the machines' exteriors were finished in polished metal. Cylinder and dome covers, handrails, bells, and whistles were golden brass. The side rods and valve gear were burnished steel. The boiler jackets were made of Russian Iron, a richly luminous planished sheet iron, often silver gray in color. The total effect: remarkably bright, ornamental machines of unsurpassed elegance. These festive locomotives were appropriate to the joyous wedding of the rails at Promontory.

May 1969

Overland Diary— 1869

Cornelia E. Comstock

We crossed the Mississippi River in the night, for which we were sorry.

Friday, October 1, 1869: Awakened this morning in Iowa. Rain and hail for more than half a day—the 18th Friday of rain in succession, someone said. One long dead level, the famed prairie lands of Iowa; no beauty for me. Soil black as coal and so muddy. At two o'clock saw a streak of light all around the horizon. Asked the conductor if that betokened clearing off. "In Iowa," he said, "yes, the rain will be entirely over in two or three hours." He was a true prophet: It cleared off beautifully in two.

While we were sitting listlessly by the windows in separate seats, or wherever we would (for only a few were in the car), Mate said to me, "Did you hear that? One of those gentlemen [in] back of me lives near Auburn Station, California. I heard him talking about it." Of course, I was interested, too, but didn't make any enquiries until he spoke to us, asked us how far we were going, etc. We found he was a resident of California, had been east to Massachusetts to see about some property he has there. The gentleman with him is from Boston, on his way to California. Both are married men and very agreeable. We were delighted to find such company, especially as the one from California was acquainted with the route over the mountains and would give us much information when we should reach the

interesting places. Heard of several on the train en route to California. One family of five, from Maine, and the Champion Billiard Player of America, John Deary—a fine-looking man but a "sport," one could tell at a glance.

Boyer River was much swollen by the rains. It is very sluggish, and a long time is required before it reaches the usual level. As we neared Council Bluffs, which are very fine, judging from our twilight view, the river overflowed the track for 3 miles. I felt relieved when we were through. The sound of the wheels, every one a water wheel, was not pleasant, for we knew the river was deep.

We crossed the Missouri River by ferry. We took rooms at the Wyoming Hotel, a very comfortable house with a pleasant proprietor. I think we were made as happy as could be by the privilege of taking a bath.

⚓ ⚓

Saturday, October 2, 1869: Ate a good, hearty breakfast after which we just had time to put on hats and waterproofs before the bus came for us. The proprietor bade us good cheer, and we were on our way to the Union Pacific depot—a full hour and a half before train time. We didn't know what for until we reached the baggage room. I don't see how the

Cornelia E. Comstock was born on July 14, 1846, in the tiny settlement of Jenksville, N.Y., and was educated at nearby Owego. On September 29, 1869, at the age of 23, she left Owego to teach music in a school at Mendocino, Calif. This article is composed of excerpts from her journal of that trip. She traveled west with a girl companion, identified only as Mate, and we pick up the journey as she nears Omaha. The portrait photograph was taken in 1890, 21 years after her trip and just one year before she died at the age of 45.

[Her grandson, Philip N. Jenner (1921–2013), a linguistics professor, edited the journal.]

baggage master keeps his temper at all. Such a crowd as there is around him, and each one anxious for his time to come. Mate came with the checks soon. No extra charge for my baggage. Twenty-two dollars extra for hers. I was glad I took only one trunk.

Messrs. Barlow and Fletcher* had sent a telegram before reaching Omaha to engage one of the Pullman palace sleeping cars, or a section, rather, in one. We might have engaged one in this place but the gentlemen insisted that we should take half of theirs, and only when it was too late did we learn that they would take no pay from us. They said our company paid. We didn't consider it worth so much. We finally were settled in our staterooms,† not to make another change until Promontory should be reached three days and two nights distant.

We are not near so tired now as when we first started. We are used to the motion of the train, and rather enjoy the prospect of a long ride in this most elegant, comfortable car. Every convenience is at hand, and a pillow ready for us when we feel like lounging. We are crossing the great Platte Valley of Nebraska—one unending, dead level without a tree or even a fence to break the monotonous stretch of plain, only once in a while a poor thatched cottage, a hut more like. Someone asked me if my idea of "love in a cottage" could be [ful]filled out here; I don't see how anyone can live here. We see a few emigrant trains away out on the plains, in the roads, I suppose. Merely a supposition, for we can see nothing to mark a road except once in a while a square piece of board high up on a post with RAIL ROAD CROSSING—LOOK OUT FOR THE CARS printed on it. Looking down, and looking closely, we find what probably may be wagon tracks but indistinct and overgrown with grass now.

Well, we are tired of looking outside, tired of reading, so we try to familiarize ourselves to the faces of our traveling companions. We four in our stateroom in the center of the car. Just in front of us, facing the west, Mr. Goetze and Hattie Sachs, the "British Queen"—our name for her—and a young lady. Opposite them, Mr. Smith and wife, Mr. Glenzer and Mr. Weyrich—these last Germans are playing euchre, the porter having just put up their table. Back of them, opposite us, a solitary gentleman of pleasing countenance wrapped around with an immense cloak of dignity, which makes us believe we shall not be favored with his acquaintance very much. Back of us and back of him, a gentleman and lady in each stateroom. Second back of us, the "Champion Billiard Player of America." Opposite him, the Webb family from Maine.

Towards evening we commence singing—keep it up for two or three hours. For a wonder, everybody's voice is clear. Old pieces almost forgotten were brought out in fine style, and we had quite an audience. A Welshman from the farthest stateroom of our coach came around with a small hymnbook, and we sang old hymns. Well, time for retiring came at last, much to our regret. From choice we chose an upper berth, and when time came to take it our small dilemma came also. Mate thought she would not wait for the porter to bring the stairs, but would climb up some other way. She attempted it, but my notions of propriety [were] being immensely fine just then. How bravely I overcame them at last! I held her back—she says she nearly broke her neck in consequence. I called for the porter and the stairs, then she compelled me

*Mr. Barlow and Mr. Fletcher are the men mentioned in the second paragraph.

†*Stateroom* was a term used briefly during this era to describe a compartment. However, this and subsequent references to stateroom apparently were made in error, since from the running description of the cars and events, it is obvious that Miss Comstock actually was occupying a section (upper and open lower berth) during her ride west.

"We enjoy the prospect of a long ride in this most elegant, comfortable car." *American Geographical Society*

to make the ascent first, which I accomplished safely, and was glad to get behind the scenes. Mate followed on, and we finally composed ourselves for sleep, which we enjoyed notwithstanding the storm of cinders that fell upon our faces all night, one of the ventilators having been left slightly open. I suppose we looked like two black girls in the morning.

Sunday, October 3, 1869: We arose—that is, as far as we could consistently, considering we couldn't sit up straight without coming in contact with the ceiling of the car—rather early, still not early enough to have the first place in the dressing room. We waited our turn patiently, remembered it was Sunday morning, and we must try to do right. Took breakfast at Cheyenne. There is no dining car on the train as we anticipated. We ran around Cheyenne a long time—the train waited for something—in search of moss agates. We found none very nice but a good many pretty stones. Mr. Goetze has to bid us good-bye here. We waved our handkerchiefs from our car window, he from a box on the depot platform, until a turn in the road took us out of sight. Oh, but the air is perfectly pure and delightful away up here (6,040 feet above the level of the sea)! Our ascent has been so gradual we scarcely noticed it. I thought we would come suddenly upon the Rocky Mountains; instead, it has only been a plain, the nicest place imaginable, it seems for a railroad, the grade is so regular.

We saw this morning some rocks to the right of us that were strangely formed. One huge boulder was, or seemed to be, a perfect pattern in stone of a mud turtle. It was monstrous—would probably weigh 100 tons; this was a rough guess made by one of the passengers. Certainly I never saw anything more natural. It lay there head towards us, slightly descending, clear-cut against the sky. Its shell was very distinct, a stone on its back—which made it more natural, for its head was thrown out just as a turtle will be with any weight upon its back. Its feet were firmly planted on the rock beneath. It looked as though it might come down and swallow us all. It was 2 or 3 miles away, perhaps farther; in that pure atmosphere it seemed very near.

We reached Sherman, the highest point of mountains which we would cross, at about noon—a strange-looking place, as all these mountain villages are. The people live mostly in tents. Soldiers are stationed all along the route. It seems natural to see so many blue uniforms. We felt sorry for them, away out in these lonesome places. Thought we would show our sympathy by singing *John Brown* and waving our handkerchiefs. Our kindness met with no response except a prolonged stare from every one of them. We decided that they had been out here so long they had forgotten the usage of civilized society. We saved our voices after this and used our handkerchiefs for more legitimate purposes.

We got off the train again at Laramie [and] took a walk, in fact a good run, around the place. The air is perfectly delightful; objects miles and miles away seem very near. The air is meat and drink. I never felt such delight as here, thought I could stay forever.

Mr. Fletcher came for us to go to the other side of the depot to see a black bear. We found the bruin very tame and docile. It would walk to people on its hind feet and take nuts or apples from them in his great forepaws. I wanted, but did not venture, to stroke his fur; I was afraid he would return my affectionate advances

with a good hugging. We saw plenty of deer and antelope. Some saw wolves but no buffalo and only this one tame bear. Well, we had to go on board at last, much to our regret.

Traveling was not quite so convenient after leaving Summit. The palace car in the rear of ours broke down in some way, and had to be switched off and sent back. Passengers were obliged to find seats elsewhere; some had to put up with the common coaches. I was so sorry for them, and thankful that we were more highly favored. Mr. Greenwood gave up part of his section to two gentlemen. One only went a little way. The other, Mr. Hatch, [was] en route for Nevada, I believe.

Mr. Greenwood commenced being very pleasant after the singing last evening [and has] invited Mate and myself to sit in his section whenever it would please us. His acquaintance commenced really by his laughing to see us get in our berth last night, and he was ready to help us down this morning. He received a severe scratch from some unruly pin on Mate's clothes while helping her. He said he was rejoiced to receive the wound because he would remember her as long as it lasted, regretted that it was not more serious. She said she thought there was too much sentiment in the coach already—there were two violent flirtations going on which had been spoken of several times. The flirtations going on were between the billiard player and a young lady belonging to the Webb family (she was anything but agreeable to us) on one side of us, and the young man who first discovered the famous "White Pine region" as being rich with silver and the young lady who was traveling with the "British Queen." Both flirtations were so marked as to annoy the passengers at times, though some fun was extracted after all.

We reached the Great American Desert today but not the most deserted part of it, I believe. Wyoming Territory has few charms except the mountain air. We sang again this evening, but it didn't sound as well as usual or as it did last evening.

⚓ ⚓

Monday, October 4, 1869: Had a siege trying to dress this morning, just as we have had all the time. Awoke to find an unending stretch of the barren desert before us and behind us—dust, dust, the alkali dust everywhere. Nothing growing but the wild sagebrush, the very lowest order of vegetation; it thrives well here.

We reached the Chimney Rocks and the famed Echo and Weber Canyons. I have wondered why no descriptions of these places have been attempted—at least I have not seen one. I learned while passing through. No words could, or all words could not, do the subject justice. We can imagine nothing more sublime, more beautiful, more terrific than the rocks that form these canyons. Chimney Rocks, Devil's Slide, and Devil's Gate are three noticeable features, but all, all is grand. The rocks assume all forms and are of all sizes. Some tower up hundreds of feet above our heads, some form almost rectangular steps for ascent, and all the time in the distance lie the Wasatch Mountains covered with snow and standing out so clearly they seem very near. This is a peculiar feature of all this mountain scenery. "Thou art so near and yet so far," I constantly thought. I stood on the platform of the car while we were passing all these magnificent views. Mr. Barlow took care of Mate, put me in charge of another gentleman, so we really ran no risk although the train was making fast time.

"It looked as though it might come down and swallow us all." *Harold A. Edmonson*

Today we have passed from Wyoming [in] to Utah. We are nearing Great Salt Lake now. Mormons are everywhere numerous in this region. Soil is perhaps a little less sterile.

Salt Lake smiles upon us suddenly. I am sorry that my ideas of Paradise will borrow coloring from the view, which we enjoy for two hours. Utah Mountains in the distance. Great Salt Lake, an arm of which we cross, lying at the foot, not a ripple visible on its clear surface—the loveliest, softest shade of blue, Heaven's ever-blue, the mountains borrowing (it would seem) the same hue only tinged more with the purple indistinctness which distance gives. I thought, "Can anything be more lovely?" I hear that Salt Lake City is an Eden, judging from the outside appearance, but like these waters, bitterness fills every place but is hidden beneath the fair exterior. The smell of the water is offensive, very, its taste sickening. Still its beauty charms the eye, yea the heart.

And so we reach Promontory at about six o'clock. We took supper here. Had a great time before going to eat, disposing of our baggage. Engaged a stateroom on one of the Silver Palace sleeping cars. Had to get our baggage checked—our satchels, I mean; they are not allowed in the cars. I didn't care for that, for the porter said we could go into the baggage room and open them when we pleased. We went into supper at last, our party (always counting Hattie, the dear little girl) and Mr. Greenwood. He is a resident of San Francisco, is returning now from Prussia, where he has been to take his daughter to be educated in German and music more especially.

Tuesday, October 5, 1869: We dressed a little more comfortably than usual this morning because these cars are built a little different from the Pullman cars. The seats are not quite so comfortable it seems to me. While we were in the ladies' dressing room having a nice little comfortable time washing, the new conductor, whom we had not seen before, stepped in and called for tickets. Mate told him she thought this was the ladies' room. He laughed, looked at her sharply, said conductors were privileged persons, he was sorry to trouble her. He is a fine-looking young man. We found afterwards that he was from Owego and desired an introduction to us. He came and Mr. Fletcher introduced him. Name, Charles Kimball. He was very entertaining, tried to make a pleasant day of journeying for us. Told us that his engineer, Charles Arnold, was also from Owego and would be glad to see us. Invited us to ride on the engine. We were pleased with the idea of traveling in that way away out in Nevada, so when we reached the next station, Mr. Kimball took us off and helped us on. We liked Mr. Arnold very well. We rode 24 miles with him along the foot of the Humboldt Mountains, by the side of Humboldt River, and through Humboldt Canyon. We made short turns and rode by deep ravines. We could see all the seeming danger from our position in the engine, which seemed to be possessed with life and judgment—it bore us so safely and steadily onward.

Chinese are numerous here as workers along the line of railroad. We finally alighted from our lofty position, returned to the coach to finish telling the conductor Owego news. He said he had not heard so much in 12 years. He is, or has been of late, a resident of New York. Was once a schoolmate of Mate's. He said he remembered her face but could not tell where he had seen it.

Indians abound all day, some of the Shoshone tribe. … They stand along by the sides of the train at every station,

waiting for passengers to throw them something. They don't want any money unless it is silver. A penny they would throw away, or one of the new five-cent pieces so common [in the] East. Some of the squaws with their papooses on their backs were so comical. If their papoose cried they would slip the strap off their heads—the whole weight of the child is on the mother's head, unbuckle the straightjacket in which the child is bound, lay it right down in the dust—the alkali dust, half a foot deep—until she should be ready to nurse it. I saw them take scraps from their dogs and eat them.

⌶　⌶

Wednesday, October 6, 1869: The day of all days! I awoke before light, told Mate I thought she had better waken and we would dress. She agreed with me, of course, and although it was very dark, we found our clothes and dressed more easily than at any time before. Had no one to help us down, so caught hold of a rod running through by the ceiling of the car and swung ourselves down without noise—for we promised to be very quiet so as not to wake the [other] passengers. We went out in the dressing room, looked at our watches, found it was only two o'clock. We laughed at ourselves but didn't care much after all, especially as after a while when the other ladies came to wash, the water suddenly gave out.

We went out on the platform when it commenced getting light. Saw objects distinctly but missed Donner Lake, much to our regret. We saw another lake, which looked beautiful, away up in the mountains. We came to the snowsheds before daylight. They were tedious enough—50 miles of snowsheds! I had no idea what that meant until I passed through. Only once in a while an opening. We were glad when we left them and were once more out in the pure mountain air. And then the view, once seen, can never be forgotten. We realized what was meant by "high rocks on one side, nothing on the other." We stood on the platform with

Messrs. Barlow and Greenwood for a hundred miles at least. The conductor came scolding along one time because we stood there, told the gentlemen it was the most unsafe thing ladies could do. He looked dreadfully stern. I stepped inside to show my ticket; he continued on with his discourse. I told him we knew it was dangerous and asked if he did not know we must run some risk for the sake of his beautiful California scenery. He was a true lover of California, I know, for he smiled and said very pleasantly, "Oh, well, if you are willing to risk it, I haven't any further objection." However, I stayed inside a little more after this, in the dressing room; only went out when the gentlemen told of some particularly fine view.

This side around Cape Horn is wonderful. We are descending a steep grade one minute, in three minutes afterwards are ascending one in an exactly opposite direction. We can see the engine and the last coach of our train at once. Oh, the scenery! There can be nothing to compare with it anywhere, I am certain.

How fast we lived all this morning—never faster in my life (not even when we were crossing the desert and took liquors instead of the water, which was terrible to the taste and worse for the stomach, just like saleratus [sodium or potassium bicarbonate used as a leavening agent]). We have to descend into the valleys, always in this life, after having been on the mountain top. Our descent was rapid. We saw a good deal of hydraulic mining on our way, learned how it was carried on. We reached Auburn at about half past nine. We are getting down into the Sacramento Valley. Everything in Nature has changed from the wild mountain scenery to wide fields and dusty roads, to live oaks instead of the mountain spruce and laurel. We began to breathe more naturally, and find when Sacramento is reached that we are extremely tired. The excitement is over

"Took breakfast at Cheyenne. There is no dining car on the train as we anticipated." *American Geographical Society*

and instead of the bracing air we have extreme heat and dust deeper than I have ever dreamed of. No rain has been here since the 18th of April.

We change cars at Sacramento, leave our easy palace car for one of the common kind on the new railroad, over which the first train went on last Saturday. We are glad to leave this city, glad to be rid of the close air of the depot and the outrageous noise of the hackmen, which almost deafens one. We have a tiresome ride before us on account of the heat and dust. We raise the windows and smother from dust; we close them and suffocate

from heat. We passed some most beautiful ranches, saw windmills—a great number of them. They are constantly drawing up water to irrigate the ranches. One naturally wonders how anything can grow in this dry climate. That grain is abundant is evident from the fact that we saw thousands and tens of thousands of bushels of wheat in bags piled up along the line of railroad. It was a sight worth seeing. It was almost as much a curiosity as to see a dozen or more Chinamen washing clothes in the Sacramento River.

We reached Alameda at about six or half past—I could not tell accurately. I looked at my watch every time and guessed. There was 3 hours and 17 minutes difference when I reached San Francisco between mine and RR time. We rode on

trestlework down into the Bay, even to the ferryboat. The ferryboat is very fine and very large, much like a steamboat, with upper and lower decks, etc. We enjoyed our ride immensely; the cool ocean breeze was refreshing. I enjoyed it so well I think I caught cold being up on deck all the time. The Bay is 5½ or 6 miles wide at this place. We crossed in about half an hour. Parted from Mr. Greenwood, who regretted our short stay in San Francisco because he would like to show us around the city. We took the American Exchange omnibus, saw the last of Hattie. We reached the Exchange at about nine o'clock. Could get no supper here and were obliged to go to a restaurant. Retired at once on our return to the hotel, glad to have a room and a genuine good bed.

October 1969

GOD MADE SNOW FOR FARMERS AND ARTISTS

John Norwood

The lonesomest sound in His universe is a blizzard wind blowing snow through ice-coated branches of spruce trees. Especially when those trees are in the throat of a mountain pass high in the San Juan Mountains along the Colorado-New Mexico state line.

Especially if the sky is black but the land is white, and overriding the screaming wind is a quietness so intense you can hear each snowflake fall.

But most of all, when that wind has just bowled you over and you are facedown in the cold smother of snow all tangled up in the blizzard, your snowshoes, and a sled rope. Most of all, when you find yourself fighting panic that is almost tangible, and a gut-twisting cramp of fear in your stomach puts the taste of gall in your mouth.

The lonesome, soughing wind is the voice of a sweet-talking siren promising warmth under the white blanket, whispering to you to quit fighting and relax in her white arms while you sleep with her—forever.

Cumbres Pass, on the narrow gauge route of the Denver & Rio Grande Western Railroad, between Alamosa and Durango. Colo., was a siren. Over 10,000 feet in elevation, the Hill was like a beautiful woman—dangerous, alluring, always humming a seductive song. In the summer and fall, soft and amorous; in the winter, a vixen.

Cumbres was a siren in the image of Eve, the result of the world's first transplant. Eve, from the moment God created her from Adam's rib, was a tribulation to man. Some of the troubles she caused are still with us. She conceived sons who were farmers, and farmers need water for their crops. She conceived sons who were artists, and artists need beauty. So the Almighty created snow to make water for the crops—snow that falls in the winter to lie clean and white over the sleeping land and to mantle the tall spruce trees. Snow: useful, beautiful—and cruel.

In the winter of 1951-1952, Cumbres Pass had snowfall enough to make 10,000 farmers happy. It lay on the tall spruce trees, and it lay on the land, drifted and torn into thousands of sculptured forms, magnificent vistas, and beautiful murals. So many, and of such beauty, that all the artists in the world could never match them.

But there were no farmers to look and gloat, no artists to see and marvel—only cold, tired, and hungry railroaders trying

Butting into a snow-plugged cut just west of Osier, Colo., Rotary OY and Mikados 494 and 499 show what winter railroading is all about in the land of the Rio Grande's 3-foot gauge. *John Norwood*

to whip the storm. And more than that—simply trying to survive.

⟂ ⟂

December 28, 1951, at Chama, N.M., located at the foot of Cumbres Pass on the west side, was one of those winter days of turquoise sky and warm breezes. The kind of day the Chinook Indians called "Old Snow Eater." Trainmen and sectionmen went about their work barehanded and in shirt-sleeves. The old snow on the ground turned to slush, then to

water. The high ridges of the San Juans toward Cumbres Pass were clear and sharp against the cloudless blue. Barometers at all our weather reporting stations showed small drops but nothing to be concerned about. Weather reports from other sources promised continuing clear skies and warm breezes.

A Chama-Cumbres Turn departed Chama at 8:50 p.m. to shuttle a string of loads to the top of the Hill. Engineer Joe Dalla and fireman Johnny Lira had been called for engine 491 to help this Turn to Cumbres, then run light to Alamosa. This

was a routine move; the weather was good and the two men expected to be asleep in their own beds long before dawn. They reported for duty at the roundhouse lightly dressed, without heavy coats or overshoes. Each carried the usual Thermos of coffee, but their only food was a sack of candy Red Hots Lira had bought with the change from his evening meal.

The Cumbres Turn had been gone from Chama about an hour when a heaving black cloud came racing in from the east, wiping out the stars as it came. From the cloud mass fell a misty rain. Those of us still awake and familiar with the vagaries of a Chinook gave the condition only passing notice as we headed for our beds. The train crews who were out in it did little more. Upon returning to Chama, the Turn's conductor mentioned to the night operator that the wind on top of the Hill was blowing hard and the clouds were hanging low and heavy. Several inches of new snow, together with the old, was drifting the setout track switches full.

None of this spelled anything to worry about. What the heck! Bad weather was expected over Cumbres Pass anytime between Thanksgiving and July 4. Long sieges or squalls of snow and wind were part of the daily fare. Most times you hated and feared the white stuff; at other times, when you were drifting downgrade and siting in a warm cupola of a caboose on a still moonlit night so bright you could read print, it was different. You could look out across the wide, white alpine meadows and see blue-black spires of spruce trees sharply etched against the white—and you didn't want to be anywhere else. It was so ethereal it took your breath away. The most frustrated people in the world must be those who have been privileged to ride across Cumbres on a calm night when the snow was deep and the moon was full. Frustrated because it is beyond human capability to put the scene on canvas.

About 3 hours after midnight the call-boy pounded on my door to tell me that the Alamosa train dispatcher wanted to talk to me. When you are trainmaster of a district on a mountain railroad, a summons like this in the middle of the night is just part of the job. Stepping into the night from the warm lobby, I was struck by gusty winds and cold rain—a rain that was no longer mist but drops and trying hard to be sleet.

Walking to the station I had that queasy feeling that foretells trouble. What the dispatcher had to tell me removed any doubts. We had trouble.

The 491, running light with Dalla and Lira on her, was overdue by the Big Horn annunciator. They hadn't called in, and the dispatcher had been unable to get either the Osier or Sublette section foreman to answer his night bell. This was worry enough without having an engine lost, for those isolated hill section foremen slept with the knowledge that when the bell rang they were wanted in a hurry.

That was the way the foreman at Cumbres responded when his bell was rung. He was only half awake when we asked him how the weather was. He left the phone off the hook while he went to look, and when he got the door open, we didn't need his report. The phone acted like a microphone, and the sound picked up was one you hear only when a real tomcat of a blizzard is blowing. The foreman finally forced the door shut, returned to the phone, and in a mixture of Mexican and railroad cuss words, confirmed our fears.

Again and again the bells at Osier and Sublette were tripped. From the strong answer-back we knew the bells were ringing, but no voices responded. I was ready to start climbing the walls, but I told the dispatcher I would hang on the phone while he checked airlines and the Weather Bureau for reports. Freak local storms over Cumbres often were of limited extent and didn't show up in the general weather predictions, but we had never before had conditions such as the Cumbres foreman was describing.

The reports we got had a sameness that made a man doubt his sanity. "Mostly partly cloudy, with rain showers extending east from the coast and a cold front that may bring snow and falling temperatures." The Weather Bureau did say that there were indications of a localized barometric low centering over the south end of the San Juans. An airline reported that a westbound pilot had encountered severe and unexpected turbulence in the same vicinity.

This wasn't any news to us—not by a long shot.

The Cumbres foreman was listening, and when all the reports had been relayed, he broke in to ask what severe turbulence was. I told him it meant that the wind was blowing like hell over Cumbres.

He came back with, "They're telling me!"

A new voice cut in and said, "But it's blowing harder here at Big Horn." The voice was the Sublette section foreman, and he was at the old unoccupied section-house at Big Horn. He told us that he and all the other men of the Sublette and Osier gangs were sheltered and had fire but no food. When questioned about the 491, his reply was that they had neither seen nor heard it.

The foreman explained that the previous day the two gangs had doubled up to transpose rail on a curve east of Sublette. Some difficulty had been encountered, and it was almost dark when they put their motor cars on the rail to go to Sublette. They were away from the pole line and couldn't report in by phone, but the Osier men intended to tie up for the night at Sublette and report their location from there.

They never reached Sublette. The first snow and wind hit as they started moving west. Both snow and wind were so severe that the motor cars couldn't keep moving. Deciding they could do better going downhill with the wind at their backs, the men unloaded all their tools and started east. The cars were able to keep moving for about 2 miles, and then it became necessary to put them in the clear and to start counting ties. They took turns breaking trail in the snow and reached the Big Horn sectionhouse about midnight. There they tore up a floor and got a fire going.

⚡   ⚡

At 6 a.m. the following morning the 491 still had not made an appearance and the storm was worsening. A snowplow train left Alamosa at 8 a.m. in the charge of T. J. Cummins, road foreman of equipment, and E. N. Haase, division engineer. They were to plow to Big Horn, pick up the stranded sectionmen, then continue westward in an effort to find the 491. There no longer could be any doubt that it was stalled in the snow some where between Cumbres and Big Horn.

Running blind against the snow and an opposing movement of uncertain

Rio Grande Rotary OY, which left Alamosa on January 1, pauses in Osier on January 4 after taking three days to plow out the last 5 miles of track immediately to the east. *John Norwood*

location was hazardous to the nth degree, but there was no alternative if Dalla and Lira were to be rescued. A veteran of the narrow gauge, Tom Cummins, was on the lead engine, and this bettered the odds.

About 40 miles west of Alamosa near the Lava watertank the plow outfit started to find snow. However, it was able to proceed without difficulty to Big Horn, and the hungry sectionmen were picked up. The plow proceeded westward with Cummins reporting from each telephone booth along the way. His reports had a frustrating uniformity. The 491 had not been found; the wind was hurricane force and driving an unbelievable amount of wet, heavy snow before it. Conditions were close to being hell.

In midafternoon Cummins reported from Osier that they had not yet found the 491 and were going on west. It was no longer a case of being close to hell. *It was hell.*

The next word from the plow again came from Osier. The time was 10:30 p.m. on December 29. The plow had reached milepost 319, about one mile west of Osier. At this point they were temporarily stuck in deep snow. After they had jarred loose, it became necessary to back into Osier for water. As the caboose passed over the west switch, it derailed on accumulated ice. Everything bad that could happen followed in rapid succession. The Jordan spreader, a small flanger, and one pair of tank wheels of engine 492 also went on the ground. Conditions had reached the point where men could not work in the storm. Fires on the engines were banked, and everyone took shelter in the Osier HQ.

At Chama we made up a second plow train, and rounded up and provisioned sectionmen to go along. Moving out eastward we found no snow for the first 5 miles. Then, at an elevation of 8,500 feet, conditions changed. Snow depth gradually increased. So did the velocity of the wind. It began to hit us, coldly and fiercely.

The day was spent slugging it out with deep drifts—the throttles were kept down in the corner while the fireboys bent their backs and moved their scoops. At times it was necessary to use sectionmen and snow shovels to dig out around the engines to free them from drifts.

Finally, just west of milepost 331, a mile west of Cumbres, we got it.

A snowslide full of trees and rock had run in a location where a slide had never run before. Before the lead engine could stop we were buried cab deep in the hard, dirty baby avalanche.

It was apparent we could not free ourselves that night. On foot I broke through to Cumbres and reported our situation. The men of the Cumbres gang then returned with me to the stuck snowplow.

We fired up an acetylene flare to better assess our situation. It was bad. More help would be needed from the Chama end to pull the buried equipment from the snowslide. Power and crews for the relief train would have to come from Durango, several hours away. We were not going to be able to break loose to reach Dalla and Lira for some time.

A council of war was held on the caboose. A decision was reached that conductor Frank Young would be in charge and, weather permitting, would try to shovel the equipment partly free while awaiting the relief train from the west. I would return to the phone at Cumbres to arrange for this relief, rest a few hours, then go on east to try to find the 491. At Cumbres on the first trip I had found a pair of snowshoes, a light toboggan, and food. Snowshoes and I were working partners of long acquaintance.

Back at Cumbres I contacted the dispatcher and found that the division superintendent was also on deck. From my description of the situation there was no question about the need for assistance, and the superintendent said he would take over and get it started. He repeated to me the news he had received from Cummins at Osier.

While I was informing the superintendent of my plan to leave Cumbres on snowshoes in a few hours, Cummins butted in on the phone conversation to tell me I was nuttier than a fruitcake and that I was talking suicide. The boss took it up and said he was ordering me not to do it. The discussion was settled by my telling them both to go to hell and hanging up the phone.

I hadn't much more than warmed the blankets and fallen asleep when the night bell rang. The superintendent had got the chief engineer down to his office in Denver and he wanted to talk to me. He didn't mince words—he just wanted to be assured that I thought there was a chance to get through on snowshoes. I told him there was.

He said, "Okay, boy. The best of luck."

I   I

A little after 5 a.m. the toboggan was loaded and I tied on the snowshoes. The first mile was sheltered by a grove of spruce; several cups of coffee and a hot breakfast rested comfortably under my belt. Cummins was right. I was as nutty as a fruitcake, for I was enjoying the feel of the wind and the motion of the snowshoes—Knees tight, hips loose, pick up the toe, and drag the tail.

There is a trite old saying, "Pride goeth before a fall." Swinging away from the tree-belt shelter into the wind funnel at Tanglefoot Curve I got the fall. Tanglefoot Curve was built to cross a steep little valley near the edge of the escarpment. All the relatively warm air from the lower elevations funneled through this gap and was compressed and spewed out in a jet. Winter and summer it was always the same. I knew it but became careless.

A dozen steps away from the trees that jet stream caught the toboggan and sent it hurtling by me, then hit me between the shoulder blades with a second blast— and I was facedown in the snow. The tail of one racquet was jammed in the webbing of the other and the sled rope was tangled in the whole mess. My pride and cockiness left with the wind that knocked me down.

Suddenly the sharp edge of panic became real. Breakfast was a cramp in my stomach and the hot bitter coffee came up with a taste of gall. Being frightened is one thing; being just plain scared is another. The instinct to survive told me to get up and beat a retreat to Cumbres and safety. But then I realized that there was so much snow, wind, and darkness that I didn't know in which direction safety lay.

Desperation generates strength, if not courage. When I finally had the webs untangled and was on my feet, I turned my back to the wind and started moving— and kept on moving. It was slow and rough. The tilt of the snowshoes told me I

was going downhill; the wind at my back pushed me along. After what seemed an eternity (actually it was about an hour) without knowledge of direction or distance, I ran into our telegraph wires. The snow was so deep they struck me across the chest. Holding one wire in my gloved hand as a guide, I kept moving and at last came to one of our high wooden snow fences and was able to orient myself.

I   I

Snowshoeing is never child's play, even on good snow when the weather is calm. On December 30 on Cumbres Pass the snow wasn't good and the weather wasn't calm. After making a few thousand snowshoe tracks in the snow, I left the snow fence and reached a point where there was supposed to be a telephone booth beside the tracks. At the time, there was only drifted snow, but using one of the webs as a shovel, I dug down and found the booth. Hearing the dispatcher's voice washed away all the lonesome and lost feelings.

Neither of us had much news. At Osier everyone was under cover waiting for a break in the storm. A couple of men had made it from milepost 331 to Cumbres and had reported that everyone was okay. Rotary OY was out of Alamosa heading west, and Rotary OM was being prepared at Chama awaiting the arrival of power and crews from Durango. We still didn't know where the 491 was, its situation, or the fate of Dalla and Lira. The phone booth was at milepost 323. If the 491 wasn't found in the next couple of miles we might have something more serious than an engine stuck in the snow. East of milepost 321 the rails are on a partly natural, partly man-made shelf high above the Los Pinos River. A derailment along this shelf could be catastrophic.

Between the phone booth and milepost 322 there was no engine. Now came the time of sweating out what was beyond each curve. One curve, two, three, four curves. The next one had to be the place or we really had something to worry about.

Rounding that last curve there was nothing to see but a smooth surface of snow extending unbroken from the low

Steadfastly plowing ahead, steam-powered Rotary OY chews through hard-crusted snow and blasts it into the cold Colorado air. The sweating bare-backed firemen inside heave coal into the hungry firebox as the stack erupts a steady stream of black smoke. *John Norwood*

hogback across where the track should be and into the valley. Dejection and a reluctance to pass this point slowed me down, and I guess I lowered my eyes a little.

The next thing I knew I was blind, coughing, and my face was being burned by something hot. Johnny Lira was throwing a scoop of hot ashes out and he didn't see me in time to stop his swing.

The 491 was completely buried in the drift at milepost 321. Dalla and Lira were tired, hungry, and sleepy, but at the bottom of the tunnel they had kept open for air, it was warm and dry.

Lira and Dalla told me their story.

Shortly after leaving Cumbres about 11 p.m. on December 28, they had noticed a low cloud moving down the valley of the Los Pinos River. They had seen a lot of these in the past and weren't disturbed. At milepost 327 they hit heavy snow. By the time they reached Los Pinos the fall was much heavier and the wind was a gale, but they kept moving.

Rounding the curve at milepost 321, they saw a wholly unexpected mountain of snow ahead of the engine, but before the brakes could stop them, they were into it, stalled and buried.

At that point they did the only logical thing for men without heavy clothing or food to do. They banked the fire, dug a ventilation shaft, closed the storm curtains, and settled down to wait for someone to come after them.

⚒   ⚒

The meal we cooked in Lira's scoop held over the coals in the firebox tasted better than a state dinner. The smoky-tasting coffee was better than a vintage wine. And it was heaven to strip off my wet clothes and stand before the firebox door and soak up heat while they dried. I learned then how Sam McGee must have felt when his partner cremated him on the marge of Lake Lebarge up in the Yukon.

Warmed through and dressed again, I left the pack of food with the two enginemen and took off for Osier. They would have to wait until I could return with heavy clothes and warm footwear before they left their cave in the snow.

If any sun had been shining so there could have been a sunset, I would have reached Osier at sundown. But there was no sun—only the low clouds and snow. But with dry clothes and a full belly the

Sometimes the rotary bites off more than it can chew. The discharge becomes plugged with heavy, soggy snow, and a man with a shovel has to clear it out. Two days later, mechanical problems forced Rotary OM to retreat for repairs. *John Norwood*

struggle from the buried engine to Osier was a breeze. I was stepping high and feeling high as I walked into the section-house. The two man-size slugs of Taos Lightning that Tom Cummins had been saving for medicinal purposes went down smoothly and then exploded like a Fourth of July in my bloodstream. I was *really* high, and feeling a lot different from when I was facedown in the snow about dawn.

During the night the soft, wet snow-flakes turned to ice pellets. The air was full of them, and they were being driven from the direction of the snowbound engine by a 50 mph wind. It was not humanly possible to face into that combination.

Near midafternoon the pellets turned to flakes once more and the wind lost part of its fierceness. I reached milepost 321 about dark, too late to try to get Dalla and Lira back to Osier that day. We ate a little and made preparations for morning.

At midnight we drank a toast of strong black coffee to the New Year of 1952. There was no steam to blow the whistle, but the wind helped us celebrate by supplying a screaming, howling uproar. During the first two hours of 1952 it blew a fury greater than anything that had gone before. Then came ear-splitting quietness and absolute calm. The only sound made by the storm was that of the feathery flakes of snow falling.

When a pale light in the east announced daybreak it was still calm and snowing. We made a last pot of coffee over the coals before we dumped the fire and drained the engine. Dalla and Lira didn't shed a single tear as we departed from milepost 321. No regrets or fond farewells were voiced by either—they just wanted to get going.

The trek from milepost 321 bordered on being anticlimactic. The recollection I have is one of plain hard work as I packed a snow trail for the two men behind me who were without snowshoes. I do remember vividly that about a half mile from the end of our trip I suffered a severe attack of *mal de racquet* [pain in

Only when the wing started scraping the rocks at the right did the crew realize that the rotary had derailed here. Rerailing was not a problem: The rotary was backed out and the wheels followed the flange marks in the ice and came back to the rails. *John Norwood*

feet and ankles caused by snowshoeing]. Stay off snowshoes and you will never experience *mal de racquet*—the most exquisite pain known to man. The only relief is to scream once in a while deep inside and to keep moving to a protected place where you can warm and knead the muscles in your calves.

We walked up to the door of the Osier sectionhouse at 10:10 a.m. on January 1, 1952. I untied the thongs of the snowshoes, stuck their tails in a snowdrift near the entrance, and right at that moment, didn't care whether I ever tied them on again.

In the meantime, Rotary OY out of Alamosa got to milepost 313 and stalled. A team of bulldozers made it as far as milepost 310 coming in overland and had to give up. Rotary OM opened the line east of Chama as far as Cresco, 5 miles west of the outfit in the slide at milepost 331. Shortly after noon the snow stopped at Osier, and a few patches of watery blue sky appeared. We immediately advised the Alamosa office of the apparent favorable weather change. A plane had been provisioned and was being held in readiness for this news. Ten minutes after our message was sent, the plane, piloted by Norman Kramer, one of the great mountain flyers, was in the air. The bombardier was a Rio Grande roadmaster.

Ten minutes after takeoff we heard the plane overhead and raced outdoors to watch the bombing and pick up the food to be dropped. Kramer and his plane came barreling in from the west through a hole in the clouds on his bombing run. Halfway to us the plane whipped over with the wings perpendicular, and big brown parcels of food spewed from the cab in door. Six bombs kicked up six craters as they hit the snow in a precise pattern.

Kramer leveled off, wagged his wings at us, and disappeared in the overcast. Minutes later Rotary OY at milepost 313 was being bombed, but under conditions much more hazardous than at Osier. Milepost 313 is in the canyon with the high rims about a mile apart. Kramer had to make his run by coming in on a steep dive from the south wall and pulling out before colliding with the north wall. Three such runs were necessary to drop the six bombs on Rotary OY. Accuracy was phenomenal. One bundle struck a tree above the cook car and slid downhill over the snow right through the open door. The cook picked up the sack, removed the protective padding, and started stowing away, the groceries. He was convinced this was the only way to have supplies delivered.

At Osier there was more jubilation. For the past 24 hours we had been on short rations consisting of unsalted, unseasoned frijoles and unsalted tortillas. We were drinking nothing stronger than hot water. Ordinarily frijoles and tortillas make prime food—if they are salted and seasoned. They don't when they aren't. The redeeming feature of tortillas is that the longer you chew them, the bigger the lump in your mouth becomes. By the time you finally swallow, your food intake has been considerably increased. Also, they're a long time in digesting.

The second day of the new year brought more blue sky and little or no wind. Kramer made two more drops of food to us at Osier. Rotary OY had moved from milepost 313 to milepost 315 and was out of the canyon. Kramer bombed them with more food too.

In midafternoon of the following day a detachment from the Army Mountain and Cold Weather Command, guided by our division water service supervisor, came in over the snow from the north. Their vehicles were two versatile DUKWUs— light sea landing craft that operated efficiently as snowcraft. They brought more food, but best of all, they gave us mobility less physically demanding than snowshoes.

As you find wherever there are soldiers, the DUKs were covered with graffiti. Among the wisecracks and bits of philosophy had been written in big letters: UNIT OF RAILWAY OPERATING BATTALION. RIDE AT YOUR OWN RISK.

We promptly took advantage of the DUK's and traded rested crews from Osier for tired men from Rotary OY. The trade was made about a mile east of Osier. The snow was so deep and packed that a hole was not to be bored through to Osier until late on January 4.

On the west side of Cumbres, Rotary OM had not been idle. All the marooned employees at milepost 331 were taken back to Chama on January 2. The next day all the stalled equipment was dug out of the slide and towed to Chama. The line west of Cumbres was ready for the OM to start plowing to a meet with the OY.

From the first light until after dark on January 5 at Osier we rerailed equipment— starting fires and getting up steam in the engines we had killed earlier—until we were ready to drop. On January 6 Rotary OM arrived at Cumbres at 10:05 a.m. and plowed a hole to the east end near the start of Tanglefoot Curve. Tunnels were dug to the doors and windows of the telegraph office, and an operator opened a point of communication. The OY working west from Osier reached milepost 321 and returned to Osier for the night.

On this date, too, the forces at Osier were counted and a selection was made of those who would remain. The rest were shuttled by DUKs to a highway head about 10 miles from Antonito. The only dissension in the ranks during this entire operation occurred while I was selecting the men who would be taken out on the DUKs. Dissension is too mild a word—it was open mutiny. Nobody, including Joe Dalla or Johnny Lira, wanted to go home.

The next day Rotary OM opened the line 2½ miles east of Cumbres, bucking deep, hard-packed snow all the way. The Osier group spent the day digging out around the 491. One pull was attempted near dark, but the dead engine would not budge. Condensation had formed ice in the cylinders and the pistons would not move. It was necessary to build fires around them to slowly heat the iron. A party in the charge of conductor George Andriko with engine 494 and a caboose was left to keep the fires burning properly during the night. The others returned to Osier for rest and water.

On January 8 Rotary OM had to return to Chama for repairs, more coal, and general reoutfitting. The two units of the Railway Operating Battalion made a round trip to the highway and shuttled in additional food. The OY spent the day redistributing the dwindling coal supply among engines and rotary. We dug nearly a carload of old weather-slacked coal from below the rotted stringers of an old coaling platform. A carload of coal is a lot of wheelbarrow loads, and it takes plenty of sweat and muscle to push that many loads up a snow ramp high enough to dump over the side of an engine tender.

One engine with a cook car ran to milepost 321 to relieve the group watching the fires and to do some more digging around the engine.

Word came back from the group at engine 491 that by morning the cylinders would be free of ice and ready to move. At daybreak we moved from Osier to release the dead engine from its cave in the snow. After arriving at the scene of operations, we cut off the cook car and bunk cars about 300 feet from the working face and tied them down with hand brakes.

The engine that was to make the pull moved to a coupling with the 491. The coupling was tried, and sand dried on a scoop in the firebox was spread on the rail behind the drivers. One final inspection was made to see that we hadn't overlooked anything and we were ready. No matter how careful you are, you can always overlook something. We didn't take into account how much work had been done around the 491 and that the fires which had melted the ice in the cylinders had to a degree warmed up a lot more metal. Neither did we take into account the skim of ice left on the rails about 100 feet east of the two engines. We surely never expected the 491 to come out of the snowbank as easily as she did.

This combination caused the only injury suffered by anyone during two weeks of hazardous work. At the same moment the 491 broke loose, the cook lifted a 5-gallon pot of boiling-hot frijoles from the stove to move to another location. The tow engine came onto the skim of ice; the engineman felt what was happening and set the brakes. The two engines didn't slow the least bit—until they came to the cook car.

The first sound heard after the bang of couplers coming together hard was a series of squawks, howls, and Mexican cuss words—all indicating pain. Came the coupling and the cook lost his balance— and his hold on the pot of hot beans. Beans and man for an instant were airborne. The beans, with a slab of salt pork in them, landed first. Next, the cook made

The fight is over, and on January 12, a train from Chama picks up the cripples and cleans the line. During the height of the storm on December 30, the author crossed the 408-foot-long, 115-foot-high bridge at milepost 319.98 on his hands and knees. *John Norwood*

a perfect two-point sitdown on the pork. The toboggan ride across the floor mounted on the hot, greasy slab of pork through the wash of hotter beans unfortunately was solo. No photographs or tape recordings are in existence to pass down to posterity.

For several days afterward at least we could say that we had the most upright cook anywhere. He couldn't bear to sit down, and what little sleeping he did was on his stomach.

We ate lunch at milepost 321—without beans—and 2 hours later we had the 491 sitting on a spur at Osier.

Rotary OM almost made it to Los Pinos, but it had a breakdown, and the crew reported that they would return to Chama for repairs at daybreak.

The return to Chama was uneventful, and repairs were made rapidly. The OM headed east again at 3:45 p.m. During this time the OY opened the drift at milepost 321 and worked on west.

At 8:15 p.m. on January 10, two ugly brutes covered with snow, icicles, and cinders stood side by side at Los Pinos. Cumbres Pass was open, and those two dirty hunks of iron and wood pushed by a bunch of mountainbred railroaders once again had kicked the Hill in the teeth. We weren't foolish enough to have any notions that it was the last round for the winter.

Just before midnight on January 12 we had moved all the equipment—including the dead 491 and Rotary OM, which was by now completely inoperative—to Alamosa. The men went home to get

reacquainted with their families. The OY outfit was spotted for resupplying and for steaming off the icicles and snow. The OM went into the backshop for heavy repairs.

Up around the top of the world, where storms are conceived and born, a second generation was in the making. The birth came on January 17. The baby was a big, sprawling, brawling brat, meaner and trickier than the one we had just put to bed.

The snowbirds flocked to the now clean and resupplied Rotary OY and headed back for another round with the Hill, that bitch. It took us until February 1 to hogtie her and to show her who was boss.

But that is another story.

Once upon a time the Jersey Central was a proud and prosperous railroad.

But no more

THE OBJECTIVE WAS TO CLEAN FLUES AND WASH BOILERS

Richard D. Johnson

To participate in the last days of steam on the Pittsburgh & Lake Erie was a rare privilege, exciting in a way that nothing else can ever be.

It was, on occasion, extremely hard work. But it was fun. My god, it was fun.

To roundhouse veterans, a young boilermaker helper ranks little higher than an atheist at a Sunday School picnic. Perhaps it is not odd for that thought to cross my mind as long-idle brain cells stir, recalling an all-too-brief period in a relatively short railroad career.

The time ended in the late spring of 1952; it began, as I remember, in the fall of '49 when I became a railroader—a boilermaker helper on the third trick (11 p.m. to 7 a.m.) at the Pittsburgh & Lake Erie's Youngstown (Ohio)—actually, East Youngstown—roundhouse.

Lucky, lucky me. The pay? A rich $1.72 per hour, with time and a half for overtime. The money was enough to pay my college tuition and living expenses; the work was tiring enough to cause me regularly to sleep through an 8 a.m. history class.

There was a lot of steam power: the sleek, powerful 9400s, just a few years old; two veteran archtubeless "teakettles" circa 1890; a seemingly illimitable supply of the husky J3-class 8-wheel switchers to handle the heavy car movements in Youngstown-area steel mills; and an occasional visiting New York Central Hudson, usually complete with dented, twisted tender water scoops. The steam locomotives were beautiful in a gargantuan sort of way. But even more beautiful was the roundhouse, all 22 stalls, with its pits, pipes, valves, and gigantic doors.

And the people. I was the youngest (17 years old), smallest (5' 6", 130 pounds) on the third-trick crew. The majority of the 25 or 30 on the night shift were old-timers—big men mostly: boilermakers, pipefitters, machinists, and electricians. They were men who enjoyed their work in *their* roundhouse, men such as boilermaker Tom Tacovich. He saved my life one night.

Tom was one of the senior men who could have worked days, but he, as the other old-timers, liked the night. He lived in New Castle, just across the state line in Pennsylvania. He commuted on any Baltimore & Ohio or P&LE train headed from New Castle toward Youngstown. When the train made a required safety stop at the always busy Center Street crossing, Tom would jump off, then hike the mile or so to the roundhouse.

On this particular night, a locomotive with ashes and fire dumped, but still under steam pressure, had moved into stall 4 (or was it 5?). Tom and I climbed to the cab, opened the firebox door to check the grates, the arch brick, the flue sheets, and the rest of the firebox. We could not close the grates. Upon looking inside we saw a huge "cinderblock" of coals against the rear firebox wall. I volunteered to take a coal pick, squirm into the firebox, break up the cinders, and knock them through the grates so we could get on with our work.

In the blacksmith or forge shop, heavy machinery was required to make and repair rods and other steam locomotive components. *Jay Williams collection*

I climbed over the 4-foot-wide pile and began to chip away with the coal pick. It was like waking a sleeping dragon—the coals burst into flame.

There I was—inside a locomotive firebox where it was (as I once measured) nearly 200 degrees Centigrade. Between me and the only way out was a wall of fire, about 8 feet wide and 4 feet deep, and a 2-foot-high pile of, by this time, red-hot coals.

The oxygen must have been burning up fast. It was damn hot. Maybe hell-hot. Tom yelled, "Get out of there, Reverend (my nickname because at the time I was studying to become a United Presbyterian preacher)!"

I replied, "I can't. I can't even see."

He swore. Loudly. "Hurry, damn it, hurry. Dive for the door or you won't be able to do any goddam thing ever." I dived, hit my head on the edge of the opening, and passed out or knocked myself out.

I woke up on the cab floor. Others told me how Tom had crawled halfway through the flames to grab my arms and pull me out. Thanks, Tom. Thanks.

I remember too Tom's regular helper, George "Happy" Harris, a wild Irishman who loved his Irish whiskey. (When he drank too much and didn't make it to work that usually meant a sixth workday for me at $2.85 per hour.)

My first night on the job, Happy came up to me. He was dressed in the customary soot-filled coveralls of a boiler repair crew; I was in my new Oshkosh B'Gosh outfit. He asked, "Are you Johnson?" After I nodded, Happy said, "Michaels [the foreman] wants you to take that hose and fill up the tank of 4207."

I grappled with the hose—about 6 inches in diameter and about 40 feet long, as I recall, and made of the heaviest rubber in the world. I dragged it, all 250 pounds or so of it, from stall 2 to stall 22 and back looking for No. 4207. The locomotive was not there, anywhere. I did see it several nights later—and when I did, my attitude toward Happy was anything but. No. 4207 was one of the P&LE's few diesels! A garden hose would have handled its water supply.

But Happy wasn't finished with his jokes. Another one took place at Christmastime. Boilermaker Guy Mazzocco had brought some of his homemade sausage. Helper "Big Phillip" Zunek had brought some of his own "Dago red" wine. Tony Mazzaro brought sauerkraut. Others brought other roundhouse Christmas-party delicacies—Italian bread, pickles, pickled peppers, ham. And Happy smuggled in his Irish whiskey.

We always had coffee (ever since I've been a heavy coffee drinker). Happy offered me a cup. It was good—and different. I took a second—and perhaps even a third—swallow before I realized that the cup was half filled with Happy's whiskey.

For me to re-create the effect on my then rather prudish Presbyterian principles is difficult, but now I wish I could enjoy a cup of the best Irish coffee with my once fellow boilermaker helper, Happy Harris.

⌐ ⌐

Big Phillip Zunek was big—about 6' 6" tall, maybe 300 pounds, maybe even

350—and a wonderfully friendly Croatian. One night an over-the-cab-window grab iron had broken. In those days, all locomotive grab irons had to be forge-repaired. Tom Tacovich got this job. He, Big Phillip, and I headed for the blacksmith shop at the "cold" end of the roundhouse (the higher numbered stalls). Tom got the forge hot. I still remember pumping the bellows. Tom heated the two grab iron pieces, transferred them to the anvil, and held them and, in turn, the shaping dies. "Hit it, Big Phillip!" he shouted, and the roundhouse echoed the resulting clang. "Hit it, Reverend!" he yelled at me. And my tremendous 8-pound sledge rang out—*ting*—through at least a 6-foot radius. That's the way it was for the next 15 or 20 minutes: CLANG … *ting* … CLANG … *ting* … CLANG … *ting*. Unforgettable.

⌐ ⌐

Back to the locomotives. This time it was an NYC Hudson (does No. 5455 sound right?). It had developed a steam failure with a honeycomb-covered flue sheet and flues plugged solid. Two helpers were assigned the task of getting her ready for a New York Central Ashtabula-bound passenger train in the morning. Len Matarazzo, who worked in the roundhouse only that winter because the next summer he became a pitcher on a Pittsburgh Pirate farm club, was one of the helpers; I was the other. Jim "Peanuts" Panozzo, a veteran boilermaker temporarily promoted to inspector, was to check our work.

And work we did: first with coal picks to break up the honeycomb; then with air through the long ¾-inch pipe, then through the shorter ½-inch pipe, to blow out the flues. We blew flues in the cold firebox until we felt as cold as the steel. Then we went to a pot-bellied stove to get warm. Back to the flues. To the stove. To the flues again.

At 6:30 a.m. we replaced the arch brick and announced, "She's ready." Peanuts checked our work and signed the release slip, and almost within seconds a new fire was blazing. In 20 minutes, steam was up. Promptly at 7 a hostler backed the black beauty onto the turntable.

Len and I cheered.

That night we returned. And so did our Hudson. She had failed about 10 miles north of Youngstown. She had limped away from the train and could only inch her way south to our roundhouse while a P&LE diesel whisked the passengers northward about 2½ hours late.

Len and I damn near cried; but we got the Hudson out the next morning—the last time I ever saw her. Perhaps she wound up at McKees Rocks, a challenge to the laggards there.

⌐ ⌐

At the cold end of the roundhouse "dead" locomotives were inspected and repaired. They were given special inspections at 30- and 60-day intervals.

A boilermaker helper often worked alone at the cold end, usually at one of two jobs: cleaning flues, or washing boilers. The objective each night was to clean the flues on two of the J3 switchers or wash the boilers on two. And there were J3 switchers always, everywhere. The first time I was assigned to this job, I barely got the arch brick down before quitting time. In a few days, though, I could completely finish two flue-cleaning jobs a night. Getting to the point where I could finish the two boiler washings in one night took longer because of the heavy, awkward hose—the same type I had dragged while looking for No. 4207.

After two or three weeks, I became almost as proficient as some of the other men at flue cleaning: knock down the bricks with the long pipe; use the pipe as a hammer to pound the honeycomb loose; let the air blow into each flue until you hear the loud whoosh that means it is open; and when you don't hear the whoosh, climb into the firebox with the short pipe, slide it into the troublesome flue, turn on the air, stand there while more soot than any chimney sweep ever saw comes blowing back at your face—until each flue is drawing.

Two locomotives. The inspection. Eventually I could clean flues on a switch engine in an hour (one of the tall-stacked teakettles would take only a half hour).

When my two were done for the night, often before 1 a.m., I would find some dimly lit corner and study, usually ancient Greek, but sometimes for an exam. Occasionally I would sleep—on a two-by-four with one end propped at the firebox door, the other end on the grates at the flue sheet. A large handful of waste made a good pillow, and the bedroom certainly was private. One time I overslept—until about 10:30 a.m. The day-shift guys, if they ever think about it, probably still are laughing.

Most of the nighttime action at the roundhouse, however, was at the hot end. There the hostlers kept the locomotives shuttling in for repairs as required and out for return to service.

The inspection pit was a half mile or so north of the roundhouse. There, too, was a boiler blowout station, manned by a boilermaker helper. We would connect the pipe, then turn the valves and blow the sediment out of boilers of locomotives that had been standing idle for several hours. I still do not know whether I ever handled the job properly. I never exploded any boilers, though, and the cab of a fired-up locomotive was a great place to stay warm on a cold winter night—a hell of a lot warmer than the roundhouse.

One other task at the blowout station was throwing six cakes of water-softening compound into each tank. Each night the roundhouse stores clerk would send up two or three cases of the compound on the front step of a switcher. Now and then the compound actually got tossed into a tender's water hatch. More often, especially during the winter, the two or three cases of water softener were thrown into a gondola headed for Republic Steel or Youngstown Sheet & Tube … or maybe into an empty hopper car bound for Connellsville for coal.

I   I

There are other stories too: of cross-country train trips, possible only because obliging conductors honored my P&LE annual pass, received after one year's service … of the night Russell (I've forgotten his first—or his last—name), the roundhouse foreman, caught me playing pinochle with the powerhouse stationary engineer and his fireman … of the

Chalk markings indicate problems that need to be fixed. This is a Pennsylvania Railroad I-1 (2-10-0) in the roundhouse at Renovo, Pa. *Philip R. Hastings*

night I reported nearly 4 hours late and was docked only a half hour … or of the night three boozed-up experts from safety came to explain why a boiler had exploded at Newton, Kans., on the Santa Fe 3 or 4 or 5 years earlier … or of prossering leaking flues … or of the time we were snowed in for 2½ days … or of the day President Harry Truman ordered the Army to take over the railroads … or of a union meeting discussion when the union shop became the rule … or of watching at dawn a B&O Mallet with a Vanderbilt tank pull a long iron-ore drag upgrade across the way … or of the simple but strong feeling when you saw a locomotive you had worked on starting out of the

yard with a long string of ore-laden hoppers for the Pittsburgh steel district.

And other stories of other days on other railroads…

But to me the beginning of railroads was not the *Rocket* or the *Best Friend of Charleston*—rather it was the last days of steam on the Pittsburgh & Lake Erie … the days immediately preceding Gateway Yard … the day I became a railroadman. And it was the marvelous men who kept those locomotives running—the men on the third trick. I am fortunate to have been one of them for a while.

September 1973

What Happened When an Ex-Flyboy Went Railroading in the Blue Mountains

James E. Satterfield

Sometimes I wonder how the old Oregon Trail pioneers felt as they neared the eastern approaches to the Blue Mountains of Oregon.

Perhaps it was with dull resignation of another mountain range to cross after months on the trail. At this stage of their journey little doubt could have existed that their mules and oxen were exhausted and their supplies were at the vanishing point. Their last rest and supply point probably had been Fort Hall on the banks of the Snake River in Idaho, some 400 miles behind them. Perhaps they were elated at merely being in Oregon, knowing they had little farther to go on their long journey. In any event, the task ahead of them was formidable, and as they camped on the sage-studded flatland near the present city of La Grande, they must have pondered how to conquer the narrow gorge of the Grande Ronde river, through which lay their route over the mountains.

Little did these hardy pioneers know that in the not too distant future the surveyors of the Oregon Short Line would be pondering many of the same questions in an effort to lay steel rails over the mountains to connect with the Oregon Railway & Navigation Company line at Pendleton. Where the pioneers went, so

went civilization in the form of twin ribbons of steel. In this historical setting did I first have direct access to the mysteries of steam railroading, mountain style. The experience was enlightening.

I I

My job with the Union Pacific was not a planned one. My intent was to fly airliners. Had it not been for the blandishments of an attractive redhead (who here shall remain unnamed) who for some reason was interested in my company, the interlude might not have happened at all. In late October 1945 I, along with some 2,000 other members of the Army Air Corps, was sweating it out at Walla Walla Air Base in Washington. The war was over, and we wanted out. The Army bureaucracy was overwhelmed with requests for discharges. A point quota system had been set up based on length of service, time overseas, and other criteria, and as a result, I was among the first to be released.

My initial act was to race to Seattle to place my application for an airline job. I was fortunate in my undertaking and was

The Union Pacific's 3500-class 2-8-8-0s were often found lugging freights in the Blue Mountains. Here, No. 3532 pulls 70 cars of an extra freight upgrade west of La Grande, Ore., in July 1948. *Henry R. Griffiths Jr.*

told that I would be accepted and would be notified when, and if, my services were required. Satisfied with this tentative acceptance, I mounted my 1941 Mercury coupe and with carefully garnered gas coupons started homeward to visit my parents in West Virginia.

On the following day, I found myself in the town of La Grande in eastern Oregon. La Grande looked like a railroad town—a couple of hotels and the usual main street with an occasional spiritual oasis with a name such as Railroad Inn or Switchman's Shanty. I was tired from my drive from Seattle, and I took a room at the local hostelry. After ablutions and a sandwich, I wandered down to the depot for a look at the trains. The first order of business was to read the trainboard. I checked the list and found that No. 17, the *Portland Rose*, was due in about 10 minutes, or 20 minutes if the message in chalk which read "10 minutes late" was to be taken seriously.

As I wandered down the platform, I noted the extensive yards and the back-shop at La Grande. This evidently was a place where considerable rail activity occurred. My thoughts were interrupted

by the sound of an engine coming fast, whistling for the yard. Five minutes later a giant of a locomotive, wearing the number 3939 and pulling 15 heavyweight head-end and passenger cars, drifted to a halt in front of the depot. It had no more than stopped when dozens of figures—or so it seemed—leaped from the shadows and placed blue lights and flags up and down the train. I looked again at the engine, whose blower sound was loud in the evening air. I could not recall seeing an engine so huge on a passenger train.

I spotted an individual who appeared to be a railroadman and inquired why what seemed to be a freight engine was pulling a passenger train. He advised me in short order: "That ain't just any engine, that's a Challenger." I didn't know exactly what a Challenger was. The engine had all the marks of a simple articulated similar to those that pulled coal in West Virginia. True, the drivers seemed a little larger and the train was a heavy load for the likes of a Pacific. Sensing my puzzlement, my friend of short acquaintance allowed that this machine was a dual-purpose engine, but on this division, it was used only to haul heavy passenger trains. The Challenger

was put on at Huntington, and it would run all the way to Rieth (wherever that was). He told me that it could pull those 15 heavyweight cars without a helper from the east to La Grande, and that was why it was used as a passenger engine. From La Grande west to the top of the hill at Meacham, it would need help. In confirmation of my friend's statements, a few moments later a big-barreled Mikado eased gently through the crossover, and with an imperceptible bump, it attached itself to the front of the train. One by one the blue markers came down, and the conductor herded 8 or 10 passengers aboard. The blowers on the two engines were wide open when the highball came.

As the markers passed me on the platform, the shrieking of the blower had become a deep-throated roar as though the reverse lever were full forward. In the space of 200 yards the train appeared to be racing toward the mountains. "Do they often leave town like that?" I asked my newfound friend. "They have to," came the reply. My friend noted that to the west were about 2 miles of level track and then a sharp curve to where the grade started at Hilgard. A fast departure was in order if a train was to best the 11 miles of 2.2 percent grade facing it to the top of the Blue Mountains. I was pleased at having witnessed such a sight, and I departed La Grande depot with the thought of sleep and an early morning departure for points east. Such was not to be the case.

᛫   ᛫

As I wandered the short block from the depot to the hotel, I noted an oasis of sorts across the street. Perhaps a nightcap would be a good idea. I entered a darkened room which had a long mahogany bar complete with mirror and pseudo gaslights. To the left were booths in which couples nuzzled contentedly. To the chagrin of my teetotaling fundamentalist parents, I had developed the habit during the war of tasting the grape upon occasion, and this seemed an appropriate place. Unfortunately, the waitress advised, in Oregon one could not simply partake as one might wish. Spirits, like almost everything else during the time, were rationed. A ration card, which was good for the purchase of one bottle every other week, must be secured. Then one had to bring his bottle to his favorite pub; the bottle was labeled with his name and was placed in a rack. Then he could ask for his bottle, pay for whatever service he required, and his beverage would be served.

On this occasion, the barmaid felt pity for me—perhaps because I still was wearing a uniform—and she told me that she would see what she could do to ease my pain. She deftly removed one of the bottles from the rack, poured some of its contents into a glass, then quickly filled the glass with Coke. After this operation she walked back to my table and placed the bracing tonic before this tired veteran. This revelation was to stand me in good stead in future months. I can only surmise how many of the local railroad population found their bottles short of spirits because of a friendly barmaid. After I left the Union Pacific and La Grande I often wondered how much of my spirits went

down the gullet of some undeserving brakeman who had learned my secret of survival.

While I was enjoying the comforts of the oasis, who should walk through the door but two recent compatriots from the Air Force. They were still in service at Walla Walla Army Air Base 120 miles away, and in their weekend meanderings, they had found La Grande. I deduced from their conversation that they did not care how long their discharges were delayed as long as they could come to La Grande on weekends. This news raised doubts in my mind as to their sanity, since the classification of La Grande as a swinging place was not justified from what I had seen thus far. I was wrong.

La Grande, I was to learn, was an unusual town. My buddies relayed the facts that, first, an all-girl school was located here; second, half the male population was still in service; and third, all the local railroaders were working 16 hours a day. As a consequence there were five girls for every eligible male. In addition, with the exception of Walla Walla, no Army or Navy bases were close. Many years had passed since I had found such favorable odds, and when my friends suggested they might be able to find me some interesting companionship, the thought of sleep after my tiring drive faded from my mind. Perhaps I should have forgone the offer, since the events of this night were to have a profound influence on my becoming a railroader.

᛫   ᛫

The evening was a huge success. Release from the Air Corps after 4½ years, plus the company of a receptive redhead, had its effect. At the local melting pot 2½ miles south of La Grande, we kept the jukebox warm with a never-ending supply of nickels (that was all it cost then). For those of us who remember, that was the day of the big bands, and most of the tunes were sweet and low. One could clasp the opposite sex in a smooth-flowing intimacy scarcely equaled today. Hard rock, had it then been in vogue, would not have led me the next morning to the door of the UP hiring office in La Grande. My lovely had turned out to be the daughter of a railroader, and she whispered in my ear that it might be possible for me to

make as much as $1,000 a month on the extra board. The experience was heady for a boy from the hills whose knowledge of girls had been severely limited. I reasoned that while I was waiting for my airline job I might as well make money in a place where my talents were appreciated by the important elements of the community.

The alacrity with which I was accepted as a student fireman surprised me. I filled out an application, received a timetable and a book of rules, and was told to get a railroad watch. The acquisition of a railroad watch in 1945 probably was the most difficult problem encountered in getting a rail job. However lucrative the trade was for the one local horologist, he could not provide a new watch or even one of moderate vintage. I was told it would take six months or longer to acquire a new Hamilton, but if I would take a used watch, he would place my order. From under the counter he brought forth something resembling a large cigar box in which rested the most outlandish collection of timepieces this side of the Smithsonian Institution. I was assured that all had been repaired and serviced and were guaranteed to be as accurate as the Naval Observatory. From the box the jeweler selected a diadem with an ornate elk etched on the front cover and a gargoyle-like steam locomotive on the back. The back opened to an inscription which read, "To Charles from Harriet, Christmas, 1912." The timepiece had huge Roman numerals and was as big as an orange. It must have weighed at least a half pound.

After paying $35—which I was assured would be applied to a new watch if one ever came—for the used watch, I learned that if one has a railroad watch one must have a chain to carry the watch. Nothing less than a 24-carat gold chain would do credit to my new Hamilton. Another $10 took care of the chain. After having paid two weeks in advance for my room at the hotel, plus my expenditures on the redhead, I realized the wisdom of my working for the Union Pacific as quickly as possible. After writing a brief note to the airline to inform them of my whereabouts and a postcard to my parents, I set about learning railroading firsthand.

After being discharged from the Army Air Corps, the author stopped in La Grande, where he stayed for several months. This photo shows downtown La Grande in the 1940s, as it looked about the time the author lived there. *Trains magazine collection*

The Union Pacific was a generous railroad—or perhaps it just needed help desperately—for it paid you while you were cubbing the road. It was necessary to learn from one end to the other that part of the road on which you were to work. This meant going both east and west out of La Grande. Our territory extended west over the crest of the Blue Mountains to Rieth, just west of Pendleton. To the east the territory ended at Huntington. My first trip was from La Grande to Huntington. Although from the cab of a simple articulated it appeared to me that we were heading south, I was quickly informed we were eastbound. As an aviator I always had assumed that to go east was to point oneself toward the rising run or until the compass read east. I knew Union Pacific trains usually wound up in Omaha, which was to the east; so as the fireman said, we must be going east.

My first trip was spent riding and observing. I deadheaded back to La Grande, and the next day I went west on a time freight to Rieth. For a week this procedure went on as the firemen tried to

explain to me the intricacies of firing a 3500-class simple articulated. First you hosed down the cab to make it clean. Next you checked for leaks in the tank. Then you went back to the cab to check the oil measuring stick on the front end of the tank to see if the hostler had filled her up. Next you made sure that your sand scoop was handy and that you had sand in a small box behind the fireman's seat. Next you ascertained that the atomizer at the rear of the firebox was operating properly. Then came the injector and the feedwater pump. Then the blower, the engine generator, and the running lights. Finally, after checking water levels, you climbed up the front of the engine to put up the flags and the markers. Most of the time these flags were white and the train bore the number of the engine preceded by an X, denoting an extra. After you climbed out on the running boards and checked the sand domes and the lines, the preliminaries were over, and if everything was in order, you were ready to go. At first firing one of these monster 2-8-8-0s did not seem difficult, but soon I was to learn that each engine had an individual

temperament and that the delicate balance between steam pressure and water level in the boiler was not easy to achieve. One consolation was that these engines were oil fired and the fireman did not have to shovel coal all day.

My first lesson came on Extra 3553 West. As I climbed aboard the engine on the ready track I was greeted by a gruff character who was to be my instructor. I could tell that he was not overjoyed to have a greenhorn on the trip. After checking over the engine I was full of confidence and set to go.

The engineer stepped aboard and his first question inquired if I had heated the oil. This was a new one. I had visions of building a fire under the tender, since there was no obvious way of heating the oil. Furthermore, the need to heat the oil escaped me. Sensing my confusion, the fireman instructor placed his hand upon a valve and said, "This is the way you heat the oil. This is a high-pressure steam line from the boiler to the tank. When you turn it on a jet of high-pressure steam is forced through the oil, warming it up." I turned the valve and heard a hissing, gurgling sound from the environs of the tank. Sensing my further confusion, my instructor noted that in wintertime the bunker C oil got thick and would not flow properly through the atomizer unless it was kept warm. To thin the oil one juiced it periodically with a little hot steam.

I next learned that nothing moves as long as one blue flag or blue light (at night) is on the train. Workmen might be anywhere on or under the train. After the blue lights and flags had been removed, the conductor highballed, and the fun began. The first order of business was to have our massive steed hot and ready to go. "Turn the blower on and shoot the oil to her," said my fireman instructor. "And don't let her pop." The pressure gauge hovered around 250 pounds and edged up as the engineer eased the Johnson bar to full forward. Eying the gauge, I reached for the injector lever to keep her from popping. "Don't do that!" came a shout. "He'll pull it out from under you."

"Who will pull what?" I asked.

"The engineer when he opens her up," came the reply. As our train eased out of the yard the engineer pulled the throttle almost full out, and the stack became a blast. The three other articulateds on the train took up the rhythm. All sound was blotted out by the roar as the heavy train accelerated. Slowly we gained momentum, and just as slowly the steam pressure began to drop. "Pour some more oil to her, and shut off that damn blower!" shouted the fireman. "See that black string on the oil lever?" he asked as a finger pointed to black twine wrapped around the oil lever quadrant. "Now!" yelled the fireman.

"Now what?" I inquired.

"Hit the injector, you idiot—and when she gets water into the boiler turn on the feedwater pump." Gurgling noises came from the boiler. The fire was a raging inferno and the steam pressure climbed back to 250 pounds. I turned the feedwater valve to a position marked by a red string, and the situation looked stable enough for me to relax a bit. I was elated. I had achieved success.

Then it happened. The engineer shoved the throttle to full closed and started fiddling with the brake levers. Black smoke rolled out of the firedoor, filling the cab and blocking all vision. "What's he doing?" I screamed.

"Turn on the blower, you dodo, and cut the oil."

"What's happening?" came my anguished wail as I grabbed for the blower.

"He's making a running brake test. Watch it—he's gonna open her up again." The engineer widened the throttle, and the steady roar of the exhaust blotted out all but hand signals. It was a nightmare. This poor novice was still struggling as the 80-car train pounded through the curve at Hilgard and struck the long 2.2 percent grade of the Blue Mountains.

As we met the ascending grade, the situation stabilized. The engines steadied to a slow rhythmic beat. All went fine until the gauge reading began to drop. A voice from behind said, "Sand the flues."

"Sand the who?" I asked.

"The flues, dum-dum." The fireman grabbed the sugar scoop, dipped into the sandbox behind the fireman's seat, and threw a scoop of sand into the firebox. Black clouds erupted from the stack. "That cleans the soot out," said my now irritated instructor. The engineer, casting a beady eye in my direction, asked if I had been one of the pilots who had fought in the war. I replied in the affirmative, hoping to regain some prestige. His reply did not help my sagging morale—he indicated that it was no wonder we had taken four years to whip the Germans.

After the flue episode I was thoroughly chagrined. Upon reaching Meacham, the fireman said he would take her on into Rieth and I could watch. Once we were on the ground at Rieth, my instructor became benevolent. He said I hadn't done too badly considering this was my first time. We grabbed our overnight bags, rode the switch engine back to the Pendleton station, and stayed in the old station hotel. The callboy roused us at an ungodly hour—4 a.m., I believe—for an extra turn back to La Grande. The job was a little easier on the way back, but more was to come before this novice mastered the art of firing.

ɪ   ɪ

A day later I was on a local freight headed east toward Huntington. I found that working a local was a long and

tiresome task—not quite as bad as some of the helper jobs on the east end but a job that, with all the starting, stopping, shifting, and reassembling of the train after picking up and depositing cars en route, kept the fireman busy. South from La Grande, the Union Pacific line was fairly level for a number of miles. Our first chore on this day was to drop two tank cars at a junction a few miles south of the La Grande yard. A pair of rusty rails meandered from the main line toward a little town in the distance. I learned from the engineer that the town was Union and that the rails were of a company apart from the Union Pacific. He called it the dummy line. Union, an old settlement on the Oregon Trail, had been bypassed by a few miles when the railroad came through. To connect with the railroad, Union built its own line, the Union Railroad of Oregon. An old four-coupled engine, referred to as the dummy, had done the work. It was retired but still was stored in a one-stall engine shed at Union. The work was handled by a small diesel locomotive bought second-hand from a lumber company. Three cars were its maximum load, and if more were on hand, two or three trips were necessary.

At the southern end of the Wallowa plain we began our mountain railroading again and picked up a helper for the climb to Telocaset. Here I got into trouble once more. My instructor had been patient to this point; seemingly he had found little fault with my firing. Our helper—another 3500 series articulated—coupled onto the rear, and we whistled off and started our climb. I had her hot, and everything was going well. The steam gauge indicated a steady 250 pounds. As the water in the glass sank lower and lower, I reached for the injector. I eased the feedwater pump on and was relieved to see the water climb perceptibly. I had been told to keep the water at about the three-quarter level or else. Nobody had explained what the "or else" meant. As we pounded uphill the pressure began to drop—240, then 230, then 220. "Ease off on the water," I was told. I turned off the feedwater pump and the pressure rose as the water level dropped. "Turn on the feedwater," came the voice. Again the pressure started to drop at an alarming rate. "Turn off the damn water," came a surly voice, apparently exasperated that I could not balance the two opposing items, cold water and steam. I was desperate. The glass was below one-half and the stream pressure was around 180 pounds. "What are you trying to do, burn the crownsheet?"

"What's a crownsheet?" was my question, barely audible above the roar of the exhaust and the clanking side rods. "Never mind, give me the damn thing!" my now impatient instructor cried. He shoved me from the seat. Things had gone too far now, and the fireman fought to keep enough steam and water in the engine. Finally we topped the hill at Telocaset, much to my relief and apparently much to the relief of the fireman.

That was only the beginning of my fights with the steam monsters, but after several trips I managed to master most of the intricacies of keeping a big articulated steaming in reasonably good fashion.

Next I took a trip on the Enterprise Branch, which runs east from La Grande in a great arc to the towns of Elgin, Enterprise, and Joseph. Our engine was a light Pacific of the 3100 series. The 60- and 80-pound rail precluded using heavy engines on the branch, although lighter Consolidations and heavier Mikes had been used at times if the traffic warranted them. The Pacific normally could handle with little trouble the 8 or 10 freight cars and a combination car on the daily mixed. Because the branch was almost entirely on the floor of the Wallowa Valley, there were few grades with which to contend. After working on the branch I was pronounced ready for the extra board.

Ex-flyboy Satterfield learned firing on UP 2-8-8-0 simple articulateds such as these. Near Pleasant Valley, No. 3530 is on the point of 64-car time freight 655, doing 20 mph with helper 3551 on the rear. *Henry R. Griffiths Jr.*

ɪ   ɪ

When we novices were on the extra board, we usually were assigned to time freights, extras, or helper turns in either direction out of La Grande. (All passenger runs were held down by old-timers with seniority.) Most of our time was spent riding herd on the massive 3500 series articulated engines.

Sometimes helper turns out of La Grande were short and pleasant. Other times they were a dreary 16 hours, much of which was spent in some desolate siding such as North Powder, Haines, or Durkee. Westbound trains usually consisted of about 80 cars and required four engines. The road engine always was a big articulated, and usually a Mike was helper up front. A second articulated was cut in midway in the train, and another articulated brought up the rear behind the caboose. If you caught the Mike or the helper in the center of the train you had to go all the way to Rieth with the train. The tail-end helper dropped off at Kamela, turned on the wye, and returned to La Grande. This was the job we unattached men wanted to catch because we would be back in town in about 5 or 6 hours and thus have more time for those interests which prompted us to start railroading here in the first place. Because of the dearth of men, our charming friends kept close check on the comings and goings of the single men on the extra board, and our return usually was well known before we hit the yard limit. As a consequence—especially if we had been

out for 16 hours we had little time for rest, and in all probability at the end of our 8-hour rest period the callboy would phone or would rouse us from badly needed sleep. We were young, however, and our occasional bending of Rule G while we were off duty seemed not to bother the Union Pacific too much.

Deadheading was an ordeal during that winter of 1945-1946. Most trains ran in sections, and the *Portland Rose* often ran in as many as four sections. This train was an anathema to us when we were trying to make time over the road with a freight. We could go in the hole at a place such as Lime, just a few miles from our terminal at Huntington, and see what seemed to be a never-ending string of passenger trains bearing green flags. When we were forced to deadhead, it was not unusual for us to stand all the way from Pendleton or Huntington to La Grande because every seat was occupied and people filled the vestibules. Unless we wanted to get back in a hurry we tried to avoid deadheading, but often we were caught by the 16-hour law and had little choice.

No one was allowed to deadhead on the streamliner *City of Portland*, which incidentally was the only diesel-powered train on the line at that time. It passed through La Grande during the wee hours in either direction, so my infrequent glimpses of the flagship were a treat. My first sighting came after we went in the hole with an extra somewhere west of Kamela. Stopping an 80-car train on the downgrade was a chore. The reason for retaining more than one engine on the descent from Kamela to Pendleton became clear as I viewed the cherry-red brake shoes during a night stop on the hill. Not long after we cleared the main we heard the distinctive burbling of the *City* as it fought upgrade. The *City of Portland* was scheduled to make the 74.2 miles between Pendleton and La Grande in 2 hours 9 minutes. This was an average of something like 35 mph over a stretch of mountain railroad that we often spent 6 to 8 hours covering in a time freight or extra. And we always exceeded the timecard schedule.

Although I had watched the operations of the Baltimore & Ohio in West Virginia during my youth, I was almost totally unaware of the many problems confronting the railroad in mountain operations. Retainer valves were a mystery to me. Their use was a necessity going in both directions from La Grande. I was curious the first time my train was stopped on the downgrade on the main line. I thought we had developed a hotbox or the train line had broken. The purpose of the stop merely was to cool the brakes and the wheels. The brakeman's task, which entailed skittering from car to car to turn up the retainers on every third car, was not easy. Because the season was winter I was not envious of their task. Since the advent of diesels over the mountains, I often have wondered if dynamic braking has eliminated or at least eased this chore for the brakeman, or if it still is necessary to make stops to cool wheels and brakes and set retainers.

One helper trip is remembered. We were assigned engine 3556, just out of the shops after a complete overhaul. Since this was a break-in run, the road foreman of engines and the shop supervisor were on hand. This congregation of people did not bother me because I felt confident to handle the old girl. Little did I know what was to occur. No trouble was encountered in getting steam pressure up to a full 250 pounds. We started out of La Grande with the usual bang that westbound trains made, and the stack was really talking as we passed Hilgard and hit the grade. Then it happened—the old girl began to lie down on us, and nothing we did could keep the steam pressure from dropping. The road foreman shoved me out of the seat and made a futile attempt to keep the pressure from dropping more. Water was swapped for steam, steam for water, and still the gauge kept showing less pressure. When the water finally disappeared from the glass, no choice remained but to get some water over the crownsheet. Down went the gauge needle, and on went the train brakes. We were 3 miles up the hill, stalled and blocking the main line. But in a matter of minutes the steam pressure was climbing again. After pumping up the train line, we were on our way. All went well for about a mile, but the pressure fell again and we stalled a second time. The pressure built back up quickly and we were off again—only to stall a third time after another mile. We wondered if we ever would reach Meacham. Something was wrong with our steed.

We climbed down from the cab. In our examination we found water dripping from the seam edges of the boiler surrounding the firebox. Someone apparently had placed the incorrect tension on the staybolts. When the engine was not working, all appeared to be in order and the seams looked tight. When it was under load, a minute separation allowed water from the boiler to drip into the firebox, making it impossible to maintain sufficient heat to produce steam. Six hours and 8 miles from La Grande we finally made it into a siding. The lead engines and the rear helper doubled the train the last 5 miles to the top. We drifted back light to La Grande in defeat.

Most of the motive power Union Pacific used out of La Grande was typical of that used in mountain railroading across the country. One unusual exception was an 80-inch-drivered Atlantic that I noted snoozing peacefully in the Huntington yards on several trips I made there. How this engine could have mastered the mountainous terrain with more than one car was a mystery to me. It carried a number in the 800 series, and I later learned it had been bought by the Oregon Short Line for fast passenger service many years before. The task of the 4-4-2 at the time I saw it was branchline service out of Weiser, Idaho, over the onetime Pacific & Idaho Northern which fol lowed the flank of Seven Devils Mountain in the Weiser River Valley.

Wintertime brought problems to the railroad out of La Grande, especially on the run to the west. To the east, few problems occurred; snow fences took care of drifts, and the rotary rarely went in that direction. Kamela, to the west, usually was buried in a blanket of white. Often the snow depth would equal the height of the engines. At Kamela, frozen switches were a problem. To keep the switches free the Union Pacific had undergirded the area with gas lines, and hundreds of little blue flames sprouted below each movable part of a turnout.

ᴵ   ᴵ

Despite the hazards of the Blue Mountains, railroading there was a pleasant experience. Early in February 1946 I received a wire from the airline instructing me to report to work in three weeks. I was reluctant to leave La Grande, but I had not seen my parents in three years. I sold my old Mercury to the local Ford dealer and bought a ticket to Clarksburg, W.Va. I kissed my lovelies good-bye, boarded the eastbound *Portland Rose*, and left La Grande and the Union Pacific for good. I always have hoped I might return. I may do so yet, and if I see a middle-aged matron who looks slightly familiar, I may give her a wink. She may not recognize my white hair, but surely she will remember that years ago some interesting times were to be had around La Grande. As I composed this article I mentioned to my dear wife of a quarter century that, before I met her, in a place called Oregon I was considered very much a ladies man. I was not prepared for her screams of laughter. I don't know what she found amusing.

June 1977

THE BEST TEN-WHEELER IN THE WHOLE WIDE WORLD

W. F. Beckum Jr.

Before the Great Depression, my dad held a regular job as flagman on Georgia Railroad trains 3 and 4, the so-called *Night Express* between Augusta and Atlanta.

The entire crew on his side of the run remained together for a prolonged period, some six or seven years. The conductor was "Cap'n" Bill Hubbard, a neat, kindly gentleman who was well liked by the other men and by the many regular passengers who rode with him over the years. Comer Jernigan, a close friend of Dad's since their boyhood days in Hancock County, was baggagemaster. "Chunk" Johnson, a very short man who always was jolly and who invariably would slap his right knee when he was enjoying a good laugh, was the train porter. Up on the head end you would find engineer Ed Ewing, fireman A. J. Kirby, and—last but not least—engine 211, a 4-6-0 Baldwin graduate of 1910. Yes, the 211 should be included because she too was a longtime regular on the run.

Following her rebuilding as a superheated engine at the Georgia Road shops in 1922, the 211 was assigned to Mr. Ewing's side of 3 and 4, and she immediately became his pride and joy. From then until 1934 when the 4-6-0s were replaced in passenger service by Pacifics acquired from the West Point Route, "Mr. Ed" managed to keep 211 with him on the *Night Express*.

The 211 was far and away my favorite too. In the fall of 1925, while I was returning home to Thomson with Dad on No. 4 from a day at the Southeastern Fair in Atlanta, I had the privilege of sharing 211's right-hand seatbox with Mr. Ed from Madison to Union Point. This was my first ride on a locomotive—to a lad of 9, quite an experience. From that night on, I too was convinced that the 211 was the very best Ten-Wheeler in the whole wide world.

✠   ✠

One clear cold night just a week or so after that memorable ride, the 211 was standing under the old Union Station trainshed in Augusta, ready to head No. 3 to Atlanta. Dad and the rest of the crew were looking forward to getting out on time at 2:15 a.m. on what promised to be a routine run. The Atlantic Coast Line and Southern connections were in, and the Wilmington-Atlanta and Charleston-Atlanta sleepers they brought had been coupled behind No. 3's coach. The local Augusta-Atlanta Pullman had been set over last and bore Dad's bright oil-burning markers. This rounded out the consist to eight cars: two express, one RPO, one combine, one day coach, and three sleepers—not a big train but a tidy handful for any Ten-Wheeler. I was not along, but Dad would tell of a trip that was any thing but routine.

While the brake test was being made, Cap'n Hubbard went into the telegraph office in the old Georgia Railroad general office building at the east end of the shed for his orders. In a moment or two Dad and Chunk, who were stationed by the coach and combine steps to assist aboard any late-arriving passengers, spotted their conductor walking briskly along the train toward them without the customary flimsies in his hand. Even from afar, they sensed that something was wrong. Sure enough, Cap'n reported that freight train No. 18 minutes before had derailed out at the 5 milepost, tying up the main line. No one seemed to know how many cars were on the ground.

Later, after it had been determined that the line would not be opened until well into the day, arrangements were made to detour No. 3 over the Charleston & Western Carolina to Greenwood, S.C., and from there to Atlanta over the Seaboard Air Line. By the time the necessary details had been worked out, the time was getting toward 5 a.m., the departure time of C&WC train 1, a passenger, mail, and express to Spartanburg, so the dispatcher issued orders designating the C&WC train as First 1 and Georgia 211 as Second 1, Augusta to Greenwood.

The C&WC engineer who was called to pilot No. 3 on the first lap of the detour showed up, walked rapidly over to the 211, threw his grip up into the gangway, and joined Mr. Ewing for a final look around. This gent no doubt had seen the Georgia's 200s around Augusta hundreds of times, but in all probability this was the first time he had ever looked one

squarely in the face. After learning that the 211 would be pulling eight cars, he shook his head and declared that she would never get such a train over the formidable Clark's Hill grade, 23 miles above Augusta. He was so convinced that he hurried off to find the C&WC trainmaster, who also had rolled out early that morning to ride the detour to Greenwood. The trainmaster too had visions of a passenger train doubling Clark's Hill and tying up his railroad in the process. Why not run the 211 as First 1 and then, after she stalled, bring up Second 1 and shove the Georgia Road train over the hill? By then it was leaving time, but all concerned crowded back into the telegraph office for a change in orders putting 211 in the lead.

At last the trains were ready to go. To quote Dad, "All the scrambling and running around finally died out and we left town." Leaving the shed, the trainmaster rode the rear platform with Dad, but as soon as they swung off onto C&WC rails at 11th Street, the C&WC man went up into the train. Dad then took a stand just inside the rear door of the Pullman and watched a new railroad unfold in the early morning light.

First 1 took water at Woodlawn, a lonely spot in the swamps on the South Carolina side of the Savannah River. The trainmaster had returned to the rear to advise Dad about the stop and about flagging while at the tank. Leaving Woodlawn, he announced that they soon would be on Clark's Hill, and he instructed Dad to remain on the rear platform and be ready to drop off with his equipment and flag Second 1 as soon as 211's speed went down to a crawl. He further stated that because of the many curves on the hill, after the train had stalled he would walk back a short distance to assist in getting Second 1 up behind them.

Getting away from Woodlawn, the pilot engineer cracked the whip, 211 took the bit in her teeth, and First 1 charged Clark's Hill.

I   I

Back down the line, Second 1—the C&WC train—crossed the river and eased cautiously up to the Woodlawn tank. What transpired then was passed

along to Dad by a friend and fellow BRT Lodge member who was running baggage on the train that morning. First 1 had just left, so the tank's counterweights no doubt still were swaying and the spout still was dripping water.

After he had spotted his engine under the spout, the engineer dropped to the ground to oil around. Looking back, he saw the porter leaning from a vestibule, and the engineer, with a big sweep of his arm, motioned the porter up to the engine. The train was short, so the porter was there within seconds.

"Step down the track away from the noise of the engine and see if you can hear that Georgia Road train on the hill," the porter was instructed.

The porter trotted down the track, pausing now and then to listen, then came to a halt and cocked his head toward the north. Back through the clear, crisp morning air came that typically sharp, ringing exhaust of a Georgia 200 hard at work—a sound that set these engines apart during all their days and, in my opinion, served as a tribute to the Georgia Road shopmen who kept them in topnotch working order. Old 211 was walking her train up Clark's Hill and letting all the world know that she had the situation well in hand After hurrying back to his train, the porter exclaimed, "Ain't no need to worry about that Georgia Road man. That little ole engine's up Clark's Hill shoutin' 'Home, Sweet Home.'"

Up the hill on First 1, Dad realized that "we were on a mighty stout pull," and he could tell as he moved from side to side in the vestibule watching the 211 blast her way into first one curve and then another that "ole Kirby is surely getting a workout this morning." Dad kept waiting for the speed to drop to that crawl indicating it was time for him to hit the ground and flag Second 1. He was still waiting when he began to notice a quickening tempo in those solid, six-wheel Pullman trucks strumming the rail joints. Shortly he saw receding to the rear a small frame depot with CLARK'S HILL signboards. Just then, the rear door on the Pullman opened and the trainmaster

Georgia Railroad Ten-Wheeler No. 211 rolls out of Scottsdale, Ga., in June 1936. In earlier years, the locomotive was a regular on trains 3 and 4 between Augusta and Atlanta. *Charles K. Marsh Jr. collection*

shouted above the din, "You may as well come on in. We've got it made."

First I had topped Clark's Hill, and the 211 was beginning to ramble.

Dad entered the Pullman, turned into the men's lounge, took a seat on the end of the sofa by the window, and—I'd be willing to bet—lit a Chesterfield. In a few minutes "Pink" Pinckney, the Pullman porter on the car who also was a longtime regular on the Augusta-Atlanta run, parted the curtains. With a broad smile on his face and a dollar bill in his hand, he said, "Mr. Beck (Beck was Dad's railroad monicker), if you'll go find the 'butch,' I'll buy us a Coca-Cola."

"Somebody given you a big tip this early in the morning?" queried Dad.

"No, said Pink. "That porter up yonder in the Charleston car was born and raised on one of those railroad section lines somewhere around here, and before we left Augusta, he bet me a dollar our ole 211 wouldn't get us over the hill. I just collected."

Dad never said much about the remainder of that trip to Atlanta, but it was obvious that he enjoyed it all, riding over foreign lines and through villages and towns he had never seen before.

🚂　🚂

The story doesn't end at Clark's Hill, however, because for weeks afterward it was rumored that the C&WC was making a concerted effort to buy the 211. The "sand house" was positive in its assertions and even went so far as to quote big

prices being offered for the engine. Engineer Ed Ewing was reported to be thoroughly alarmed, often visiting the Augusta roundhouse during his off hours to see if the 211 was safe in her stall.

Of course the 211 never was sold to the C&WC. In my youth the rumors of her sale disturbed me, but as I grew older and was better able to evaluate sandhouse news, I decided that no such deal ever had been thought about, at least not in any official way. But do you know what? Even at this late date, a small, youthful voice inside me keeps saying, "It *could* have happened. After all, she *was* the very best Ten-Wheeler in the whole wide world."

March 1978

F. Axtell Kramer Jr.

9,900 TONS

Bill Smith

On April 9, 1964, I was called as fireman for northbound Gulf, Mobile & Ohio freight No. 28 out of Iselin Yard in Jackson, Tenn., at 9:30 p.m.

When I arrived at the bullpen of the caller's office, I was pleased to learn that Ralph Burkeen was to be the engineer. Ralph and I had worked well together on numerous occasions.

When we boarded the "motors" (as diesels were termed on our part of the GM&O), I found that we had four brand-new GP35s in our trust: Nos. 609, 607, 608, and 605. We backed onto our double and began to pump up our train line. When we had completed the air-brake test, the flagman brought our train orders and instructions. Our yellow sheet read "192 loads, 4 empties, 9,900 tons. One short for Davis. Pick up 14 loads and

3 empties off south end of passing track, Union City."

After we coupled up our head-end double, and a switch engine had coupled our rear-end double, Ralph drew down the train air to equalize the brake-pipe pressure. With the train all together, our head end stood just north of Main Street in Jackson, while the caboose and pusher were more than 2 miles to the south, downhill and across the Forked Deer River. Ahead of us was the long pull up Jackson Hill.

Ralph started the train with no trouble. As he increased throttle to fourth notch, the amp needle went to the post (1,500 amps). Thinking that perhaps one

GP30 No. 502 leads southbound train 33 south of Pomona, Ill., in December 1971. The 500s were common power on mainline trains prior to the ICG merger. *Steven Mueller*

unit was not loading, I made my way through the dust and sand. Shortly I reported to the head end that all motors were loading.

The motors settled down to 1,150 amps and a steady 2 mph. At that point Ralph asked if I thought they would "take another notch." With thoughts of the next 2 miles of 2 percent grade, 15 switches, two crossovers, and five road crossings, I said that I would not increase amperage.

We called Iselin Yard office and asked for another helper. None was available. A mile and a half and 45 minutes later, we went by Conalco. The speed climbed to 6 mph. Ralph worked the throttle to eighth notch, and we began to roll. And roll we did—there were too few empties with open doors to catch crosswinds and slow us down.

On the GM&O, big trains were the rule rather than the exception. These were not unit or specialized trains—they were merchandise freights operated by

timetable schedule. A train of 150 or fewer cars was a rarity and was sometimes referred to as "duck soup." Frequently, during soybean season, No. 29 or No. 31, after picking up 100 or more loads, would leave Corinth, Miss., with 16,000 to 17,000 tons.

Trains of this size were made possible by dieselization, which GM&O accomplished in the late 1940s (the first large road to do so). The ease of handling these big trains, at least out of Jackson, Tenn., where I worked, was made possible by two factors: a superb roadbed and a group of the finest engineers to be found anywhere. Ice in a train line would be a serious factor with more than 125 cars, but such extreme weather was rare in the South.

The trains were pulled by standard blocks of power that seldom varied. First, the standard had been five 700s (Alco FAs) and their B units; after they were scrapped in the early 1960s and until the Illinois Central Gulf merger in 1972, the standard was four 500s (GP30s) or 600s (GP35s), or three 900s (SD40s). The

Alcos, although they had less horsepower, could run faster, but the 900s could do a better job overall of handling the trains.

On only one occasion do I recall a 900 slipping. It happened on a foggy night as I was leaving Corinth on No. 29 with 202 cars and 15,000 tons. As I increased power from seventh notch to eighth notch, the leading motor's front wheels slipped, but luckily, the train did not part. This would not have been the case with the Alcos, for when one wheel slipped, the power dropped on all units, and a severe lunge was experienced as power was restored.

When the GM&O dieselized, most of the steam-locomotive engineers were approaching retirement. The young extra-board engineers and firemen had worked only a few years and so grew up with the diesels. Only a few of the older engineers successfully made the transition from steam and short trains to diesels and long trains.

Later, another factor, which seemed to be a rarity, entered. Most of the younger engineers allowed their firemen to do half the running. As the firemen worked with different engineers, the firemen would take the improved techniques learned with one engineer to others. Soon, most had learned what not to do, and—at a time when other railroads would not allow their firemen to touch a throttle—GM&O's young firemen were qualified to run years before promotion.

The spirit was unbelievable. At the ends of our district's runs, in Tamms, Ill., and Okolona, Miss., the crews would spend hours going over train-handling procedures, train orders, and rules.

With big trains, the challenge was always there. I don't know what the record length for a GM&O train was, but No. 32 came into Jackson one time with 267 cars. After I was promoted to engineer, I often hoped that I would someday leave Iselin on No. 29 with 300 or more cars.

Let me point out that I am not taking a position on the pros and cons of long trains, but rather on the manner in which they were operated. When many railroads were having problems moving much shorter trains over the road, on our railroad, broken knuckles and pulled drawbars were extremely rare.

Almost anyone can operate a 100-car train. The difficulty increases significantly with 125 to 150 cars, and with 175 or more, operation is very exacting and tedious. Our axiom was "Always start in time."

To successfully handle a heavy, fast train, an engineer must employ concentration, consistency, and subtlety. Power and air must be used in discerning amounts. On a 200-car train, advancing a throttle too rapidly or making too heavy a brake application and release is foolhardy and terribly unforgiving.

For example, when I would approach Davis (North Cairo), Ill., southbound at approximately 60 mph on No. 33 to make a set-out, I would make a brake-pipe reduction of 15 pounds at the north end of the passing track, which was 175 car-lengths from the set-out switch. This action calls for commitment and follow-through. The closing rate with a long, heavy train of 10,000-plus tons is very fast and demands precision execution. When the brake application is made, one

should reduce throttle to sixth notch. At 45 mph one should reduce to fourth notch, and at 35 to second notch. At 30 to 25 mph one must release the automatic brake, close throttle to off position, and bunch slack with the independent brake. The train speed then will be about 15 mph, allowing the head brakeman to drop off. One must again activate the automatic brake to stop the train at the predetermined spot.

Normally, the brakeman will have to take only a few steps, make the cut, and give a "go ahead." I noticed that in this situation, the older engineers sometimes did not follow through with their commitment and really fouled up. Most of them would shut off the power several miles away and roll their train to a stop. Then there were those who invariably would use the engine brakes excessively and overheat the wheels. Needless to say, dynamic braking helped the marginal engineers more than it helped the good ones.

When the track was good, we ran fast. But with the demise of the passenger trains on our end of the GM&O, the track was allowed to deteriorate. Speed limits were reduced to 35 mph, making train-handling much more difficult. But we learned to cope. Amazing as it might seem, we operated those long, heavy trains from terminal to terminal at 35 mph with no more than a 1 mph differential. During most runs, a glass of water in the caboose would not have tipped over. The few broken knuckles or pulled drawbars usually occurred on trains operated by the same few engineers. Often I wonder if there are any other engineers around the country who can drive in 200 cars and stop within one car-length of their selected spot.

⌶   ⌶

North out of Jackson, the heaviest train normally would weigh about 12,000 tons. Many trains had 20 to 40 cars of alumina or superphosphate on the rear that would hang on hogbacks and push hard downhill. We called them "sinkers." But our train of April 9, 1964, with those four new GP35s, rolled nicely at 50 to 60 mph.

Before we arrived at Union City, the chief dispatcher called and instructed us to cancel our pickup. This suited us, since we knew we did not need any more tonnage to tow up over the Cairo bridge.

I took the controls at Union City. As I drove in eighth notch at 25 mph through that sleeping town and uphill to Cayce, Ky., I realized even more the heaviness of our train. When we made the hill at Cayce, we began to roll once more.

Our conductor, Doc Warren, came in on the radio at Columbus and told me to stop the engine at Berkeley and back the train up to let the flagman look us over. This was a standard practice before the installation of hotbox detectors.

As I drove down Columbus Hill at 55 mph, I made an 8-pound brake reduction with the 26L brake approximately 3 miles from the Berkeley depot site. To stop a long, heavy train you must make a reduction sufficient for all brakes to equalize and release. You must also stop the train stretched over a series of hogbacks so you can back up.

Within the next mile and a half our train speed dropped to 45 mph. I made another 7-pound reduction and reduced throttle to sixth notch. The brakes now were tightly applied to 1,576 wheels. When the speed dropped to 35, I reduced throttle to fourth notch. *Blam!* The train ran in on the motors with such force that it almost knocked the three of us off our seats. Knowing that I had braked the train properly, the thought flashed through my mind: *9,900 tons, hell!*

After I had stopped the motors where the depot once stood, and the brakes had released on the caboose, I had to take slack forward twice. On the third attempt I got the train moving southward (a train this size is easily jack-knifed if there is sufficient head-end motive power). The "flag" looked over both sides and found nothing amiss, so we started north again.

The block at Winford Junction was green, so we moved onto the TCS-controlled Illinois Central main line, over which GM&O had trackage rights for 11 miles to Cairo Junction, Ill. (GM&O also owned one track for 4 miles of this segment, between Wickliffe and East

Cairo.) Our next, and hopefully last, obstacle would be the Cairo bridge over the Ohio River. This main line was double track, but the bridge was single track and trains ran over it in coveys. When approaching the bridge from the south with a heavy train, an engineer had to have it under control for a possible stop. Also, he had to be able to start pulling hard as soon as possible if the bridge trackage was clear. The approach was curved, which greatly limited visibility.

The approach signal was clear, and I went up the ramp in eighth notch at 20 mph. By the time I reached the first main span, our speed was down to 10 mph. I reduced throttle to sixth notch and lower amps to avoid slipping and tearing the train apart on the severe grade and curve. I then saw what I least wanted to see—the block at the north end of the bridge was yellow. This meant that the crossover switch was lined to head us up the southbound main before crossing us over to the GM&O main at Cairo Junction. Illinois Central special instructions told us to stop and receive permission from the IC dispatcher before making this move.

I told Ralph that I had no intention of stopping at that moment unless he overruled me. He agreed. We both knew that the chance of starting our train again in one piece would be almost zero. Cairo bridge is no place to deal with broken knuckles or drawbars at 3 a.m.

Later, I told Hewitt Wilson, the fine IC traveling engineer, what I had done. Instead of reprimanding me, he complimented me and said that he would have done the same. We realized that the rule had little effect on IC train movements because the IC did not pull the heavy trains we did, so we asked Mr. Wilson to help us get the rule changed. With his assistance, and that of Joe Willett, GM&O's rules examiner, the instruction to stop for the yellow block was dropped.

At Cairo Junction we picked up our clearance card and a yellow sheet that instructed us not to set out the one car at Davis. We then rolled the last 16 miles to Tamms, doubled our train over, and put off at 5:35 a.m.

We were called to go back on No. 33 at 6:50 p.m. that same day. Our head brakeman, V. C. Thompson, entered the shanty,

Slower than the old Alcos but "better at handling trains" were trios of SD40s—900s or "Redbirds." *J. Parker Lamb*

handed me our orders, and said, "Trainmaster Lewis called Iselin and got on them about that tonnage figure."

"He did?" I responded.

"Yeah," said Thompson, "he said it took almost three trains to get over Alto Pass with what we brought in here. We had 14,791 tons!" He looked at me a moment, puffed on his pipe and said, "By the way, you and Ralph did a fine job of getting it here in one piece."

As I acknowledged the compliment, which in itself is a rare thing among railroaders, a wave of euphoria swept over me. For the second time in 24 hours, that unspoken thought flashed through my mind: *9,900 tons, hell!*

The Gulf, Mobile & Ohio is no more. The long, fast trains are no more. No longer does No. 33 follow IC No. 9, the *Seminole*, out of Cairo and beat it to Jackson. I look at the weed-grown old GM&O main line and wonder "Did I really come the 130 miles from Tamms to Jackson, across the Cairo bridge, with 189 cars in only 3 hours 21 minutes, including three stops?"

Most of the fine engineers who handled those long trains are retired or gone, but the top two of the bunch, Paul Kilzer and Guy Taylor, still are around. Hopefully they will be for a few more years.

July 1978

YES, I DID WANT TO RUN A RAILROAD

Ron Flanary

The night could not have been any darker.

As the 50-car train of ballast moved slowly along one of the two mainline tracks of Southern's subsidiary Cincinnati, New Orleans & Texas Pacific, I struggled with the long metal pipe used to crank open the ballast-car doors. From the railroad's viewpoint, the wee hours of the morning was an excellent time to spread ballast. The nocturnal lull in rail traffic resented ideal working conditions for the Operating Department, and salaried employees who drew no overtime pay could be used. From my viewpoint, the time was terrible. This was early Monday morning, and I knew daylight would find me still on the property, preparing for a full day of track inspection and routine maintenance. That flange lubricator near Kings Mountain would have to be repaired. The slow-ordered turnout at South Fork would need tamping. There were no two ways about it—the railroad was operated by a group of sadists.

I plodded along with the moving train, constantly regulating the ballast flow, but as I pondered my fate, my mind was not totally on the task at hand. I failed to see an empty, half-crushed metal spike keg and stepped right into it. Losing my balance, I tumbled down an embankment into a thick growth of briars. It was there and then that I made up my mind to leave the railroad.

Even though the survey of railroad management-training programs, entitled "So You Want to Run a Railroad," by Harold Edmonson in April 1970 TRAINS, made some negative points, there seemed to be no question: I wanted to pursue a position in management with the Southern Railway. I had weighed every alternative and considered each pro and con. I was well aware that life as a railroad official included long, tiring, and erratic hours, frequent moves, and often very harsh working conditions. Edmonson's article focused attention on the sometimes tenuous relationship between railfans and rail executives, but he extolled the virtues of being "rail knowledgeable" and the advantage this gave the modern fan over other, less-informed college grads who might be pursuing the same job.

Even from my earliest memory, I had had a strong attraction to the flanged wheel upon the steel rail. Beginning with childhood impressions of steaming L&N "Big Emmas" and N&W Y's in eastern Kentucky and southwest Virginia, I had always been totally engrossed with what I thought was man's most outstanding guided-movement system. For these reasons, I jumped at the chance to make railroading my career. During my railfan pursuits I had developed a great deal of expertise in the field. Rules 99 and G were no strangers to me. I was attuned to the seemingly insignificant differences between a late F3 and an early F7. I was

Management trainees found themselves in a variety of positions gaining "experience" in real railroading. *Carter Siegling*

familiar with every conceivable form of train order. Railroading was the perfect job, right? Wrong!

I was to find that working one's way up the railroad managerial ladder could be quite difficult. After two separate doses of railroading, it was to become apparent that—at least for me—to turn one's hobby into one's job effectively killed the former. Employment as a management trainee offered a myriad of opportunities. On the Southern, trainees were most often assigned to the Office of the Chief Engineer. The Southern reasoned, quite correctly, that you had to learn the basic ingredient of railroading—trackwork— before the rest was of any real importance. Other avenues to managerial positions with Southern Railway included training programs in the Sales or Mechanical Departments. But the most exciting route was through Maintenance-of-Way.

Life as a management trainee was seldom dull. My first job was in English, Ind., under the watchful eye of a youthful red-haired track supervisor, himself a graduate of a Southern training program. He was quite talkative, virtually bubbling over with helpful inside hints which could make my training period easier. But within a week, I was to find out that railroading was not at all the romantic adventure I thought it to be. It began with 14-hour days in the Indiana sun, swinging a spike maul interspersed by numerous trips to the water bucket. The latter job seemed to be the only one I was able to perform with any degree of proficiency during my first few weeks. I avoided use of the spike maul, preferring instead to tamp ties or tote tools. These tasks required less skill and therefore didn't make the fact that I was a greenhorn quite so obvious. But railroading was heady stuff, and my fascination for the job grew as I became accustomed to Southern's "hands-on" policy for trainees.

During my stay on the Louisville-Huntingburg section of the St. Louis Division, I was assigned for three weeks work with a fellow named Swanson, a short, fat ex-Pennsy yard clerk who somehow had convinced the Southern he was

an excellent trackman. Swanson was in charge of what must have been the railroad's oldest and most decrepit pneumatic tamper, known locally as the "smoothing machine." For the benefit of the uninformed, a tamper is a piece of maintenance-of-way equipment which jacks either rail or both rails up to the proper level and then tamps the ballast under the ties to maintain that level. To do this, a series of small spade-shaped teeth on both sides of the tie pound the ballast in place like so many small jackhammers.

The process always would be the same. Swanson would saunter up the track for some distance, throw down a cushion salvaged from a derelict motor car (track speeder), and, on bended knees, eyeball the offending rail back toward the tamper. Acting on his hand signal, Paxton Barker, the tamper operator, who was of equal obesity, would jack the rail up the prescribed distance and commence with the tamping exercise.

After the first ties were secured, it was merely a matter of bringing the track structure on either side of the initial tamp up to level. My job was to help two track laborers shovel loose ballast into the small cavity created by the raised ties so that the tamper would have plenty of rock with which to work. On rare occasions I got to operate the tamper itself (under Barker's watchful eye) and even level the track—if Swanson had indulged in a heavy lunch and couldn't bend over. The job, even with just a normal day's work, produced no small amount of blisters and backaches, but I couldn't really complain, for my apprenticeship was proving to be most fruitful.

After a weekend respite in which I spent much time pondering my newly found skills, I returned to find a rather precarious situation developing. Swanson only had two flagmen and Barker to attack a job which ordinarily would require the services of a larger work force. The Southern's already thin maintenance-of-way troops on the St. Louis line had fallen on hard times. Welded rail was being laid near English, a work train was spreading relay 130-pound jointed steel through New Albany, and the red-haired supervisor was off sick.

We were told to correct a section of tangent track on the main line which had fallen out of cross-level for some distance. Upon arrival at the scene it became painfully apparent to us that Southern's last surfacing operation in this area had probably been completed just after the last regular use of steam power.

Swanson stationed himself on the cushion and beckoned Barker to raise the north rail at its lowest point. After the prescribed level had been reached, Swanson's pudgy arm waved an "all stop." I stared forlornly at what must have been a 4-inch gap between the bottom of the tie and the roadbed. This can't be, I told myself; I *can't* be the only shoveler on the railroad. But there was nowhere to hide, so I began shoveling what ballast I could find, plus loose dirt, twigs, rocks, empty beer cans, and whatever else was handy in a vain effort to reach the level of the ties. Barker merely watched. It was taking five minutes of my shoveling for every 30 seconds of his tamping—a ratio certainly not in my favor. I staggered into the shade to

die quietly. I had taken my shirt off to cool down a bit, and by so doing, I had also managed to get a sunburn of considerable magnitude. The tangent was in worse shape than ever. We had managed to make a pronounced hump on the north rail—enough to require a 15 mph slow order until reinforcements could arrive the following day. My bones creaked and groaned on the way back to the motel, and I reflected that my learning experience that day had been vivid. Yes, being on Southern's management team was great fun.

Of all my experiences with the tamper crew, the strangest began on the day I returned to work after a weekend visit to my home. Stashed in my car trunk was one of my favorite pieces of railroadiana—an old L&N single-note steam whistle salvaged from the car shop in Loyall, Ky. Barker and I attached the hooter to the tamper's main air reservoir and installed a long rope for activation of the valve lever. After rechecking the train lineup for the morning, Swanson found enough track time for us to begin work, so we departed for the job site, a curve reelevation assignment near Temple.

As we approached the first highway crossing outside of town, Barker used his new toy officially for the first time. His imitation of a Walter Dove grade-crossing solo was exquisite. I could have sworn it was the ghost of one of Southern's Ps-2 Pacifics on the St. Louis local. The supreme compliment came when we rounded an uphill curve about a half mile beyond. There, perched on the bank above, was a contingency of perhaps 10 people—all wondering, no doubt, what manner of machine was passing before their eyes. They had obviously thought the likes of 4501 was ascending the hill. Swanson, Barker, and I were all quite amused by the incident, but, true to form, that was to be my last laugh for yet another tiring day of ballast-shoveling.

I   I

One of the more palatable assignments a railfan-railroader can receive is an order to actually ride a train. In this regard, railroading is much like the Army: the less desirable the job, the better the chance a lower echelon has of doing it. Welded-rail trains on the Southern fell into this category.

I likened my status, or rank, on the railroad to being a Second Lieutenant in the Army. You command absolutely no one. You are a rookie officer, meaning that every other officer, save one of your peers, is above you in terms of rank, and employees below you couldn't care less. In fact, the railroad trainee often has to deal with a considerable amount of dislike for "college boys who know it all." With these points in mind, the neophyte railroad executive often could find himself seated in the rear unit of a five-unit consist acting as official messenger for the Maintenance-of-Way Department on a welded-rail train.

Rail trains were not all that bad, for they gave me the chance to take in the music of five F units throwing sounds off the Tennessee mountains on the hill north out of Oakdale. As the roar of the F's 567s filled my ears, I could only guess as to what it must have been like to perch upon the left-hand seatbox of an Ms-4 Mike, northbound on Florida perishables during the halcyon days of the Rat Hole. Even more vivid was the thought of the original EMD FT as it toiled up the same grades.

My job was to look back over the train for anything out of the ordinary. This was particularly important in the movement of welded rail and its accompanying equipment. Southern must have thought that two extra eyeballs scrutinizing the cargo couldn't hurt.

My first rail train, in 1970, was the most memorable. Combination Gang No. 3 had just finished putting the finishing touches on 7-plus miles of new 132-pound heat-treated welded rail between English and Tazewell, Ind., and I was selected to accompany the train loaded with the old rail back to Atlanta. We departed English in the wee hours of the morning with five old freight Fs on the point. Now bear in mind that by 1970, 20-year-old F units on the Southern were feeling the effects of "lick-and-a-promise" maintenance practices. As we began descending the hill from Duncan to New Albany, the young extra-board engineer slapped the transition selector into dynamic braking and notched back on the throttle. Every unit died immediately. In the ensuing din of engine alarm bells,

Author Flanary found escorting rail trains wasn't bad duty—provided the locomotive brakes were working properly. *William J. Husa Jr.*

the engineer released sufficient air to retard our progress so that we eventually came to a stop on the Ohio riverfront near New Albany, Ind. It was determined that further use of the dynamic brake would be ill-advised.

After a lengthy stay at the Kentucky & Indiana Terminal's Youngtown Yard in Louisville (shared by Southern, B&O, and Monon) we again were under way for Atlanta. The relieving crew took heed of my warning not to use the dynamic brake.

The trip from Louisville to Danville was uneventful.

At this point in my employment, I had yet to see the CNO&TP in the flesh. I had probably expected too much, for at first sighting at the junction north of Danville known as SJ Tower, the line turned out to be just a rather deserted stretch of CTC-controlled double- and single-track railroad. At Danville, my train and I inherited the stereotype hogger. Clad in a billed straw hat, starched work shirt, a pair of matching pants with the bottoms pinned

together, and the longest stogie I've ever seen, he ascended the steps of his 7,500-hp mount. He was my idea of what surely must have been the engineer who regularly charged south out of Danville with a Wimble smoke duct-equipped Ps-4 on the point of the *Royal Palm*.

He began scavenging around in his grip and extracted two rather unusual items. One was a metal throttle extension, which could be attached with two set screws, and the other was a long pull rope with a wooden handle salvaged from an old power mower. He attached this latter device to the whistle cord to facilitate the proper quilling of the Nathan five-chime above. By using these devices he could (1) personalize his locomotive and (2) assume a more comfortable position by not requiring himself to lean forward to add a throttle notch or to blow for a grade crossing.

As we departed from Danville, I busied myself with introductions and began a barrage of old Rat Hole questions. The strategy usually was not to let

the old-head railroaders know that you were a fanatic, but this situation demanded interrogation. I finally got around to advising our engineer about the malfunctioning dynamics.

"Son, I've been runnin' these engines since before you was born and I don't need some smart ass to tell me what to do."

End of interrogation. As we topped the hill south of Moreland, the hogger came back a notch or two on his Tom Swift throttle extension and the Fs really started to ramble. The distant signal for Palm, where single track became double, displayed a yellow approach indication. The throttle was eased off, and the selector placed in D again. At the first notch, all five units shut down again to the attendant clatter of alarm bells at 55 mph. We sailed through the 45 mph turnout at Palm onto No. 2 track, the diverging route, with me struggling to keep my place in the brakeman's seat. Under a very heavy application of air, our stereotype hogger stopped his charge directly in front of a small country store near Geneva.

As the color came back to my knuckles, the old fellow silently got up and descended from the cab. After reaching the ground he looked back up.

"Hey, son, how 'bout a dope (Kentuckyese for a soft drink)?"

"Don't mind if I do," I gleefully replied.

After our impromptu snack, we departed central Kentucky the very best of friends, me respecting him for his image and he for my "comprehensive locomotive expertise."

⚒   ⚒

One of the most frequent assignments I was given was track inspection. At one time or another I managed to cover most all of the Danville-to-St. Louis line as well as the CNO&TP on either a motor car or hi-trail truck. There was always an element of fear that went along with operating a motor car. The operating management of the railroad maintained that there was no—repeat, *no*—excuse for a motor-car accident. If an automobile hit you at a crossing, you should have anticipated the collision and stopped beforehand. If a wheel fell off, you should have exercised better preventive maintenance. If you derailed, excessive speed was the cause. No excuses, period. At one point during my working days, one track supervisor even had the misfortune of running his large gang type car head-on into the local—on a branch which saw only one train a day! He did what any enterprising official might do. A contractor's backhoe was quietly summoned to the scene of the collision and the remains of the car were buried near the right-of-way with appropriate last rites. Since no injuries had occurred and damage to the local's Geep was minimal, the matter was kept quiet and probably never reached headquarters. Self-perpetuation was everyone's concern.

One realization that hit home in a hurry during my CNO&TP tenure was the unusually heavy (at least for the South) traffic patterns. It was bad enough to be assigned to the crew of a local freight or *dolly* (CNO&TP lexicon for a local coal drag) trying to buck northbound "per diems" headed for Cincinnati, but being responsible for piloting a yellow hi-rail against the flow of traffic was a real challenge.

Track inspection is a vital necessity on any railroad, and Southern placed the utmost emphasis on it. I vividly recall one training film shown in Atlanta (during one of my infrequent trips there for classroom instruction) which dealt specifically with the importance of track inspection. The film cautioned assistant track supervisors, who ordinarily did this work, to not get so infatuated with rail and tie conditions that they forgot where they were going. This happened to two poor souls in the deep South once, and they propelled their speeder through an open drawbridge! The film reenacted this humorous tragedy, albeit without passengers.

The priority assigned to track inspection, however, was often forgotten in the face of revenue tonnage. Running a non-revenue motor car against the flow of traffic on a line as heavily traveled as the CNO&TP was an ordeal. Depending on how his day was going, conversations with the dispatcher could be good or extremely bad.

"Flanary at Cumberland Falls calling the CNO&TP dispatcher at Somerset."

Long wait; no answer.

"Flanary at Cumberland Falls calling the CNO&TP dispatcher at Somerset."

"This is the CNO&TP dispatcher, Flanary; clear No. 2 track immediately, and call me after seven trains."

Now, this was disheartening. Situations like that often would crop up, and I soon found myself either waiting out the trains or inspecting the suddenly busy segment on foot. For some reason, the chief engineer frowned on the latter. Not to be outdone, I soon realized that most dispatchers would give a fellow a break if you played by their rules. On one such heavy-traffic day, my helper and I had been lucky enough to get the single track from Woods, just south of Somerset, Ky., to Grove and the double track from there on to Tateville. There we busied ourselves

repairing an inoperable flange lubricator (*rail greaser*) while northbound tonnage rolled by on adjacent track No. 1. After the freight passed, we hurriedly finished our work in hopes of obtaining clearance over the single track to KD Tower.

"Flanary callin' CNO&TP dispatcher at Somerset."

"Go ahead, Flanary."

"I'm at Tateville and would like to go on south to KD Tower."

Deathly silence…

"How long'll it take you to get there?"

I knew what was coming. The DS was ready to run trains. Visions of a 10-train wait danced through my head.

"Nine minutes."

More silence.

"It's against my better judgment, but copy an order."

Now, it was a crooked 7.4 mile jaunt uphill to KD Tower, and Southern Railway rules strictly forbid a motor car or rail truck to exceed 35 mph. A quick calculation will show that you would have to average about 50 mph to make 7.4 miles in 9 minutes. The DS also warned us not to stick his northbound PC runthrough. We tore out of Tateville like a K4-powered New York & Long Branch commuter leaving Red Bank. Up the ascending grade to KD we roared, our hi-rail bounding from side to side with every joint. My helper was speechless. I looked at the track racing beneath me in a vain attempt to pick out flaws. Finally, we saw KD, with the switch lined for No. 2. I slowed down to allow a walking check of the No. 20 crossover, then quickly pulled into the clear. And none too soon. The dynamic brake whine coming from around the bend and the accompanying churn of the CTC-controlled switch machine were positive indicators that indeed, we hadn't stuck his northbound PC run-through. A quick exchange with the engine crew, the prescribed once-over, all-black to the cab, and we were on our way, albeit more sedately.

At Oneida, Tenn., that evening, we rolled up to the depot, pulled up the flanged wheels, and prepared for our return to Somerset on the highway. As we pulled away from the crossing, the rear

Track maintenance was a common assignment for Southern management trainees. *William J. Husa Jr.*

end of the hi-rail began to wobble uncontrollably. An inspection revealed the cause. The highway tires were mounted on hub extensions designed to bring the gauge out to 4 feet 8½ inches. But the lug holes on the extensions were larger than the bolts which held them on. On the left rear extension, all but two had been completely sheared off by the movement of the loose hub. I was absolutely weak. I vowed to never again impersonate a Metroliner. This brush with disaster left its mark; I had learned an unforgettable lesson. To make sure, I even walked the Tateville-KD Tower section that night to see if I had missed anything during my wild ride. The fact that I found a rather severe low spot which I had not noticed lent credence to my newfound theory that track inspection and speed did not mix.

I I

As a management trainee, one soon realized that weekends were not sacred. Saturdays and Sundays were just days 6 and 7. Time and time again, I found my weekends occupied with ballast trains, derailments, and assorted catch-up work. It was on such a weekend that Leonard Smith, assistant track supervisor at Somerset, and I were called upon to stripe the track from Winfield, Tenn., to Pine Knot, Ky. Now, the Southern's rail-laying crews rely on a thin white line painted 28¼ inches from the inside of either rail (the exact center of tangent track, if it's gauged properly).

To streamline its Maintenance-of-Way Department, the railroad during the regime of President D. W. Brosnan had hired a number of mechanical geniuses to design mechanized track maintenance equipment. One of their grotesque creations was known as the striping machine. This mechanical aide was merely a push car with a gasoline-motor-operated paint pump feeding an adjustable nozzle, which pinpointed a stream of paint to the ties below. To achieve said thin line, one merely loaded the canister with water-based paint from the local hardware store and adjusted the nozzle to the right or left to the desired center line. The machine then was slowly towed down the track by some form of power, spraying the thin line as it went.

On the Saturday in question, Leonard and I arrived at Pine Knot with a gallon of white water-based paint, a straight pin (to clean the nozzle), 5 gallons of water, and the hi-rail truck. We prepared the machine for its weekend mission, laboriously loaded it into the back of the hi-rail, and went to Winfield. Upon arrival there, everything was in readiness. We railed the striping machine and the hi-rail on a spur and called the dispatcher for clearance.

"We'll need to run the striping machine from Winfield north to Silerville and then up No. 1 to Pine Knot, if you can give us clearance."

The usual waiting period followed.

"I've got a bunch of southbounds coming, but copy an order."

Eureka! After repeating the order, we stepped out onto the main with me in the

A Southern ballast-cleaning train rolls along the Rat Hole Division near Dry Ridge, Ky., in July 1971. *William J. Husa Jr.*

driver's seat of the hi-rail and Leonard manning the striper. As we slowly made our way toward Pine Knot, Leonard gunned the gasoline engine and motioned for me to go faster. I depressed the accelerator, and our pace quickened. Another motion for more speed. I responded with 10 more mph. At every crossing and switch I would slow down and motion for Leonard to raise the nozzle and negotiate the obstacle. Near the state line, tragedy occurred. A broken tie, its splintered remains jutting high in the air, had been passed over unnoticed, and it stuck the paint nozzle of the high-stepping striping machine. I looked back and saw Leonard covered with white paint, his ghostly form waving a frantic washout. The thin white stripe now was a white boulevard stretching from rail to rail.

After we got the machine shut down, we had to come to grips with the situation: an incapacitated striping machine, a half-finished job, an impatient dispatcher who wanted his track back, and Leonard's white paint job. We got off at a nearby grade crossing and relinquished the track

to revenue freight. Leonard was hopelessly covered from head to toe with latex paint, now dried. He looked for all the world like an angel sent to deliver me from my earthly woes on the railroad.

By the time we got the striping machine repaired, the dispatcher wouldn't answer our repeated calls. All of the trains on the CNO&TP suddenly had converged on Silerville. At 9:45 that evening after 15 trains had passed, Leonard and I finally limped back to Pine Knot. He kept trying to tell me that it wasn't my fault, but I wasn't listening.

I   I

As I climbed back up the hill from the briar patch to the ballast train, my mind was made up. The railroad was fine, but I felt my future lay somewhere else. My career, which had lasted a mere 10 months in all, had taken me to such never-never lands as Princeton, Ind., where the old steam backshop still stood; Oneida, Tenn., where the Tennessee Railroad's RS1s still burbled; and Cincinnati, for one last look at CUT. The decision wasn't easy, but I felt it had to be made; things weren't getting any better.

At the time the numerous mishaps which had happened to me on the railroad had seemed like so many small tragedies. Only in retrospect can I find humor in those experiences. Railroading in the flesh just wasn't as palatable as I thought it would be, so I elected to abandon my short career for new pursuits while I still was young. But I do concur with Harold Edmonson's position that "a growing force is on the move." Young railfans indeed are moving into top management positions on most every major carrier. For many fans, a management career has proved to be the gratifying realization of a lifelong dream. But other enthusiasts have found, like I did, that actually working for a railroad isn't the kind of job they want to face on a day-to-day basis. But others who have become dissatisfied possibly would agree with me that they're richer for the experience and for having had the opportunity to taste such high adventure. If there's one thing I miss, it's the sound of those five laboring Fs on the grade out of Oakdale. For that alone, my Southern Railway career was all worth it.

A REPUTATION FOR RELIABILITY

W. A. Gardner

January 1979

My first close-up look at an E7 locomotive was late in the afternoon of an early fall day in 1945.

Earlier the same day I had gone to work at my regular job at the Pennsylvania's Enola enginehouse, with no suspicion that for the next six months I would not be back there again. A phone call from the master mechanic's office just after noon instructed me to go to Harrisburg, report to the general foreman, and expect to stay awhile to get the maintenance procedures set up on a new diesel locomotive arriving later that day.

Harrisburg was a madhouse. The superintendent of motive power, master mechanic, assistant master mechanic, general foreman, and assistant general foreman were all over the place to see this new marvel that was finally going to relieve the poor old war-weary K4s and put them to pasture, or at least onto slow locals, for a well-earned rest. Was the diesel the new marvel? By no means. It just so happened that the same day the diesel was to arrive was also the delivery date for the first two of an order of 50 T1s. Occupying the two tracks nearest the office, so the dignitaries did not have too far to walk, were the 5501 and 5502, hissing and humming at anyone who dared to come too close.

On my third or fourth try I finally managed to get the general foreman's ear for an undivided 45 or 50 seconds—long enough to find out that the diesel would arrive in an hour or two and would be stored down at the electric track. A General Motors man was down there, I

was told, and I should go see if I could help him. A machinist, an electrician, and a laborer would be provided the next morning if we needed them. End of instruction period.

Don Fricke, the EMD maintenance instructor, was indeed at the electric track (where GG1s were serviced and dispatched), and he seemed relieved that finally someone had arrived who was willing to acknowledge that he existed and was even willing to talk to him. The westbound passenger fleet had started to arrive by this time, and the electric-track personnel were too busy watering and arranging GG1s to do much more in the way of communicating than to ask him to move when he got in the way.

Fricke's joy at my arrival did not last long when it quickly became evident that he knew much more than I did about what was going on. I did learn from him that two E7 units, the 5900 and 5901 (both As), were on their way light from Chicago. Apparently the PRR had bought them with the intention of using them on a Florida run out of Chicago, but arrangements for this train fell apart at the last minute. Fricke had been all set to help with the maintenance at Chicago until two days before, at which time he had been told to go to Harrisburg as quickly as possible. The locomotive would be sent there as soon as it was delivered from La Grange, light, since there were no fueling stations, and its original fuel supply would have to last to Harrisburg. This left no margin for such frivolity as pulling a train, much less heating it (the steam generators, on a cold day, could consume more fuel than the engines). At Harrisburg, the diesel would temporarily share the GG1's fuel facility.

This remained the sum of our combined knowledge for the rest of that day. In due course the locomotive did arrive, and as people kept climbing off, I decided someone had made a mistake—they should have stopped at the passenger station first. Three EMD instructors, two special-duty men from Philadelphia, two road foremen, and almost lost in the crowd—the engineer and fireman all unloaded from the 5900 and 5901.

We squeezed the two units onto the supply track, set the hand brakes, secured the engines, turned off the lights, locked the doors, and went home. The dispatcher had told us there were no immediate plans to use the locomotive, and everyone who had sufficient knowledge or authority to change that was too busy with the T1s to be concerned with a puny 4,000-hp diesel, so we might as well quit for the day.

⚓ ⚓

The next morning we got a little more attention while the crowd waited for the 5501 to be towed back from Newport, Pa., about 30 miles away, where both airpumps had failed and were not able to be restarted because no one knew where the steam control valve was and couldn't find it in the dark. The 5502 had made it all the way to Pittsburgh but had derailed in the station. It wasn't expected back for a couple of days. Oh, yeah—about that diesel.

We were finally told that the plan was to run the 5900-5901 on the *Red Arrow* to Detroit, but that this schedule could not be started until a fuel station was set up at Mansfield, Ohio, which would take about a week. This fuel station, to be duplicated at Harrisburg, would consist of a tank car with a filter and pump mounted on its running board. Meantime, the locomotive would be broken in by running to Altoona and back on whatever train the dispatcher chose, since it could go that far, and that far only, and safely get back without running out of fuel.

Sure enough, sooner or later at some time during the day, we would get a call to

have the units ready for a certain train, and off they would go to Altoona. Ten to 18 hours later they would be back. This went on for eight days, with one day off for finding and correcting a cab-signal failure. The motor-generator set which reduced the diesel's 74-volt battery potential to the 32 volts required by the steam-engine-type cab-signal equipment lost a bearing and had to be repaired.

This rather leisurely pace left plenty of time for Fricke to teach me what I needed to know, and I'm afraid I took advantage of him, but we did manage to remain friends.

What maintenance is required?
What tools do we need?
How do you take this or that apart?
What does that relay or contactor do?
How can a running test be made to ensure that everything works?
How much oil should be available? How soon do we change it?
How do you wash one of these boilers (they didn't even call them boilers, but steam generators instead)?
Is it safe to wash the trucks with the steam-engine washing machine, or will it hurt the motors?
And on and on and on. Fricke never gave up, even when he had to say, "I don't know, but I'll find out." He always did, too, coming back a few days later with the right answer.

In due course, our fuel station arrived, and, we were told, the one at Mansfield was also in place. Detroit, here we come. Seven months of Harrisburg-Detroit one night, and Detroit-Harrisburg the next, followed, without a road failure and with very few problems, even minor ones. Starting with full fuel tanks, the units could make Mansfield on the westbound trip, fuel there, go to Detroit and return to Mansfield the next night, fuel again, and make it home. There were a couple of close calls, once when the *Red Arrow* got caught behind a freight derailment and later when one of the cars gave trouble, both on cold nights with high steam usage, but the E7s always got home.

In the first few weeks the job became almost boring, but about the time we were getting really familiar with the machinery, a few minor fuel and oil piping leaks showed up, giving us the excuse to take something apart. About the third week, one of the automatic brake valves

became more difficult to operate, and we thought: Good—we're going to get to see what's inside that big pile of iron that Westinghouse calls a 24L. No such luck. We had no spares yet, so Westinghouse changed out the brake valve during the station stop in Pittsburgh one night.

Our first chance to do something important came when one of the air compressors (two-stage, two-cylinder machines driven from the front of each of the four engines) started squealing for attention. The high-pressure cylinder's pretty suede gray paint also turned to an ugly brown, giving us a good idea of where the problem was. An hour's work had the cylinder and piston on the floor and the mystery solved—a scored cylinder. While the storekeeper took the cylinder to the local truck maintenance garage and had it honed, we got the spare piston and rings ready. A clean-up, oil change, and another two hours to put things back together, and off to Detroit went the E7s once more. Two of the other compressors later did the same thing, but by now that, too, was getting boring, and we managed to do them in half the time.

Our first real chance at the engines came in a morning inspection when we discovered water dripping down inside one of the cylinders. Fricke allowed as to how the gasket had probably failed, but the only sure way to know was to remove the cylinder head and look. Now, to us steam types, "Remove a cylinder head" meant at least eight hours of hard, dirty work, and the units not going to Detroit tonight. Fricke laughed and sent the laborer to the storehouse for a gasket, telling us if we'd go to work instead of talking, we'd be ready to put it in before the man got back. As usual, Fricke was right, and we had time to drink coffee while we waited. The work was all done before lunchtime.

Our first experience with taking the units into the roundhouse was at the third monthly inspection, still called *boilerwash* by all the PRR people. The boilers, or rather steam generators, were slowly but surely scaling up from the hard Ohio water they were getting every trip. The Altoona Test Department had been consulted, and they told us an acid wash was in order, which they would perform

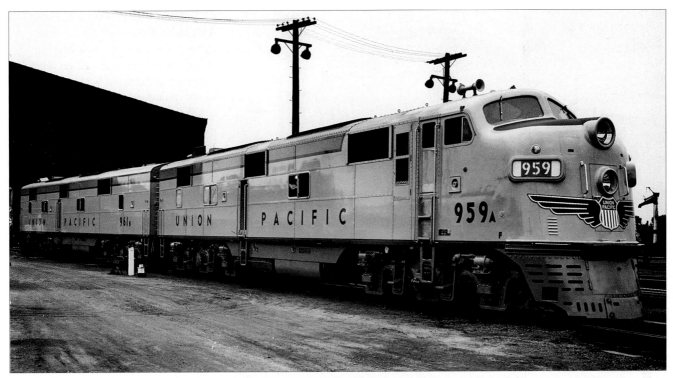

An E7 delivery to the Union Pacific involved more personnel problems than locomotive issues. *Union Pacific*

for us. This meant both units in the house for four hours, where the equipment the test people assembled would have power and an ample supply of water.

The general foreman acted as though we had asked for at least his right arm, and maybe both of them, but after the correct amount of ranting and raving, he finally agreed we could have two tracks for four hours, no more. By the way, where had we done the last two boiler-washes? On the storage track, of course. "You mean those things have never been in the house in three months?"

"Right."

"Hmm. OK." The poor man had good reason to be frantic. By now he had 30 T1s, with at least 15 in the house every morning and four or five more waiting to get in, and not all tracks were long enough to hold one. To make matters worse, the poor old tired K4s that the T1s were supposed to relieve but couldn't, could not be squeezed into the house to get the attention their duties demanded, and their usually reasonable failure rate was headed for the sky.

ɪ ɪ

A basic fact came to light when the E7s were six months old. I decided the wheels were beginning to look rather worn and took down flange and tread wear measurements with my gauges. Flange wear looked

quite severe. I had been puzzling over how we were going to handle wheel work, since the steam-engine drop tables certainly were not suited to removing diesel wheels or trucks. I called on the general foreman with my measurements and pointed out to him that in another two months we would be in violation of the legal wheel wear limits if something wasn't done. He knew I was crazy and told me so, since the locomotive was only six months old. Everyone except me knew wheels last at least 1½ years.

I pointed out to him that the units had traveled 69,000 miles, and then he had his "crazy" suspicions confirmed, taking great care to point out to me in the most elementary terms that of the 30 T1s in service, the one with the highest mileage in the same period of time had run only 2,800—yes, twenty-eight hundred—miles. Therefore, I, the speedometers, the wheels, and probably the whole world must be crazy. He did agree to come look at the wheels, however, which he did the next day. He had to agree they were worn, but it must be that GM had used soft wheels. He had never heard of wheels wearing out in six months and just knew it wasn't possible. The basic fact? The dramatic difference between steam and diesel availability and reliability.

Yes, the wheels did get turned before they became illegal, but it was by no means an easy job using the steam-engine-type drop tables. Wheel-truing machines were, of course, unheard of in those days. Enola helped by doing one unit while Harrisburg did the other.

A short time later, I left the PRR and went to work for EMD, having decided that in spite of the one new diesel to 50 new steam ratio I had just observed on the "Standard Railroad of the World," EMD really had something there, and it might be a good idea to associate myself with them.

ɪ ɪ

My acquaintance with E7s continued almost immediately, for I was assigned to the delivery of some on the Union Pacific. One of my colleagues and I played a rather dirty trick on an overbearing, newly appointed diesel supervisor while on that job. The UP always took the precaution of running new units on a local from Omaha to Cheyenne and back, to make sure the bugs were all out before giving the newcomers an important assignment. We, therefore, found ourselves riding an A-B-B consist pulling a six-car train on a slow schedule west out of Omaha, gross overpowering to say the least. Everything

EMD's E7 earned a reputation as a reliable, dependable passenger locomotive that didn't require much shop time. *Glenn J. Williams*

was going well until we got within about 10 miles of Grand Island, Neb., where the diesel supervisor told us he intended to get off and wait for us to come back. It seemed he had a girlfriend there he thought needed his company.

We were in the cab admiring the scenery when the supervisor came in from the engineroom and asked what was the matter with the No. 1 engine in the second unit. We replied that 5 minutes before, when we had checked, nothing had been wrong. "Well," he told us, "it's not loading now." We went back to look, and sure enough, it was not. A brief inspection of the electrical cabinet soon turned up the problem—a paper match stuck into a starting contactor interlock, thus preventing completion of the circuit to the generator field contactors. The interlock's purpose is to prevent completing the field circuit until the starting circuit is opened. We disgustedly pulled the paper match out, and the engine loaded up again as the generator went back to work. I was about to throw the match on the floor when my buddy stopped me. "Put it back," he said, so I did, not yet understanding what he was up to. He got a short electrical jumper

out of his bag, reached in back of the panel, and clipped it around the interlock terminals. The engine loaded again, although the interlock was still "bugged."

We then went back to the cab and told our would-be tormentor nothing was wrong. He, of course, immediately hot-footed it back, looked at the interlock, saw the match still in place, and then didn't know what to do. By the time he had pulled it out and put it back, with no effect, two or three times, we were coming into Grand Island and he didn't dare get off. After we left there, with him still aboard, one of us kept him busy elsewhere while the other went back, took off the jumper, and threw away the match. The supervisor went back later, stuck another match in the interlock, and, of course, the engine unloaded again. He never did figure out what happened, but we hoped he had even more trouble explaining to the girl why he didn't show up. He didn't bug us anymore on that trip, or on any other.

 🚆   🚆

It was almost a year later when I next got aboard an E7, this time on the New York Central. I was assigned to a delivery of F3s at Buffalo, N.Y., and was asked by

the local road foreman if I knew what a particular engineer could possibly be doing to cause a rough-handling complaint, always at the same place, shortly after leaving the depot westbound. Similar complaints against other engineers handling the same train did not occur. I suggested we take a ride with this man and maybe we could figure it out.

An E7, in common with all the other EMD E models, had two completely separate power plants. The No. 1 engine-generator set powered the two motors in the front truck, while the No. 2 set provided power for the rear truck. For better tractive effort, the motors were series connected at starting. The motor connections changed to parallel automatically, under control of a voltage sensitive relay, after a reasonable speed was attained. The speed at which this occurred depended on the gear ratio. Since it was practically impossible to set all the relays exactly alike, each power plant would make this transition when its own relay picked up, and even though there was a loss of power when this happened, since all the remaining power plants kept pulling, the effect on the train could not be felt.

A few days later the road foreman called me, and we boarded the train to see how this particular man managed the seemingly impossible. The operating rules called for a running brake test shortly after leaving Buffalo. Most crews would make this test as soon as they got up to 10 or 15 mph, but this man waited until he was above 25. He then finished the job by reducing the throttle to notch 7 (8 is full speed) right after he applied the brakes. He had been told it was poor practice to power brake in the eighth notch. Satisfied that the brakes were OK, he released, but, again being careful, he did not advance the throttle to 8 again until he was certain the brakes had fully released. By now the train had accelerated to well over the normal transition speed, but with the throttle in 7, none of the generators had yet reached transition voltage. Now came the clincher. He advanced the throttle to 8, all the engines speeded up, all the relays picked up at once, and all six power plants (we had three units) made transition simultaneously. If there were any pieces left on the dining-car tables, it wasn't because the locomotive hadn't tried its best to shake them off. There was a severe run-in as the series power contactors opened and all power was lost, followed by a severe run-out a few seconds later when the parallel contactors closed and all power was restored. The cure was simple: The engineer was instructed to start his running brake test at a lower speed and have it finished before he reached transition speed.

Unfortunately not all problems were solved as easily. One I got involved with concerned a complaint that a certain unit would trip the ground relay intermittently, always while going around a curve to the right. Inspections and tests turned up no reason. The ground relay's function is to detect a high-voltage ground. When it trips the main generator, field circuits are opened to avoid what could be massive damage to the motors, generator, or cabling at the point where the ground has occurred. It must be reset manually to restore power Several rides on the offending unit failed to disclose the trouble until someone suggested that it be ridden at night with the lights off. Possibly when the ground occurred there would be enough of a flash to know where to look. Sure enough, after several boring miles of nothing happening, and as usual on a curve to the right, the relay tripped, and I thought I saw a minor flash in the bottom of the electrical cabinet. I poked around in the area for a while and saw nothing unusual, but then we went around another curve and I saw something move in the bottom of the cabinet. Fishing down under the cables, I pulled out a metal flashlight that apparently someone had dropped and either didn't know it or couldn't find it. When it rolled to the left (on the right-hand curves) it shorted a cable terminal to the deck. End of mystery, with further proof of the folly of using metal flashlights near electrical equipment.

Author Gardner's first E7 experiences were with the first two of the model delivered to the Pennsylvania Railroad, Nos. 5901 and 5900. *Pennsylvania*

I I

E7s gained a reputation for reliability, good riding, and—with a few exceptions—easy maintenance. The batteries on the A unit were under the cab floor, and no one cared much for the backbreaking job of flushing them (filling with water), and even less for the job of changing them when it was necessary. As the units got older, it was found to be wise not to spend too much time lounging in the area next to the traction-motor blower chain cases. When the chain decided to break, it frequently would come through the case and wander around the engine room before coming to rest. It was not a good idea to be in its path when this happened.

The units had impingement air filters that had to be removed, cleaned, and oiled periodically if the engine intake air was to be kept reasonably clean. No one stood in line to do that job, either.

The first time I walked through an E7 engineroom I thought someone had found an excellent surface for the floor. It was cast aluminum plates, with a carborundum type material imbedded in the surface. It was impossible to slide your foot across it, even if it was oily. When these floor plates had suffered through 10 or 12 years of heavy foot-stomping, however, they got very smooth, and with some oil on them it was like trying to walk on greased ice. You almost had to grab hold of something to stop. The plates could have been changed, of course, but no one was willing to spend that kind of money on a unit near the end of its economic life.

The E7 was the most popular of all the E models. Out of almost 1,300 Es, 511 were E7s. Several factors had combined in early 1945 to make this so. The War Production Board material restrictions had been lifted, and materials once again were available. There was a pent-up demand for passenger locomotives, since none had been produced for three years. War-worn passenger power, and trains, would have to be replaced if the railroads had any chance of retaining a reasonable share of the passenger business that had fallen in their laps because of the war. Finally, a good, proven design was ready. The E7 was a minor evolutionary step from the E6, which had been well-tried. The FT nose and cab were used for a more standardized construction, but most of the rest of the design features were neither new nor untested. The unit could be safely predicted to be a success, which it was. E7s could be found on the head end of almost every name train in the country in the next few years, and they stayed there for some time, even after higher horsepower E8 and E9 models came along.

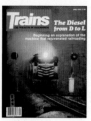

April 1979

M. A. McGrail

BOILERWASH EXTRA

LLoyd Arkinstall

On a spring evening in 1942, the Pennsylvania Railroad engine crew dispatcher's phone call brought my feet down smartly from the porch rail.

Through the side of his mouth that was unoccupied by a gnawed cigar, he ordered me for a 9:30 p.m. light-engine move out of the Meadows (N.J.) enginehouse for the Trenton shops. Grabbing my still-shiny engine bag, I went my way, rejoicing in anticipation of a leisurely tour of duty.

At the Meadows enginehouse sign-on point, the "bench committee" was in full cry, for there were crews from Enola and Potomac yards eloquently griping about everything from leaking combustion chamber staybolts to lumpy seatbox cushions.

Oblivious to the uproar, a burly, steady-eyed engineman completed his unhurried perusal of the bulletin board, and then proceeded to sign the register covering the light-engine move. I signed next, puzzled by the provision made on the sheet for *three* firemen. Finally, two other characters, who had been in no tearing haste to sign, filled the remaining two slots.

In response to a meaningful nod toward the door from our engineman, who obviously took a dim view of small talk, we filed out into the soft spring night and threaded our way between rows of slumbering, hostled brutes to the west end of the ready tracks. Headed out was the 5705, a G5 Ten-Wheeler, coupled to two H9 Consolidations. Harry Gordon, the engineman, assigned my two colleagues to the H9s as "watertenders," instructing them to close the double-heading cocks, set the lubricator valve and cylinder feeds for road running, put the reverses in full forward gear, check their night flagging equipment, and light the tank markers on the rear. Beyond that, he suggested quite forcibly that they keep their sweaty little hands off the throttles. He and I then proceeded on to the G5 which, like the two H9s, was also a boilerwash candidate headed for the Trenton shops.

I had never been aboard a G5, and consequently, the abnormally high flush deck, at first, seemed unsettling. She had the usual PRR horizontally split, hand-bomber firedoor on vertical runners, which might require a protective heel in the fire to prevent sticking from expansion. To minimize this irksome phenomenon, some innovative soul had attached a tin cup of graphite grease to the firedoor air-cylinder pipe. With passenger gas coal, the protective heel in front of the firedoor ring also served to keep one's overalls a degree or two below the flash point.

ɩ   ɩ

After we had stowed our gear in our respective seatboxes, Harry ignited the conical engine torch at the firedoor, reached for the long-necked oiler, and climbed down to prod around. I blew down the water glass and try cocks, cracked the blower, and barred up the bank fire. I next set the lubricator feeds and followed this by cracking the compressor steam valve to slowly build an air cushion before fully opening the valve. Finally I tried both injectors, which primed and caught reassuringly.

Before loading ice and drinking water into the right tank bulkhead, I checked my equipment: coal pick on the coal gate, scoop, slice bar, and hoe (the stoker jobs substituted clinker hooks for this tool, which the graybeards called a scraper). Spare scoop, shaker bar, red and white lanterns (which I lighted), and a steel-handled monkey wrench all occupied the left bulkhead. Fusees, torpedoes, and spare waste were in the seatbox. Finally, tucked behind the left injector delivery pipe, was the deck broom.

I had just finished checking the tank level and trimming the incipient avalanche that an overzealous coaling-tower hostler had produced,when Harry, crouched beside the tank with his flaring torch, called for the water scoop to be lowered and raised. Having finished his groundwork, he climbed aboard and proceeded to inspect the firebox interior, using the scoop as a smoke deflector Satisfied, he next made a hefty automatic-brake application, lapped the brake valve, and, Hamilton in hand, determined that brake-pipe leakage was not unreasonable. With an assist from the rear watertender, a standing brake test followed. One detail remained, the outbound cab signal test rack, toward which we lumbered slowly. I climbed down and, as I worked the selector switch on the stanchion, the cab acknowledger bleated with each more restrictive aspect. Happily (in jargon not then coined), all systems were go.

There was a slight grade from the Meadows ready track to GY (now Karny) Tower at the west end of the yard. The two heavy Consolidations, with sniffing valves a-wheeze, gave ground very grudgingly. Any coy notion that I had entertained about a leisurely light-engine move was fading fast. While a novice fireman, I had listened with almost eavesdropper intensity when old heads discussed firing techniques peculiar to each class of engine, variations in coal, and survival in general. Praise for G5s was sparse indeed; they were usually dismissed as having the riding qualities of wheelbarrows and the smoke-producing potential of Mrs. O'Leary's cow.

I did, however, gather that their draft tendencies made it all too easy to plug the forward openings under the arch bricks, which promptly produced an utterly discouraging steam-gauge reading. Since I had never fired this class engine in my brief career, my sole option was to act upon the hearsay recommendation of the most credible of my elders. In effect, I had nothing to fear but hearsay itself; and, a hundred-mile round trip of on-the-job training!

Perhaps in my innocence, I overreacted a bit to the nature of our tow, but the charge that I baled into that firebox was at considerable odds with the firing manual's ideal. I built up the sides front to back, practically climbed into the box stuffing the rear corners, and climaxed this production with a huge coked-up heel in front of the firedoor.

ɩ   ɩ

Instead of routing our clanking caravan over the steam-operated swing bridge spanning the Passaic River onto the WP freight branch, the Movement Bureau decided to mainline us on the old passenger outbound engine track, over which high-wheelers with mounded tanks and wiped boiler jackets had once trundled to their rendezvous with westbound jack-rod motors at old Manhattan Transfer. Fortunately, the night was moonless, for G5s—lacking, among other niceties, combustion chambers—were notoriously smoky. On a Ringleman Smoke intensity chart (prominently posted in enginehouses) my stack emissions would have rated Condition 5, which was basic black.

The old outbound light-engine track, once under the highline main, paralleled the DL&W right-of-way fence all the way past Hudson Tower (old Manhattan Transfer), whose operator turned us loose on No. 4 main. Dock Tower at the Passaic lift bridge crossed us over onto No. 3 track. We went straight through Newark's Market Street Station with firedoor cracked and bell hammering. Upon clearing the Newark trainshed, my engineman yanked the slim bar throttle wide and settled down to running the engine with the reverse lever The cracking exhaust modulated into a staccato chop as Harry, head cocked in a listening attitude, sought the working notch. By the time the engine truck tugged us into the gentle superelevated curve at South Newark Hunter Tower, our stack's output had flattened into a hissing roar Looking back at our "train," I found the furious low-wheeled rod action to be a sobering sight. Our uproarious passage by Waverly Yard and Lane Tower elicited a sampling of whistle catcalls from our well-wishers.

So far, the boilerwash-bound 5705 had responded favorably to my scoop-flailing efforts. I had been banging my shots off the side sheets and short-firing the center over my steamboat heel, letting the fierce draft pull the charge forward. I had even managed to lift the pop once for morale purposes. The scuttlebutt appraisal of the G5 had been realistic; she was rough, dirty, and incredibly smoky. To risk a generality, I believe a hand-bomber fireman wore out more brooms than the average housewife. Since G5s were flush deckers (with the firing deck and seatbox platforms on the same plane) extra broom vigilance was required to keep the loose coal level below the runner's shoetops. After the glare of putting in a fire at night, the brief sweeping interval gave one's night vision a moment to unscramble.

Our ecologically ruinous extra charged onward, bending into the graceful S curve over the Jersey Central at Elizabeth, straightening out at South Elizabeth's Elmora Tower, where the four-track main enlarged to six. Since two track pans had been reinstalled at Linden, Harry informed me that we would top off the tank in passing.

Many of the older tenders still had their original manual waterscooping gear intact. Long, Johnson-barlike levers protruded up through a deck slot and terminated between a smooth double quadrant with locking-pin holes near the forward stop. A finger-thick pin was attached, on one end, to a short length of chain. The whole mechanism was counter-balanced, after a fashion, and with the engine standing still, a fireman could raise and lower the scoop without undue strain. Scooping water at speed, however, produced a lashing effect which made this simple maneuver fracture-prone. Old-timers had minimized this peril by attaching a stout rope lanyard to the lever handle. When lowering, they pulled the pin and let the lanyard slip through their gloved hand, as scoop contact with the

water whipped the bar against the rear quadrant stop. As they approached the end of the pan, they tugged on the knotted end of the lanyard as the scoop rode up the graduated end of the pan, thus holding the monster captive while they reinserted the locking pin.

Bearing down on the Linden pan marker light, I recalled this gem of pioneer ingenuity as I lifted the little scoop air valve's locking plate on the right tank bulkhead. Possibly concerned about my depth perception, my engineman informed me in a conversational yell that he would give me a whistle toot to lower the scoop and another to raise it. The pan marker light flashed by the gangway, Harry tooted, and I lowered, all according to script. However, seconds before his next toot, the tank manhole cover was slammed against its overflow stops, venting a torrent that enveloped the lead H9, refreshing the watertender in its passage through the open cab running-board doors.

I   I

So far, we had received varnish treatment, three vertical amber lights appearing above our track at each gantry with almost monotonous regularity. I caught a fleeting, gangway glimpse of my hometown, Rahway, which seemed compressed and was quickly gone. We clattered through Union Tower's bustling six-track interlocking, briefly obscuring the tower itself in our passage. Mercifully, our smoke plume and epic cinder fallout was absorbed by the darkness. To keep a G5 on the peg at sustained hard running, required (at least, in my case) a firing rate that crowded the fire and produced a smoke pall that rivaled a refinery blaze. Since the firing deck was but slightly behind and above the third drivers, the resulting rough ride at speed challenged a novice fireman to remain standing, let alone to fire with any degree of accuracy.

In all fairness to the PRR, the passenger gas coal from the Meadows coaling tower generated a heat that would melt Hell's hinges, and no one short of a fireman of unique ineptness could entirely fail to hack it in the matter of producing steam. The low-volatile coal used by yard, peddle, and transfer jobs, however, often separated the men from the boys.

Bearing down on Colonia, we approached a long eastbound freight stopped on the adjacent track. As instructed, I forewent my seatbox respite and stood peering around the backhead for a possible fouling deckload. Suddenly, too close to appear in my engineman's scope of vision beyond the smokebox, a trainman materialized from between the cars and wildly swung us down with a fusee. "Washout!" I yelled, and my runner's left hand flicked out like a frog's tongue and dumped the air. Unlike big-holing a conventional train at speed, the combined braking force and cylinder compression of the three locomotives stopped us in a comparatively short distance, and the bobbing approach of the fusee-bearing trainman provided theatrical lighting for our little tableau. The brakeman crunched to our gangway and puffed, "Something dumped us. I'm walking the train. Watch for fouling gear until you clear our hind end." During our leisurely passage by the remainder of the train, however, our headlight beam revealed nothing amiss, and we resumed speed after passing the red-and-white-lantern-equipped flagman. I had half expected my impassive engineman to ask where I had picked up the salty term *washout* for emergency stop, but he graciously settled for a speculative look which might have passed for amusement.

Successive westward towers Edison, County, and Midway continued to ply us with clear boards until, finally, after we scooped water at Plainsboro, Nassau tower at Princeton Junction reminded us that we were not No. 29, the *Broadway*, but rather a boilerwash extra, and ground us to a jostling halt at the home board.

Naval warfare has been described as long periods of waiting interspersed with eruptions of violent action. The same observation might well be applied to road-freight service in general, and special moves, such as ours, in particular. We lay smoldering for over an hour while varnish jobs slammed by in both directions with the frequency of a Manhattan subway rush hour. A huge trackside privet hedge nearby exuded a cloying sweetness that failed to enhance our enforced stay. The operator finally relented and allowed us to continue with our methodical pollution,

The Pennsy's class G-5 Ten-Wheelers had a reputation as rough-riding, smoke-producing locomotives. *Harold K. Vollrath collection*

without further interruption, to the Trenton shops where our pit arrival was cheerlessly observed by a third-trick firecleaner.

I   I

After a several-hour layover, during the small hours of May 2, 1942, the pit foreman decreed that we were to return to the Meadows with a freshly boilerwashed G5, 5724, and an H9 whose number I failed to record. As with the Meadows departure, Harry and I prepared the G5 while the two babysitters relaxed in the tow's cab. A short time later, we lay waiting for the signal to mainline us eastbound. My fire was ready and I was pleasurably psyched-up for a return workout when up clambered one of the watertenders. He insisted upon firing back. Why he hadn't manifested this consuming desire *before* I prepared the engine so nettled me that I resisted the idea. However, he clamored so long and piteously that I finally appealed the case to my engineman, confident that he would tap me. Much to my chagrin, Harry's shrug eloquently indicated that whether Sim Webb or Mickey Mouse fired back was immaterial to him, but that someone had damn well better provide the steam for him to get this show back to Jersey City.

To this day I regret not having unloaded while there was still time and not having assumed the unoccupied seatbox of the tow. Instead, lacking the advantage of hindsight, I slumped on the seatbox while my relief went through the motions of examining my fire. He was broad-beamed, a bit overweight, and in dire need of a shave. In a matter of minutes, we were given the railroad, and Harry went to work on the G5 in a very spirited fashion.

Almost from the first exhaust, my relief seized the scoop, tramped on the firedoor treadle, and began to shovel with the wild abandon of Jawn Henry versus the steam drill! I stared in open-mouthed disbelief! Lord, how he baled coal, like a veritable Iron Fireman, until the deck resembled a strip mine in mid-passage. The inevitable happened with chilling swiftness; the slender hand on the Ashcroft steam gauge swung steadily left and downward. The Iron Fireman finally slid the scoop under the coalgate, made a token pass with the deck broom, and stumbled toward the seatbox. I moved forward to share the box, onto which he slumped, sweating profusely, and panting, "Guess I got her a little too heavy." A minute or two pounded by, the steam pressure continued to fall inexorably, and still this pooped clown made no attempt

to get off the box. I looked across the cab at Harry, who was looking across at us, or rather, at me. He was not smiling! That blew it. Righteous indignation hyped the old adrenalin into full glow. Harry had tacitly sanctioned this slob's firing, and now, to maul a cliche, I was to pull this fat copout's chestnuts out of the fire!

Pulling chestnuts would have been vastly preferable to pulling coal out from under arch bricks. Harry had of necessity slowed down and managed to keep the crownsheet covered. When the air compressor could no longer cope with the feed valve's demand, he could resort to running in full release to keep the brakes off.

The mound of green coal jammed under the arch bricks was awesome. I would hoe back furiously until the scraper became an incandescent blob, pull it out on the deck to cool, then go at it again. And again. The coal I had hoed back burned in the rear grate area, but the stoppage robbed us of the evaporative surface of the lower course flues. Finally, after miles of this pyromanic drudgery, I partially cocked the front grates and asked Harry to widen out and briefly fullstroke her. He complied readily enough, and this drastic therapy started the breakthrough. He throttled down and hooked

Pennsylvania G-5 No. 5720 has a full head of steam as it awaits its next assignment at the Camden, N.J., roundhouse in March 1955. *Don Wood*

up again while I centered and secured the front grate linkage. After one last exploratory pass with the hoe, I slid this poor distorted implement back over the coal gate. Constant close-range firedoor exposure had reduced me to a parboiled state, and after the hoe workout, the scoop seemed a civilized tool indeed.

The steam gauge, that barometer of a fireman's well-being, was again on the rise, as was the crownsheet's coverage. In my singleness of purpose. I had lost all track of surrounding. A glance to the right into the predawn grayness revealed our accelerating progress through the New Brunswick passenger station. To my left, my seatbox was totally obscured by the rhythmic, jostling mass of the Iron Fireman, deep in slumber with a beatific smile on his grimy, stubble-covered face. My initial impulse was to prime the deck hose and blow him off the seatbox, but I prudently rejected this as a bit theatrical. Then too, the prospect of this misfit's sabotaging my fire a second time had a sobering effect. From a utilitarian standpoint, he was peaking out at maximum efficiency as he was. Besides, with the return of full boiler pressure, Harry's renewed vigor was all but eliminating my need for a seatbox.

So, between putting in fires, I rode the gangway watching the dawn come up, not in Kipling's thunderous manner but more like an art-deco poster with pinkish cloud undersides. It was more than adequate. After our inauspicious start, Harry did his stack-busting best to make a creditable showing. The watertender on our low-wheeled tow must have found the vibration level stimulating, for with apron banging and cab windows rattling, he kept a low profile.

So went the remainder of our return leg, a clear-board outing all the way Leaving the high line at Hudson Tower for the Meadows' inbound engine track, the view of the Manhattan skyline, in spite of the roundhouse haze, was detailed. Once sharply again, our pit arrival elicited no cheery greeting from the firecleaners, a morose lot at best. The Iron Fireman, having earned nonperson status, wordlessly slunk off the engine and regrouped with his co-watertender. As Harry and I trudged through the cinders to the crew room, they were last seen homing in on the roundhouse cafeteria and its promise of exotic, leaden fare.

WHAT'S THE PROBLEM UP THERE, UNION?

October 1981

Paul D. Schneider

Mainly, it's a funnel. The interlocking plant at Union Avenue in Chicago, that is.

You see, between South River Street in Aurora and Union Avenue in Chicago on the Burlington Northern, there are three main tracks, numbered from the north beginning with No. 1. From Cicero east, a freight line, main track No. 4, joins the inevitable march toward MP 2.1, the west limits of Union Avenue interlocking. After that, it's all downhill, so to speak, toward Chicago Union Station.

Because, as BN's Special Instructions so dispassionately point out, "Between Roosevelt Road, MP 0.8, and Union Avenue interlocking, MP 1.4, there are two main tracks, on which movement of trains in either direction will be governed by signal direction." Which means that *four* tracks at the west end of the plant turn into *two* tracks at the east end.

In other words, a funnel.

But that's not all. Union Avenue is the western end of the St. Charles Air Line, the jointly owned (Illinois Central Gulf and Chicago & North Western) line that bridges the South Branch of the Chicago River to connect the BN and the North Western with the Rock Island and ICG's Iowa Division at Clark Street interlocking. Toss in the Canal Street wye—the connecting tracks between BN and Conrail—and what you have is pandemonium. Sheer chaos.

Union Avenue is an interlocking plant that looks like it was laid out by a drunken baboon with a blunt crayon. Monday through Friday mornings, it's subjected to BN's commuter rush, followed by practically everything possible: overloaded Conrail drags out of CR's 55th Street Yard for Cicero, underpowered BN drags headed the opposite way, entire Amtrak trains being turned on the wye, ICG-C&NW coal trains in and out of the North Western's Wood Street yard, BN wash trains, Amtrak revenue trains, North Western switch runs thrown in for good measure … and who knows what else.

In 1972, when I was a naive and impressionable young railfan, I rolled by Union Avenue tower on Amtrak's *San Francisco Zephyr* at a particularly frantic moment and wondered what kind of person the BN could have dragged in kicking and screaming to work that madhouse. Seven years later, as suburban train 202 stops to let off the extra operator temporarily assigned to first trick Union Avenue, I know. Me.

There are certain irrefutable truths about Union Avenue tower: There are 144 levers in the 60-foot-long machine, and the machine itself built by General Railway Signal, is Model 5 Form B "similar in many respects to the Form A machine," according to the GRS service manual, "yet built on an entirely different frame." Even the notation scratched into that frame—Wired by J R Smith 8/31 IN THE DEPTHS OF THE DEPRESSION— ascribes a hard reality to the place.

What is harder to define is the ambience about Union Avenue. There's an intangible feeling that the tower is some stoical spectator at a giant outdoor movie, while the operator jumping up, pulling levers, glancing out at the numbers on passing locomotives and jotting them down—is the animating force behind the spectator's eyes, taking in the flickering montage of time and events ... and trains. It's 7 a.m. ... and you can almost *feel* the place holding its breath.

ɪ　ɪ

Yes, indeed. I've discovered myself humming snatches of an Elvis Costello song, "Waiting for the End of the World." Not a particularly optimistic number, considering its title, and certainly not in the proper spirit of things at 4 minutes past 7, waiting for the "dinky parade"—the suburban rush, that is—to begin.

But a minute later No. 204 hits the bell at the west end of the plant on main 2, and I'm up and pulling levers, lining up the signals for a straight shot down 2 to Union Station. It's roughly 4 minutes from the time an eastbound hits the bell at Kedzie Avenue until he pops past the tower, unless he makes a stop at Halsted Street, which 204 does. Figure him by the tower around 7:10.

"Hello Union?"

Wait a minute; what's that? Hello? I hear a voice calling me from the speaker above the desk. The odds are that it's the Chicago Union Station operator at Harrison Street, but I would not bet on it. There are seven lines tied into here through the one speaker: Union Station, the 14th Street coach yard, the outside plant phones, the BN East End dispatcher, the Baltimore & Ohio bridge on the Air Line, the BN wash rack, and the

Conrail switchtender on the south end of the Canal Street wye at Lumber Street. Until you fine-tune your ears to the idiosyncratic sounds of each voice on each line, you're playing the speaker on intuition.

"Hello Union?" Hmmm ... he sounds concerned. He's probably wondering what's happened to the BN operator. Well then, it's time for action! I glare at the maddening array of lookalike toggle switches in front of me and, without flinching, depress the one marked CUS.

"Union," I say, bracing myself.

"Ah, Union!" The Harrison Street operator sounds relieved. "Two-ninety-one on track one."

Well, that's just fine. Train 291 is an empty equipment move that starts the day as 202. It will now flip back to Downers Grove and reoriginate as 234. CUS OS'es [reports] the outbound dinkies to me, and I OS the inbounds to him.

As a matter of fact, as I line up 291 straight through on track 1 westbound, 204 is accelerating from its Halsted Street stop. This time I mash down the CUS switch with an air of cool indifference. "Here's two-oh-four on track two at …"—I glance at the clock—"7:10." On the advertised.

"Two-oh-four on two at 7:10 … all right." A pause. "Say, who *is* this, anyway?"

About the time I'm reaching for the switch to tell him, 204's engineer decides to wind out his power—rebuilt E9 9912— for the short sprint into Union Station. I hold back. All attempts at rational communication are wiped out by the exultant roar of 9912's twin 645s, a deafening wave of sound that shakes the tower by the throat.

The windows stop shaking. The sun catches a corner of 204's bilevels as it leans into the curve toward the depot. OK, let's try it again.

The door behind me crashes open.

"Oh, no. Not *you*?"

"That's right. It's me." The joker standing open-mouthed in the doorway letting the cool air out is our signal maintainer, Larry.

"And I thought there'd be an operator here this morning," he mocks.

Ignoring Larry's remark, I hit the CUS switch and introduce myself to the Harrison Street operator, who tells me that his name is Bo and that he's the swing man, and asks if I know what's happened to the regular first-trick man up here.

Ah … a touchy question. The first-trick operator, the guy who trained me to work this madhouse, has been bounced out of here for almost mating a westbound dinky with a track inspection car. Rather than go into the painful details, I tell Bo that I'm not sure what's going on.

"That's for sure," deadpans Larry.

7:17. No. 206 glides past on track 2 with 9911 pushing; 295 flips back toward Congress Park on track 1 with 9912 to reoriginate as 230, and Larry and I exchange insults on the relative ineptitude of our respective crafts. Then there's a new development. The East End dispatcher rings to tell me that there's an eastbound Conrail freight, designated BNEL-0 [BN-Elkhart] just out of Cicero for 55th Street. Power: 3376, 3377, 3362, and 3378, four fairly new GP40-2s.

No. 212 has already hit the bell on track 3 when the telephone rings again. This time it's one of Larry's numerous lady friends. He decides to accept the call downstairs in his "office." That's fine with me.

"Who needs the maintainer, anyway," I call after him jokingly.

ɪ　ɪ

Suburban trains 210 and 212 present a problem. No. 212 hits the plant on track 3. The only way to get him onto track 2—the old funnel problem again— is by running him over switch 109. Which is no big deal … except that 210, a nonstopper, hits the plant at the same time 212 does, and switch 109 has to be lined the opposite way for his straight shot down 2.

When I was breaking in here, I would foul this one up royally. Train 212 would hit, and I'd rush over to line him up. Then 210 would pop up on track 2 … 212 would go by, slowing for his Halsted Street stop as 210 rocketed by … and I'd be flying across the room to throw switch 109 for

A worm's-eye view of a light engine on K track (middle) between Amtrak 380 (left) and dinky 240. *Paul D. Schneider*

210, whose engineer would be barking over the radio that he had a red board and would the operator at Union Avenue *mind* lining him up?

Now I know better. I just line up 210 first. After he's by me, I line up 212. Very simple.

It's the same thing this morning. After 210 flies past me, I walk to the middle of the interlocking machine, reach for 109's lever, and yank on it to line up 212.

But the lever doesn't budge.

Hmmm … sometimes these old levers get stubborn. I whack it with the palm of my hand and yank again. Nothing. Sweat breaks out on my forehead. "Uh, Larry?" I call, depressing the Plant switch, hoping that he'll hear me downstairs. No reply. Now 212's hogger is calling for the signal over the radio. "Yeah, I know you're out there," I mutter, glaring at his headlight through the window. What does he think I am, blind?

All right now, let's not get excited. I know it'll only make matters worse. I must stay cool. I must not … "LARRY!"

The telephone rings. I jerk the receiver from its cradle. "Larry?"

"What is it, Schneider?"

"Larry, switch one-oh-nine won't pull and two-twelve is sitting out here!"

"Oh, that's all right, Schneider," drawls Larry. "Who needs the maintainer, anyway."

A few seconds later he's calmly surveying the levers, poking at relays, trying to ascertain the problem. I get on the radio and inform 212 that we've got signal trouble, which seems to pacify him for the time being. Finally, Larry announces that he has to go outside and check the switch itself.

"Here's two-ninety-seven on one, Union," says Bo.

Yipes! I leap to the levers and line him up westbound. Whenever a crisis hits at Union Avenue, you expect the rest of the railroad to shut down until it's rectified. Not so. As a matter of fact, a glance at the west end of the track schematic board reveals 214 on track 2. I might as well line him up, seeing as 212 isn't going anywhere for a while.

There is no problem when the Conrail drag shows up on 4; I just line him down to the tower and hold him until I get an OK from the Lumber Street switchtender to let him on down the wye.

At 7:35, dinky 216 hits the bell on 2 … and I'm beginning to worry. The Burlington Northern prides itself on its superlative commuter service, and this pride is reflected in its concern over tardy trains. An operator who has delayed a dinky receives a calm, matter-of-fact telephone call from an official downtown. An operator who delays dinkies once too often will end up at Eola yard, where he'll be allowed to clear up branch-line trains and feed waybills into a computer. I don't want to go to Eola.

But wait … Larry's waving to me! He wants me to try the switch; 216 is hollering about the yellow board he's coming up against, but to hell with him. I grasp the lever. I close my eyes. I yank.

It pulls.

Aha, 212 is lined up! Fired with victory, I pull the signal for him and, with two toots of his horn, he's moving. It's 7:37, and he's 7 minutes late, but still, he's moving.

⚋ ⚋

The best thing about westbound dinkies is that their E units are on the point leaving the depot. The BN's E units are an especially delightful breed anyway, with their sweeping bands of green and white. No squat F40PHs for this operation—nothing but Es, long and lean and leggy, 100 percent pure. Nos. 9900 through 9908 are E8As, 9910 and up are E9As, but the distinctions end there. All are former CB&Q units, rebuilt by Morrison-Knudsen in Boise, Idaho, in 1973 and 1974. EMD 645-engine components upgraded the venerable 567 prime movers that had seen so much service on the *Zephyrs* (and dinkies), while Cummins equipment was installed to provide head-end power for the Budd gallery cars, allowing retirement of generator-coaches. No other stable of commuter locomotives in the United States can match the class of BN's.

Larry flings the door open and, muttering about foreign material in the switches, flops on an easy chair. I walk the length of the machine, clearing signals and pulling out switches 109 and 110. Train 203 is the last westbound move on track 2 until 205 at 8:51, so for the next hour I can use track 1 for eastbounds. Throwing 109 and 110 effectively turns the plant into a double-barrel shotgun pumping dinkies off of tracks 3 and 2 into the depot on tracks 2 and 1.

I've already checked with Lumber Street on the feasibility of moving this BNEL-0 sometime in the near future. He had to check with 21st Street, 21st Street had to check with 55th Street, 55th Street had to check with 51st Street, 51st Street had to check with the Pope. Now, half an hour later, the switchtender calls me. "OK, let him come, but keep him going once he gets his speed up."

Gotcha, Chief. Let him come once he gets it up. I throw the signal and look out the window to see if the BNEL-0 is moving. Sure enough, a smear of dignified exhaust, hardly more than a smudge above the 3376's turbocharger stack, tells me that he is. A minute later, the four matched 645s of the new EMDs are shaking an audible fist at the Alco-loving operator, their screaming turbochargers threatening to shatter every window in the tower. Apparently Larry's had just about enough of this hot action. Rising from his chair, he announces that he's going down to the ladder tracks at the west end of the plant to watch Jesse, the section foreman, change out a frog on switch 19. "Think you can handle things OK from up here without me?"

⚋ ⚋

Why, of course I can. It's now my second day and, short of a few *minor* problems, I'm doing a bang-up job.

"Nealy?"

Ouch. That's Warren, yardmaster at the 14th Street coach yard. He uses the Q line to talk to me and to Nealy, his switchtender. Unfortunately the Q line is much louder than the other six lines, and if you turn it down you lose all volume on the others. Stand next to the speaker when Warren is on, however, and you can kiss your hearing good-bye.

"Hello Union?" bellows Warren. I depress the Q switch and ask him what's up.

"You'll be getting two light engines down three lead for one, then two down four for one. After that I've got two-ten's wash train for the wash rack."

Wash train? What day is this? "Are you washing trains today, Warren?" I inquire stupidly. There's a long pause at the other end of the line. ...

"That's right. Who's this?"

I introduce myself for the second time in two days. I'm not offended, though. I figure Warren's got a lot on his mind down there at the coach yard. Still, I'm not too enthused about the wash trains. "It'll be a while before I can get them through the dinky rush, Chief." Like maybe not until second shift, after I've gone home, is what I'm thinking.

"Well," retorts Warren, "I've got to get this guy in there. I've got the five-forty-three with an eight-car wash behind him, and later on, I'll have a bunch of light engines going down there. Lemme know when it opens up, up there."

Right.

Don't get me wrong. I think clean commuter trains are great. It's simply that in the middle of the rush, wash trains can tie up this plant like a hangman's noose. And we *know* what happens when the operator delays a dinky.

Then again, when you hold up a wash train, you have Warren's steady barrage of questions blasting over a speaker. "What's the problem up there, Union?"

The first light engine, 9907, slips out of the coach yard on 3 lead. I pull two switches and three signals, and 9907 runs up to K track on the schematic. From where I'm standing, I can see the unit beneath the I-94 bridge. After he stops behind the signal, I run down the previous lineup—it takes about 10 seconds—and line him back down K to lead 1, where he'll pick his way through the coach yard to the engine facility, which is known even today as the Zephyr Pit.

The dinky rush continues to move past me with the smoothness of hot butter tipped downhill. Meanwhile, back at the Light Engine Movement Department, 9910 has been tucked away by 8:20.

"Union!" thunders Warren, "can you handle this guy?"

It sounds like Warren's getting anxious. Well, what the heck ... I guess I can squeeze his wash trains in; the next dinky isn't until 8:36.

This is the proverbial lull before the storm. The rush slacks off for a quarter of an hour and, while I'm taking the wash train off the north leg of the wye and down 5 track to the wash rack, Bo calls and asks if I can handle Amtrak train 56's wye move. I tell him that it's OK to send him down the north leg of the wye behind Warren's washer.

8:33 ... and I'm looking down at Conrail 8444, an ancient SW1. Every inch of its tapered black body is shaking with the effort of lugging 56's wye through the

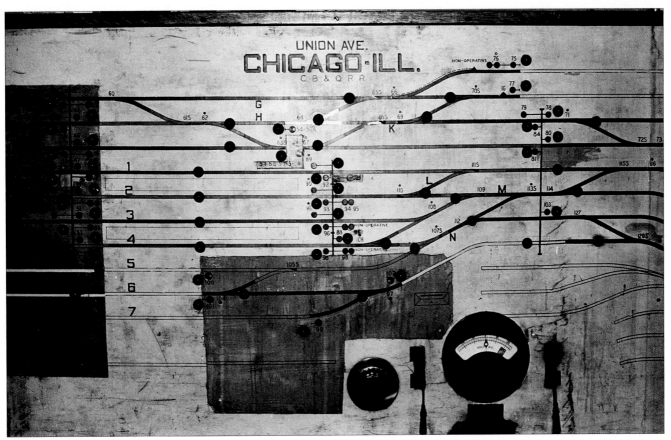

Schematic of Union Avenue interlocking. At left (west), mains 1-4 are BN high iron from Cicero, with tracks 5-7 the wash rack. Halsted Street platforms are between 1 and 2, and 3 and 4, to the west of the tower. At top, tracks G and H feed to C&NW Wood Street yard. At right (east), from top, are two tracks from St. Charles Air Line and B&O bridge, leads from the BN coach yard, two mains from Union Station, and tracks from the Canal Street wye. *Paul D. Schneider*

plant. Amtrak has two or three Geeps assigned to its 18th Street enginehouse, but for some curious reason, all of the wye moves by here rate these antediluvian EMDs. Which is fine by me. I *like* SW1s. Sure, there are zillions of them on Conrail, but now that EMD has announced it will no longer stock parts for the 6-cylinder 567 the SW1 has, how much longer do you think they have left on this road … or on any other Class 1, for that matter? Sure, I'm a diehard Alco enthusiast, but I can appreciate a survivor when I see one.

After it stops, I line the 8444 back down the south leg of the wye. From the operator in the tower it's more than just a signal. It's a salute.

I   I

The problem with Amtrak trains 391 and 380 is, quite simply this: They tend to be in the same place at the same time, much like suburban trains 210 and 212.

Unlike the two dinkies, though, the Amtrak trains move in opposite directions: 391 is outbound to Carbondale, 380 inbound to CUS.

Bo wants to know what track he should send 391 out on. Oh, well. "Put him on one, Bo."

You see, there is no direct route into Union Station for Amtrak trains that utilize the former Illinois Central main line into Chicago. Consequently, they have to back into the depot after taking the St. Charles Air Line over from the ICG connection at Clark Street interlocking. It's a time-consuming move, but it's the only way to get these trains in and out of the depot. Sigh.

When the B&O bridgetender up on the Air Line rings me twice, I accept the call without enthusiasm. "Hello Union," he says brightly. "Number three-eighty comin' your way."

Rats. "What track?"

"Westbound."

Of course. Still, there's no need for me to panic. So what if there's a light engine screaming for the signal down there on 4 lead? Let him eat cake. A nervous glance to the east reveals the tail end of 391 backing toward me—three Superliners and a GE P30CH. It's a losing combination esthetically, if you want to know the truth, but it sure beats an F40 and three Amcoaches. The stubby 391 rumbles past me, clears the signal, and stops. The headlight of the big GE glares at me.

So go ahead and glare, turkey. A second glance out of the window shows 380 tiptoeing down the Air Line. It's regrettable that the laws of nature allow but one train on one track at one time, cornfield meets notwithstanding. Today, 380 takes the square. I throw him the signal and stand back to watch him pass 391.

With three Amcoaches and an F40, 380 proves to be the disappointment of the hour. Nonetheless, I crank off the OS to Bo, first lining 380 back toward the depot. We'll make it at 8:55. By 8:59, 391 is on its merry way to the ICG main.

The hour between 9 and 10 a.m. is relatively calm. By 8:39, with the passing of 242, the dinky parade is pretty much over with, and once 380 and 391 are out of the way, you can kick back and tear into your lunch … with only the occasional burst of activity to intrude upon your R&R.

"Hello Union?"

Pushing aside my yogurt, I depress the Plant switch and find a C&NW engineer on the other end. He's got an empty WEPX coal empty going back to the ICG. Can I let him go?

After checking with both the Wood Street yardmaster and the B&O bridge on the Air Line, I tell him yes. The bridgetender has informed me that there's a westbound Rock Island transfer waiting at Clark Street to use the Air Line, but that the empty Weppix should come first. It doesn't make any difference to me, so I line up the North Western train.

He eases by a few minutes later with 115 empties behind the 879, an SD40, and—of all things—Union Pacific 2810, a U28C!

I   I

Wash trains, wash trains, wash trains. I think that's Warren's hobby. He collects wash trains. Then, after he's got about 10 of them, he sends them down to me.

Between 10 a.m. and 10:40, I handle *three* additional wash trains, including two sets of three light engines. The only complication arises when Amtrak 348, the run from Quincy, rockets through the plant at 10:14, followed by dinky 246 at 10:15.

"What's the hang-up up there, Union?"

"Just a couple of those pesky through trains, Chief. I'll have them out of your way in a jiffy."

At 10:30, a treat: the Rock Island transfer that trundles down the Air Line is in the hands of the 418, one of the Rock's rare C415s! Good Lord, I wonder … how could the Rock, a road

noted for re-engining its 244 Alcos with EMD engines while completely ignoring the application of the 251 prime mover in road freight units—how could *the Rock* have ended up with 10 C415s? You could almost as easily imagine MoPac with C628s.

Don't misunderstand me. I'm certainly not complaining about the Rock's Alco fleet, particularly since the units are assigned to the Chicago area. I think they're great … but to be fair, I don't have to stock parts for the little monsters.

10:36. … Good heavens, it's the B&O bridge again, announcing the imminent arrival of Amtrak 58, the *Panama Limited*.

Well, good. Would it be that 391 and 380 were as easy to deal with as 58. Just line him off the Air Line down 2 main, wait for him to stop, and then line him back down 2 to the depot. Simple as pie.

Lumber Street phones with a call on an ELBN-3 with four units: the 2539, 2715, 2797, and 2762. Hey … that's a pure GE lashup! Conrail's been something of a drag since it started gorging itself on potloads of GP and SD40-2s. The best place to find a Conrail F unit is at Joe Pielet's scrapyard out in McCook across the tracks from EMD, and as far as the Alco situation on Conrail in 1979 is concerned, well … I'd rather not talk about it. A pure GE lashup, though—that I could handle.

"And behind him," adds the switchtender, "are these light coal engines back from the GM&O."

Boy, that floors me. It really does. Some of these old-timers talk like they're living in a corked bottle from the '50s, a place where mergers haven't taken place, where the Burlington still takes coal trains to the GM&O, instead of the BN taking them to the ICG. Eavesdropping on the dispatcher's line, you can hear them talking about the Nickel Plate transfer. I suppose it doesn't matter how much Cascade green or Conrail blue or NW black you slap over engines or on paycheck stubs. To the guy yanking couplers or switches or waybills out of boxes somewhere on the old system, it's still going to be the Burlington or the Pennsy or the Nickel Plate. And probably always will be.

Yes, well … reality beckons in the form of 58. Why, if I dared to compare what I've heard about Illinois Central's *Panama Limited* to *this* train—this Amtrak collection of two P30CHs and Amcoaches—I might get downright depressed. It is not the function of the operator at Union Avenue, however, to pass judgment on what rolls over these switches and takes these signals. No, sir … just line 'em up off the Air Line, wait for 'em to stop, and line 'em back into the depot.

Except that, a minute later, I'm still waiting for 'em.

To back up.

Lumber Street's call snaps my head around to the east window. "Here's that ELBN-3, Union." Ah, yes … there they are, four shuddering GEs crawling painfully around the south wye. Still shaking my head over the *Panama*, I line the freight straight through on 4, then drift back to the desk.

"Say, Bo … this *Panama* won't take the signal to back up. Do you have a radio up there?"

He doesn't, but he suggests the next best thing … that I call the ICG train director and have him talk to 58. That's a good idea. I mean, what could be wrong with this train? Maybe he has air problems. Maybe both GEs died simultaneously. Still, the nagging suspicion remains that somehow—I'm not sure how, but somehow—I've screwed up. But how? Maybe if I check the…

"Union, how about this wash train off the north wye?" *POOWWW!!!* A double-knuckle fist of Warren the yardsmasher punches me right in the side of the head.

That's it. I can't hear anything out of my right ear! I reel away from the desk speaker, holding my hand over my ear, trying to keep my balance…

Wait … what's that? The telephone! I can still hear! I jerk the receiver off its hook.

"Union."

"Is this the Burlington Northern Union Avenue?"

"Of course it is," I retort. I mean, why does *everyone* ask that? How many bloody Union Avenues could there be in this town?

Rebuilt E8 in the wash rack west of Union Avenue. "I think Warren just collects wash trains." *Paul D. Schneider*

"This is the ICG train director at Markham."

"Yeah, well, I'm glad you called, man," I burst out. "What's this stupid number fifty-eight doing here? He's got the stupid signal."

"Well, yes. Union … but be claims that he's lined *into* the C&NW yard there."

I stare at the receiver for what seems to be a painfully long period of time. In front of me, through the north window, I can make out the rounded carbody lines of the 2539, a U25B still in Penn Central paint. Another part of my consciousness tells me that this is the ELBN-3 chugging past me. That's nice.

"Hello Union?"

I might as well face up to the inevitable. I raise my eyes to the track schematic. Ah, yes … reality. If 58 had indeed been on 2 main where I had intended to send him, then the track indicator light on 2 main would be lit. It is not.

"I, uh, think I see the problem," I mumble into the phone.

"OK, Union, great." The train director seems remarkably nonplussed over the entire incident. But then, he's not the one who has to back up the Air Line.

It takes 58 *four* moves to accomplish what *two* moves should have accomplished and, when the power stomps past the tower, I find an excuse to be elsewhere. Like in the bathroom. After all, there is no reason to show myself to the engineer of 58. He might be … well, *distressed*.

⊥ ⊥

What goes on at Union Avenue for the rest of first trick? It varies from day to day. Some things are consistent, like the dinkies. And some are not. Freights come and go in both directions, and some of them breeze right through the interlocking, while others—like this PIBN-5 here—take a little longer.

There are several reasons for delays. Freights are held out of yards by irate yardmasters, or they have air problems. Some are underpowered, which means they have a hard time lifting their tonnage out of the natural bowl in which the Canal Street wye resides. Some are detained by other things—like this PIBN-5.

"What's the problem with this Conrail guy, Union?"

I've decided that Warren can't be the 300-pound gorilla I imagine him to be—it's just the effects of the speaker, right? He's probably an OK guy with a nice wife and a bunch of swell kids. Nonetheless, at this stage of the game, I'd like to shoot him.

I don't know *what* the Conrail's problem is. The light engines and ELBN-3 both went down 4 track without any problems. Now, at close to 2 p.m., this train is stopped dead in the middle of the plant, effectively blocking Warren's wash train from leaving the wash rack.

"Beats me," I reply innocently. "I think he has air problems."

There's no response to that one, but then again, I don't expect any. Then I hear something that sounds vaguely like a tape recording of Mickey Mouse being squeezed through a vegetable strainer. Wait a minute … that's Larry! "Larry? Are you there?" I holler into the Plant phone.

Unit coal train off freight main 4, bound for ICG and Joliet. "From the CB&Q to the GM&O … as it will always be." *Paul D. Schneider*

"Yeah, Schneider. … Say, this Conrail engineer wants to talk at you." I tell Larry to put him on.

"Is this the operator?" asks an unfamiliar voice. "This is the engineer off this PIBN-5. Say, are you *sure* you want to line us up this way?"

What is this, some kind of joke?

"What are you talking about? What way?"

"Why … through the wash rack."

No … no, I didn't intend to do any thing of the sort. And when Frank, the second-trick operator, arrives 40 minutes later, I refrain from telling him the whole terrible story: how PIBN-5 had to back up out of the wash rack lead, how he lost his air twice, how he blocked Warren's wash train for 30 minutes, and how the temperature in the tower dropped 20 degrees each time the yardmaster got on the speaker to ask what the problem was.

Frank has seen a lot of changes in this East End over the last 30 years. In immediate postwar years, according to Frank, there were towers at Roby Street, Kedzie

Avenue, Cicero, La Vergne, Congress Park, Downers Grove, Eola itself, and West Eola. There were 250 operators on the First Subdivision seniority list alone.

That impressed me. We're lucky to have 50 now, and the only manned towers left on this end of the BN are Aurora tower and, of course, Union.

Congress Park long ago lost its manned interlocking plant to CTC, but Frank ended up as agent there when "the Park" became a COMPASS computer reporting station. When BN cut the job in 1979, Frank bumped into Union, where he'd worked years before as an extra telegrapher. He says he has pictures of the place back then … of steam-powered Pennsy transfer drags and quicksilver Q *Twin Zephyrs* … and one of these days he'll bring them in to show me what it was like. I'm dying to see them.

The tower itself has seen a lot of changes. Long before gallery cars and Cascade green, Union Avenue was there, dusted by coal smoke and exhaust from 8-cylinder Winton 201-A prime movers, reverberating to the sounds of the Q's De La Vergne-engined Baldwin VO switchers and matched A-B-A F3s. Frank

tells me the New York Central used to handle transfer trains with four-unit covered-wagon sets, handsome locomotives graced with lightning stripes. I don't doubt it.

"Are you getting the hang of the place now?" he asks.

"Oh, yeah, sure," I lie cheerfully. "No problem at all." Except for when the Amtrak official called to ask *why* 58 was so late getting into the depot. But what the heck. "I like it here," I add impulsively. "I really do."

"Oh, jeez, yes," Frank agrees with a smile. "It's a helluva place to be, isn't it?"

There's a sudden swell of engine noise outside the window, carried along by the high-pitched whine of Electro-Motive turbochargers. "That's the *Zephyr*," I tell Frank hurriedly. "I already lined him up."

The SDP40F leading Amtrak No. 6 seems to knock the air aside as it whacks past the tower. It's followed by another SDP … a rebuilt E9B masquerading as a heater car … then an unbroken stream of stainless steel bucking along on 2 main, headed for Union Station.

Frank's right, you know … about this place. It's a helluva place to be.

Recollections of an Omaha Brasspounder

Ken C. Brovald

June 1982

Railroading uses a language foreign to many.

Not only does railroading have a spoken jargon still peculiar to it today, but before the advent of two-way radios, employees in one location would work all day without actually speaking to other employees elsewhere. They used a mysterious language—the telegraph.

I grew up along the Great Northern main line on the North Dakota prairie, where the only connections to the rest of the world were the track and the telegraph. Watching tonnage rumble westward during World War II stimulated my interest in this mysterious language. I would gape as the local GN agent/telegrapher sat at his bay-window desk and wrote something on paper that had been "said" to him through the clicking instrument in the square box, then reply similarly with his fingers. He would have the answers to my questions. "Extra 2551 will meet number 9 here" or "Number 83 has the 2031 [a huge 2-8-8-2] today." The trains provided the entertainment; today, with no local passenger trains and few local freights to watch, small-town life must be a bore.

Almost 10 years were to pass in my transformation from a wide-eyed farm lad to a railroad telegrapher, but my destiny seemed to be to join the ranks as a

brasspounder, also known in the trade as a telegrapher, a Morse man, or simply an op (for telegraph operator). One succeeded to each title through the years, from a *tyro* (apprentice) to a *ham* to a *telegrapher* to—finally—a *brasspounder*.

Learning the Morse code of telegraphy seemed simple enough … all I would have to do was learn 26 letters, 10 numbers, and a few punctuation symbols and translate them into dots and dashes. Could telegraph be hard work? I was to learn it takes years to master it.

The 40-hour workweek became effective September 1, 1949, and as a result, the railroads were in immediate need of thousands of additional employees, particularly in the stations and telegraph departments as relief telegraph operators. The roads could reduce some stations to a 5-day workweek to avoid extra hires, but for operational reasons, many mainline facilities had to be open continuously, 24 hours a day, 7 days a week.

To fill the demand, a number of schools were established all over the country to train people. In a relatively short time, hundreds of young men and a few women attended classes in Morse. Those proficient enough soon passed the required test of 15 words per minute in code and an examination on the Consolidated Book of Rules; they were then ready to work for a railroad.

In August 1949, I attended the Gale Institute telegraph school in Minneapolis (where my instructor was Ronald V. Nixon, who has contributed many photos to TRAINS). After I completed school, my big day arrived just one day before the 40-hour law took effect. The Chicago, St. Paul, Minneapolis & Omaha Railway—the Omaha Road—called for a number of relief men, and I joined their ranks. I carried this message:

This will introduce Ken C. Brovald, newly hired Western Division telegrapher. Mr. Brovald will report to Bingham Lake, relieving the telegrapher on third trick, commencing 12:01 a.m., Aug. 30, 1949. (signed)
Geo. R. McGinty, Chief Train Dispatcher

Armed with these credentials and a big brass, hollow-cylinder switch key which would open any freight-room door on the Omaha Road, I began my telegraph career.

I   I

Third trick (shift), midnight to 8 a.m. The mysterious telegraph was clicking as, shortly before midnight, I entered the sacred inner sanctum of the depot office in Bingham Lake, Minn., a nondescript small town on the Omaha's Twin Cities-Sioux City main line. The second-trick operator turned over the transfer sheet, and the station was mine. At last, I was a real railroadman charged with the responsibilities of copying train orders and messages to be delivered to passing trains.

The station was typical of small-town depots. A wood shelf table was built into the bay window, allowing a view down the track in each direction. There was a rolltop desk, a pot-bellied, coal-burning stove, iron bars at the ticket window, wooden cabinets on the walls, and a wooden contraption of a chair, its four legs stuck in green glass insulators substituting for rollers (but better suited to slide on the rough wood floor). A typewriter set in a sunken table blended with the telegraph instruments.

BI BI BI DI … the dispatcher (located at Western Division headquarters in St. James, Minn.) called on the wire, repeating the two-letter code for my station and identifying himself. I reached for the key, but my hand immediately froze into nervous immobility—my first attack of a "glass arm." I finally opened the key and feebly answered … I BI (I am ready; station code).

Quickly, the wire sputtered to life: 19 CY 3 WEST (three copies of a Form 19 order for a westbound train). This was manual-block territory, with the order-board signal in front of the station displaying the direction of control. This prevented a train from entering a block until it received an order or a clearance card indicating the track ahead was clear of opposing trains.

I set the signal against eastbound traffic and acknowledged on the wire SD WEST (signal displayed for westbounds), that I was ready to copy. I pulled a carbon set of 19 forms from their pigeon-hole cabinet. The code came through slowly, as my ears and mind laboriously strained to catch each letter and translate them into English on the form:

C&E NO 201

BI

NO 201 MEET NO 210 AT HERON LAKE
NO 210 TAKE SIDING

G R M

(Translation: For conductor and engineer of train 201 at Bingham Lake…) I repeated the order to ensure accuracy, and the dispatcher made it complete, authorizing the signing of his initials. The whole process took a while, but with much patience from the dispatcher, I had copied my first live train order. I delivered it to the westbound train, No. 201, known as the *Nightingale*. I was oh so proud of my skills, helping to keep the railroad system operating by my membership on the team, as the trains rolled through the night past my station to more important destinations.

I reported to the dispatcher that the train had passed my station. This was done by the simple symbol OS, probably the most widely known and used telegraphic code. Apparently no one is sure of its exact origin, but it is believed to mean *on sheet*. I keyed OS BI 201 132 (symbol that the train has passed, reporting station's code, train number, time).

There was some dispute among operators as to when a train should be OS'ed. A fast passenger train would be by in a minute, but a long freight might take 5 minutes or longer. Most operators reported the time when the caboose passed the station—i.e., when the operator no longer had control to stop it.

I   I

The railroad industry had a system of promotion in the working ranks which was known as *bid and bump*. In my time on the railroad, I found this system of straight seniority to be most equitable in aiding one's promotion into better positions. No politics, no squabbles, no extra proof of ability to perform were involved.

If a job on your division was closed, or if a telegraph operator with considerable seniority was bumped from his post by someone with more whiskers, a chain of relocations was set into motion. The system was sometimes harsh and ruthless, but rules were rules and no one complained bitterly. An open telegrapher's job was posted by circular letter issued by the division superintendent's office. Qualified telegraphers interested in the position would bid their seniority against others, and the applicant with the most service time would be granted the assignment. This would put the successful bidder's former job open for another round of bids, and the whole process for everyone to relocate into new positions would take months.

During my first 2 years on the Omaha, I worked 51 stations (some more than once) in Minnesota, South Dakota, Iowa, and Nebraska.

"You'll love the station," said the Chief (chief dispatcher). The agent in Thurston, Neb., was due for a vacation, but no extra relief men were willing to take the assignment. My name came up in line, and I caught the next train south. Thurston was the first town north of Pender, and both were in the Winnebago Omaha Indian Reservation.

My first successful bid station was in February 1951 at Winside, Neb., where I would listen on the radio to John Carson, who was from nearby Norfolk (locally pronounced *Norfork*).

A subsequent move gave me the station at Spencer, S.D., a busy branch-line point of some 500 population serving a farming community. The main shipper was a hard quartz rock quarry, from which thousands of carloads of rock were being sent to the Missouri River for the Pick/Sloan flood-control power dams being constructed at numerous points between Omaha and Bismarck, N.D. The Omaha Road was a key artery in the supply of the concrete sand, fill rock, and rip-rap for those dams.

The Omaha Road was born as the Tomah & Lake St. Croix in Wisconsin on April 1, 1863, and after expansions and consolidations acquired its full CMStP&O name on May 25, 1880. The Chicago & North Western purchased a controlling interest in the Omaha as early as 1882, increasing its investment to 93.6 percent by 1925. The Omaha remained a separate corporation until 1957, when the C&NW absorbed it. When the Omaha built into the prairie frontier, Dakota was still singular, not having achieved statehood (that came in 1889). When I arrived in Spencer, I found some station hardware still labeled *Dakota Territory*—or simply DT—almost 75 years after the fact!

The agent's duties at Spencer were typical. The public knew little about waybills, tariffs, fares, junctions, or routings, and it was the local station agent to whom the public turned to conduct business with the railroad. It was he (or she) who made up the bill of lading when freight was to be shipped, or issued the tickets when people were to travel. A bill of lading, the primary document which ran the railroad, was the legal contract from which a waybill was prepared, the goods were moved to their destination, and the shipping charges were assessed.

In the depot's tariff case were stacked the books and sheets of the rates and rules from which the agent determined the charges for shipping or traveling. The freight tariffs in Omaha depots revealed the products of the prairie: grain, milk and cream, wool, livestock, rock, sand, and gravel. Inbound shipments included lumber, cement, coal, fuel oil and gasoline, and farm machinery. As newer tariff forms appeared or changes in old ones were made, the old, unused stock simply

The telegraph key was the basic implement for any operator. Operators would acquire high-quality keys and take them from job to job. *George H. Drury*

stayed in their slots in the case, gathering dust and turning yellow—mute testimony to the railroad's metamorphosis.

The telegraphy field had two general categories: the **commercial field**, which included those employed by Western Union and commercial press wire services, and **railroading**, which employed more than the others combined. The paths would cross in many places. In small towns, the railroad station usually was also the Western Union outlet, and the 24-hour railroad office often extended the commercial company's limited hours.

In railroading, *telegrams* and *messages* were synonymous, the terms being used to distinguish between Western Union and railroad company communications. Western Union telegrams offered the greatest variety of news and hence kept the local station agent in the thick of local information. The most challenging were telegrams from foreign countries in native languages. I had a sense of satisfaction when a telegraph I copied in Swedish was found to be correct, although before it was delivered and read, I had no idea what it said. Perhaps the most difficult task of a railroad telegrapher was the distressing duty of delivering a telegram telling of a death in a family.

Passengers sometimes tested the patience of an agent/telegrapher. One

Omaha Road agent who handled tourists in the summer was heard to remark, "After handling people all summer, I'm glad to see the sheep, and after six months of sheep, I welcome the people again."

Prairie towns usually had government grain bins controlled by the Commodity Credit Corporation (CCC), built to store grain during periods of low prices. The farmers sealed the grain for a fixed price and placed it in the bins. Some years, very little grain would be shipped, and these were dry years for the Omaha Road. But as soon as the price was better, several years' crops might be shipped, and the Omaha (and other roads) would have to scramble for 40-foot boxcars. Telegraph messages would flow to and from the railroads' general offices placing orders for cars and supplies. In the grain belt from Canada to Texas, with thousands of local grain elevators all shipping as fast as they could to take advantage of the good market, massive car shortages would result. Prompted by prairie members, Congress would call for an investigation of the inefficient distribution system, asking for more controls. Congress did not seem to realize it was a government agency, the CCC, that caused it.

Each road, in turn, would call their own cars home, as ordered by the Interstate Commerce Commission, causing a massive redistribution of empty cars. The system would break down in the morass of red tape. Grain would pile up at major terminals from Duluth to Houston, and as the grain flooded the market, prices would fall, ending the car shortage as fast as it had begun. Even today the situation is not fully rectified.

I   I

Most small-town depots shared the same odor, caused by a combination of oily floors and acid smoke from the coal-burning stove inside, and creosoted ties and the passing steam locomotives outside. The pot-bellied stove burned locomotive coal, high in sulphur acid. Ground into a powder, it fused into massive clinkers, and the stove belched every hour like the Old Faithful geyser. But its strong heat kept the wooden depot buildings warm during the most fierce winter storms.

Winter on the North Western system seemed to prove that one's loyalty to one's home area is unshakeable. The radio would report that, say, Chicago was paralyzed by a crippling snowstorm, so I'd inquire on the telegraph to the Chicago office. Response: Milwaukee got it worse. Milwaukee, in turn, would report just a light snow but add that Green Bay really got clobbered. The Green Bay operator would then put my query to rest by replying, "We were hardly hit, but they really got it in Chicago!"

Out on the prairie, winter operational problems would sometimes haunt the small-town depots. Snow and sleet would accumulate on the lineside wires until they snapped, cutting communications until a lineman could work his way down the line on a track motor car. Extreme cold, coupled with drifting snow, would fill the cuts out in the country, and if the snow wasn't cleared soon after the storm, the white stuff would become crusted and hard-packed. The wedge plows would go out, ripping through town to gain enough momentum to break through the first cut beyond. Occasionally, snow thrown clear by the plow going through town would slam into the depot, breaking windows and filling the office with its own drift.

As did many prairie railroads, the Omaha found it desirable at some locations to have an agent/telegrapher present at all times, and the live-in depot became commonplace. In an age of corporate paternalism, the arrangement was mutually acceptable to employee and railroad, eliminating the problem of searching (and paying) for housing. Usually that type of station was a two-story structure with living quarters on the second level. For agents at stations without the feature, the pay scale usually compensated for the necessity of rent money.

Stations were required to report the local business situation each morning by telegraph to the local division office; this was the CS (car summary) of cars needed, on hand, or ready to move. Weather or unusual situations were reported on appropriate forms. Automobile/train accidents and personal injury reports were rushed to headquarters at once. Incoming messages were copied on "clips," half sheets of yellow paper which were kept at the ready on the depot typewriter.

Train consists were sent ahead of a departing train to the next yard where the cars would be switched or reclassified. The sending station would alert all interested offices by the symbol 23 (all stations copy), and the list would go to all stations at once, heavy with abbreviations. The operator would roll a 5-copy carbon into the typewriter, and when the code came crashing through the resonator box, accuracy would be paramount, for there was no time to erase errors. A sample:

OMAHA JUNE 18 1952 910 A
TRAIN 18 4051 4054 6505 4087 (engines)
98 15 5330 (loads, empties, tons)
MILLER (conductor)
1 ARTX 28310 R 50 SPUDS SUFALLS
(reporting marks, car number, type [refrigerator], commodity, destination, interchange)
2 GATX 17332 T 24 MTY STP GN
(empty to Great Northern, St. Paul)
3 PLE 22147 B 60 I/S MANKATO
(iron/steel)
4 CO 14573 B 51 CD GD DO
(canned goods to Mankato [ditto])
5 RBNX 80381 R 56 BEER DO
6 NYC 72121 B 72 LIQ STP NP
7 UP 53481 F 79 MCHY STP SOO
8 GN 20664 B 40 LDRS MPLS
9 IGN 14362 B 42 RBR MPLS

Morse code was not read like a book; it was heard, and listened to, like good music. It had a stylish beat; it was an inanimate companion but not dull or spiritless. With the sounding bar clicking like castanets and repeaters adding their own metallic notes, the composition was complete. Each word, especially the more familiar ones, had an unmistakable, individual sound.

You did not hear names of familiar places (CHICAGO, OMAHA, MANKATO) as letters, rather as a word; they had a bounce, a roll, that was recognized immediately. Proficient operators read all chatter in rhythm. To the lone operator at a small-town station, sitting under a blob of pale yellow light at his desk, wearing his green eyeshade, the talk of the telegraph was a friendly, echoing sound. He was oblivious to the other sounders chattering in unison on the table; he knew by the sound that it was through traffic (relay) that did not concern him.

To the public, ignoring a chattering wire was the same as not answering a ringing telephone, but more often than not, when a message was transmitted by phone, the operator would tell the sending office to "give it to me on the wire." The wire was easier to work; it made sense, eliminated trivia and rhetoric, was no-nonsense.

I   I

The wires strung across the countryside, hanging on cross-arms, were generally referred to as strings, referring not only to their frail nature but to their tying the stations together. Each wire was for a specific purpose and was assigned to exclusive use: Western Union telegrams, dispatcher's circuit, general message wire, and high-speed message wire (tied directly to the general office). Most stations had three wires, some only one, but the more important points had as many as 10 strings wired in. All were connected to a resonator box by the use of a selector jack box where the wire to be used could be isolated from the others. Woe be to anyone who used an exclusive wire for purposes other than intended. The offending operator would be told to "Get off. Get your own string to play with." Message traffic would become so heavy

Small-town depots all had a similar appearance. Note the tobacco can tucked into the telegraph resonator box (to the right of the operator's head), the phone on the scissors extender, the beat-up wood desk, and the Western Union wall clock. Most such buildings shared an odor from oily floors, stove smoke, creosoted ties, and locomotive smoke. *George W. Wickersham II*

This 1947 view shows a train arriving at Chadron, Neb., typical of the small-town stations worked by author Brovald. *Fred H. Ragsdale*

that certain wires were dedicated to select offices. It became an exercise in attention to listen to the mainline sounders, all clicking at once, to pick out the one calling your station. Experienced operators had an ear tuned in (or in vernacular, "Had my head cut in") and could identify who was calling and on which string.

Stations were equipped with a circuit test patch board, a simple device made with vertical copper strips in which were cut notches, placed in a wooden frame, attached to the wire circuits. It was a game among old-timers to trick innocent new operators into washing the copper strips—to "clean the board"—when the wires were not responding perfectly. I never fell for such a trick, but for those who did, it was said that sparks flew from the seat of their pants. The voltage was not strong enough to do harm, but the experience immediately

made a crusty veteran out of a naive newcomer.

Even into the 1950s, many prairie stations were not wired with electricity, with artificial light being provided by kerosene lamps. The telegraph resonator sounder, however, needed current to work, and that which powered the mainline telegraph wires could not be used owing to differences in volts, amperes, ohms, and resistance. Local current came from a wet-process Blue Vitriol battery, which produced a small electric charge from two glass jars filled with a mixture of blue vitriol copper and zinc crystals added to water, in which were placed a negative and positive copper and zinc foot. The interaction created enough current to power the telegraph.

A characteristic of this battery was that the more it was used, the stronger the charge, until the acid ate away the metal foot. It required constant maintenance and caused a mess. To get the most

out of the code, frequently used words and phrases came to be coded in a system known (for its creator) as the Phillips Abbreviated Code. Knowing this code separated the hams from the "bonus men." The list of abbreviated symbols was long and required extensive attention to master. Some samples:

1 Wait a minute
12 Do you understand?
25 Busy
30 End of transmission
73 Best regards.

There were some expletives, too, such as SOB and GTH, which need no translation.

Weather affected the electrical impulse of the telegraph. During rain or in high humidity, the amperage would increase, causing the magnetism on the sounder bar to intensify, but all that was necessary to bring the dual magnets in harmony with the contact finger was a simple adjustment of a thumbscrew. And, no telegraph office was complete without a Prince Albert tobacco can placed in the resonator box to amplify the sound. What would we do today if we still had telegraph but no tobacco cans?

Telegraphers adopted a *sine* that identified the person and was accepted as a signature. Dispatchers issuing train orders always identified by their three initials, a practice still done today (and also seen wherein all railroad officials go by just their first two initials rather than using a first name and initial). Likewise, this abbreviated nomenclature is still evident in the two-letter coding of railroad location points, dating from the telegraph code adopted for use within a company—a code generally not interchangeable with other roads owing to duplication. This system long predates the computer and the adoption of a national universal machine language.

The legendary ambidextrous telegraph operator who could send a message with one hand, copy with the other, and talk to a third person—all at once—forever eluded me. He was always on another division or was someone's brother-in-law—a phantom. But the telegrapher was a skilled and important member of his community, in a key position for information since all big news traveled by telegraph.

No two Morse men were alike on the wire, for the style of one's "fist," as it was known, took on an individuality as recognizable as his voice. Each operator's personality could be read by his fellow telegraphers. Just as nature knows no duplicates—snowflakes, leaves, fingerprints, faces, voices—Morse key "voices" were never alike. Some would send as smooth as silk, while others were rough and sounded like buckshot in a tin pail.

Most operators were comfortable at 30 to 40 words per minute, although there were always a few around who could burn it. The highest recorded speed at which anyone received Morse was 75.2—that's over 17 symbols a second—achieved by Ted R. McElroy in a tournament at Asheville, N.C., on July 2, 1939.

Every operator wanted to be known as a good op and would equip himself with a speed key, a bug (so named by the

trademark of the Vibroplex Company which made the instrument, a patented sending device). Although other companies made them, the name *bug* became standard nomenclature. A bug was not company issue—each person bought his own and carried it with him from station to station along with his bedroll and a change of clothes. The bug took on the personality of its owner, some being chrome-plated with platinum points or having jeweled movements. Others were off the shelf, but all performed the same duty. A bug relieved the operator of hand fatigue caused by long and continuous use of the hand key.

The adhesive that bound the far-flung ranks of operators together was the Order of Railroad Telegraphers, or ORT. Early on, there was no requirement to join the fraternity, but in such a tight-knit society as railroading, not joining was tantamount to living without eating.

To become a first-class telegrapher, you had to master more than the alphabet. There were all the common punctuation marks, plus the symbols on a typewriter keyboard, plus many abbreviations for words and phrases—all designed to promote speed. A typical conversation:
TS KC (This is Ken Cliff.)
ES (Yes?)
U CMG OVR (You coming over?)
ES TMRW 2 (Yes, tomorrow at 2.)
GD C U TN (Good; see you then.)
73 (Regards.)

Operators carried their Morse with them, of course, and they even made keys out of knives and forks, tapping out impatient messages to their wives when dinner was slow in coming to the table. Ops often spoke in monosyllables—the habit of saving time and words ran deep. When friends were summoned to the deathbed of an operator named Charles Phillips, he is said to have told them "No use, boys, no battery, no current, zinc's eaten away, no time to galvanize now, guess I'll cut off."

I   I

Each day at 12 noon Eastern Time, every depot shared an experience when the Naval Observatory in Washington, D.C., would mark the hour by a signal sent simultaneously to every railroad

office. The signal would begin two minutes before the hour, allowing every office sufficient time to plug into the time circuit. The signal would register a series of dashes until precisely at the hour, when the circuit would click closed. The signals kept the nation on time, and the public came to rely on railroad time as being accurate.

On personal timepieces (watches), accuracy was just as important, and railroaders checked them every day to conform with the time signal. If they did not jibe, they were adjusted or repaired. So much pride was taken on this accuracy that the unwritten standard was "When the signal says 12 noon, all three hands on your watch should point straight up."

Of the many offices on the Omaha Road I worked, one of the busiest was Ferry, Neb. It was small but important, being just across the Missouri River from Sioux City, Iowa. The Omaha Road owned the bridge, but the Burlington and the Great Northern used it as a connection between their lines. The bridge was not strong enough to carry a long, heavy train, so they were broken into small cuts on each side of the river. A steady stream of movements rumbled across the single-track structure, bouncing to and from the yards on each side like a ping-pong ball. Indeed, these moves were known locally as *pingers*. The telegraph train-order office at Ferry became a meat grinder, a hot seat, in keeping three roads' dispatchers happy.

I worked my share of third tricks, when the rhythmic click of the Seth Thomas mechanical wall clock (the standard in most stations) blended with the staccato chatter of the sounder to keep the operator company. The unhurried *tick-tock* measured off the night in slow cadence and created a comfortable feeling during the lonely hours. Often, a telegrapher at a not-so-busy outpost would spend the long night playing a game of checkers with an equally lonely friend miles away on the division ... using the telegraph to register every move. Some ops were women, and we have no idea how many romances were sparked by the telegraph.

The comforting sounds at the depot desk had to be left behind, though, for

Operators had to brave the elements to hoop up orders to train crews in all types of weather. *Richard Steinheimer*

periodic checks of the yard tracks, where in the middle of a cold, dark night you could hear all kinds of strange noises. More than once I sprinted from between two rows of railroad cars to the safety of the glow of a street light or station platform lamp, seeking refuge from a (usually) imagined peril in the yard.

One day at Le Mars, Iowa, where the Illinois Central agent took care of his and the Omaha's trains, a long westbound Omaha train of empty grain cars took a siding to meet an equally long eastbound. The westbound cut some grade crossings to permit auto traffic to cross, but some less important streets remained blocked. An enterprising local policeman decided to make a case of city against railroad, arresting the conductor. The policeman then called our division superintendent, citing the amount of ransom to release the prisoner. In a rage, the Super challenged the law, saying, "Keep him there. We don't pay blackmail." The conductor was released.

One night at Alton, Iowa, a train had a locomotive failure, making it necessary to reduce tonnage. The dispatcher sent the usual message to the train crew, with instructions to set out nonperishable and non-time-sensitive cargo. Among the cars set out was a load of fence posts; there was no advice that it was of importance. Next morning, in reviewing the night's activity, the Super discovered that the fence posts had not arrived and called the night workers on the carpet for the offense. Turned out the Super had assured a local lumber dealer in St. James that his shipment would arrive without fail. Thereafter, whenever a train reduced tonnage, the messages added "except fence posts."

Gene Autry, the cowboy singing star, at one time was a telegrapher for the St. Louis-San Francisco (Frisco) in Oklahoma. After he gained fame, he visited crippled children's hospitals, and one such tour brought him to Sioux Falls, S.D., on the Omaha Road, where I was working a relief job. Before his departure, Mr. Autry stopped by the depot, and as I was preparing to copy the orders for his train to Minneapolis, he asked permission to talk with the dispatcher on the wire. I granted it, and with a flair recognized only by experienced operators, Mr. Autry cracked the wire, saying, "This is Gene Autry in Sioux Falls." In the usual no-nonsense manner, the dispatcher replied, "And this is Santa Claus. Now what." After a few exchanges, the chit-chat ended and Mr. Autry copied his own running orders.

When the opportunity came for me to work a high-speed telegraph relay position in the dispatcher's office at St. James, I accepted. A relay job was sort of a telegraph message switching center, whose operator's job was to copy reports from online stations and send them to other offices. The op was an assistant to the dispatcher and division superintendent. It was a demanding job, and my lack of exposure to the work almost led to my disqualification. But I kept with it. Enough reports would pour in every day to the division headquarters to keep a bank of telegraphers busy. The reports were in a symbol code where a word would mean an entire sentence, and quick response to identify the symbols was necessary.

Later, I successfully bid in as third-trick wire chief in the general offices in St. Paul. This exalted throne was the goal of many brasspounders, since it was the heart of the system's telegraph network. The positions of wire chief and train dispatcher were the top of the telegrapher's career.

On a railroad, one does not resign or retire. He "pulls the pin" or "takes his pension." Pulling the pin is a maneuver describing the end of a run, when the coupling pin is pulled up and the engine uncouples from its cars and leaves, to go to the barn (round house) or just tie up (park for the night). My 10 years of employment as a railroad telegrapher were enjoyable. I pulled the pin on May 30, 1959, to go on to other endeavors, never to recouple, but the flavor of railroad operations still surges through my veins.

Generations of Americans grew up with the familiar sound of the telegraph, but today, few of our 220 million citizens have heard its mystic chatter. It has been drowned out by the prosaic but dull-sounding children of automation, the teletype and computer. The electromagnetic telegraph instrument and code were invented and perfected by Samuel Finley Breese Morse in 1844. His name, enshrined in the code, became the synonym for the telegraph; he was the common patron saint for all of us brasspounders.

IN THE VIOLET HOUR

Paul D. Schneider

At the violet hour,
when the eyes and back
Turn upward from the desk,
when the human engine waits

—T. S. Eliot, from "The Waste Land" (IV. Death by Water)

Dying. The Chicago, Rock Island & Pacific Railroad Company is dying. You're quite cognizant of this, and still … you're amazed. Amazed.

After all, this was the granger that had taken seed at 22nd Street in Chicago on October 1, 1851, as the Rock Island & La Salle Railroad Company, It had blossomed into a 7,500-mile system covering 14 states between the Great Lakes and the Gulf of Mexico, between the eastern fringe of the Rocky Mountains and the Mississippi River. No tea-kettled short line this; this was one of the big boys—a thumping, Class 1, 4-foot 8½-inch gauge railroad titan.

And now the titan was drawing its last breath.

The events that brought the colossus to its knees by January 1980 seemed to happen with the inevitability of dominoes falling. First, the Rock's clerks (members of the Brotherhood of Railway and Airline Clerks) walked off the job on August 28, 1979, in a dispute over retroactive pay. Members of the United Transportation Union followed a day later.

So on September 20, President Jimmy Carter issued an executive order creating an emergency board in the disputes between the Rock Island and the BRAC and the UTU; an order which, theoretically, suspended the strike and required everyone to revert to the status quo for a minimum of 60 days.

The UTU complied with the law. But not BRAC. Thumb to nose, BRAC president Fred Kroll sniffed that be wouldn't send his people back to work unless they received the prevailing industry wage scale and full retroactive pay.

Strangely, the Carter Administration did nothing in the face of this refusal.

Then, on September 26, the Interstate Commerce Commission served its Rock Island directed-service order which authorized the directed carrier, the Kansas City Terminal Railway, to pay the prevailing wage scale, if paying the prevailing wage was what it would take to get BRAC members back to work.

BRAC members returned to work.

So on October 5, 1979, a task force made up of officials from the 11 lines that owned the KCT—plus the Rio Grande and the Southern Pacific—took over responsibility for operating the Rock under the 60-day directed-service order.

If the Rock was a crippled giant floundering about in a shark-filled sea, then the ICC's directed-service order was just so much blood in the water. For with their sense of smell pricked, it was just a matter of time before the sharks closed in on their convulsive victim and kicked off a horrific feeding frenzy.

And there were plenty of sharks. There were the Rock's railroad neighbors who, despite their repeated bleating over the overbuilt rail network in the Midwest, were anxious to sink their teeth into significant portions of the Rock's "redundant" flesh. There was chief creditor Henry Crown, a very big fish indeed, who'd been snarling for years that the property was patently unreorganizable and should be liquidated. There was BRAC, which may have felt that a sure-thing victory was in order after its bloody setback in the 82-day Norfolk & Western strike of 1978. Then too, there were the sharks in Washington, the ones that had repeatedly sneered at the notion of bailing out the Rock—who just may have seen a politically painless way to eliminate what they clearly saw as a redundant railroad.

No … you don't believe that the Chicago, Rock Island & Pacific Railroad will survive directed service. So in January 1980, you decide to cover as much of the Rock as you can within a two-week period, talking to people in an attempt to understand how this—the collapse of their railroad—has affected them.

⚎ ⚎

'Coz when I see that union man walking down the street
he's the man who decides if I live or I die,
if I starve or I eat
Then he walks up to me and the sun begins to shine
then he walks right past and I know that I've got to get back in the line

—Raymond Douglas Davies,
from "Get Back in the Line"

Manly, Iowa. His name is Delos Werle. He is the second-trick operator at Manly, Iowa.

Your Rock Island public-relations brochure touts Manly as being an important operating center on the Des Moines Division; a trucker at the restaurant near the intersection of Highways 65 and 9 describes it as a town full of railroaders, "Soon to be *retired* railroaders!"

Delos Werle is one of them.

"I'm used to talking to people. I used to run an ice dock down here when I first hired out. You know, when I hired here it was just for the money; I needed a little extra money … I wasn't gonna work for no railroad all my life!

"I worked down here, and it was during the time of the Depression or right after it, and these guys were riding boxcars, you know. And we're out there running up and down cars, looking down bunkers—you know what a bunker is? Well, they put ice in the ends of these old refrigerator cars. OK, we're up there—a bunch of us knuckleheads, you know, looking down—telling how much ice, how many inches down. Some guy's writing it down, and all these bums are passing through the yard, you know. Well, hell … I used to set and talk to all these guys, see.

"Oh God … you can learn a lot from everybody. I never pass up anybody. 'Cuz you can learn an awful lot. And you get used to talking to people.

"I worked at that ice dock until they tore the doggone ice house down. I was down there about 18 years, and then they tore the damn place down. They quit … all them perishables.

"We used to ice as many as 75 to 100 cars a train. Of peaches. Oh yeah, we got all that business. Cherries, grapes, celery, and lettuce all winter. We'd ice that celery all winter. Ice kept the frost out of it. I never did really get that through my head how that worked. But it worked.

"You know, our problem is right out there, those two strips of cement; that's when our troubles started. We had good business until they started that. Cheap fuel, fast … man, a truck can get it there overnight, and it takes us three days or more!

"And people don't understand that we're paying for our competition! That's

right! Every damn town we go through, we pay taxes out the nose! 'Course, that trucker's gotta make a living too, I suppose … but I don't want to be feeding him!'

"That truck deal is what wrecked us.

"And then we were so sure we were gonna merge with that Union Pacific. This would have been a *real* railroad with that UP, boy. Let me tell you … from what I've seen of that UP … oh! That's a railroad and a half!

"But there was too much red tape. Red tape in the courts, and pretty soon the Rock Island's gone downhill, and the UP—when they could've had us—they said, 'Sorry, can't afford the repairs.'

"Now that Kansas City Southern; if they get up here, look out! 'Course the North Western says, 'Oh, the competition will be too bad!' But the Rock Island's always been here, and they've never complained about our competition. So why not let the Kansas City Southern in?

"One thing that the Government claims that they will not have—ever—is another Conrail. Because in the paper—I think the Sunday paper—they said that they would not make another Conrail out of the Rock. All they've had is problems with Conrail. They still have … it's just not successful.

"But I can't see them letting the whole railroad just disappear. No, it'll be here … this railroad'll be here. And somebody'll fix it up, and you'll read, when you're 50 years old, about the history of how the Rock went down and somebody else took it over and think: Could that have been possible? That it was in *that* kind of shape? And they'll be running 80 miles an hour down here. You know.

⚎ ⚎

Iowa Falls, Iowa. It is 1 p.m. A bloodless winter's day. We're between Popejoy and Dows, Iowa, alongside the Rock Island's Subdivision 12A branch line between Iowa Falls and Estherville. Train No. 340 is a varicolored rope twisted taut between you and a point just beyond the next dip in the tracks, ambling across the snowy sweep of the central Iowa farmland. No. 340's Geeps and jumbo hoppers imply an agreeable harmony with their environment.

This is the heart of the Rock Island Railroad. And the lifeblood it pumps is grain.

Iowa Falls, Iowa. The back room of the Rock Island's depot there. Prior to directed service, he'd been the agent at Dows, Iowa. His name is Bob Tallahson.

"OK. You start there at Dows—he loads grain trains. Clarion handles grain trains. Get up here to Bode—they've got grain trains. West Bend, Klemme—grain trains. You get up to Estherville, and then you go up to a place called Superior, right up there on Highway 9. They load grain trains.

"But you see a loss of potential on these lines. This guy at Thompson has the elevator, the equipment, and plenty of track. He could load unit trains … if we could get into him. But we haven't got the cars, haven't got the track fixed up enough.

"These co-ops are owned by the farmers. The farmers get together, they pool their money, and they form a co-op. Then they go out and build it and hire a manager to run it for them like this Mark Friedow up at Klemme. He markets this grain for the farmers, trying to get the best deal for them on their grain.

"Let's say that I've got some corn now. I can sell that corn to a broker for, say, 30 cents a bushel for May delivery.

"So the co-op manager books his equipment. He's promised to deliver this corn to the broker by May and—if he fails to do so—he gets penalized. Very badly. By the broker.

"So to prevent this sort of thing from happening, the co-ops lease their own cars. Now they know how many cars they have to work with. They can turn around and sell grain with the assurance that it will be delivered in May.

"These co-ops want to move this grain, to make a profit. They don't want to hang onto it. That's how to make their money.

"That's why everyone's upset about this problem with the Rock Island. If we close down, they're going to have to truck it to the river to be shipped out on barges. I mean, they'll get so mad at us they won't even ship it on another railroad. They'll go to the expense of trucking it all the way to the Mississippi River.

Rock Island train 340 switches cars at Dows, Iowa, in January 1980. *Paul D. Schneider*

"This guy at Thompson … he got so fouled up with us that he shipped two barge loads himself. It was expensive, but he had to get rid of it. He was getting into a bind. No other choice.

"When we were on strike, I talked to this one trucker who was just shuffling corn in a big loop between Ventura and Britte, between Klemme and Garner. That's a tremendous waste of energy!"

Weren't supervisors running trains during the strike?

"The only one that we know of up here that did get grain moved was West Bend. They did take care of them. Klemme may have got one train.

"We take it everywhere. Most of our stuff goes down to the Gulf for export. Houston, New Orleans … they've all got loading points. It just depends on which broker buys it.

"Up through here—this area that we're talking about—is a very, very rich grain area. You're talking good Iowa bottom-land. And this guy in Superior draws from a tremendous area up in Minnesota too. Corn and soybeans. You bet.

"And these elevators; I mean, they're a big business in their town. Like Klemme

… Klemme elevator is, probably, the biggest thing in town. It keeps the town. It's the main employer.

"If you kill the railroad, you've killed the whole town."

From the top of the Klemme Co-Op's elevator, the whole thing is simple. And mythical. For the gigantean elevator is Argus, the hundred-eyed guardian, while the sleepy town of Klemme is Io, the woman entrusted to the giant's care.

From traffic manager Mark Friedow's point of view, the matter is more pragmatic than poetic. "What we're concerned with here at Klemme is no rail service, because we've got over 2 million bushels of grain contracted for to be delivered to the Gulf, you know, in 75-car trains. So if we don't have service, we're gonna be right up the creek. That's our first problem. Secondly, we're geared up to move pretty good volumes of grain through here. And we count on rail.

"We've got three 75-car units that we're trying to run year around; that's our goal. If they turn one and a half times a month, we'll ship four trains."

Rock Island train 34 rocks and rolls its way into the yard at El Dorado, Ark., in February 1980.
Paul D. Schneider

What's the usual turnaround time to the Gulf these days?

"Oh when the Kansas City Terminal first took over in October, we had three trains turn in about 14 days each. But that was unusual. We're up to a 20-, 25-day turn now to the Gulf and back."

And that's not too good?

"Well, if they could hold it to between 15 and 20 days—maybe 18—we'd be happy. We can live with that. Thirty days, though … that's too long. We've got our own hopper cars—quite a slug of them—and if they don't turn faster, our freight costs rise. We pay a certain fee per month, see, and the only income that we get back is the mileage credit based on loaded miles that those cars run. Well, hell … if they only turn around once a month, they don't get enough loaded miles.

"The worst it got was between January and March of 1979. That was snow—heavy snow—last winter. We had one train. Sixty or 65 days to get to the Gulf and back. The first six months of last year was the worst winter I've ever seen. All that snow. The wind would blow from the north one day and drift it in; the next day they'd plow it out, and it'd drift the other way."

"We couldn't store grain then because we couldn't buy it. We went out of the market. We could have shipped by truck, but all of our handling margin would have been eaten up, and then some, if we'd done that. Right now—going 75 cars to the Gulf by rail—you're looking at a 50-cent rate over 1,200 miles. Just to truck a bushel to Des Moines costs 25 cents. And that's just a hundred miles. We couldn't hack that.

"We've been involved in the Iowa Falls Gateway Shippers since its inception, and we've dumped a lot of money into track repair. But the Rock Island's never maintained it once it's been upgraded. What we need is a railroad that'll come in here with the finances to maintain the damn stuff. Doesn't do any good to rehabilitate the track and then let it go to hell again. And with the tonnage that we're moving, you know … you're gonna have the repairs. Once you start moving 75 cars of 100-ton jumbo hoppers full of grain, you're gonna tear up some track now and then.

ALL AGENTS … C/O OPRS
ALL FRT SALES REPS—SOME VIA TELEX
ICC DIRECTED SERVICE ORDER 1398 (SUB. NO. I) DATED DECEMBER 3, 1979, DIRECT-ING KANSAS CITY TERMINAL RAILWAY COMPANY TO PROVIDE SERVICE AS A

DIRECTED RAIL CARRIER OVER CERTAIN LINES OF THE CHICAGO ROCK ISLAND AND PACIFIC RAILROAD COMPANY EXPIRES AT 11:59 P.M. ON MARCH 2, 1980 … ACCORD-INGLY, KCT AS THE DIRECTED RAIL CAR-RIER HEREBY PLACES CRI AND P EMBARGO NO 6-80 WHICH PERMANENTLY EMBAR-GOES ALL COMMODITIES AND CLASSES OF TRAFFIC TO, FROM OR VIA ALL STATIONS OF THE CRI AND P RR … WITH NO EXCEPTIONS.

"Anything that the railroad people feel won't be off of the property by March 8 will be embargoed; that's how I under-stand it. We hear that we'll be able to load late into February because our stuff will be going off of the Rock Island at Kansas City."

But after that, you're up in the air?

"Right."

And I imagine that the shippers are pretty torqued off about the whole mess?

"Well yeah, I guess they're as cranked up as they've ever been. A lot of us have been cranked up for too damn long.

"I mean, I don't think it's right that our entire livelihood ends up resting on last-minute decisions. I mean … my gosh, last September is when the ICC started the directed service. Now they've gone over five months, and they're just now getting around to getting bids in on the damn thing. They're gonna shut it down in three weeks, and here they are finally taking bids. Why didn't they start sooner?

"So what do we do? We're just sup-posed to sit out here, right? You know, you can scream—you can write your sen-ators, call your congressman—but after a while you get tired of that. I think that that sort of thing can do some good—I think it helped us to get the directed ser-vice—but here we are, up to the wire again.

"Here's an elevator in the middle of Iowa trying to determine whether we should go ahead and buy corn for March delivery, and we don't even know if we're gonna have a railroad! Now are we just supposed to drop out of the market and say, 'Well, farmers, we're sorry; we don't know if we're gonna be shipping by rail or not. You just sit on your hands until March 8 and then—if we're still in busi-ness—well then we'll buy your corn. But until that time, you can just sit on it. We're sorry, but that's the way it is.'

"The farmer's option is to go to another elevator on a line that's running … the North Western, the ICG, the BN, the Milwaukee … if those lines have the capacity to handle the additional business.

"Course, you dump us out of the picture and you know what's gonna happen around here. Everybody else is gonna say, 'Hey! That Klemme's out of business!' They'll know that there's gonna be ten million bushels of grain out there that we're not going to be handling, so they take a little more margin. And the price to the farmer drops down."

If all else fails, I suppose that the next step would be a shipper-owned line?

"Sure. You have an alternative.

"We don't intend to just lay down and die. We'll never let that happen. We can't afford to. We've got millions and millions invested in the equipment and the facilities to load big grain trains. We'll fight to the bitter end."

I   I

'The Rock' is an insurance company. This is the Rock Island Railroad.

—Agent at Herington, Kan.

Herington, Kansas. Long fingers of jumbo covered hoppers crunching over icy switchpoints. A lonesome, asthmatic U25B brooding over its fate. The treble sound of picks and shovels shattering hard-packed snow and striking pavement.

Eleven-thirty in Herington, Kan. Fifteen degrees above zero. Too damned cold.

You're down on Highway 4 at the north end of town with the Herington maintenance-of-way gang waiting for train No. 537-11, the local to Salina, Kan., to assault the snow-clogged 49.4-mile Subdivision 21A branch line for the first time in over a week. Steve Lewis is the gang's foreman. "But don't let this fool you," he says, tapping his white hardhat, "I'm just a working stiff like the rest of the gang." The rest of the gang comprising, from left to right, Gary D. Brown and Don F. Sauer.

When you mention that you're thinking about chasing the local up the branch, they tell you that they'll be doing pretty much the same thing in the way of

softening up the line for the roundhouse punch of the 537-11's big snowplow. "Why not follow us?" suggests Steve. "Be a lot easier than trying to follow the line on your own."

Without a second thought, you agree. And, in that moment, it doesn't seem quite so cold out.

Despite your expectations, there's no fireworks when the maw of the plow bites into the snow on the other side of the highway crossing. "Hell, they don't need no big plow up front in the first place," mutters Steve. "That little plow on the engine coulda handled this stuff."

No matter. The motive power behind the plow is nice enough: GP38-2 4304 (*The Loyal Shipper*) in the Ingram Administration-inspired blue and white, and U25B 223 in the somber maroon and yellow. A minute after the caboose clanks past, you're charging west—then north—behind the gang's battered orange Ford pick-up truck.

Fifteen, 20 minutes later. Standing a little ways back from the next crossing, watching 537-11 float across the snow-socked Kansas farmland, the thought strikes you that, despite the significance of Herington as an operating center (it's the junction of the Missouri-Kansas Division—the old Golden State Route—with the Southern Division gateway to Oklahoma, Texas, and Arkansas), the Salina branch is more representative of the region.

Because this, Steve tells you, is wheat country. The elevators scattered up and down the line are like the transformers on a tinplate model railroad, providing power for the local in the form of thousands of carloads of wheat. Unplug the grain and you unplug the train. It's that simple.

Conversely, there's a vicious twist to this concept of the Salina branch as the Rock's main nerve in the area. The juice that keeps that nerve humming is the juice that's burning it to a crisp. The higher axle loadings are wreaking havoc with the physical state of the plant. The track is shot. Listening to Steve, you remember Mark Friedow's words: "Once you start moving 100-ton jumbo hoppers full of grain, you're gonna tear up some track now and then."

Steve says that he doesn't have the supplies that he needs to maintain the

line. What sort of things does he need?

"Oh, you know … just the minor things. Rails. Ties. Spikes."

You nod your head glumly. Sadly, you've heard this song before, and it's not the one about the Rock Island Line being a mighty good road. It sounds more like Elvis Costello's "Accidents Will Happen."

Eventually, someone in an official capacity decides that that big snowplow is hardly necessary to get the local up the line. While 537-11 sets it out on a siding near Pearl, Steve suggest breaking for beans. Everyone concurs.

Pretty soon you're sitting down to eat at Marianne's on Sunflower in Pearl, talking about the BRAC strike with Steve and Gary (Don having elected to eat his boxed lunch out in the truck). Steve figures that the Rock's clerks will never see their back pay, that a lot of them will be lucky to be working after March 31. You nod your head and stab at your food.

Strike stories … about a guy Steve knew who'd been on picket duty in Abilene, Kan., when a Santa Fe train showed up on the joint AT&SF/CRI&P track there. This guy—Buzzy—was a real union man. He saw that Santa Fe train moving, and he saw red. Climbed right up on the lead unit and asked the hogger if he knew just what the hell a picket sign meant? That Santa Fe man not only knew what it meant, he knew where Buzzy was going to put that picket sign if he didn't big-hole his train pronto. What happened then? "Why, that hogger backed his train right the hell up!"

Oh yeah, the strike was tough on Rock Islanders—especially in Herington. Herington's a railroad town; but most of all, it's a Rock Island town. When the owner of a local five-and-dime said something about caring first about the welfare of the townspeople and secondly about the damned Rock Island, a bunch of those same townspeople almost lynched him. His business dropped off to practically nothing, and he had to apologize for what he'd said. Herington being, after all, a railroad town … and a Rock Island town. Period.

An innocent-looking notation in the Rock's Special Instructions for Subdivision 21A of the Missouri-Kansas Division reads "Between West Abilene and East Salina trains will be governed by timetable and rules of the UP Railroad." While the information is quite valid—the Rock Island does, in fact, have trackage rights on the Union Pacific between these two points—it is deceiving. It is like the bland "Fasten Seatbelts" that flashes above your head before your airplane heads into some tricky turbulence; it hardly prepares you for what is to follow.

What follows on the joint CRI&P/UP track west of Abilene is nothing less than astonishing … and exhilarating. It is February 11, 1980—the eve of the Rock Island's destruction—yet can you believe this scene? The Salina local is skirring over the sun-slicked desolation of the Kansas winter scene, its unrelated, variegated, multicolored diesels dropped into the slot and floating along at 50, 60 mph; looking for all the world like the embodiment of the first movement of Beethoven's Fifth Symphony … triumph incarnate … and exultation!

You wonder, in particular, if the 223 is rejoicing in this sudden crank of speed over the railroad that, but for the ineptitude of the ICC, would have been its savior. Remember that roundhouse foreman in Des Moines? He told you that the biggest problem with the Rock's GEs were their turbos; that you had to wind the U-boats up into the seventh and eighth notch to keep the turbos well-lubricated; that they were probably best suited for flat-out running over 40 mph.

Well, according to the speedometer on your car, the 223 is popping along at a good 20 mph over that foreman's recommendation … and doing just fine, thank you.

Salina. Finally. Steve's gang meets up with the Salina maintenance gang. Foreman is James "Jim Bob" Pryor. Gang is nicknamed "Pryor's Polacks," much to Pryor's amusement. Several disparaging remarks exchanged between the two foremen. All in jest, of course. The two are obviously old friends.

While everyone pitches in on a snowbound switch, you drift over to the Salina gang's truck. End up talking to Santiago Mascareno, who's sitting inside the cab. His son works for a power plant somewhere. Figures that the kid will have a pretty secure future. Leastways, better than his old man's. Thirty years ago, he wouldn't have believed that he'd ever feel that way about a career on the railroad.

Times change, though.

It's getting late now. Three-thirty, four p.m. Time to move on down the line. You almost regret having to leave these guys.

You decide to try to preserve something of the moment on film before the light fades. A group portrait, then. Everyone goes along with the suggestion. Someone coaxes Sandy out of the truck. You frame both gangs in the viewfinder of your camera … set the aperture … focus.

Don Sauer, Sandy Mascareno, Gary Brown, Tom "G.I. Joe" Dunlop, James Pryor, Steve Lewis, Troy "Radar" Johnson, and the illustrious Mister Bryant. In the moment before you trip the shutter, you see these eight as something special and eloquent; the avatar of the real Rock Island Railroad.

Click.

⚏ ⚏

El Reno, Oklahoma. Leon Willingham is the superintendent of operations at the Rock Island's El Reno, Okla., car shop. He is an equable, level-headed sort of fellow, the very model of stoicism in the face of an impending disaster.

Leon tells you, right off the bat, that the morale around this place isn't anything to write home about these days. "Most of these guys don't know if they'll have a job or not next month."

He points out that even if another railroad takes over the Rock's operations in the El Reno area, there's no guarantee that they'll keep the car shops going. The rumors here indicate that the Katy is interested in the Houston-El Reno-Herington main line—maybe even the Santa Fe—but neither road has any use for another car shop. Leon figures that their best bet is to hope that a private contractor steps into the picture. "Of course, they'd probably pay a lower wage," he says. Which is no surprise, considering that wages have always been somewhat lower south of the Mason-Dixon line. But, as a carman had told you earlier, "Sure, they might only pay eight bucks an hour. But if it was steady work—if it was a good company—I'd take it."

Put it another way: In June of 1979, there were 370 people employed here. Today that figure is something like 97. If you were one of those 273 workers—your livelihood chopped off, a mortgage hanging over your head—would you settle for $7.50 or $8 an hour if it meant a steady five days a week … after week … after?

Walking through the facility with Leon, you're engulfed in a wave of "new image" blue. It looks like the entire 150-acre car shop has been lacquered in the Rock's robin's-egg blue paint: doors, signs, hardhats, rolling stock, forklifts. You're almost afraid to peek into the lavatories.

The new color was another wrinkle of the Ingram Administration, according to Leon. A revamped image for a revitalized railroad. He claims that their next twist of crinkum-crankum was to paint everything white. You bet. Tells you that, that group of Warren & Ouachita Valley cars were just delivered in white. "They had a lot of money to throw away on new paint," he says shortly.

There's a quick red glare to Leon's remarks, as if the door to a firebox has swung open. Intrigued by this chink in the man's phlegmatic armor, you turn and ask him if he believes—as others do—that the Ingram Administration milked the Rock Island Railroad dry?

He looks at you carefully, his eyes narrowed. Then the door to the firebox bangs shut. He shrugs his shoulders noncommittally. "All I know is this: I watch a lot of cars go out of here brand spanking new—and turn up a few weeks later wrecked." He nods his head in the direction of the main line. "They must have been having a lot of derailments out there."

⚏ ⚏

Long ago it must be,
I have a photograph
Preserve your memories,
they're all that's left you

—Paul Simon, from *Bookends*

El Dorado, Arkansas. We're halfway down the throat of the Rock's Southern Division on Subdivision 38. To the north, just across the creek dividing the two properties, is the El Dorado & Wesson, a

6-mile long, all-Alco short line; to the east lies the Missouri Pacific's yard.

His name is Bynum O. Blackmore. He is, to your way of thinking, the epitome of the traditional Southern gentleman: soft-spoken, dignified, cordial.

He is Number One on the Southern Division engineer's seniority roster.

"I hired out on November 29, 1945, at Little Rock. Transferred down here in April of 1946. That was just after World War II.

"I started out firing on steam. Alcos and Baldwins both. I've worked with a good many steamers—the 2600s and 2700s, the 3000s. We used to use those high-drivered 5000-series engines on our passenger trains. They were a 4-8-4 type.

"We used to have Alco diesels down here in the yard. The RS2 and 3 types. Oh, they were good engines! Rugged. You could walk away with the whole yard with an Alco. They weren't as slippery as these Geeps we're using now; they could *pull!*

"For the last year or so, we had our own engine here in El Dorado, the 838. Just a little bitty EMD switcher, but we had her painted up in the blue like the 4463 out here. Boy, did she look sharp! There's a picture of her in the back room. She's gone now; they moved her to Little Rock after this directed-service thing.

"I plan on retiring this August. I'm the last qualified passenger engineer on the Southern Division."

He introduces himself as Bruce Nelson.

He is the prideful owner of the *Pike's Peak*, one of two club-dining cars off of the old *Rocky Mountain Rocket*. The coach—painstakingly refurbished by Nelson and lined, from one end to the other, with Rock Island memorabilia—reposes in genteel retirement on a siding within sight of the Rock's El Dorado depot.

He is the third-oldest clerk/operator in seniority in El Dorado. He is 56 years old.

"I've got about 36 years with the company. I was 21 when I hired out. I'd just gotten out of the service. I was working over in Memphis in a defense factory when a distant cousin sent word through my dad that the Rock Island was hiring. So here I came.

A local behind a GP38-2 assaults the snow on the Salina branch west of Pearl, Kan., for the first time in a week. *Paul D. Schneider*

"I went to work as a yard clerk. This building used to be a clerical office; the yard office was up there," he waves his hand toward the east. "They tore the yard office down. They used to have a big mechanical shop here years ago; man, they did all kinds of work here! Had a big roundhouse, too—I got a picture of that roundhouse, over there in the coach. Shows those old steam engines sitting at the roundhouse.

"I have a picture of the business car that we were using on the Rock Island before this directed-service thing happened. The president of traffic was down here with his wife, entertaining shippers, and they parked it right next to mine on the rip track. I talked to the two guys that worked on there—the cook and the attendant—and asked them if they wanted to see my *Pike's Peak*. 'Hell no!' says the cook. 'We spent all the time we intend to spend on that damn car! We don't ever want to set foot in it again!'

"Well, I finally talked him into going up there. Well, he couldn't believe his eyes! He says, 'Oh my, lemme go get so-and-so!' John, I believe he called him. The president of traffic. 'Lemme go get John, I want him to see this!' See, he couldn't believe what I'd done to the inside of that coach, how it looked. See, when I got it, it had an old green color paint in there and it looked just … horrible. This John ended up over there, and he just admired that *Pike's Peak*. I made their pictures while I had them over there. They just couldn't believe their own eyes.

"The sister to this coach here has been cut up and scrapped. So this is the only one—the only club-dining car left that was on the *Rocky Mountain Rocket*."

When you ask to see the picture of the 838, he takes you into the back room and points out two color photographs under the glass top of someone's desk. They show a jaunty blue SW8 with the words THE LITTLE ROCK painted proudly across its carbody.

Everything south of Biddle Yard in Little Rock, Ark., turns out to be The Little Rock, something akin to a paper railroad without the reporting mark status of, say, the Warren & Ouachita Valley. "But we were an independent railroad," says Nelson. "Had our own locomotives, our own people, separate accounting, the works.

"And we made money for them too. That's because we're a year-around operation down here; always have been. We

Little Rock's SW8 switcher: "Just a little bitty EMD switcher, but we had her painted up."
Paul D. Schneider

ship a lot of chemicals and pulpwood products out of here. We aren't seasonal like the rest of the system. Man, I wish they just would have left us alone.

"But after that directed service happened, that was the end of The Little Rock."

You mention that, to the best of your knowledge, there isn't another switcher like the 838 anywhere on the system. Certainly not with that slogan emblazoned across its side. It is, you say approvingly, a unique little engine.

"Man, were we proud of that little goat! Had a local firm paint her up special for us. We kept her in tip-top shape, too. But now…" He shakes his head ruefully. "They'll probably run her into the ground up there in Little Rock."

You mention that you might make a stop there on your last swing homeward. "Well, if you see that 838, you take a picture of her. She's special."

A misty Thursday morning. The main office of the El Dorado & Wesson Railway Company. You close the door on the sound of E&W 21 gulping down the cool morning air and sit down across from the short line's general manager and president.

He introduces himself as H. D. Reynolds Jr. A mirthless, businesslike man, he tells you, by way of a preface, that the E&W is a railroad run "with common sense and practicality." His words aren't hyperbole; they are gospel truth. His whole demeanor says so.

He outlines the E&Ws dilemma in short, broad strokes: All of their traffic from on-line industries—lumber, poultry, chemicals—is funneled through their sole physical connection with the Rock Island. When the Rock collapses, the E&W stands to be completely isolated from the outside world. "That," points out Mr. Reynolds, "is why we're negotiating for 1,500 feet of Rock Island track to make a connection with the Missouri Pacific."

He ticks off what he feels are the reasons for the Rock's messy demise: a loss of business after World War II due to bad management, a deplorable physical plant and subsequent derailments, and—his mouth turns down at the corners—the worst labor contract in the United States.

You wonder aloud if he's referring to full-crew laws. But no; he tells you that the E&W regularly uses four-, even five-person crews. He hints that the problem isn't one of numbers; it's something else, something less tangible. "Let me put it this way. The people in this area—if you give them the inspiration, you've got the world by the tail."

Inspiration. You stand next to E&W's immaculately maintained Alco S2, tripping on the laughing sound of its 539 prime mover, and recall the words of the two Rock Island employees who'd held their little blue switcher in such high regard.

The people in this area—if you give them the inspiration, you've got the world by the tail.

Mr. H. D. Reynolds Jr., meet Messrs. Blackmore and Nelson.

A train has the two great attributes of life, she thought, motion and purpose; this had been like a living entity, but now it was only a number of dead freight cars and engines. Don't give yourself time to feel, she thought, dismember the carcass as fast as possible…

—Ayn Rand, from *Atlas Shrugged*

Epilogue. March 30, 1980. Late on a Sunday afternoon. You stand alone at the edge of the Rock Island's Blue Island yard on the south side of Chicago. Staring out over a motionless sea of Rock blue rolling stock, searching for an off-line car.

There are none.

Down by the remains of the roundhouse, Dick Jensen's ex-Grand Trunk Western 4-6-2 sits twisted in a rictus of frozen immobility, its black cab windows staring vacantly at a nearby Rock Island C415. Orphaned sons of the same mother. The center-cab Alco shudders in dreamless sleep.

You're not exactly sure why you decided to stop here on this cheerless spring day. To hear the muffled drum? To walk the dead march? It doesn't matter anymore. Tomorrow, the 31st of March 1980, your official permission from the Rock's PR department to be on the property will finally expire.

But then, so will the Chicago, Rock Island & Pacific Railroad.

October 1984

THE 10:30

Don L. Hofsommer

There were few lights: one atop the water tower, a couple down at Callender Grain's South Elevator, a handful of street lamps, a saucy red and blue neon sign at the beer joint, and the perky illumination marking Fry's Jack Sprat store.

Yard lights dotted surrounding farms, and here and there headlamps of motor vehicles searched crude gravel roads. Far to the south, at least 5 miles, lights of Gowrie danced on the horizon. Except for these, and the sparkling stars above, plus the itinerant but happy signals of lightning bugs along the right-of-way, it was dark.

The nighttime was complemented by a summer's silence. Yes, frogs chirped across the way in a small farm pond, crickets sang their voluntary serenade, and occasionally the rails emitted a mysterious and unmusical clank as they imperceptibly contracted in the relative coolness following a hot summer day. There were other fugitive sounds emanating from the venerable depot nearby, but they could be detected only by pressing an ear to the window of the operator's bay. Then could be heard the soft but regular chatter of relay telegraph instruments—their magic bewildering to all but the operator and, of course, Callender was only a daylight station and thus he was not on duty. The fact that the old wooden depot was without light, that nobody was there to read the code, made the nearly inaudible sounds even more mysterious, more ghostlike. What news was being transmitted? Where were the men who were sending and receiving?

A car or two and then several parked in front of the depot and nearby as the final tinge of sun in the west yielded to night. It was ten o'clock. There were soft conversations and occasional laughter among those who gathered. Some lingered in their automobiles—doors wide open to facilitate circulation; others shuffled here and there along the cinder platform without apparent purpose. Few braved the warm, dark, and austere waiting room of the depot.

Most were idling in the time-honored way of small-town residents of the period. They were present simply to witness drama incident to the coming and going of "The 10:30," the nightly train up from Des Moines or, more correctly, Minneapolis & St. Louis Railway No. 3.

Frankly, it was not much of a train, certainly not when compared with the *Corn Belt Rocket*, *City of San Francisco*, and *Midwest Hiawatha*, the fine trains of the Rock Island, North Western, and Milwaukee, whose rails The 10:30 had crossed earlier in the evening as it coursed its way northward across Iowa toward Callender. Generally No. 3 consisted of a gas-electric car providing power as well as Railway Post Office, baggage, and express facilities; a mail storage car; and an elderly coach (with straight pipe-to-track commodes and Baker heaters). Not much of a train. Those who were there to meet it referred to No. 3 as the puddle-jumper; the ride it offered, they chuckled, was anything but smooth. Yet in those unhurried days before interstate highways and jet aircraft it was all they had—and it *was*, after all, a connection to the outside world from the fertile countryside of Webster County. Ironically, its residents subjected themselves to something of a contradiction. As much as they made fun of it, those uncomplicated souls had a deep affection for The 10:30.

Actually, No. 3 was due at Callender at 10:18, not 10:30, but the train was frequently a bit tardy and that, no doubt,

Change came to The 10:30 after the season described in this story. Stainless-steel Budd coaches replaced wooden cars in 1948, and overnight trains 3 and 4 became daytime runs 1 and 2. Here, No. 2, behind a GE-29, pauses in Callender in fall 1950. *Don L. Hofsommer*

explained the local moniker. It made little difference to those who congregated around the depot. Many involuntarily began glancing down the track as early as ten o'clock, increasing in this nervous activity as train time approached.

The flickering lights of Gowrie confused the issue as less skillful observers mistook one or more of these for the headlight of The 10:30. Less frequently in this nightly routine, the crowd was categorically befuddled when a train from Rock Island's Sibley-Gowrie branch exercised trackage rights over the M&StL at the north edge of Gowrie. Kids did not rely on visual perception alone. They put their heads to the rail and periodically proclaimed the imminent arrival of No. 3, this important information divined from sounds they had heard in the steel. Adults indulged them. Ultimately, some sharp-eyed citizen espied a golden-yellow glimmer far down the track. The color, he contended, was qualitatively different from the others down Gowrie way and, besides, this particular light had not been there before. It must be the train, he asserted. His confidence evaporated, though, when the glimmer strangely disappeared.

Soft conversations resumed after this false alarm. Topics were neither varied nor complex.

"How are your crops?" the elevator man inquired of a farmer.

"Where does the Ladies Aid meet this week?" one of the wives wanted to know.

"Did you get any rain last night?" one farmer asked another.

"It was mighty hot today," said someone to nobody in particular.

Then the conversations of frogs, crickets, and humans ceased as, suddenly, a headlight—yes, the headlight of The 10:30, and it was more yellow than other lights rose—as if pulled by a string when the onrushing train lifted itself out of the drainage ditch bottoms beyond the South Elevator. Those who had been visually inattentive were presently galvanized by the urgent sound of the GE car's wounded-goose whistle—one long blast, the traditional notice given by trains passing yard limit boards, and then two longs, a short, and a long grade crossing alarm just as the train glided over the road in front of the depot.

As soon as he had stopped his train, the engineer casually moved from his right-hand control station to the left doorway, on the depot side. Only the dimly lit gauge lights in the cab, and the headlight staring dumbly forward, offered illumination. He leaned against the door jamb, surveying the activity back along the train, a cigarette dangled carelessly from his hand. A brief moment to relax. "It surely stays hot—hotter up here than out there," he shouted to a man and his small son who had wandered up to the front of the train. "That's Iowa in July," shouted the man in return. The engineer smiled and nodded his agreement.

Shouting in this instance was proper etiquette. Indeed, it was required for any conversation in and about the GE car, for the irregular if hearty reports from the gasoline engine's exhaust drowned timid forms of expression. Back over the cab, colored fingers of blue and yellow erupted from the stack. It was, it seemed, an audiovisual symphony, played as accompaniment to the human activity occasioned by the presence of No. 3 in this ordinary, pleasant Midwestern village. However, the mighty

tattoo could last but briefly. After all, Callender was only one of four dozen station stops the train was obliged to make on its nightly passage from Des Moines to Fort Dodge to the great city of the north—Minneapolis. Express and mail were quickly deposited in and retrieved from the sagging freight house, passengers were detrained and boarded, letters were handed to the RPO clerks for posting aboard the train. The miscellaneous curious—there were lots of these—stood off on one side, out of the way, and exchanged small talk with the trainmen.

It was over as quickly as it had begun. An up-and-down signal from the conductor's lantern told the engineer that his hiatus was ended, that it was time to go. He spun his cigarette to the ground, waved to the man and boy, and returned to his seat-box. Two long blasts from the GE's air horn acknowledged the conductor's highball. The engineer closed the throttle, released the air brakes, moved the controller to its first position, and re-opened the throttle. A growing volume of yellow and blue color at the stack was mixed with a more orderly and authoritative crack-burble-crack exhaust. The loud report echoed off the Middle Elevator and then the North Elevator; when the train cleared the passing track, the engineer shifted his controller to an advanced series and the train gathered speed. Red markers at the end of the coach garnished a narrowing ring of light that encircled the image of the train as it moved off into the darkness and another stop, at Moorland, 6 miles northward.

Silence quickly returned, violated only by the frogs and crickets who again asserted their nocturnal dominion. A few persons lingered at the depot, but presently, they sauntered over to the town pump in front of the S. Hanson Lumber Company yard for a few additional moments of conversation. The rest pointed their Fords and Chevys toward home.

An important ritual had been maintained. Callenderites understood that The 10:30 provided not only useful transportation and communication services, but they also knew, implicitly, that it represented continuity and a form of glue requisite to any community. That is why townspeople and their country brethren had met the train, had gone to see The 10:30. And on the evening of the morrow they or their kindred would be there again.

Arthur F. Knauer

THE BEST
TRAIN-WATCHING SEAT

George H. Drury

The Boston & Maine of 1951 was an intensely busy railroad and an eminently watchable one.

In September of that year I got one of the best train-watching seats on the B&M—perhaps one of the best anywhere.

The Walter S. Parker Junior High School in Reading, Mass. (named for a former superintendent of schools), is just west of the railroad—in those days it was Boston & Maine's double-track Portland Division main line. Between the main

and the school were a roundhouse and a coach yard for storing suburban trains overnight and a station called Reading Highlands; the Reading depot, 12 miles from Boston, was a half mile south.

Nearly all the classrooms in the school were on the east side of the building, and the rooms were arranged so that with eyes left and a little craning of the neck I had a view across the football field to the tracks. It didn't take long that first day of seventh grade to learn that the desirable seats were next to the windows, nor did it take the teachers long to learn why I thought them desirable.

Indeed, a few teachers encouraged my hobby. Mrs. Rice, who taught arithmetic, brought me copies of the B&M employees' magazine from her daughter, and Miss Day channeled my energies into building a Strombecker *DeWitt Clinton* for the school's science museum. It may still be there. Miss Beattie knew that any extra-credit pictures I painted after hurrying through the assignments would be of trains. Some teachers didn't notice—Miss Becket, for instance, whose music class on Monday afternoons coincided with the arrival of the local freight behind an 0-6-0. Shop and gym classes (when the latter were held outside) were unstructured enough that I could watch the action without fear of reprimand.

Mrs. Sudak's English class was an exception. I was madly in love with her and I watched her, not the trains. If nothing else, I learned how to spell *unrequited*. Another exception, a briar patch in this Garden of Eden, was social studies with Miss Hunt. Not only did she tell me to sit back down, eyes front, and never do that again in her class, but she rearranged the desks so they faced the corridor wall. In fairness, I should say she wasn't an absolute Wicked Witch of the West. I could always count on her to buy an official Boy Scout Christmas wreath.

I don't recall the attitudes of the eighth and ninth grade teachers with such clarity, but by then, I was familiar with the trains and could miss one now and then. Also, I had become a less-obvious train-watcher.

⊥　⊥

I should recount a typical day's activity. The times and the consists are indelibly printed on my memory. As I coasted down Woburn Street to the crossing I was greeted by the 7:56 to Boston, waiting to pull onto the main after the passage of the 7:52. Both trains—for that matter, all

the local passenger trains—were powered by P-2 class Pacifics. The 7:52 was made up of ex-Pennsy P54 coaches. (In the 1940s, B&M had gone shopping for secondhand steel coaches to replace some of its open-platform wooden cars, and they came home with an eclectic group of cars from the Pennsylvania, the Erie, the New York Central, the Reading, and the Lackawanna.)

I usually watched the 7:56 pull down to the depot, and that left me with just enough time to pedal the rest of the way, put my bike in the rack, remember my locker combination, and take my seat in Miss Day's homeroom. The school day began with the reading of a Psalm (by order of the Commonwealth of Massachusetts, which dates this narrative as surely as do the P-2s and the wooden coaches), and with the 8:33 pulling out of the last track in the coach yard and backing to the Reading Highlands depot, while on the main line there passed in quick succession an outbound local for Haverhill, an inbound express from Dover, and train 8, the *Gull*, from Halifax and Saint John. The 8:33 then followed No. 8 to Boston.

A few minutes later a mail and express train for Portland zipped past. Trains to and from Portland were in the care of B&M and Maine Central E7s, almost always singly, except that the *Gull* often had B&M's lone E8 on the head end and sometimes two E7s, back to back. Even if I couldn't see it, I could recognize the E8 by its sound, growlier than that of the E7s.

The next busy spell came during third period, and class schedules varied from day to day, so I could compensate in math class on Wednesday for what I didn't see in social studies on Tuesday. The rush began with the arrival at Reading Highlands of a local. The Pacific cut off, ran around the combine and three coaches, all woodies, and pushed them up to the station. Then it stopped on the roundhouse lead for a drink from the tank, turned on the electrically driven table, and recoupled to its train. Meanwhile, on the main there were three expresses within 20 minutes: the *Beachcomber*, which had left Portland

at 6:50, right after the *Gull*, and stopped everywhere until it reached suburban territory; the *Kennebec*, for Portland and Bangor, with an E7, one each maroon-striped stainless-steel combine and coach, heavyweight parlor-buffet-lounge, and another stainless coach; and the *Casco* from Portland, three American Flyer coaches and an unexplainable New Haven combine (its olive green paint unique in a full day of maroon) behind an E7. Add an outbound local after the Kennebec and the departure of the inbound train from the Highlands, and it's a wonder I learned anything academic in third period.

Then it was time for my favorite, train 2914 from North Conway: a P-3 Pacific with Delta trailing truck and fancy red lettering and four cars brought up by an ex-Pennsy baggage-RPO the same size and shape as the P54 coaches. No, I can't explain why it was my favorite.

It was fortunate that things dropped off after the passage of the *Pine Tree* from Bangor—several head-end cars and a full complement of stainless steel. I say fortunate because the cafeteria was on the west side of the building. I was usually back in class in time to see the *Flying Yankee*, which often included a blue-striped Bangor & Aroostook coach bound for Van Buren, 476 miles from Boston (lest you forget how big Maine is, that same rail distance from Boston will put you 20 miles beyond Washington, D.C., or 20 miles short of Buffalo, N.Y.).

⊥　⊥

The afternoon belonged mostly to the local freight. Tuesdays through Fridays it was *High Car*, which worked from Boston out to Reading, North Wilmington, or Lowell Junction, backed to Wakefield Junction, and then went up the Newburyport Branch and over to Salem with all the cars that were too tall to go through the Salem tunnel. *High Car*'s power was a K-8 2-8-0.

On Mondays enough high cars had accumulated over the weekend that a second train took care of the local work: *Morning Glory*, powered by an 0-6-0 and

A local freight with soon-to-be replaced 0-6-0 No. 443 switches cars at Reading, Mass., on a cold February day in 1953. *S. K. Bolton Jr.*

brought up by a short caboose, rather than a long one like *High Car* had. The freight usually had to scuttle into the team track or the coach yard to get out of the way of the Portland-bound *Casco*, a mail and express train. (The only other freight through Reading was a late-evening Boston-to-Portland train whose southbound counterpart bypassed the town and entered Boston through Wilmington.)

That was it for the school day. On the way home I encountered an inbound local at the crossing and waited for the next outbound one. Between times I talked with an incredibly patient crossing tender, who told me about train numbers and locomotive classes and division assignments and the system timetable and the double-clapper bells of the ex-Portland Terminal 0-6-0s.

During those three years there were also special events. B&M built a new wooden water tank at Reading Highlands and put down new rail on the main line, so there were work trains powered by 0-8-0s and small 2-8-0s and even diesel cranes. The local passenger trains were taken over by diesels: BL2s, GP7s, and RS2s and RS3s. The freight train got an SW8 after a short period when it ran behind a New Haven RS. I never did figure that out.

Then it was time for high school, far from the tracks and on the same side of them that I lived on. I lost my daily contact with the railroad. RDCs took over suburban service while I was in high school and then picked up what was left of the withering Portland service while I was in college.

In the summer of 1959, B&M rerouted Haverhill and Portland trains over the New Hampshire route to Wilmington and up the Wildcat line (B&M's original route, incidentally) to a connection with the Portland Division south of Lowell Junction. It was a summer in which I commuted to work in Boston, so I was glad to have more reliable service, even if train-watching in Reading had become a dull affair. Boston & Maine's decline began about the time I moved far away. I wasn't around to watch. It's just as well.

The Walter S. Parker Junior High School is still there, and so are the seats. They're not much good for train-watching, though.

June 1986

DISASTER DU JOUR, AND OTHER STORIES

E. W. King Jr.

"It's a high-visibility job," Rock Island General Manager Bill Pasta had said, looking at me from across his desk high in the Rock's general offices in La Salle Street Station, Chicago, during that interview in late November 1976.

Maybe he thought he was playing his trump card, but if I had known what was coming, that comment might have turned me off.

After the creation of Conrail, the department I worked in at the United States Railway Association was phased out at the end of October 1976. I had sent a resumé to the Rock Island, which had resulted in the interview with Pasta. Two jobs were offered—a road foreman of engines and the manager of suburban operations. I wasn't interested in being a road foreman—I'd done that for 10 years elsewhere, but I'd never been involved with commuter operations. I took them up on that one.

🛤   🛤

It's amazing the thoughts that can cross your mind at a stop light. Early one fine, late-summer morning in 1979, I was on my way from my apartment to the Rock Island's tower adjacent to the Blue Island station to watch the morning rush-hour trains. As usual, I would pick one to ride downtown to my office in the track-level concourse of La Salle Street. I

climbed the steps to the tower and greeted third-trick operator Bob McGarry and trainmaster Harry Andersen. Harry was marking down the arrival times of the late evening trains of the day before and calculating the on-time percentage, and he smiled broadly in announcing the previous day's figure to be better than 97 percent.

"Everything's smooth, no problems," McGarry told me as he punched up a route on Blue Island's modern, entrance-exit interlocking machine. And indeed, to the west of the tower and station, the Suburban Line trains were departing on time, curving to the left to commence their halting, stop-every-four-blocks trips through Morgan Park and Beverly Hills 8 miles to Gresham, where they rejoined the main line for the rest of the 17-mile run to La Salle Street. On the mainline side—where the trains from Joliet, 40 miles out, made their Blue Island stop—as train time neared, little knots of commuters were forming exactly one coach-length apart, a ritual seen hundreds of times a day on commuter railroads around Chicago and elsewhere. If the engineer failed to stop the doors right in

A new RTA F40 arrives at Blue Island with a train of "Jesse James" coaches in that period before the Rock had received its new RTA bilevel coaches. It's running west on the eastbound track; the westbound was out of service for rebuilding. *E. W. King Jr.*

front of those little knots, he'd get a few hundred dirty looks as the commuters walked by his cab-car window upon arrival downtown. But that day, all was well; no engineer was missing his spots for the stops, and the trains of bilevel gallery cars, pushed into the city by the Regional Transportation Authority's new EMD F40PH diesels, were right on schedule. In a fleet operation such as this, woe betide the train that becomes late—the commuter will catch the first train that appears after he gets to his station, so the late train will get its regular customers plus those of the next train.

This summer of 1979 was a far cry from the days in 1977 and 1978, when I would awaken to the alarm and wonder what disaster of the day was going to

befall the Rock Island's patient commuters, and what we'd have to do to overcome it.

I I

Like the day Amtrak derailed on the diamonds at 16th Street Tower, where the St. Charles Air Line route of Illinois Central Gulf—used by Amtrak to reach the old IC main line to Champaign and beyond—crosses the Rock's main. We'd had to run our evening rush through the old Rock Island coach yard, around the northwest leg of the wye, and out on the Air Line toward Union Tower, and then back around the southwest leg to our southbound track. Besides delaying all our trains, this operation turned them around. But one great advantage of push-pull trains is the speed with which you can turn 'em around if you have to; all the

crew has to do is cut out the controls on one end, then walk to the other end and cut them in. Next morning, all our trains came into La Salle Street engine-first.

ICG had an inordinate number of derailments on and near that crossing, owing to sharp S curves in the area; a particular villain was the coal train interchanged with Chicago & North Western, especially when the train was operating wrong-main. Officials were so paranoid about this move, which usually took place early in the afternoon, thereby causing maximum discomfort to the evening rush hour anyway, that the ICG terminal superintendent himself would be there to oversee it. I told him, only half jokingly, that if his coal train hit the turf, he'd better be under it.

Or the morning that the first of the two trains we stored on ground level behind the freight station at Joliet derailed trying to get up to the main line, which is elevated above street level. We quickly collared a set of Blue Island push-pull equipment and ran it out the north main line as far as Tinley Park to try to take up the slack. Even though road foreman of engines Bob Barcus and the crew got the stored train rerailed quickly, both trains were delayed and the service disturbed.

Or the bitter cold, snowy 1977 morning the phone woke me up before the alarm clock got around to it. The engines used on the Blue Island trains spent their nights in the roundhouse there, and Charlie Pitts, the Blue Island superintendent, had bad news.

"The turntable's frozen," said Charlie. "We can't get the engines out of the house."

The hostler had gotten one engine out—the one in the stall lined up with the lead track on the other side of the turntable. The rest were stranded.

"Well, Charlie, what can we beg, borrow, or steal from you good folks in the freight department?"

A lot of commuters went to Chicago that morning cold, and they went in the dark too. They were pulled by GP7s, U-boats, and EMD switchers, none with any capacity to provide steam for heat or to generate electricity for lights. But we got our riders to work. The Joliet line commuters? They never even knew there was a problem.

With the help of a section gang's truck, the turntable was worked free in time to let us deadhead the engines downtown for the outbound evening rush.

⌐ ¬

When I joined the Rock Island in January 1977, I quickly found out that I was the *de facto* curator of the country's largest operating railroad museum. All but a couple of the trains operating out of Blue Island on the Suburban Line were equipped with the steam-heated, 2500- and 2600-series "Jesse James" (or Harriman) open-window coaches from the mid-1920s. Some commuters swore that there were holes in them from bullets and arrows. The cars would seat 100 hardy souls and stand nearly a hundred more. One Joliet train was equipped with the 1949 AC 2700-series coaches, ostensibly air-conditioned but still steam-heated; these center-double-vestibule Pullman-Standards also would seat about a hundred (officially, 100 to 102). There were enough bilevel cars to equip a couple of the Blue Island trains and the remaining Joliet runs, a fleet about equally split between the stainless-steel Budds of 1965 and the Henry Crown-red smooth-side Pullmans of 1970; these would seat an average of about 155 in relative comfort (by the book, as many as 162).

To pull this melange, we had a mixture of EMD cab units: three F7s, 675-677, equipped with 480-volt auxiliary generators for head-end-power to light and air-condition the gallery cars; 630, the world's last active E6, also HEP-equipped; a half dozen or so E7s including B-unit 610, last active E7B in the world (all the E7s were steam-equipped to heat the old coaches); and a motley collection of E8s and E9s, some of which were refugees from Union Pacific (about half the 8s and 9s were steam-equipped, half HEP). The steam-generator-equipped units were fitted with a 64-volt generator in the back end to power the lights in the Jesse James cars. To switch at La Salle Street and at the 51st Street coach yard, we had more antiques, two 4800-series SW1s from a group of five—some built before World War II—that had come from Illinois Central through Precision National in 1969.

The RTA had already ordered enough new F40s and Budd bilevel cars to replace everything except our two switchers and, of course, our own bilevels (which were in generally good condition), but the delivery date was more than a year away, and we needed immediate help. RTA had the Chicago & North Western send a four-car bilevel train over to us—a cab-control car and three trailers. We assigned an F7 or an E8 to handle this train, where its bright red paint could clash happily with the traditional C&NW yellow and green. North Western didn't waste its good stuff on us—of the hundreds of trailers it operated, we got three of the oldest, Nos. 2, 7, and 13, all from the first batch built in 1955 by St. Louis Car Company. Cab car 176 was a little better—it was a 1960 Pullman. We were glad to get them, though, whatever the age or builder; we put them in an all-day Blue Island cycle where they could rack up significant mileage and help with each rush hour.

⌐ ¬

Back to 1979. Since everything was going well, I picked out a Suburban Line train to ride into the city and climbed up on its F40 on the rear end. Why the engine instead of the forward end? It's a bit cramped to ride in the cab compartment of the lead car with the engine crew, and besides, the little F40s put on quite a show. A suburban engineer will peel the throttle right out into Run 8 after getting the highball and catching the slack, and I liked to watch the load meters go to the peg when the ugly little EMDs responded. And even with six or seven loaded cars, an F40, after coming through the slip switches at Gresham, would easily top the hill toward Englewood at 60 mph.

On other days, I rode the train, following the train crew as they checked tickets and cut cash fares.

The late Don Sale was a very amiable, patient conductor, a veteran who was respected and liked by his regular riders and coworkers. But one of Don's semi-regulars, a well-dressed man, sometimes tried to beat him out of a ride by telling him that he had nothing smaller than a $50 bill, hoping that Don would let him ride without changing the thing; our trainmen and collectors weren't required to change anything larger than a 20. But

The world's last E6 in revenue service, Rock Island 630, arrives at Blue Island on the main line, crossing Vermont Street with its two-car local—just about all the train it could make time with. *E. W. King Jr.*

Sale, recognizing that this would be unfair to the other 800 or so of his riders that dutifully paid their fares, would patiently write out a chit so that the man could get his change at the La Salle Street ticket office. Of course, the commuter complained vigorously, "I don't have time for that rigmarole."

Finally, even Sale's patience wore thin, and he got ready for the high-roller. After tendering his next 50, the commuter gained considerable weight—he got off the train with a disgusted expression on his face and 47 or so Susan B. Anthony silver dollars for his change!

I'd like to report that that cured the big-bill commuter, but it didn't. He *was* cured, though, about a week later when he offered Sale another 50—Sale reached in his pocket and rattled his loose change

purposefully with a smile on his face, and the commuter put his 50 away and came up with the required fare in singles.

⚏ ⚏

We eased into La Salle Street right on time, and I looked up at the open gridwork that was used to support the roof slabs. The Rock Island trustee had decreed the slabs' removal after several of them had cracked and dropped onto the platforms, fortunately without causing injury. But I remembered the problems that we'd had with an open depot in the winter.

"The whole damn depot's full of snow, Ed." This was the cheery prospect facing me after I arrived at Blue Island Tower one winter morning. John Sullivan, the first-trick operator at Polk Street Tower at the south end of the La Salle Street platforms, was on the horn. We had

known that this was going to happen, but at that time, we had no means of doing anything about it other than praying for summer.

"How many tracks can we use, John?"
"Just two—the straight-in tracks from the mains."

"The section crew there yet?"
"Yeah. I'm having them clean the crossovers between the mains first."

"Good."

Well, the commuters were delayed again, but they all got into La Salle Street. We pulled two trains into each track and unloaded them, then backed them out on the outbound main to the 51st Street coach yard, meantime running two more trains into the tracks to unload.

At the time, we only had two small section gangs, and when we anticipated heavy snow, we split them up to keep the interlockings open. They reported to their assigned towers about an hour before the first train was due. The La Salle Street forces came in early too to clean platforms.

By the evening rush, we had five tracks available for the outbounds, with decent platforms, and we got everyone home in reasonable shape.

Commuters are no less creatures of habit than anyone else. If Joe was accustomed to catching his 5:08 Suburban Line train home on track 6, he was quite justified in expecting it to be there every day. Changing track assignments of outbound rush-hour trains was akin to moving the furniture in a blind man's house, but sometimes it couldn't be helped. Such occasions required constant announcements on the station PA system, as well as manager of stations and services Bob Mielzynski in the concourse with the bullhorn.

ɪ ɪ

I hear tell that in winter, the North Western used to put the locomotive on the inbound end of the first consist to head for Chicago on its Lake Geneva (Wis.) commuter branch line (later cut back to Richmond, Ill., and now McHenry), the better to plow snow with, rather than a bilevel cab car. Not so with the Rock, with its open-country or elevated right-of-way. Engineer Oley Gilbert customarily ran our first Chicago-bound train out of Joliet, No. 400, a bilevel consist, and from the time I arrived at the Rock Island until the big strike ended the railroad in 1980, Oley Gilbert came to Chicago, breaking trail in the deepest of snows with his cab car. He must have been a frustrated rotary plow operator. "I felt her raise up a little when I hit that drift, but I just widened on her and we came right through."

In the morning, the steps and escalators at La Salle Street would be inundated by a steady stream of commuters sallying forth to do battle with the world of commerce. Many of them worked or

traded at the nearby Chicago Board of Trade or the Options Exchange, and in the evening rush, some of them would wend their way home poorer, not richer, from the day's action.

Several of the Rock's train and engine crew personnel had taken jobs at the CBOT after they got enough seniority to hold a job of one trip in in the morning and out in the evening. Notable among these were the aforementioned Don Sale and engineer Chester Ballard. The latter was noted for his genial, outgoing personality and his "Japanese stops"—his riders said that at each stop, there occurred a lurch that caused all the seated riders to bow toward the engine.

I went downstairs to the ticket office and checked in with Bob Mielzynski. Bob kept a very capable finger on the pulse of such things as ticket sales, budget performance, the suburban stations, and the complaint file.

The latter was very fat in 1977, and it got fatter during the winter of 1977-1978, but the arrival of the new equipment, implementation of monumental track rehabilitation programs, the presence of our very own section crews to troubleshoot problem areas not covered by the rehab, and considerable work in the areas of car cleaning and some cosmetic work on La Salle Street Station all had had a gratifying effect. By 1979, complaints were rare.

I decided to ride a midday train to Joliet and back, to get a look at the stations and some of the trackwork that was progressing on the main line west of Blue Island.

ɪ ɪ

Out of Englewood one day in 1977, the 630, our prima donna E6, had struggled and grunted and groaned and gotten its two-car outbound midday train up to 60 mph at the top of the hill. Our young hogger made one application and lapped the 24-RL brake, shut off the throttle, and folded his hands in his lap. His hands hadn't moved when the train came to a halt at the Gresham station with the doorway of the first car right opposite the stairwell.

"Can you do that every time?" I asked, impressed.

"I make four round trips a day on this midday run," said he, "with 12 stops in each direction. That's 96 station stops a day. If I couldn't do it every time by now, I'd be ashamed of myself."

The 630 was something else. It was not what you would call an ideal suburban locomotive, being slow to load up and quick to slip once it did … but then, it wasn't built for this work. Glenn Monhart, where were you when we needed you? (Glenn and his wife own restored Atlantic Coast Line E3 501.) We tried not to have to use 630 on the long Joliet trains, especially the "Bankers"—the 5:11 p.m. hotshot, eight bilevels, first stop Tinley Park. An F7 couldn't hack that one, either, so we tried to keep a good E8 or E9 on it.

The 5:16, the Joliet train that followed the Bankers out, first stop Midlothian, was another long consist. It was supposed to have 13 AC cars, but there came a time where beleaguered master mechanic-car Stan Globis could not scrape together enough ACs that were serviceable—the floors were falling out of them, for one thing, so we had to fill the train with 2500s. We had used back-to-back E7s on it, and they did a creditable job. The F40s were delivered before the new RTA bilevels, so the Authority leased enough non-push-pull bilevels from Amtrak (the old C&NW intercity cars built by Pullman-Standard in 1958 for the *Flambeau* and *Peninsula* 400s) to equip the 5:16. But we had no way to turn engines at Joliet, so we still had to use two units back to back. There was a short period in early summer 1978 when we used the F40s on the Jesse James cars, which made an amusing sight. The irony was that the F40s had no 64-volt power supply for the lights, or steam for the heat; the new bilevels came, though, before the days grew short enough to need lights or cool enough to require heat.

ɪ ɪ

On my midday trip back from Joliet in 1979, we had an F40, and it booted us out of Blue Island past the coach yard.

"Scoots" meet at Blue Island on the Suburban Line. Westbound (left) in pull mode with Jesse James coaches meets an eastbound in push mode with bilevels at Vermont Street. *E. W. King Jr.*

The Suburban Line rehabilitation and the Blue Island coach yard had been two of the RTA's most badly needed projects. After the work was done, the Blue Island facility might have been the only coach yard in the world with body tracks good for 50 mph—all welded rail, new ties, deep ballast. If that sounds like wasteful overkill to you, think about it for a minute—the yard would not have to have much maintenance before about 2010 or so. Before the rehab, shoving trains into the yard through the old ladder track at Vermont Street, just north of the Blue Island station, produced enough derailments, especially in the winter, to be more than an occasional source of stomach acid.

The story was the same for the Suburban Line itself. When I joined the Rock, the entire branch had a 15 mph limit; I

had nicknamed it "the dirt road." It wasn't until the snow melted in early March 1977 that I found out how appropriate my nickname was.

But the rehab was properly done. One track was taken out of service and removed down to the subroadbed, then rebuilt from scratch. When that track was completed, the other was done the same way. There was hardly enough reusable material worth taking the trouble to reclaim. The new tracks were good for about 80 mph, but they had a 30 mph limit, not unreasonable considering that each train stops every four blocks.

After we got through the slip switches at Gresham, the F40 got us up to 60 on the new welded rail before we got near the top of the hill. North of Englewood, we went along at 40 on a part of the line not yet rehabbed; our section gang had, however, installed enough new crossties in this segment to make it decent.

We passed the 51st Street coach yard and the 47th Street diesel shop (known as the "Rocket House," or to some, the "Launching Pad"), each of which had required some trackwork. Master mechanic-locomotive Tony Orsino had said that when an engine went over the Rocket House trackage, the track looked like it was alive. This complex only had one track into it, and a derailment at the wrong time and place could delay a lot of commuters … and did, once.

We passed Root Street Tower, where a wye goes out over the Dan Ryan Expressway; this was used to turn the older diesels each day for their outbound trips on the steam-equipped trains.

One of the more embarrassing delays we had experienced occurred when a rather new tower operator lined the engines off the wye onto the northbound track through the crossover and, due to a distraction, forgot to return the signal lever to normal while the circuit was occupied. This locked up his plant; he could not return the lever to normal and run time to reset, and those old switch machines had no provision for hand operation. Five early afternoon rush-hour trains were stacked up at Root Street before a signal maintainer could fight his way through 5 p.m. traffic to unlock the plant (we had no maintainer assigned to evenings at Root Street). By the time the evening rush was due, the operator had no conflicting movements and so should have been able to set his interlocking for fleet operation on the main lines and just keep score.

I I

As I walked back to the office after an on-time arrival, trainmaster Jim McCarthy met me with some bad news. "The 2:20 is sitting at 69th Street and can't go across the bridge. The Chicago Police called just before he got there and said that an oversized semi had struck the bridge and not to let anything across until it was inspected. The roadmaster is on his way." I had missed the radio call—my train must have just made it across before the police call.

The long and short of it was that the bridge was OK, but the semi died—and another trainload of commuters was delayed by the "better safe than sorry" department. It was a bargain, compared with a more famous incident.

Hernan Solarte was a Rock Island bridge engineer who really liked his work. He was into bridges. Every workday morning, Hernan would look out of his inbound Jesse James coach window and admire the box-section support structure of the Chicago Transit Authority's Dan Ryan Line bridge over the Rock Island just south of 12th Street. On the bitter cold morning of January 4, 1978, something didn't look just right to him. Hernan came bursting into my office, saying it looked like the CTA bridge was cracked; he used my telephone to call his counterpart at the CTA. Shortly after ten o'clock, the bridge was inspected, and sure enough, three piers were cracked. The busy Dan Ryan Line was summarily shut

down, and the Rock Island trustee properly said, "If they won't take anybody across that bridge, we won't take anybody under it." So we were shut down too. We did take our equipment out of the station, to the 51st Street coach yard.

Solarte later received a commendation from the City of Chicago for observing a potentially catastrophic situation and doing something about it.

This incident served to illustrate one advantage of having an organization like the RTA to coordinate things in an emergency. RTA arranged for the ICG's electric suburban line to run extra trains for us and to honor Rock Island tickets, taking our commuters to Blue Island, the end of an ICG electrified branch whose station was just across Vermont Street and our main line from our Blue Island station. In the afternoon rush, we put one freshly serviced train at our Blue Island station and lined up the remainder of the Joliet trains on our westbound main line alongside Blue Island Yard. As the ICG trains came in, the Rock commuters walked across the street and boarded a Rock train; as one train loaded and left town, we moved the next one into Position A. On the Suburban Line, we put a set of push-pull equipment on each track and gave each train exclusive right to use it between Blue Island and Gresham. They loaded passengers off the ICG and went as far up the Suburban Line as they needed to unload, then returned to Blue Island.

In the morning, the operation was in reverse. Our Joliet trains came into Blue Island and disgorged, the passengers going across the street to catch their ICG connection. We then moved each train up to 51st Street for servicing. In the off-hours, we operated a shuttle service to connect with the ICG. A few Joliet passengers might have taken advantage of the other commuter service there, two daily trains on ICG's "diesel line," the former GM&O "Plug" local route.

We operated that way for 4 days while the CTA erected a temporary falsework to support the bridge until permanent measures could be taken. These were the only four days that I experienced in my tenure at the Rock that we couldn't complete our job, and it was due to conditions beyond our control. We might have been

late often in those premodernization days, but we were never shut out. And in this period, there were many instances when the N&W couldn't get out of Orland Park or the ICG had wire trouble, or even when the mighty Burlington had problems on its three-track speedway—times when the RTA bused those riders over to the poor old broken-down, much-maligned Rock Island. Often during those times, our trainmen would come into the office and tell of the trains being so crowded that they couldn't even get through to lift transportation—and the Rock's men were real professionals, often seeming to move through crowded trains by a process of osmosis.

I I

There was a certain amount of pride involved when one could stand at the bumping posts in the evening after all the day's work was done: trains cleaned, engines serviced and backed onto the trains in time to have the air-conditioning get a head start on getting the cars cooled (we had no 480-volt standby at La Salle Street), reports done, budget figures entered and compared with standard, Lost and Found inquiries answered (*No, this is just the Found; the Lost is still out there somewhere.* [Every commuter was said to have three umbrellas: one to leave at home, one to leave on the train, and one to leave at the office]), and nothing left to do but watch the homebound weary toilers streaming through the gates and the trains moving out on time.

At 4:40.00 p.m. the green coaches of the first rush-hour Suburban Line train move away from the bumping post in response to conductor Ed Trebelhorn's highball. At 4:40.20, a nicely dressed young lady bursts through the gate and gives chase, high heels and all. Halfway down the platform she gives up and comes back toward the concourse, breathing hard and moving her lips silently.

"Thanks," I offer.

"What for?" she asks, angrily. 'That train might never have left if you hadn't chased it out of here."

Even after her irate glare turns into a rueful smile, the better part of valor keeps me from asking the obvious, "Can we count on you for tomorrow?"

Rock Island E8 652, the *Independence*, arrives at Blue Island on its way west with the two-car *Peoria Rocket*; it would not live up to such a speedy name on the Peoria Branch's 25 and 10 mph, rock-and-roll track. This Bicentennial paint scheme was designed by a group of Chicago railfans. *E. W. King Jr.*

At 5:11.00 conductor Merle Strutz closes the doors on the Bankers and punches out a two-short highball on the communicating buzzer. At 5:11.20, Strutz opens the door to see why there has been a disturbing lack of forward progress … just in time for the puffing, panting fireman to climb aboard Strutz's rear car, rush upstairs, and go back to the engineer's cab compartment. When the train was brought in from 51st Street, the crew hadn't centered and removed the cab-car reverse lever—the reverser on the locomotive was thus locked in the inbound position. Only a second after the fireman gets there, the Bankers is on the move.

Next morning, a very embarrassed engine crew tells me about this in the office. They never did it again, but we started spot-checking cab cars, just in case some other crew was in a hurry to get to the coffee shop between runs.

I also liked to watch the evening rush from Polk Street Tower. In 1977, it had been no real treat—fingers crossed, hoping that all the switches worked and nothing went on the ground; but by 1979, roadmaster Howard Buchanan's section gang had put enough crossties in the throat switches and elsewhere to take the worry out of it. In 1977 or 1979, it was a treat watching second-trick operator Earl Luchs playing that old pistol-grip plant like an organist hitting hot licks from Bach as he got 'em out of town.

The most impressive thing about my three years on the Rock Island was the sheer dedication of the railroaders. *Much-maligned* is an overworked term, but it was completely applicable to the Rock Island commuter service until the Regional Transportation Authority's improvements could be felt. But the people who made the service work never let the maligning get them down. The

number of times in those three years that the poor old Rock ran when others didn't is the proof.

⚓   ⚓

Commuter, obviously an elderly lady in an agitated state, on the telephone at midday during one of Chicago's heavier snowstorms: "Sir, is the Rock Island going to be running this evening? Somebody said that they heard on the radio that you weren't going to run."

"That's wrong, ma'am. We brought you downtown this morning, and we'll take you home tonight."

And we did.

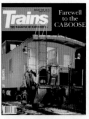

August 1990

THE END

William Benning Stewart

It wasn't really that his teachers had told him that a freight car was not beautiful. But they had told him that Keats, Shelley, the Taj Mahal, the Acropolis, Westminster Abbey, the Louvre, the Isles of Greece, were beautiful. And they had told it to him so often and in such a way that he not only thought it true—which it is—but that these things were everything that beauty is.

—Thomas Wolfe, from *The Web and the Rock*, 1937

Looking back, I can't fault Frank Holland for his skepticism. During the golden, late summer days of 1966, friend Frank and I were, it seemed, still achingly far from reaching our majority, yet sufficiently aged to have almost every curve of approaching adulthood carefully charted. But as September neared, we became increasingly restive as we contemplated the academic maze and social minefields of Indiana University's fast-approaching fall semester. Mindful of Mark Twain's admonition against letting one's schooling interfere with one's education, we charted a daily agenda marked by the pursuit of girls, the purchase of pizza and cheeseburgers, and the exploration of the world with the aid of a snazzy new Plymouth convertible. Each of those activities, I recall, was accompanied by the amplified beat of the Beach Boys and other Top 40 artists on the Sport Fury's AM radio.

But my version of the "Little Deuce Coupe" that summer was an eight-wheeled, 35-foot-long red relic dating to the turn of the century. No dual-quad carburetors, no straight pipes, no four-on-the-floor … ah, but what a set of wheels.

At an early age, I had lost my heart to the winsome wooden cabooses of the

Nickel Plate Road. Weekday journeys to school and Saturday visits to a lumber yard with my father were regularly enlivened by the sight of passing NKP freights, and the solid roll of their 1100-series crummies—solid old hacks ennobled with a scripted reassurance of NICKEL PLATE HIGH SPEED SERVICE—sealed my belief that the rear of a freight train was invariably as interesting as the fascinating machinery on the other end.

Within a decade of those early encounters, my beloved 1100s were living on borrowed time, and purchasing and preserving one for use as a personal study became one of my most sacrosanct objectives. A nervously typed teenage inquiry to Nickel Plate's Cleveland headquarters during 1964 brought a gracious response and an invitation to examine the recently retired 1138, still awaiting disposition in the division point yards at Charleston, Ill. The ensuing journey was a wonderful introduction to the west end of Nickel Plate's storied Clover Leaf District, but the 1138, aged and infirm, appeared past the point of salvation.

Two years later, I distracted Holland from the pursuit of a strawberry blonde with electric blue eyes and a decidedly

The Nickel Plate Road's cabooses proudly advertised the railroad's fast freight trains with Nickel Plate High Speed Service lettering. Here, a wooden NKP caboose trails a freight near Avery, Ohio, in July 1957. *Don Wood*

non-Midwestern moniker (Frank, what *was* her name?) long enough to accompany me on an inspection trip to the NKP shop city of Frankfort, Ind., where one of the last 1100s sat forlornly on the RIP track of successor Norfolk & Western's back lot. While I busied myself with critical analysis of the 1137's thin flanges and drooping end platforms, Frank departed to secure shakes, burgers, and fries at a nearby drive-in, biding his time with daydreams of the elusive blonde (*Yvette? Yvonne? Lydia? Sonja?*).

Such are the perils of youth. My passion for the 1137 proved to be as short-lived as Frank's fondness for the blonde. I can't speak to the source of *his* discomfiture, but mine came with an N&W

mechanical officer's pronouncement that the 1137 would need substantial shopping before she could be pronounced fit to amble down a main line once more. Sadly, I see now that his perspective was based on standards for slack levels of 5,000-ton trains; my goals were simply to find a friendly siding for the car, polish the once proud High Speed Service proclamation, light the kerosene markers, and conjure up visions of a night ride to Charleston from the cupola cushions.

On that warm afternoon at the western Nickel Plate citadel, it was simple enough to envision a recently shopped 1137 heading west again at the back of a Berkshire-powered manifest, to watch her gathering speed as twilight burnished the rails of the Clover Leaf, to see her

heel gracefully to the reverse curves at Veedersburg as darkness enveloped the train. It was even easier to picture myself on the back platform awaiting the operator's "all black" highball as the car clattered over C&EI's double-track diamonds at Cayuga, listening later from the cupola for the hollow rumble of the deck girder bridge high above the Little Vermilion River, absorbing the abundant, toothsome tastes of traditional freight railroading served by a swaying caboose rolling headlong through the middle of an eastern Illinois night.

In a cornfield meet between such dreams and the realities of AAR interchange rules, my affair with the 1137 met the fate of most romances at age 19; she met her destiny (a fiery end in the Frankfort back lot) while I ruefully returned to the university, where Professor Zinninger's literature class would introduce me to the caustic wit of H. L. Mencken and the Baltimore bard's sage observation that love, like war, is easy to begin but hard to stop.

I want to confess right now: I'm a sucker for cabooses. Something about them has always captivated me, ever since I was one of the kids waving eagerly beside the Southern Pacific tracks two blocks from my boyhood home in California. Maybe it's their toylike quality or their look of fragility and vulnerability, especially in contrast to the snorting beast at the front of the train.

—Donald Dale Jackson,
"Cabooses May Be Nearing the End of the Line,"
Smithsonian magazine, 1986

It's safe to presume that fragility and vulnerability weren't T. B. Watson's adjectives of choice when he persuaded a master mechanic to add caboosedom's first cupola to his Chicago & North Western waycar in 1863. Early cabooses—the name derives from the Dutch *kabuis*, for ship's galley—tended to be humble shanties on flatcars or boxcars hastily remodeled to provide space and shelter for rear-end train crews. Legend holds that conductor Watson encountered such a car with a hole in its roof during a run across Iowa. Elevating himself through the opening at speed, he became so taken with the view of his train and the passing landscape that he was moved to devise plans for the glass-enclosed observation post which forever distanced the caboose from all other transportation conveyances.

Cupolas not only advanced the safety and productivity of train crews but also gave a curious public a better look at the men who had signed on for railroading's great adventure. Engineers and small-town telegraphers probably enjoyed greater status as heroes to small boys, but a wave from the rocking red ark at the end of a train was to become a happily

anticipated element of trackside life for males and females of all ages in every post-Civil War generation. "It has an upstairs and a downstairs, a front porch and a back porch," went one woman's succinct analysis of the caboose's architectural and social charms. "And it's cute."

To plowing farmers, commuting workers, or any of life's multitudinous varieties of sidewalk superintendents, the rear-end trainman's friendly acknowledgment of momentarily intersecting lives, careers, and fortunes added a melodic note to otherwise mundane workdays, a signal of accomplishment as pronounced as the arrival of the newspaper on the front porch or the blast of the plant whistle at five o'clock. As a part of the fabric of one's hometown, the caboose easily outranked innumerable politicians and sweethearts in popularity and longevity. And, in the era of billboard boxcars—when Westerners speculated as to whether Phoebe Snow was a gentrywoman on the order of Alice Roosevelt Longworth and Easterners wondered how a railroad that ended in Colorado and Wyoming could correctly claim to go "Everywhere West"—the caboose provided a brief paragraph of summation to the multi-messaged travelogue of a passing freight. The coming of the automobile age only heightened public anticipation of the caboose's arrival: For idled grade-crossing grammarians it offered an exuberant exclamation point at the end of a fast-stepping time freight, the long-awaited period of a plodding coal drag.

The seemingly universal public affection for the caboose may be at least partially ascribed to its omnipresence during railroading's golden era. At its peak during the Roaring Twenties, the caboose family numbered more than 25,000 members, ranging from the four-wheel bobbers of short lines and switching roads to mass-produced fleets of waycars operated by carriers that counted their route mileages in five figures. To patrol the Pennsylvania Railroad's 10,499 miles of track in 1930, for example, the Standard Railroad of the World employed 2,983 look-alike cabin cars. Executing the same type of work over the Canadian Pacific's longer but less-densely trafficked system of 15,057

miles called for the use of 1,345 vans. The number of cabooses employed by medium-size roads was no less remarkable: 1,234 on the 5,550-mile Baltimore & Ohio, 677 on the 7,452-mile Missouri Pacific, 270 on the 2,077-mile Boston & Maine. 130 on the 1,223-mile Nashville, Chattanooga & St. Louis.

In its busiest hour, the caboose was a daily sight on railroads throughout North America, bringing up the rear of mainline manifests and local freights, riding the spindly wooden trestles of the Colorado narrow gauges, serving as primary elements of mixed trains on short lines and branches of major systems, shepherding the freight of a surprising number of interurban lines. Wherever freight-carrying rails and human activity crossed paths, it was a rare day which did not see at least one encounter between man and caboose.

There were people who always waved, or at night they'd flick a porch light on or wave a lantern in the barnyard. I believe that's gone now. We'd look for that, look forward to it. We never knew them, but we'd give them names like Mabel and Harry. It was just a friendly gesture. If you didn't see them you'd wonder what happened. You'd see the kids every year and watch them grow up.

—John Bragg, retired B&O conductor,
Smithsonian magazine, 1986

For the men on the other side of the cupola, careers aboard cabooses often fulfilled many boyhood dreams if not every adult expectation. No one questioned the lack of monotony that came with the job: assignments at every hour of the day or night, a back-seat view of every imaginable lifestyle, an appreciation of how each trackside enterprise functioned. Added benefits included admission to the fellowship of an exclusive men's club and the prospect of savoring a long-simmering, caboose-stove-cooked pot roast or spicy Mulligan stew—hearty fare far removed from the drab offerings of most division point or tank town beaneries—at the end of the long workday.

Lantern in hand, the conductor of a Winston-Salem Southbound train stands by his caboose as his train prepares to set out cars for interchange at High Rock, N.C., in 1956. *Philip R. Hastings*

The pay wasn't bad, either, particularly in light of the freedom the job offered from the dawn-to-dusk routines known to most who waved longingly from trackside. For both onlookers and employees, the caboose touched a national nerve, the pervasive desire to be going somewhere else, preferably with dispatch and some sense of abandon.

To the unknowing eye, life aboard the caboose seemed disarmingly agreeable and straightforward. The conductor, master of the train, tended to his waybills and wheel report beneath the cheery glow of a chimney lamp. The brakeman, when not called upon to throw switches, couple cars, or protect the rear of his train, gazed down idly from his post in the cupola, never failing to acknowledge a trackside

salute between routine glances at the running gear of his charge and studied examination of approaching signals and passing trains.

In truth, the railroad remained a dirty, dangerous place to work, and the successful start of every journey carried with it the prospect of an uncertain end. For every dozen trips completed without incident, there were a few untold others marked by vicious storms, pulled drawbars, derailments, encounters with hobos, and myriad other contretemps. Shifting loads, engine failures, grade-crossing accidents, and delays caused by other trains could also make for a long day. In the worst winter weather—those days when even regular wavers didn't appear at their windows or trackside posts—a few minutes spent flagging in a blinding blizzard

could make a man compose love songs to a No. 14 Sun Beam Railway Cabin Car Stove as he strained to hear four shouts from a distant locomotive whistle, relieving him of his dreary post.

Still, "the other side of the job," as railroaders called return journeys, brought balance to what outsiders saw as a vagabond existence, and enforcement of the Hours of Service law lessened the weeklong caboose encampments that marked the industry's early years. For all its frustrations and hardships, life aboard cabooses forged a common bond. Over time, trainmen of the 1,001-caboose Chicago, Milwaukee, St. Paul & Pacific and the one-crummy Gainesville & Northwestern came to realize their occupational kinship with conductors and brakemen of such distant pikes as the Bangor & Aroostook, Atlantic Coast Line, Gulf, Mobile & Ohio, and Sacramento Northern, developing an ofttimes fierce pride in their calling and their respective companies. A New York Central conductor once told me he regularly tossed inoperative lanterns from his caboose as it crossed the highest bridge on his division, not from anger or distaste but because he and his colleagues felt the schedules of their busy railroad and the safety of its employees couldn't be compromised by faulty equipment.

Once indoctrinated, few men of the caboose turned away. "I'd be there yet if they'd let me," John Bragg told *Smithsonian* of the railroad his peers referred to as the "Best & Only." "Hell, they had to drag me off."

After sitting on a siding in the 95-degree central Texas heat for more than an hour, Jake Batson's caboose is hot enough inside to bake bread. But the 60-year-old conductor talks as if his car at the rear of a freight train were a palace. "You won't find many cabooses this nice," Batson says, pointing to an enclosed flush toilet. "Seats are real comfortable too," he adds, motioning toward the raised cupola.

—Fred W. Frailey,
U.S. News & World Report, 1985

In its starring role as railroading's blue-collar business car, the caboose was called upon to play a variety of roles capably and confidently each day. A well-equipped waycar came equipped with sufficient desktops to process the conductor's paperwork and still set a table for a flavorful feast proferred by his brakeman-*cum*-cook. The trademark cupola, progressively refined over the years, adeptly performed its starring role of rolling lookout post, while ample interior seating, bunks, sinks, and storage space were cast for the caboose's supporting roles of traveling command center and train-crew Pullman. To meet its lesser-known but vital roles as emergency vehicle and enforcer of the Book of Rules, every crummy carried a remarkable assortment of nooks and crannies designed to efficiently house a fascinating inventory of spare coupler knuckles and pins, rerailing frogs, chains, jacks, blocking, first-aid kits, tools, torpedoes, fusees, flags, lanterns, cotton waste, and coal oil.

From its inception, the multifunctional caboose challenged carbuilders to effectively mix contemporary materials with the rugged demands of round-the-clock, rear-of-the-train railroading. Over the span of a dozen decades, caboose architecture evolved from homegrown carpenter Gothic to a sophisticated if industrial blend of welded steel and carefully arranged interiors. Milestones along the way included the pioneering development of bay-window cars by the Baltimore & Ohio and Milwaukee Road, the arrival of all-steel cabooses (cars especially appreciated, one would think, by crews sandwiched between heaving helper locomotives and 10,000-ton coal trains on uncompromising mountain grades), and the latter-day advent of all-electric, roller-bearing, cushion underframe, and train-radio-equipped cabins. (How many postwar grade-crossing observers concluded—after reading the lightning-bolt-braced noun RADIO in Railroad Roman lettering on a passing bay window—that the conductor was tuned in to *Don McNeil's Breakfast Club* or *The Arthur Godfrey Show*?)

In common with other capital expenditure aspects of railroading, the caboose's fortunes rose and fell with the prevailing economic health of the earners. War, depression, and the crummy's perennial nonrevenue status combined to keep elderly hacks on the rosters of many roads well beyond their prime, but cost efficiency and safety were convincing arguments for new models when the money was available. That feast-or-famine approach to caboose building often produced fleets spanning the better part of a century in age and application, as on the Rock Island, whose postwar roster included contemporary cupola and bay-window models, outside-braced wooden rebuilds from caboose-short World War II, traditional wooden crummies, and a collection of memorable transfer cabs with wide-open, roof-mounted crew benches, accessories capable of making today's FRA and OSHA inspectors cringe.

In the last act of its long-running pageant, the caboose adopted colorful costuming traditionally reserved for its patrician, passenger-train counterparts. Some Rio Grande patrons may have mistaken that carrier's pinstriped, gold-and-silver postwar cabooses for a following second section of the *Prospector*. Elsewhere, streamlined Coca-Cola red, cream, and blue cabooses added a flash of color to the tail of Wabash time freights in the Corn Belt, while elegant aluminum-and-Chinese red saddlebag-cupola waycars of the mid-1960s brought the *elan* of the *Zephyrs* to the back of many Burlington manifests.

Ironically, its final incarnation found the caboose reverting to the fundamental cab-on-platform style dating to its earliest years. During the 1970s Missouri Pacific and future merger partner Union Pacific both embraced that tenured design known to prehistoric crummies and generations of transfer cabs in metropolitan switching districts. In its CA-11 class, UP eschewed tradition for cost efficiency and crew productivity, producing what may well have been the industry's most efficient caboose. But, inside that contemporary cabin car, foam-padded corners and shoulder-harness-equipped seats linked the CA-11 to the railroading of conductor Watson's time as they spoke of inherent deficiencies soon to be recognized as the caboose's fatal flaws.

*Let me sit on the right-hand side,
A-hold of the throttle and Johnson bar,
And make our rough, wild hogger ride
At the other end, on the old waycar.
Just watch him try to stay in the hack
When I start the train with the air and the slack,
And hear him holler when his head I drove
Right in behind the crummy stove,
And as the train goes into the sag,
Knock him out with the slack in that drag.
And let him lay there on the floor,
Afraid to stand up, for fear he'd get more.
I'd head right in on the longest track,
And cut her off a long way back;
When the hogger walks in, to him I'd say:
"Well, how was the ride you got today?"*

—B. H. Terry, "Put the Hogger in the Crummy,"
Railroad Magazine, 1941

Modern steel cabooses, such as Erie bay-window C300 in 1953, included such improvements as on-board radio (with RADIO EQUIPPED lettering and lightning bolts) and electric lighting (note the generator below and to the right of the bay). *Erie*

In *Workin' on the Railroad*, an engaging anthology of first-person railroad tales, editor Richard Reinhardt observed, sagaciously, that if railroading was "inaccessible, complex, and cold-blooded to outsiders," it remained, for three-quarters of a century or more, "the most glamorous adventure on earth. … The long-drawn whistle of a passing freight called hundreds of thousands of small-town boys from the hills and prairies, and the reality of working on the railroad seldom disappointed those who survived its hazards." But the hazards were immense, especially to the rear-end men who necessarily entrusted their lives to the adroit judgment of engineers—both on their train and the next one following—and a daily mixture of good dispatching and good luck.

Its charm and heritage notwithstanding, the caboose—essentially a box on wheels, perforated with openings and filled with obstacles for its occupants—was an inherently dangerous vehicle to board and ride. Caboose lore is filled with stories of smashups, injuries, and deaths brought about by short flagging, over-looked meeting points, switching errors, derailments, and train break-in-twos. Rear-end collisions were a leading cause of premature retirement for cabooses, but an overturned oil lamp could quickly incinerate a wooden car, and a track washout could spell doom for even the sturdiest steel crummy.

At the start of the rear-end trainman's workday, rolling thunder from the head end announced that the hogger was flexing every muscle of the iron horse to stretch the dozens or even hundreds of

feet of slack which reposed in the draw-bars of a motionless train. Slack could throw a man from a platform or cupola, smash him into bulkheads and tables, and break enough bones to abbreviate his career at an early age. The problem was exacerbated at speed when slack ran in and out on grades, bobbling a conductor's pen on his wheel report at best, bringing him considerable bodily harm at worst.

Equally dreaded was the urgent hiss of the train air going into emergency, a sudden, darkly ominous prelude to unfolding and potentially grievous events. For the men of the caboose, the longitudinal, ceiling-mounted handhold installed aboard most waycars was not an appliance of mere convenience.

Cabooses improved in style and comfort over the years, but the conditions that typically brought them and their riders to grief remained. In addition to the potential disability or death of trained and tenured employees, the destruction of a modern steel caboose—whether through wreck, fire, or grade-crossing accident—could represent a loss in excess of $75,000. As time and technology began to revamp traditional railroading, management came to see the caboose as a high-cost, high-risk anachronism from another era, one kept alive largely through prevailing laws and labor agreements.

To the perfectionist there can exist no symphony without a coda, no finished repast without the benediction of cognac. So to the railroad perfectionist there can be no train, in the technical sense and as an [a]esthetic entity, without a caboose complete with markers. There are, shamefully enough in a degenerate age, transcontinental Pullman trains without observation cars. There are also pork chops without applesauce. Either is more thinkable than a freight, whether redball manifest or modest local, effacing itself on passing tracks for every other train on the employees' card, without a crummy.

—Lucius Beebe,
Highball: A Pageant of Trains, 1945

"What's small and cute," teased Desiree French in the pages of *Forbes* magazine during 1982, "rides at the end of a freight train, and wastes maybe $400 million a year?"

Working railroaders and a universe of caboose lovers already knew. By 1980, Class 1 railroads owned 12,884 cabooses—about half of the fleet that was functioning in the waycar's heyday—and operated them 431,788,000 miles. But every mile operated (on average, 92 per caboose per day) cost the carrier as much as 92 cents. Management had been mulling over the money to be saved by not buying (at an average cost of $80,000 each), running, or repairing cabooses, not paying for the extra fuel required to haul them at the back of otherwise revenue-producing trains, not paying for lost-time injuries brought about by caboose mishaps, not purchasing supplies and paying other ancillary costs associated with their operation and upkeep.

In the age of the microchip, with computers processing much of the conductor's paperwork and trackside detectors assuming the brakeman's lookout chores, the caboose's remaining functions consisted largely of providing seating for trainmen, an operable air-brake gauge for their occasional examination, and brackets to carry marker lights or other rear-end indicators. The technological success of the end-of-train black box (could it only be coincidental that the first ones were really red?) made the unthinkable of Beebe's time practical if not particularly pleasant, and a 1982 agreement between the United Transportation Union and the carriers at last sent railroading's greatest goodwill ambassador to join many of its end-of-the-train peers on permanent layoff.

One winter night the general manager and I were coming up through Abo Canyon on a freight train. His business car was at Vaughn, and we were riding in the waycar. Sitting in the cupola, about all we could see was the red light of the signals as we struggled up past them and the marker lights of the thundering helper engine just behind us. The racket having made conversation difficult, after a short time I climbed down and pulled up a chair in front of the stove. The conductor was busy at his desk, and the rear brakeman was up in the cupola with the general manager. For all practical purposes, I was alone.

The waycar stove glowing cheerfully through the open ashpan door, the bubbling coffee pot on its top, the half-full coal bucket, a lighted red lantern nearby, and the intent figure of the conductor writing in his train book—all of these made a scene so typically "railroad" that I began thinking about the lifetime I had spent in the business.

—Joseph A. Noble, *From Cab to Caboose*, 1964

Even in its waning hours, the caboose remains for tens of thousands of railroaders, train-watchers, and the ghosts of their predecessors the premier icon of railroading's rugged grip on the psyche. Long after the last caboose has left active duty on American's for-profit railroads, the much-loved, much-maligned caboose—*crummy, doghouse, buggy, chariot, throne room, parlor, brainbox, palace, perambulator, glory wagon*—will survive on tourist carriers, in museums, and as elements of banks, motels, summer cabins, fast-food emporiums, and innumerable other enterprises.

Generations as yet unborn will be drawn to the sinuous lines and seductive invitation of the caboose's curving grab irons, as eager to climb aboard and learn its stories of adventure, distance, destiny, and danger as were their fathers and grandfathers. Let the managers of America's railroad museums resolve to professionally exhibit their cabooses and to authentically equip them with the way-bills, torpedoes, employee timetables and grips, chimney lamps, chewing tobacco, and other essential accoutrements of their active days. And let the operators of our excursion railroads forever offer those who seek it the opportunity to rise to the cupola cushions, to savor a reverie of clickety-clack broken only occasionally by the clatter of a trailing-point switch, to squint through the forward window in search of the mystical high green once known to every caboose lover along every track.

It was a perfect night for a train … When the whistle blew and the call stretched thin across the night, one had to believe that any journey could be sweet to the soul.

—Charles Turner, *The Celebrant*, 1982

A hazy ochre harvest moon rose over the Indiana prairie that crisp November midnight, effusing a mottled orange glow on the twin ribbons of the Nickel Plate. The chill breeze carried a bracing blend of autumn's aromas as it rustled the telegraph lines, trampled cornstalks, and the few remaining leaves of the red oaks bordering an intersection of the railroad and a curving country lane.

To the south, at the foot of a brief but pronounced grade, twin blades of a depot

The conductor and flagman aboard a Seaboard Air Line caboose work on their paperwork as their train rolls through the night sometime in the early 1950s. TRAINS *magazine collection*

train-order board reached silently for the night sky as the surrounding village retired. One by one, distant lights in bungalows, farmhouses, and outbuildings blinked off as the moon ascended through splotchy cirrostratus clouds. Only the occasional sound of a pickup truck, grinding through its gears at the highway crossing in the village, punctuated the night wind.

On the horizon, the staccato sweep of a Mars light forecast the town's daily drama, the evening flight of time freight 82. Swaying beams of light exploded around the superelevated curve a half-mile south of the village, suddenly spraying the depot and grain elevator across the track with bursts of intense yellow-gold, silhouetting the train-order board and putting pickup trucks and

trackside observers on notice that the day's premier performance, however brief, was fast approaching center stage.

The banshee wail of Nickel Plate's high-pitched horns seemed to knock the frost off the ties and ballast as flashers began their cadence at the highway crossing. Only moments elapsed before the Geeps repeated their urgent cry and crested the grade at the country road, their blurred, black-and-yellow passage seeming to suggest nothing less than the urgent dispatch of propeller-driven military aircraft. Behind the fleet-footed power, a quartet of mechanical reefers growled past, followed rapidly by squadrons of squeaking boxcars, trundling hoppers burdened with loads of stoker coal, empty flat cars with looseload strapping flapping in the wind, the *roomba-*

roomba-roomba-roomba of a gondola with a flat wheel. With a split-second highball from a brakeman's lantern in the cupola, NKP 1111, the venerated *Four Aces* revered by generations of Indianapolis Division crews, rushed by to be quickly swallowed in the hazy mists of that memorable night.

Tangy scents of coal smoke from the 1111's stove and kerosene from its cupola-mounted markers drifted back in the wake of 82's thunderous passage, leaving a soul-satisfying aura with those who shivered on the timbers of the crossing and watched until the twin dots of red blinked out beyond the crest of the next grade.

LAST CHANCE

August 1993

John R. Crosby

Early in 1948, Pennsylvania Railroad President Martin W. Clement announced that "by May of this year we expect all our important east-west passenger trains will be diesel-powered west of Harrisburg."

True to his word, soon hordes of pin-striped diesels began to arrive from La Grange, Eddystone, Erie, and any other place that could slap together a diesel-electric locomotive. It seems that the Pennsy, in its rush to dieselize, bought them all.

With the arrival of the new power, it was not long before the Pennsy's T1 steam locomotives, then only three or so years old, were relegated to pulling secondary trains. I was firing such a run between Fort Wayne, Ind., and Crestline, Ohio, and return. Even our unglamorous trains, many bereft of names, now regularly sported diesels on the head end.

The best evidence of this was the way that passenger engine crews dressed for work. Most of us had discarded our overalls, work shirts, and bandannas in favor of slacks and sport shirts. Some of the old-timers persisted in wearing their Oshkosh or Carhart overalls, but they were looked down upon as hopeless fossils by we of the younger crowd.

While I had joined the slacks and shirt crowd, in the bottom of my grip I still carried a pair of goggles and gauntlet gloves.

On the day in question, my engineer and I were awaiting the arrival of No. 43. The train was due into Crestline at 2:23 p.m., and was a typical secondary train of that era. The normal consist was about 14 cars of storage mail, Railway Express, and Railway Post Office cars, a combination car (coach-baggage, or *combine*), and two coaches. The train originated in Pittsburgh and wound up in Chicago, making stops every 23 miles or so. On this run, the only significant revenue was produced on the head end, not in the coaches.

About 1:43 p.m. we received word that No. 43 was running some 45 minutes late, and was steam powered. We were being assigned a T1, and would we kindly get ourselves on the 5536. Reluctantly we walked out of the roundhouse and searched for our engine. Way over on a back ready track we finally found it.

What a pitiful sight! The engine and tender were coated with thick layers of grime and soot. At any place where steam was discharged, either by design or by accident, streaks of gray dripped downward. Some wag had cleaned off the numbers on the side of the cab. This had been done in such a fashion that each number looked as though it was in an oval frame. To verify ownership, the flanks of the tender proudly displayed the letters PENNSY. The LVANIA was totally covered by dirt. The rubber diaphragm between the cab and tender was in shreds or missing. On the engine, various inspection covers were missing, giving it a curiously hollow appearance. The casing around the stacks was gone and they showed up quite clearly.

I had anticipated that the cab would not he very clean so I had scrounged up a large ball of cotton waste. Climbing up into the cab verified my suspicions that it was a filthy mess. About the only clean spot was the engineer's seatbox, where the hostler had sat while coaling up the engine. Harry, my engineer, using the privileges of seniority, remained on the ground and hollered up to me to get him a long oil can. I handed him one and began to get busy with my cleaning. It was quite evident that this engine had been sitting around for some time with the cab windows open to the elements and whatever dirt happened to be in the area.

I turned on the injector, then the squirt hose, and tried to wash down all of the dirt that I could dislodge with water. The balance of the crud I attacked with the waste. While I did achieve some degree of success, there was still a lot of dirt in the cab as Harry climbed up the ladder. He was very careful not to touch any place that I happened to miss in my cleaning operation. He spent a few minutes carefully wiping off his seat, and the various valves and levers that he would he operating.

Satisfied with his efforts, he sat down and began testing the air brakes, whistle, hell, water pump, etc. While he was busy with his chores, I got the fire ready. Surprisingly, considering how long the engine had been sitting around, the fire was in fairly good shape. It did not require much to get it to my liking.

We were now ready to back down to the station. Harry turned on the bell, gave three short blasts on the whistle, opened the cylinder cocks, and then cracked open the throttle. We started to back up,

Pennsy T1 No. 5526 roars through Van Wert, Ohio, with the eastbound *Manhattan Limited* in 1947. The 4-4-4-4s would soon be retired in favor of diesels. *Richard E. Dill*

blowing out large amounts of water through the open cylinder cocks. At Riley Street I saw that the dwarf signal governing our movement off the ready track to the running track was displaying *restricting*, allowing us to continue our reverse move. We continued to back eastward until stopped by the signal guarding access to the main line. We sat here for some time until we heard the unmistakable sound of a Pennsylvania chime whistle. No. 43 was finally in town.

A few minutes later, a pair of bedraggled K4s slipped by on their way to the roundhouse. As soon as they cleared the interlocking, I could see the switch points flop over for our movement; this was followed by the signal changing from *stop* to *restricting*. I called the aspect to Harry, and we backed down to the train, rumbling across the tracks of the Big Four's Cleveland to Columbus main line. As we coupled onto the train, I noted that our conductor was standing on the platform with a clearance card stating that No. 43 had no train orders. He also let us know that today we had a total of 15 cars. It was quite obvious that his major concern was that of maintaining as much distance as possible between himself and this dirty hulk of a locomotive.

The car inspectors coupled the air and signal hoses, and then the steam heat connectors. Harry ran the air test while I fed coal to the fire. At 3:40 p.m., 1 hour and 15 minutes late, the communicating whistle peeped twice, and we were finally on our way. Harry turned on the bell, opened the sanders, and pulled out gently on the throttle. With a T1, you did not yank open the throttle unless you wanted the engine to slip, sand or no sand. We slowly began to move, again rumbling over the Big Four diamonds. At about 20 mph, Harry made a running brake test. He released the brakes and opened the throttle a bit more. We had a 40 mph speed restriction around an S curve through the yard. Once clear of it, Harry got down to business, and the 5536 began to accelerate just as its designers had intended.

In spite of its cruddy appearance, this engine was still in good mechanical condition. As the speed increased, so did the flow of cinders, grime, sand dust, and other debris into and out of the cab. Evidently there were some nooks that I had overlooked in my cleaning efforts. It was indeed fortunate that I still had my goggles available. While our eyes were protected from the flying dirt, I cannot say the same for our slacks and sport shirts.

Bucyrus was our first stop, only 12 miles west of Crestline. We drove into the station in a cloud of sand, dust, and blue brakeshoe smoke. After a few minutes, during which mail, express, and a few passengers had either been loaded or unloaded, we started another dash to Upper Sandusky, all of 18 miles farther west. This was followed by stops at Ada and Lima. During the Lima stop, we filled the tender to its 19,000-gallon capacity.

The farther west we went, the better the big T1 performed. Our speed passed 90 several times. Now, before anyone reading this gets excited about the speeds mentioned, and cites the fact that the legal speed limit for passenger trains on the Fort Wayne Division was 79 mph, let me quote the road foreman at the time, one James A. (Pappy) Warren: "If you can't make up time without worrying about the speed limit, I'll get someone who can."

      I   I

Our last scheduled stop was in Van Wert, Ohio. Again, Harry drove into the station, making a precise spot so that the various mail and express carts did not have to move far to find an open door. He called me over to his side of the cab and said, "Johnny, this may be our last chance at one of these beasts. What do you say about us seeing just what she'll do between here and Fort Wayne?" As he spoke, I noted that his face was completely covered with dirt, except for the two white circles behind his glasses.

My deferential reply was, "You're the boss. My side of the cab is still attached to yours."

He nodded in reply to my answer, and issued a warning. "You'd better get ready, 'cause we're going to move out of here."

With this bit of information, I began to work on my fire. I grabbed the No. 5 scoop shovel and filled in the back corners of the firebox. I shut off the stoker jets and ran a big wad of coal into the firebox, right in front of the firebox doors. When finished, I felt satisfied that I was ready for what was to come.

With the first peep of the communicating whistle, Harry turned on the bell and sanders. A second later came the second peep. He cautiously opened the throttle. The first six or so exhausts were relatively gentle *chuffs* as we began to move. One of the exhausts blew a perfect smoke ring. When Harry was satisfied that we had a good supply of sand under the drivers, he pulled open the throttle a little further. Until then, the sounds of the exhaust had been drowned out by the sound of the whistle, but no more. The exhaust began to snap and crack out of the twin stacks. The presence of nearby warehouses and lumber yards created a pronounced echo effect so that each exhaust was multiplied as it bounced back and forth from building to building. This was the ultimate in stereo. With the heavy throttle, the engine began to rock slightly from side to side.

We rounded the curve at Estry Tower, and now between us and Fort Wayne lay 31 miles of perfectly straight track. As soon as we cleared the Cincinnati Northern diamond, Harry pulled the throttle wide open. The engine began to quiver, and it was easy to note the acceleration. With a good supply of sand, there was not a hint of a slip, although I did note that Harry kept his hand on the throttle in anticipation of such an event. As the speed built up, he began to move the reverse lever from the corner up toward center, in effect shifting from low to high gear.

The busy U.S. 30 crossing slipped by with the speedometer showing 78 mph. Soon the needle showed 86. In spite of the large demand for steam, I had no problem in maintaining 300 pounds steam pressure. This was not necessarily due to my prowess as a fireman, but rather to the fact that the engine was a free steamer. I cracked open the firedoors to check the fire. I was satisfied to note that its color was a bright yellow-white. The coal that I had put into the back corners and in front of the firedoor was long gone.

Dixon is the location of a cast-iron post indicating Ohio on one side and Indiana on the other. We did not have much time for reading as we were now running along at 96 mph. Harry had now moved the reverse lever to within just a few points of being vertical. He was kept busy blowing for road crossings. At our speed, there was not too much time from the passing of a whistle post until the crossing showed up.

We bounced straight through the Monroeville crossovers at 108, with the needle still unwinding. West of town we hit 110. The T still had some reserve left. The only problem we had was with dirt and soot. This was compounded by coal dust from the tender.

At Maples the speedometer needle quit moving. We were now covering a mile in 30 seconds—120 mph!

We blazed by Adams Tower with the engine and tender each trying to go their separate ways as they passed over crossovers and siding switches. The operator beat a hasty retreat as the breeze we created tried to blow him over. Clearing the interlocking, Harry applied the brakes and pulled our speed down to a more respectable 80. We slipped into town, stopping at the coal dock for a load of coal. With the tender full, we made our final dash of a mile to the Fort Wayne station.

Arriving there, we got off and headed downstairs to the crew room. The passenger crew dispatcher, Chet Glant, met Harry as he turned in our timeslip. "Harry, the dispatcher wants to talk to you upstairs." So without cleaning up, we both went up to the dispatcher's office.

      I   I

The DS eyeballed us, shaking his head in wonder. Somewhat sarcastically he asked, "Which one of you two clowns has a pilot's license?" He paused for dramatic effect and continued, "You guys were certainly flying low today. According to your times by Estry and Adams, it took you all of 17 minutes to cover 27 miles. Now my math is nothing to brag about, but that averages out to something like 95 mph, and that from a station stop."

Neither of us offered any comment. He looked at us for a few moments and closed with the admonition, "Don't do this again." As we walked out he grinned and added, "Good job, guys."

That did turn out to be my last trip on a T1. With the proliferation of diesels on passenger trains, there was little call for maintaining much of an extra passenger board. About the only business was that of pulling dead, or nearly dead, Baldwin diesels. So when the engineers' board was cut, I wound up back on freight with Q2s, J1s, and F3s. But that is another story.

March 1995

John B. Corns

THE WALK OF A QUEEN

Kevin P. Keefe

The dream, though old, is never old. ...
Did you see an old woman going down the path?
I did not, but I saw a young girl, and she had the walk of a queen.

—William Butler Yeats, from *Cathleen Ni Hoolihan*, 1902

Years from now, business historians doing research about the railroad boom of the 1990s will discover that Norfolk Southern Corporation more than held up its end of the deal. If they look closely at a given year, say 1993, they'll see that NS earned $772 million in net income, or $5.54 per share, and established an industry-leading operating ratio of 75.6 percent. They'll also discover

that, just one year later, NS broke thousands of hearts.

NS Chairman David Goode's decision in October 1994 to scuttle one of America's most ingenious and beloved corporate public-relations campaigns—otherwise known as the NS steam program—meant that December 3 would go down in the history books. What was to have been just another in a decades-old series of excursions out of Birmingham, Ala., literally became the fan trip to end all fan trips. Anyone who cared about NS steam or its two star performers—Norfolk & Western 4-8-4 No. 611 and 2-6-6-4 No. 1218—had to be there for the last public excursion behind steam. As the word spread in early November, the phone began to ring off the hook at the home of Carol Clark, tripmaster for the sponsoring Heart of Dixie Chapter, National Railway Historical Society.

For photographer John Corns and me, the implications of December 3 were personal as well as professional. Trains would have to cover the event, of course; this magazine has followed the steam program faithfully for 30 years.

But we would have gone anyway. Like a lot of other folks who barely missed the end of the steam age, the trips run by Southern Railway and successor NS were as close we ever could get to the real thing. There was a tangible difference between NS and virtually all other steam operators. On NS, it was a *railroad* running the train, a big railroad, with big engines and a big schedule. Over the years, steam ran on the system with such streetcar-like dependability that it was easy to forget it was a tiny part of NS, something not on a par with unit coal trains and RoadRailers. John and I love steam, so we often headed south to sample the pleasures of 4501, 610, 611, 1218, and most of the program's other engines. Besides, John grew up in Ironton, Ohio. As a child, he had seen N&W's marvelous machines, and they were in his blood.

That's why it felt so familiar, so right, to be on the platform of Washington Union Station on the evening of Thursday, December 1. We were headed for Alabama on Amtrak train 19, the *Crescent*.

The *Crescent* is a rattletrap these days, but we still enjoyed the ride, made all the more memorable by our surprise dinner companion, James A. Bistline, the retired manager of steam operations for NS. Much to the chagrin of the dining-car crew, we occupied our table for the better part of two hours, exchanging

stories about 4501 and Graham and Bob Claytor. At various moments, I tried every reporter's tactic I'd ever learned to see if I could draw Jim out a bit. You see, we'd heard rumors that Bistline was upset about Goode's decision, and he's still a major NS stockholder, and there is this campaign to change Goode's mind, and…

Nothing doing. Not by accident did Jim Bistline graduate *summa cum laude* from Duke, or earn a law degree at Columbia, or work his way up to the posts of general counsel and assistant to the chairman at Southern. He's smart, savvy, diplomatic, a good soldier … all the things that make for a gentleman in the best sense of the word. Jim Bistline wasn't going to let a nosy editor get him to say something he might regret.

Bistline did say that he was surprised by the swiftness with which the curtain fell, but he also spoke convincingly of some of NS's justifications—the lack of management people in the field, the interference with crowded main lines, the threat of liability. "It was a tough decision for Goode," said Jim Bistline. Fair enough, we said, and we retreated to the sleepers.

* * *

The gorgeous weather in Birmingham seemed to be mocking our mission when we arrived the following morning. At the Avis counter downtown, the headline in the morning *Birmingham Post-Herald* was a rude awakening: "Iron Horse is Put to Pasture," it said alongside a color photo of the 611. The story brought a reflexive, revealing outburst from Bistline. "Gosh darn, that's so sad," he said with emotion. I thought of his diplomatic comments the night before in the diner and couldn't help feeling that here was the real answer to our questions.

Our next stop: Irondale, on the east edge of Birmingham, site of NS's huge Norris Yard and site of the company's steam shop. At first, the atmosphere was tense as an obviously stressed steam crew tried to go about their work servicing the 611 amid a small crowd of railfans. Photo opportunities were limited, but John did manage to finagle some time on the sunny side of the engine for a portrait.

The J gleamed after a fresh application of clear-coat.

After a while, the tension dissipated as other NS insiders drifted out of the shop building. Carl Jensen, NS steam manager until a month before, looked relaxed and fit for someone who must have been experiencing some mixed emotions. Also on hand was his successor, Doug Karhan, and Preston Claytor, son of the late Robert Claytor, NS chairman and the patron saint of 611 and 1218. Other members of the engine crew gathered, and everyone was delighted to see Bistline and, later, Bill Purdie, retired master mechanic-steam. There were handshakes all around, laughter, and frequent glances back at the engine. It was like one of those funeral visitations where the warmth of renewed friendships momentarily eclipses the sadness at hand.

* * *

Saturday arrived amid gathering clouds. A huge crowd was on hand at the site of Southern's old Terminal Station, now a no-man's land of freeway ramps and empty lots. The railroad and Heart of Dixie promised a prompt 8:30 a.m. departure, but passengers lingered longer than usual around 611. The scene was chaos. Parents and children climbed on the front of the engine. Heart of Dixie volunteers straightened out last-minute ticket snafus. Fans poked around in the futile quest for a clean shot of the engine. One guy even scalped tickets. Was this 611's swan song, or an NBA game?

In the eye of the storm was Heart of Dixie's Carol Clark, one woman who was definitely going to have a hard time getting through this day with dry eyes. She'd already spent some time answering reporters' questions, and she was learning that it isn't easy. "I'm trying to express my disappointment without any bitterness," she said with a weary smile.

It will never be much solace to them, but Heart of Dixie members will always be able to claim that their last trip was a smash hit. Buoyed by its status as the last steam run (NS ran one more public trip,

Like a pilotfish shadowing a great whale, TVRM 2-8-0 No. 610 poses with 611 in the rain at Chattanooga. *John B. Corns*

with diesels, a December 10-11 Asheville, N.C.-Chattanooga excursion), it sold out quickly. Clark said the chapter could have sold several hundred more tickets for a Sunday trip, but NS gave the group a firm *no*. As it was, 1,000 people bought tickets for 611's last performance, and nearly every seat on the 24-car train was filled. The train included most of the standard NS excursion cars that were not damaged in the September 28 collision at Lynchburg, Va., and two private cars: *New River Valley*, owned by veteran NS car-maintenance contractor Sid Bailey, and *Kitchi Gammi Club*, a heavyweight Pullman restored by Chuck Jensen (Carl and Carol's son) and his partner, Chuck Akers.

The trip got off on a sardonic note when our car host welcomed his passengers. "How many are on your first trip with us?" There was a big show of hands. "Unfortunately, it's your last," he said. Up front, 611's whistle pealed off a mournful "amen" as she got a wheel into the train and we headed for Tennessee.

𝕀   𝕀

The trip to Chattanooga confirmed what veteran NS steam-train riders have known for several years: If you want to see the engine, don't ride the train. The 611 was all business, moving the train northeastward at the politically correct 40 mph. The ride along the old Alabama Great Southern through the long valley which flanks the Beaver Creek Mountains is pretty much a straight shot, with few curves to provide a glimpse of the engine. There were no photo runbys—customer service wasn't a high priority with NS, at least not on this day.

But the outbound trip was not without its pleasures. John spent most of the time up front in the first car, close to the engine. I wandered the train, sampling for the last time the bustling life aboard an NS steam excursion. The vendors in the two commissary cars, Heart of Dixie's 4527 and North Florida Chapter's 676, were doing a brisk business in 611 souvenirs. At one point I ran into Bill Crawford of Boston and Jim Fetchero of Charlotte N.C., fellow members of that curious fraternity known as "mileage collectors." Together we lamented some of the big ones that were undoubtedly going to get away with the demise of NS trips. My own heartbreaker: Bluefield to Iaeger, the heart of the N&W Pocahontas main line.

There was also time to stare out the window and watch the mountains go by. Over the years, this route between

Birmingham and Chattanooga has been a great locomotive proving ground. In steam days, this was home for Southern's 4-6-2s and 2-10-2s. With gentle grades and a workable distance, it's been the perfect place to take restored engines out of Irondale for shakedown cruises. In recent years it's hosted some pretty big newcomers, everything from Texas & Pacific 2-10-4 No. 610 to Chesapeake & Ohio 2-8-4 No. 2716 to CP Royal Hudson No. 2839 to N&W 611 and 1218. As we rolled through Attalla, Keener, and Fort Payne, I wondered how many of the locals were aware of what they have been so privileged to see for the last 30 years.

Not long before our arrival in Chattanooga, some old friends in *New River Valley* gathered 'round Carl Jensen for an impromptu ceremony in which several NRHS directors presented him with a plaque and a handsome gold Hamilton railroad watch. It was a personal moment that an outsider could only begin to appreciate. There is a special bond between the NS steam team and the various sponsor organizations around the system, a bond that has been tested many times in difficult circumstances. Now, all the good times and hard times came together, fused into a bittersweet moment a of affection and gratitude. Executives in Norfolk may not appreciate it now, or ever, but the kind of goodwill displayed that afternoon was a demonstration of great public relations, pure and simple.

⚊ ⚊

Whatever lighthearted air there was aboard the train vanished when 611—and the rain—arrived in Chattanooga. Our train backed into the tourist destination known as the Chattanooga Choo-Choo, a.k.a. Chattanooga Union Station, and most passengers trundled off for lunch and shopping.

Some of us, though, turned toward the head end. For most, this would be the last chance to ponder a hot 611 up close. The great 4-8-4 stood regally in the rain as a swarm of photographers jockeyed for position. As if to provide a perfect contrast, Tennessee Valley Railroad Museum's ex-Army 2-8-0 No. 610 pulled up alongside before taking some passengers on an optional excursion. The 610 is a handsome little machine, but it was dwarfed by 611's immense boiler, its 70-inch drivers, and its swank roller-bearing rods.

Suddenly someone spotted Jim Bistline, who, camera in hand, was trying to blend in with everyone else. Like all railfans, Jim couldn't resist the impulse to take a few more photos. But Bistline soon rediscovered the price of celebrity. A throng of photographers formed an arc around him, and, with 611 in the background, Jim graciously posed for several minutes of pictures.

Carl Jensen stood nearby, and he wasn't going to escape the paparazzi, either. Before long, both men were coaxed to walk up to the front of the engine for one last pose. Jensen suddenly bounded up the steps to the running board and grabbed the two ceremonial white flags on both sides of 611's smokestack. He scrambled back down the steps, handed one of the flags to Bistline, and together the pair waved a salute to the crowd.

⚊ ⚊

The trip back to Chattanooga came in darkness, and just as well. The mood throughout the train was somber, reflective, even among the several hundred passengers for whom this was a less-than-personal disaster. Call them civilians, or "daisypickers," but these are the folks who put the *public* in public relations. As I strolled through aisles, I thought of the tens of thousands of everyday people who, thanks to the steam trips, have come to know something about Norfolk Southern. The company itself acknowledges that something on the order of a million people have ridden since 1966.

At the rear of the train, Jensen, his family, crew members, and their NRHS friends settled in for a melancholy evening. A man and a woman serenaded the group with acoustic guitars and old railroad songs, but that only served to deepen the gloom. There were plenty of tears on board. Behind us, the rain glinted in the glow of *Kitchi Gammi Club*'s inspection lights.

As the hour grew late, I felt more and more like an intruder, so I headed forward and found a deserted vestibule. There, with the rain flying in through the open Dutch door, I watched and listened as 611 rode out its last miles.

It was a revelation. Town after town loomed out of the swirling darkness. Hundreds of bystanders stood witness along the right-of-way, waving forlornly in the steady rain. It was obvious that many of them had been out for quite some time. Down, down we rode, through Springville, Argo, and Trussville, 611's sonorous whistle oblivious to its fate.

There was a great commotion when we came to a stop in Birmingham. Weary passengers filed off the train. Then, as if on cue, the skies opened up, sending passengers scurrying for their cars.

John and I made our getaway too, but we couldn't resist one long, last look at the engine. Gluttons for punishment, we drove back out to Irondale a couple of hours later. We camped out on a park bench under the sidewalk canopy in front of the darkened Irondale Cafe, the folksy eatery which inspired the movie *Fried Green Tomatoes*. Finally, at around 1:30 in the morning, we heard a brief blast of 611's whistle. The great engine appeared at the throat of Norris Yard and slowly, almost silently, drifted past. The rain had stopped, but the cool night air was heavy with moisture. Immense clouds of steam hovered over the engine as she tiptoed through the switchpoints in a scene of machinery and magic. It could have been an O. Winston Link photograph.

⚊ ⚊

Epilogue: Just like Norfolk Southern said it would, 611 hustled back to Roanoke the next week with nary a note of celebration. I'm glad I missed it. I have it second- and thirdhand that the journey home was conducted with little more than grim determination, and that NS was none too solicitous of the folks who came out to say good-bye to the engine. As an admirer of David Goode's company, I'm disappointed to hear this, but perhaps it's to be expected. Norfolk Southern says it has its customers in mind, and I must believe them. But in my mind, all the art museum and symphony donations and TV commercials in the world will never match 611's masterful ability to call people to the railroad.

John C. Lucas

Twenty-Four Hours at Supai Summit

Fred W. Frailey

To discover what makes BNSF's Santa Fe Railway tick, you can go to the system operations center in Schaumburg, Ill., hover over the shoulders of train dispatchers, and eavesdrop on conversations of corridor managers.

Then you can follow up with a visit to the system's executives in Fort Worth, Texas, for a bit of the Big Picture. You'd indeed learn what makes the Santa Fe tick.

Or, you can go to Supai summit.

Strictly speaking, Supai summit doesn't exist. Out here in northern Arizona, some 10 miles west of where you now stand, there was once a siding called Supai [SOO-pie]. From Supai it was all

downhill on a 2 percent grade to sleepy little Ash Fork in the valley. The grade was Santa Fe's biggest challenge in Arizona. Then in 1960 the railroad built the Crookton Cutoff—starting at Williams Junction, 4 miles west of where you are—which consigned both Supai and Ash Fork to the secondary line going to Phoenix. Today when railroaders refer to the crest in the brief grade of the transcontinental main line at milepost 371 (from Albuquerque), they call it Supai summit. That's where you are now, at 12:01 a.m. on Thursday, May 23, 1996. And that's where you'll stay for the next 24 hours, waiting.

There's not a railroader alive who doesn't know how to wait—it goes with the job. You who just like to watch trains go by know all about waiting too. But while waiting today, let's do more than watch trains. Figuratively speaking, let's poke around and see what these trains really carry. Let's discover where they came from and when, where they're going and why, and when they'll get there. Consider this account of 24 hours at Supai summit as a sort of status report on transcontinental railroading on the eve of the millennium, based upon what goes by when you simply sit and wait.

I I

Listen: you hear it laboring up the eastbound grade from Williams Junction, whistling for Bootlegger Crossing 2 miles to the west, then easing off just as it crests a hilltop and comes into view around a 1 degree curve on the southernmost of the two main tracks. Now the spectacle bears down, ditch lights making the onrushing train seem like some nighttime avenger from hell. In a moment it is upon you: three wide-nose General Electric locomotives in Santa Fe's historic red, silver, and yellow colors, pulling a mile-long platform atop which ride 93 truck trailers and 10 containers. In a relative instant it is gone, its rear-end device emitting a red blink until the last car rounds a curve a quarter mile to the east. Quiet returns, for awhile.

The third train, P-FRCH1-21, and the sixth, 9-991-22, will look very much like that first train, 1-981-21. All began in Northern California within a seven-hour span. All are totally intermodal. All are headed for Chicago. But they couldn't be more different. Each does a different job.

Train 1-981-21 (guaranteed intermodal, Richmond-Chicago, originating May 21), is dedicated to less-than-truck-load (LTL) motor carriers: Roadway

Express, Yellow Freight, Consolidated Freightways, Arkansas Best, and Overnite, to name a few. This train left Richmond, across the bay from San Francisco, precisely on time the night before at 9 p.m., with 14 carloads of trailers. At Fresno, 190 miles later, it added 42 more cars, primarily food products. The entire train will arrive at the new Willow Springs terminal, 17 miles southwest of Chicago's Loop, 85 minutes late tomorrow afternoon. (How do we count cars on an intermodal train with tables of varying length? Santa Fe counts permanently coupled, multi-platform intermodal cars as more than one car, based on an 89-foot standard; thus, a three-well double-stack unit would be two cars, and a five-well unit would be three cars.)

Outwardly identical to the 981 is P-FRCH-21 (priority intermodal, Fresno-Chicago), which goes east past you at 12:37 a.m. The big difference is the noise of refrigeration units as this train glides by. The base load of P-FRCH is food from California's Central Valley. Tonight it carries 40 cold trailers of celery, broccoli, peaches, potatoes, oranges, lettuce, and grapes, plus unrefrigerated trailers and containers of wine, dairy products, and bakery products; sugar, dry milk, and mixed foods. P-FRCH will follow the 981 by several hours' time all the way to Chicago.

Any Santa Fe employee would know that the third train, 9-991-22 (guaranteed intermodal, Richmond-Chicago), is special, because of the 9 prefix. This means United Parcel Service. Sixty-four of 9-991's 75 trailers hold UPS goods, picked up at the UPS terminal at North Bay, 5 miles south of Richmond. As for 9-991, it is *hot hot hot*—due at the Chicago UPS facility next to the Willow Springs yard 56 hours, 15 minutes after leaving North Bay, at an average pace of 45 mph. Some perspective: The best schedule Union Pacific can offer on trailer traffic between Northern California and Chicago, on a route 225 miles shorter than Santa Fe's, is 13 hours slower (Stockton-Canal Street Chicago train STCST). This edition of 9-991 got out of North Bay 3 minutes ahead of time yesterday morning, passes you at 1:47 a.m., 43 minutes to the good, and after overtaking both P-FRCH1-22 (on double track near Grants, N.M.) and

1-981-21 (on double track near Coal City, Ill.) will reach Willow Springs tomorrow afternoon precisely 1 minute late. The train flits across the railroad like a gazelle.

So no, none of the trains you will see today comes off a cookie cutter. Proving the point, the second train of May 23 is an interloper—eastbound Southern Pacific double-stack train F-LBBP2-21 (foreign line, Long Beach-Bedford Park Chicago). For the next two months, SP will be detouring two intermodal trains each way a day over Santa Fe between Colton, Calif., just south of San Bernardino, and Vaughn, N.M., between Belen and Clovis, because of the double-tracking project work on SP's Sunset Route.

One other train of note passes you before a lull in the wee hours. It's 9-198-21, the premier Chicago-Los Angeles run—and yes, another United Parcel Service hotshot. It goes by at 1:32 a.m., more than an hour in front of its schedule, and 60 of its 91 boxes (trailers and containers) belong to UPS.

How 9-198-21 got to you is a story in itself. Every morning at Willow Springs, terminal manager Don Foltz and his trainmasters pore over the list of eastbound trains that will arrive for unloading during the next 24 hours—typically there will be nine—and decide which set of equipment will be sent back west for each westbound train. Explains Foltz: "We have four tracks broken down into eight strips, with center crossovers. The whole place is built for speed. We dump trailers on one side and load from the other. And we don't have a lot of time to massage the equipment. The push is on to get the trains, every one of them, out on time. I play with a lot of pressure."

The 198 train, due out of Willow Springs each day at 4:45 p.m., contains two blocks, or parts. Most of its cars are on the first block, for Hobart Yard in Los Angeles. Behind that rides the Barstow block, which on some afternoons contains many 28-foot Roadway Express trailers. For optimal loading, these "pup" trailers require an 89-foot RTTX car, which has three stanchions, or fifth wheels, rather than the customary two. So Foltz and his people will favor for the 198 an inbound train that has RTTX cars on its east end.

On Tuesday morning, May 21, train 1-891-19 arrived from Los Angeles ahead of schedule, at 7:15 a.m., and was used to build that afternoon's 9-198-21. Santa Fe accepts trailers for 9-198 until 40 minutes before its 4:45 p.m. departure—an extremely tight cutoff, or deadline—so how could Foltz know how many flatcars would be needed? "Based on past experience," he replies. "For instance, we know that each day of the week has a pattern of its own, each month has a distinct pattern, and that business increases toward the end of each month."

As it turned out, only seven pups showed up for the Barstow block, to be spread across four RTTX flats. Light engines came from Corwith Yard and had the 5,538-foot-long train out of Willow Springs at 4:59, 14 minutes late. By the time, almost 35 hours later, that 9-198-21 rounds the curve just east of you and hustles by, it has recovered that lost time and another hour to boot. It will get to LA 2 hours early, having whizzed 2,190 miles from Willow Springs in 47 hours.

With Bill Williams Mountain as a backdrop, the *Southwest Chief* blasts through the sag at milepost 372. *John C. Lucas*

This is nothing short of phenomenal. The fastest freight train of all time, Santa Fe's *Super C*, was scheduled the 2,201 miles between Corwith and Hobart in 40 hours flat between 1968 and 1976. What *Super C* had that 9-198-21 does not was a top speed of 79 mph (versus 70 today for Santa Fe intermodal trains), a short train (typically 15 cars, versus 9-198's 60), and herds of horses (usually 10 hp per ton, versus 3.6 hp/t on 9-198 this morning).

Now, 20 years after the demise of *Super C*, Santa Fe is reexamining that train's premise of super-fast service for a premium price. Will a true successor to *Super C* reappear? Replies Don McInnes, senior vice president and chief operations officer of both Santa Fe and parent Burlington Northern Santa Fe Corp.: "We're continually being pushed by some customers to improve performance while lowering costs. I'm not sure what will happen, except that eventually speeds will be increased." (Despite the merger of their parent companies in September 1995, BN and Santa Fe still operate independently as separate railroads, pending negotiation of new labor union agreements.)

The possible catalyst for 79 mph freights: United Parcel Service. UPS wants a three-day Los Angeles-New York City train. This would allow it, for example, to pick up packages in LA on Monday afternoon and deliver them in Manhattan on Friday morning. Right now it comes close. Q-LANY (guaranteed, Los Angeles-New York) has a cutoff for receipt of trailers of 4:30 p.m. at San Bernardino, near the UPS Ontario (Calif.) sorting facility. Departure is 6:55. A train departing Monday is due into Conrail's Englewood intermodal yard in Chicago 51 hours later, at midnight Wednesday. This train leaves Englewood as Conrail's TV-10 at 1:30 a.m. Thursday, arriving at North Bergen, N.J., across the Hudson River from Manhattan, at 8 a.m. Friday. This is about as fast as these two railroads can move today, but still 8 to 10 hours too slow for UPS to achieve its goal.

Each Wednesday, S-CHLA (double-stack, Chicago-Los Angeles) leaves Corwith with 19 five-well stack cars outfitted with experimental electronically controlled brakes that can be set and released instantaneously, rather than sequentially, car by car, as is now the norm. "Speed is what we need," says Rollin Bredenberg, BNSF's vice president-transportation, and electric brakes are crucial for 79 mph running. There isn't a whole lot more time to squeeze out of the Santa Fe. But we think we can get LA-Chicago down to 44 hours." Reminded of *Super C*'s 40-hour schedule, Bredenberg replies, "Oh, I know. But I'm talking about something you can nail down every trip." Presumably, Conrail would also have to cut running time.

This morning's version of Q-LANY passes you as morning begins, at 5:50 a.m., 1 hour, 55 minutes ahead of schedule. Roughly one-third of today's train will be delivered directly to Conrail before midnight tomorrow—the blocks for North Bergen (leaving on TV-10) and Harrisburg (leaving on MAIL-8M). The rest of this train will be set out and dumped (intermodalese for unloaded from the flatcars) at Willow Springs.

🚂   🚂

By five o'clock, a cloudless sky begins to light up in the east. Somewhere a coyote howls. Two robins begin morning vespers from their perches in the tall Ponderosa pines that dominate this part of Kaibab National Forest. The canopy of stars turns off its lights until only Jupiter remains. And in the west, Bill Williams Mountain emerges from darkness to loom directly over the right-of-way until the railroad bends north toward the town of Williams, 5 miles from your spot. This is a time of utter and complete tranquility.

In six hours you've seen 13 trains, 10 of them intermodals. Precisely two-thirds of the 51 Santa Fe freights you will see today carry nothing but trailers and containers. These 34 intermodals today are not short (they average 115 trailers or containers each), burdened by empty moves (94 percent of the boxes are loaded), or hauling leftover business nobody else wants. Indeed, almost half of Santa Fe's transcontinental intermodal traffic is extra-fare.

It wasn't always like this. When Santa Fe inaugurated *Super C* in 1968, this was the railroad's sole intermodal train. After *Super C* succumbed, due to the loss of its core contract for carrying mail and parcel post, Santa Fe had two other transcontinental trains each way a day dedicated totally to trailers—one each to and from Los Angeles and Richmond—and some trailers rode conventional trains. Thereafter, this business continued to grow, but profitability was not great, particularly when rates began to crater after railroads were deregulated in 1980. Michael W. Blaszak, an attorney formerly in Santa Fe's Law Department, puts it quite

nicely: "The way we did if in the old days—with 40-car trains—you just don't make any money."

One of the first things Robert D. Krebs turned his attention to, upon becoming chairman of Santa Fe in 1988, was to get his intermodal traffic out of that rut. And the person he fingered to accomplish this was McInnes, then a 19-year Santa Fe veteran who had worked his way through the Operating Department. A measure of McInnes's success in this assignment is that he now oversees all train operations on the BNSF system.

What he did right—in retrospect, an act of genius—was to segment the intermodal business into different levels of service and to convince customers to pay for what they got. "The traditional way of doing things," McInnes says, "was to put everyone's trailers on the same train. But we looked around and said, 'This is crazy.' Some trailers, when they reached LA on a westbound train, got unloaded and sat for three days. We were running the hell out of trains and puffing up our costs when we didn't have to."

No prototype existed for McInnes's new intermodal service unit and his pay-for-service vision. After all, this had been the downfall of *Super C*—everyone appreciated superior schedules, but few would pay extra. "Some consultants told me we were creating something that was too complex," says McInnes. "We felt that to manage costs properly we just had to have these various service offerings. The other thing we did was to expand our terminals to enable us to haul the business we were *later* offered. We had to stay ahead of the curve. We couldn't wait for the business to come to us, let service decline, and only then spend the capital. That's what was wrong with railroads—we let service standards go up and down like a yo-yo." In the 1990s, Santa Fe has opened huge new intermodal terminals at each of its three major hubs: Chicago (Willow Springs), Southern California (San Bernardino), and north Texas (Alliance, north of Fort Worth).

With the new pricing structure came Santa Fe's alphabet soup of train symbols. For intermodal traffic, the pecking order goes from Q (guaranteed) to P (premium) to S (double-stack). For each type of

train, there's a separate price—the Q shipper paying most and the S shipper least. Within each of these three levels of service, shippers might get a price break because of high volume or even which days of the week or month they offer their trailers and containers.

Who uses the Q trains? First and foremost, United Parcel Service, which accounts for one-fourth of the Q train trailers and containers that pass you at milepost 371 today. UPS even gets its own set of symbols. For more than two decades, until the McInnes plan was fully implemented in 1993, Santa Fe identified its through freights by a three-digit code. The first digit was the area of origination for instance, 1 being Chicago, 3 Kansas City, 8 Southern California, and 9 Northern California, the third digit was the area of destination. And the middle digit described the type of service, from 0, 1, 2, 3 (general service) through 8 and 9 (intermodal). This created the anomaly of trains 198 and 199 going in the same direction—198 from Chicago to Los Angeles, 199 from Chicago to Richmond.

Its unconventional nomenclature served Santa Fe well until it had to further differentiate trains, by status. UPS traffic people, however, liked the numbering system and asked that trains carrying its business not be resymboled. Would Santa Fe refuse its best customer a simple favor? So Q trains that are primary United Parcel Service runs still have three-digit numbers, and a 9 prefix on their hottest days, which is every day for 9-199 and 9-991 and most days for the others. Average them together, and 13 trains you see today whose base loads are UPS trailers (the numbered trains plus Q-LANY, Q-NYLA, Q-ALLA9, Q-WIPX9, and Q-WSST9) will have left their starting gates an average 2 minutes ahead of time and will arrive at the other end 12 minutes ahead of the clock. Performance like this isn't just good; it's better than perfect.

The rest of the Q trains bear an alphanumeric code—Q, then the two-letter city of origin abbreviation, two-letter destination code, section and day of the month of origin. So eastbound QRIAL1-21, which passed you at

4:41 a.m., was a guaranteed-service train from Richmond to Alliance, the first section to depart May 21. (The guarantee, by the way, is not that you get your money back if your trailer is late, but that a Q train is guaranteed to have priority over every other freight train on the railroad.)

Other big users of Q trains are the U.S. Postal Service, truckload trucking companies such as J. B. Hunt Transportation, and the LTL truckers. The LTL people gather small shipments and, just like railroads, schedule their service. They simply have to get their trailers to destinations by specified times, and the reason they're willing to pay a premium price to ride a Q train is that Santa Fe runs the wheels off these trains and really does honor its service commitments. Once again taking May 23 as a microcosm: Of the 21 Q trains to pass milepost 371, 12 will reach their destinations ahead of schedule and the average train will arrive 32 minutes late. Take away three abject underachievers among these 21, and the typical Q train would finish ahead of time.

Santa Fe, however, doesn't measure service by how well trains adhere to schedule. Instead, it sets a scheduled arrival time for every freight car, container, and trailer it receives. The schedule a trailer gets hinges on two things: what time it comes in the gate and whether its owner pays for Q, P, or S delivery. The term for this is *service scheduling*, which is monitored by Santa Fe's proprietary software. "We sell a particular commitment to a customer, not a train," says Chuck Schultz, senior vice president, intermodal and automotive. "If you come with a load and expect it to be at the other end, ready to be picked up, 72 hours later, then our system will decide what train to put it on. So depending upon the time of day we get it, there may be only one train that can meet the service schedule, or there may be five or six. If we have five or six choices, we'll spread the business out and take advantage of capacity."

Upon joining Santa Fe's intermodal department in 1993, Bredenberg was "absolutely shocked" by how well this system works. "You can look at your whole railroad," he says, "and see what's on schedule and what's in jeopardy, based on

With three blondes on the point, train S-ALLB6-21 rolls west through the almost mile-long, 1 degree curve at milepost 376. *John C. Lucas*

each shipment's individual goal. With shipments that are in trouble, you can instantly see what you're going to have to do to achieve service on them and which ones you're going to have to write off because there's no way to do it. People can make an informed decision. So when you're in Los Angeles at Hobart Yard and have a bunch of trains coming in and competing for strip capacity, you'll know which train to put in there first—which train has the highest leverage."

The next 13 trains you see today, between 6:03 a.m. and 12:25 p.m., include no fewer than five of the Q trains. Two merit special mention:

9-197-21, passing you 10 minutes late at 7:19 a.m., bears witness to the vitality of Santa Fe's line between Williams Junction and Phoenix. These 209 unsignaled miles, dispatched by track warrant and containing just four sidings longer than 6,000 feet, are visited by four trains in each direction on a typical day—five if you count the Arizona & California Railroad, which has trackage rights on the lower 58 miles between Matthie and Phoenix. And the queen of them all is three-day-a-week 9-197, which covers the 1,890 miles from Willow Springs in a scheduled 26 hours, 15 minutes. Today's run, which includes 18 UPS trailers, will beat its schedule by more than two hours.

Q-WIPX9-23 follows five hours behind 9-197 on the Phoenix Subdivision, or *Peavine*. This train starts in Winslow,

the crew-change point 87 miles east of you, solely to handle UPS trailers that originate in North Texas on Q-ALLA. Sometimes it's wise not to add to congestion in Winslow by making the handoff there. So today a single GP60 locomotive (set out at Winslow by M-PXBE1-22, as we discover later) leaves there a half hour behind Q-ALLA, picks up its train—22 trailers on 12 cars—immediately after Q-ALLA deposits it on the siding at Darling, just east of Flagstaff, and scoots down the Peavine, arriving in Phoenix well ahead of time.

You get a sense of what separates a Q train from a P this morning from two westbound trains. P-CHLA1-21 goes by at 7:04 a.m.—all 7,133 feet of it. J. B. Hunt accounts for 50 of the 157 containers and trailers. Up front, three of General Electric's redheads—a C40-8W, C41-8W, and C44-9W—provide a mere 2.3 hp per ton, and P-CHLA1-21 is struggling up the hill. Now more than 7 hours late and getting later almost by the mile, it will recover time only because of a generous 6 hours of padding in its schedule between San Bernardino and Los Angeles. This trip will consume 68 hours.

Arriving in LA tomorrow just 18 minutes behind P-CHLA1-21 will be Q-WSFA1-21, out of Willow Springs with 51 late-evening trailers from an array of LTL truckers. It left Chicagoland

15 hours after the P train, but is within 2 hours of it at milepost 371. WSLA is loaded with power—so much that its trailing GP60 is left off line west of Kansas City, the other three GP60s supply 5.2 hp/t, and this train gets so far ahead that even a 2-hour delay west of you at Seligman and a 1-hour hit waiting to enter Barstow won't keep it from getting to the end 2 hours ahead of time, in 53 hours. This is what your extra money gets you on a Q.

Intermodal shippers to whom price is more important than time use the S trains—the double-stacks. There are two distinct types. The first is the original kind: those long, stately processions chartered by steamship companies and taken up entirely by one (or sometimes two) logos. S-ALLB6-21, by you at 8:50 a.m., is such a train. It came from Alliance Yard in Texas and is headed to Long Beach with nothing but K-Line's red containers. Oh, the miracle of padded schedules—it will enter Los Angeles essentially right on time, then reach Long Beach, 42 miles away, almost 9 hours early. This is done, of course, to make sure the train is on the dock when its ship comes in.

The other kind of S train is epitomized by S-CHLA1-22—the trainset with the electro-pneumatic brakes. A giant of a train, 6,800 feet long and weighing 7,300 tons, it's running almost 6 hours behind schedule behind a skimpy 1.7 hp/t and will reach milepost 371 shortly before 2 a.m. tomorrow. Its big shippers are intermodal marketing companies (IMCs) with names you've probably never heard of—Hub City, Alliance Shippers, Riss Intermodal, and Railvan, to name a few. They broker truckload service at whatever price they can get while still achieving the volume they need to qualify for the lowest possible price from Santa Fe. The IMCs account for about half of the 229 containers on S-CHLA1-22. The other half is an assortment of steamship containers making its way back to the dock. S-CHLA is allotted 68 hours, versus 48 hours for 9-198 from Willow Springs and P-CHLA's 63 from Chicago.

So you pays your money and you makes your choice—big bucks for the Q, a deal for the P, and a steal on the S. How

well does this work commercially? Today, almost half—44 percent—of the containers and trailers passing milepost 371 are aboard Qs, the most expensive. So customers are willing to pay for what they get. Don Ainsworth, president of Reebie Associates, a consulting firm that tracks intermodal shipments and costs, estimates that railroads now carry 91 percent of all eastbound and 93 percent of all westbound boxes between the end points of Chicago and Los Angeles—in other words, darn near everything. And Santa Fe totally dominates that corridor. It highballs 8 to 10 intermodal trains each way per day just between Chicago and California (not counting those from Birmingham, Dallas-Fort Worth, Houston, and Kansas City) and hogs almost all the premium-priced traffic.

And the competition? SP has three and sometimes four Chicago-LA trains a day (none between Chicago and Oakland), but they run on 70-hour-plus schedules. American President Lines supplies Union Pacific with two and occasionally more Chicago-LA trains each way a day, scheduled at between 59 and 78 hours, depending upon the day of the week. But there isn't much else happening for UP across what Ainsworth calls the "optimal corridor" for intermodal service, and Union Pacific is getting clocked by Santa Fe's times between Chicago and Oakland despite UP's shorter route.

⚓   ⚓

Dry. Bone dry. So dry that when your boots touch the grass, the blades don't bend but audibly snap. So dry that volcanic soil seems to disintegrate beneath your feet. So dry that Lake Davenport, which your maps insist is just on the other side of the tracks, has gone *poof!* Northern Arizona, always arid, hasn't had it so bad in decades. Forest fires 40 miles to the east, near Flagstaff, cast a dull haze over the entire region, and there are moments when you can smell the smoke particles that have blown your way. This morning the governor of Arizona orders people off public land in surrounding Kaibab National Forest. A roadblock is set up near Bootlegger Crossing, and all that keeps you from being thrown out is that you're on Santa Fe's private property and don't budge from it. Even so, a friendly U.S. Forest Service employee

bounces his big truck down the right-of-way road just to find out who you are and what you're doing.

The climate bears mention because railroads are at the mercy of wind, fire, flood, tornado, mechanical failure, and human error. Three times during the prior six months a red strobe light revolved above a train dispatcher's work station in Schaumburg, meaning that someone had keyed in the number 9 on a VHF radio and sent the emergency tone—a prelude to word of calamity. The first occurred December 20, 1995, at 9 a.m., after westbound Q-NYLA1-19 plowed into the side of eastbound P-SBBH1-19 (San Bernardino-Birmingham) as the latter train was entering the siding at Tejon, N.M., 4 miles west of Vaughn. The conductor of Q-NYLA perished.

Awful events like this simply crush the morale of railroaders. But they can't go home and mope. The railroad wouldn't reopen for 28 hours. Dozens of trains were then coming toward Tejon, and some, such as 9-199—holiest of holies, loaded to the gills with San Francisco-bound UPS trailers—were beyond the point of being easily rerouted.

From the BNSF operations center in Fort Worth, Rollin Bredenberg, who had been a vice president and general manager of Southern Pacific, picked up his phone and activated the Old Boy Network. He asked of his former colleagues in Denver that SP accept four of Santa Fe's westbound UPS trains on short notice from the interchange track connecting their main lines at Vaughn and get them to Phoenix (9-197-19), Colton (9-198-19 and 9-398-19, destined for Los Angeles), and Bakersfield, Calif. (9-199-19, for Richmond), as fast as possible. To their credit, Southern Pacific crews ran 9-199 as if it were their own *Memphis Blue Streak Merchandise Forwarder.* As it happens, Santa Fe and SP use the same dispatching software, and on a monitor plugged into SP's network, BNSF people in Fort Worth (where Schaumburg dispatchers eventually will relocate) watched in fascination as a superpowered 9-199 bore down upon and then was allowed to pass MBSMF, SP's premier train, in the desert west of Gila Bend, Ariz.

The second disaster, on February 1, was a runaway train—H-BALT1-31 (high priority, Barstow-Los Angeles). Its brakes would not set when starting down Cajon Pass from Summit, west of Victorville, Calif. "I gave it a little more air … but we continued to gain speed," engineer Lester Foster later testified from a wheelchair. "I put the train into full emergency, but it continued to gain … 40 mph … then 45 mph … the last thing I recall, we were doing about 65 when we passed under Interstate 15." H-BALT1-31 piled up near the bottom, killing Foster's conductor and brakeman and breaking Foster's back. More detours. But this time 50 Federal Railroad Administration inspectors descended upon Southern California, mostly in Barstow, and pretty much tied up Santa Fe's primary western classification point for weeks with tests, inspections, and orders for corrective action.

Next was an act of God: At 1 a.m. on April 28, P-CHLA-27 was literally blown off the track by tornado-force winds just west of Wellington, Kan., at Milan. Almost a mile of train—130 trailers and containers—was strewn across a cut, whose narrow confines stymied the cleanup. The line was reopened 31 hours later.

In the meantime, trains scattered every which way. Seven trains detoured via Boise City, Okla.—that is, from Kansas City to Newton, Hutchinson, and Dodge City, Kan., Las Animas, Colo., and then 235 miles south on the Boise City Sub to Amarillo, Texas, rejoining the main line, or vice versa.

Six trains stayed on the north line via La Junta, Colo., all the way, up and over Raton and Glorietta passes. (Capacity of the La Junta-Albuquerque section is limited by the small number of available crews; the normal frequency of freights is two each way a day.) SP hosted eight trains on its Golden State Route between Hutchinson and Vaughn. Six detoured on Burlington Northern between Avard, Okla., near Santa Fe's former crew-change point of Waynoka, and Perry, Okla., on Santa Fe's line to Texas, thence north to Kansas City. Two eastbounds ran southeast from on BN from Amarillo to Fort Worth, then north on Santa Fe to Kansas City. Three other eastbounds were routed from Clovis to Sweetwater, Texas, on Santa Fe, to Fort Worth on Union

Ending a dry spell of 1:14, P-LAKC1-22 is the first of three eastbounds to pass MP 373 within 19 minutes. *John C. Lucas*

Pacific's El Paso line, and then north again on Santa Fe.

That's 32 trains in all, and except for two trains of empty automobile cars that took the Sweetwater bypass, all were intermodals. In every nook and cranny from Kansas City to as far west as Winslow, Santa Fe began stacking 37 boxcar, automobile, and unit trains until service could be restored through Milan.

To help the railroad react to the unexpected, Santa Fe maintains a Service Interruption Desk in Schaumburg. "Basically, we get involved with anything that will cause grief to the railroad," explains Ed Chapman, who captained the office in May. Some interruptions are of the sort you wouldn't normally think of. "Just the other day," says Chapman, "we had a planned computer outage. It was supposed to last 90 minutes, but instead went on close to 5 hours. Dispatchers were faxing track warrants, and conductors couldn't get train lists. Nineteen trains were delayed because of that."

Today Chapman's office will spread word of just three service interruptions, none of which even remotely affects trains going by you at milepost 371. But you don't know this at the time, and you begin to think something is amiss. Instead of a

flood of trains, you get a trickle from eight o'clock until four, only 11 trains. On the radio, Dee Harrah, the dispatcher in Schaumburg controlling Winslow-Seligman, commiserates with some eastbound engineers. She's running a single-track railroad between West Perrin (milepost 386) and East Doublea (MP 392) because of three broken rails on the south track found by a defect-detector car. To make a bad situation worse, the power switch at Doublea won't work.

Well, they've got to get here sometime, so it's the waiting game. Grosbeak birds sing in the pine trees. They and the ever-present wind blowing through the needles of the Ponderosa create a gentle symphony that entertains you as the afternoon wears on.

The dam breaks just before four o'clock, and among four trains that pass in a 34-minute span are two attention-grabbers:

Q-LAAL1-22 (guaranteed, Los Angeles-Alliance), by at 4:07 p.m., is not noteworthy in itself. But oh, its big brother! Saturday morning's extra section of this train is a real silver bullet. Q-LAAL9 leaves Los Angeles at 2:30 a.m., and in San Bernardino gets UPS trailers whose goods are destined for next-day delivery in Dallas-Fort Worth. How is this possible if the train must travel more than 1,500 miles? Because for parcels picked up in Los Angeles on Friday, "next day" in Dallas is really Monday. Operating on a 40-hour schedule from San Berdoo, more than four hours faster than that regular Q-LAAL1, the Saturday morning version of this train reaches Alliance, 19 miles north of Fort Worth, at 12:25 a.m. Monday, in plenty of time to have packages on delivery trucks by eight o'clock.

9-698-21 is the Birmingham-Los Angeles train begun with Burlington Northern via the Avard gateway in summer 1994, just before the two railroads discussed merging. Bredenberg calls this "the *Memphis Blue Streak Merchandise*" and means it. "Southern Pacific's MBSM is not really the MBSM anymore." To understand that statement, you have to go back to 1979, when SP revived the moribund *Memphis Blue Streak*, whose symbol hadn't been used for a decade, because United Parcel Service wanted a super-reliable, two-nights-out train from Memphis for its growing business from the Southeast to Los Angeles. The *Memphis Blue* soon supplanted the original St. Louis-Los Angeles *Blue Streak Merchandise* as Southern Pacific's spare-no-effort train.

By 1993, however, competitor Santa Fe knew that UPS was unhappy with the erratic performance of the *Memphis Blue*. Its schedule had no rubber; everything had to go right for it to reach downtown LA in time for UPS to deliver the next morning, and too often it didn't. Seeing his opening, Krebs got involved. Working directly with now-retired Burlington Northern Chairman Gerald Grinstein, he arranged for Santa Fe to be given haulage rights over BN to Memphis and Birmingham. Haulage rights means Santa Fe sold the service, then paid BN to run the trains east of Avard. Santa Fe not only secured the UPS business out of Memphis, but also that of J. B. Hunt, which had run its Birmingham-Los Angeles trailers via Kansas City Southern Railway to Dallas, thence Santa Fe. And to handle this premium business, it added a pair of *numbered* trains a year after the supposed end of numbered trains—a little favor to UPS.

Everything has not gone right with 9-698, though. "It was very unreliable

under the haulage agreement, premerger," reports Bredenberg. "BN's internal measurement of how well they ran trains did not include the performance of the Santa Fe haulage trains, so you can guess what happened."

In an interview last year, Krebs said he finally had to tell key customers such as Hunt that they were free to go elsewhere until Santa Fe and BN could get their acts together. UPS stayed, but Hunt returned most of its Birmingham-LA business to the original KCS-Santa Fe routing.

You've been waiting for 9-698 a long time today. Scheduled past Williams about noon, it finally appears at 4:27 p.m., with five locomotives supplying an extra-generous 5 hp/t. It had left Memphis 80 minutes ahead of time with a short train of UPS, Hunt, and Overnite trailers and containers, and went great guns until reaching Clovis last night. There it waited five hours to exchange boxes with a late-running Q-ALRI1-22 (Alliance-Richmond). By then it was 90 minutes late. Then it tarried in Belen during the refueling while mechanics tried to revive a dead locomotive, only to give up and order a replacement unit brought over. And near Grants, it was stuck waiting for S-LACH1-21 on the other main track to inspect its train after an emergency brake application. Later, a heroic performance between Williams and Barstow, in which more than two hours would be recovered, will be squandered by delays getting through Barstow.

The pace is picking up, but as afternoon segues into evening the train you've waited for above all others—the train that is unique on Santa Fe and perhaps unique to all of American railroading steadfastly refuses to show itself at milepost 371. Where, oh where, is the wine train?

⚒   ⚒

Mr. and Ms. America: The next bottle of California wine you uncork—that next oaky Chardonnay, spicy Zinfandel, or fruity Cabernet Sauvignon you sip—quite possibly traveled Santa Fe some of the way. Every intermodal train that comes from Northern California today (except for 9-991) is laden with the stuff: 7 trailers of wine aboard 1-981-21, 14 on P-FRCH1-21, 23 on S-RICH1-21, 18 on Q-RIAL1-21, and 15 on P-RICV1-22. This

stuff adds up. Each 48-foot container holds 1,237 cases of wine, and each case holds 12 bottles, meaning that 1,142,988 bottles of wine have gone past you today, *so far.*

That's right, there's more. Yesterday morning at 2:48 a.m., in the north end of the Central Valley, at Modesto Empire Junction, adjacent to scores of packing sheds and also to the Gallo winery, two diesels—SF30C 9535, rebuilt from a U30C, and SD45-2 5822—eased train H-MOSR1-22 (Modesto-Streator, Ill.) into motion. Every one of its 52 cars held food or wine. At Fresno, while Californians ate breakfast, it added 10 more cars to the rolling banquet. Then in Bakersfield, where the train is classified for the run east, it left behind some vegetables and wine destined for Los Angeles and Phoenix and took on as many more cars of spuds for points east. H-MOSR1-22 embarked from Bakersfield at 7:45 p.m. last night, tarried awhile in Barstow for an engine swap, recrewed in Needles at 10:16 this morning, and just disappeared.

You've spent idle moments today imagining this 63-car grocery store and wine cellar: 10 cars of oranges, 9 of catsup, 8 of potatoes, 7 of canned goods, 4 of carrots, 1 of butter … and 24 of wine. A 60-foot insulated boxcar carries 4,041 cases of wine. That's another 1,163,808 bottles, or 2,306,796 in all. This is mind-boggling. If Santa Fe trains were to carry this much wine all 250 business days per year—and maybe they do—this liquid would equal about two-thirds of all U.S.-grown wine consumed in this country.

In the last lingering light, at 8:25 p.m., as S-MCLB5-21 (double-stack, McCook-Long Beach) trundles west past milepost 371 on the north track with its Maersk and K-Line containers, a headlight appears on the south track in front of Bill Williams Mountain, coming east. Lead unit SD40-2 5091 is upon you before you can make out the train behind the headlight, and when you do, you know H-MOSR1-22 is finally here. What a sight: 4,105 feet of cushion-underframed, insulated, and refrigerated boxcars (the latter lettered SOLID COLD). Except for 13 cars to be set out two days hence in Fort Madison, Iowa, for delivery to Chicago, the entire train will interchange to Conrail a mere 24 minutes late, at 11:24 p.m.

The five-unit mix powering that jack-of-all-routings train, H-DVBA, sparkles in the evening sun at 6:52. At the point is SD75M No. 242.
John C. Lucas

May 25, at Streator, 90 miles southwest of Chicago. From there, it will use Conrail's Kankakee Belt to reach Elkhart, Ind.

H-MOSR has the longest route of any non-intermodal train on Santa Fe and is easily the most distinctive train of any sort on the property. But it was only the 10th train so far today to bear the H (high priority) or M (manifest) prefix assigned to boxcar trains. The difference between an H and an M boxcar train is one of degree. Most M freights feed traffic to the H freights, which tend to have longer routes than the M trains. In either case, the rate that shippers pay is the same.

The boxcar train is not a dinosaur—not yet, at any rate. But what a contrast this is to April 1977, when Santa Fe dispatched a boxcar train from Barstow to Kansas City, and Kansas City to Barstow, every two hours on the hour—this in addition to boxcar trains to and from Texas and the young corps of intermodal trains. Today it's the intermodal shipper who has a choice of cutoff times to make trains. The boxcar shipper usually has but one train per day available between any pair of cities. This is best illustrated by the destinations of H and M trains sent east from Barstow: trains H-BADV (Denver),

H-BAKC (Kansas City), H-BATE (Temple, Texas), H-MOSR (Streator), M-BAAL (Alliance), M-BAKC (Kansas City), and M-BAME (Memphis). Converging on Kansas City, the number of eastbound boxcar trains increases, but believe it or not, just one conventional freight per day is scheduled in and out of Corwith Yard in Chicago—*the* railroad capital of America.

There may not be a lot of these boxcar trains now, but like the wine train, they're an interesting bunch. Example: H-DVBA1-20, which goes by you at 6:52 p.m. It's the heaviest (9,550 tons) train you'll see today, and coming up the grade toward milepost 371, 1968-vintage SDF45 5951 (Santa Fe has added the SD symbol to the original F45 designation) is roaring its unmuffled lungs out in the center of the five-locomotive consist. But consider this: Of the 99 cars on this train today, only 8 (5 containing Coors beer) started out in Denver. Indeed, leaving Denver, most of this westbound train was destined east or south. Those cars were pulled at Pueblo for M-PUNW (Newton, Kan.) and M-PUAM (Amarillo). Leaving La Junta, H-DVBA1-20's shortened 37-car train had a grab bag of traffic—10 cars for Albuquerque or before, 8 cars of paper

waste for the Apache Railroad at Holbrook, Ariz., 4 cars of frozen meat for LA, and various other odds and ends.

Reaching Winslow at 1:20 p.m. today with but 32 cars, train H-DVBA cleaned out the yard, leaving three hours later with 67 more, most of them loads that had collected there—paper, tin, feed, plastics, lumber, furniture, ingots, fertilizer, potash, automobile parts, and even toys. H-DVBA is a through Denver-California train in name only. It's more accurate to say that this is a Denver-Pueblo train, a Pueblo-Albuquerque train, an Albuquerque-Winslow train, and a Winslow-Barstow train bound together by a common symbol, if not common cars.

⚒   ⚒

From above your head, the robins have sung their evening vespers. From the meadow across the tracks that used to be Lake Davenport, a coyote howls again and again. For what—a drink of water? There is none. On Interstate 40 a mile to the north, you see lights of passing trucks, which go by at the rate of about one per minute each way.

Trains are passing you, too, about three per hour. The big surprise is 9-199-22—day in day out, the train that this railroad dotes upon most. The surprise is that it doesn't look as it ought. Its 76 trailers include 58 UPS trailers, but when 9-199 passes you at 8:52 p.m. you have to look hard to find a single UPS-owned trailer. Rather, they all appear to be leased, and pretty scruffy at that. You'd never know this train is first among equals.

Tonight's 9-199 isn't long—a modest 4,109 feet—and is sufficiently overpowered by its four units—a GP60M and a trio of B40-8Ws—to have taken on more traffic, or so it seems. But Santa Fe's intermodal business unit saw things differently. On Mondays and Wednesdays 199 picks up UPS trailers at Kansas City for the North Bay terminal near Oakland, and yesterday being Wednesday, someone must have wanted to ensure a successful run. So at 1:32 p.m. yesterday, 28 minutes ahead of an on-time 9-199, Willow Springs high-balled advance section 8-199-22, with only 10 cars, carrying trailers for Yellow, Consolidated Freightways, Roadway, and Hunt—all for Stockton. At Kansas City's Argentine Yard, it added the UPS trailers for North Bay, 11 of them on six cars.

This left 9-199 a clear path all 2,492 miles to North Bay, and thus empowered, it kept time with the exactitude Santa Fe used to expect from the *Super Chief*, dead on time leaving Chicago and Kansas City, 1 minute late passing Emporia, 12 minutes ahead from Wellington, 5 from Belen, 6 from Winslow, and so on down the line. Advance section 8-199 got out of KC. still 35 minutes ahead of the main train. But 274 miles later, at Harper, Kan., west of Wellington, its headway had shrunk to just 9 minutes. So 8-199 took siding down the road a few miles and let 9-199 by. It passes you 40 minutes behind 9-199. As it turned out, 9-199 got to North Bay with 5 minutes to spare, while 8-199 got the trailers to Fresno and deposited the KC UPS trailers at North Bay 25 minutes late—in other words, as soon as 9-199 got out of its way.

Let's not pretend otherwise: You're beat. When midnight mercifully arrives, in company with transcontinental train Q-NYLA1-22, its three Warbonnet GE engines, and a 4,100-foot train of UPS,

U.S. Postal Service, and assorted other trailers, nothing pleases you more than the thought of finally getting the good night's sleep you didn't get last night.

What did you see? Fifty-six trains—51 of them Santa Fe's own freights (plus 3 SP detours and Amtrak's *Southwest Chief* each direction). For this time of week at this time of year, that's 6 to 12 trains less than the norm. For example, you missed Los Angeles-Kansas City 893, the only transcontinental train permanently routed via Albuquerque and La Junta (to pick up Albuquerque UPS trailers and avoid congestion on the southern route); S-CHLA1-21 with its electronic brakes; and 9-799, a UPS shooter assembled in Clovis from North Bay cars set out by LA-bound trains from Alabama and Texas. All will pass after midnight.

What you did see seems representative of Santa Fe's trains and traffic: 26 eastbound freights and 25 westbound. By service type: 21 Q trains (including numbered UPS shooters), 6 P trains, 7 S double-stackers, 8 H boxcar trains, 5 M boxcar trains, 3 V automobile trains, and one local. Of 192 locomotives on these 51 Santa Fe trains, 83 were redheads in Warbonnet dress, 101 were blondes in yellow and blue (1 passed twice), and 8 belonged to other owners. The intermodals carried 1,747 trailers and 2,158 containers, virtually all loaded. The five biggest truck customers were Hunt (533 boxes), UPS (483), Yellow Freight (91), Consolidated Freightways (76), and Schneider National (74). Strung end to end, these trains plus the SP detours came to 2,653 loads and 524 empties, weighing 240,847 tons, and stretching (if placed end to end) 50 miles.

And what have we learned? The morning report distributed to Santa Fe executives at dawn tomorrow will contain this: 95 percent of the trailers and containers reaching their destinations this day met their service-schedule parameters, as did 77 percent of the merchandise cars. Admittedly, not many of the cars and boxes you saw got to the end of the line on Santa Fe this same day—that will occur sequentially over several days. But it's a good measure of where Santa Fe stands in terms of satisfying customers.

In general, shippers got what they paid for. The UPS trains—numbered runs plus

Q trains with a 9 after the city-pair letters and Q-NYLA and Q-LANY—left almost to the minute and arrived the same. Q trains as a whole left on time and arrived a half hour late, which for most shippers is the same as on time. P trains left on schedule and, on average, arrived 90 minutes off. S trains, thanks to the padding that several of them had at the dock in Long Beach, as a group made up gobs of time. Among boxcar trains, the high-priority H trains got started later but lost less time en route than the prosaic M trains. The boxscore:

	Trains	Leave	Arrive
UPS trains	13	2 minutes early	12 minutes early
Q (including UPS)	21	8 minutes early	32 minutes late
P	5	4 minutes early	90 minutes late
S	7	152 minutes late	28 minutes late
H	8	129 minutes late	299 minutes late
M	5	13 minutes early	212 minutes late

Some would say that watching trains go by for 24 hours at Supai summit while listening to robins sing and watching stars twinkle in the night sky is a pretty silly way to take the pulse of a huge business enterprise. They can point to statistics such as trends in revenue per ton-mile, ton-miles per employee-hour, the percentage of shipments arriving within their service schedules, and hours of work lost to personal injury, not to mention earnings per share. And of course, they would be absolutely right, up to a point. But such statistics are built train by train, mile by mile, from events that take place right in front of your eyes. The conclusion you reach here at milepost 371 is that, all in all, Santa Fe had a pretty good day on Thursday, May 23, 1996. And so did you.

Philip R. Hastings

GOIN' LIKE 60!

John P. Hankey

Sixty miles per hour was fast running on my old road, the Baltimore & Ohio.

By the time I made it onto the engines, management regarded 55 mph as the top velocity for freights. A few men on passenger jobs saw the other side of 60, but on a road as serpentine as ours, even their fast running lasted only a few miles.

There was a rhythm to it. The B&O planted its lineside poles 60 to the mile, a pole each second. A fine running train literally was like clockwork—*whoosh, whoosh, whoosh, whoosh*—the pole line keeping time with the second hand. On the west end, past the mountains, the boys in the flat territory had it easier and ran faster. But they too knew the beat.

I wondered then, and still do, why 60 mph has a cachet—the kind of symbolic value matched only by 100 per, which was never even remotely legal on the B&O. I would listen to the men who came before me, and how they ran their Time-savers and QDs and Trailer Jets as fast as

they needed to go to maintain the schedules. They understood, in ways we now have lost, what 60 mph meant.

Parsing the term helps only a little. *Sixty* is a remarkably useful number, divisible in many ways. Although once the basis of its own scheme of counting, now it nestles uncomfortably in the base-10 number system perfected by classical Romans.

A *mile* is also a Roman concept, roughly a thousand paces. In medieval Britain, a mile represented anywhere from 5,000 to 6,000 feet. Elizabeth 1 fixed the mile at its present length at about the time England began colonizing the New World. A *foot* was, of course, based on the length of the human extremity—a convenient, but unreliable, unit of measure.

Hours are equally problematic. Ancient Babylonians, Mayans, and others had the patience to watch the heavens long enough to invent a reasonably workable calendar. A day divided into 60-minute hours and 60-second minutes made the most sense. Is there an underlying physical basis for the mile or the hour? Absolutely not—our reckoning of distance is merely a tradition.

But turn the idea around, and it is easy to see what 60 mph meant to Americans of the 19th century, and why the Railway Age burst forth so enthusiastically. From the beginning, we recognized that the railroad was powerful. Not in the political or economic sense, although that would come in time. We quickly realized that railroading meant speed, and speed shrank distance. If wide-open spaces made it possible to imagine a new nation unlike any other on the face of the earth, it took a tool as powerful as the railroad to make a continental "United" States a reality.

In the early 1830s, at about the same time that de Toqueville was making his prescient observations of politics in the United States, France sent Michel Chevalier, a trained engineer, to investigate America's new preoccupation with railroading.

"The American type … is devoured with a passion for movement, he cannot stay in one place," he noted in an 1834 letter published in Paris. His arch conclusion was that "The Americans have railroads in the water, in the bowels of the earth, and in the air. … The benefits of the invention are so palpable to their practical good sense that they endeavor to make an application of it everywhere and to everything, rightly or wrongly."

The train was a time machine to 19th-century Americans, as disorienting as it was exhilarating. It didn't physically alter the size of the republic. But it rapidly, irrevocably, fundamentally changed our perception of space. The fleet-footed 4-4-0s chewing up the miles across the Great Plains or delivering commuters to the heart of the city were not impressive for their inherent power, but for their ability to annihilate time and distance.

Because trains could traverse 60 miles in as many minutes, Americans demanded that they do so. That was in part our national character, and in part because the expanding frontier presented such daunting spaces to knit together. Theodore Judah recognized the fact in 1857, in his plan for a transcontinental railroad: "However well we may be satisfied with the present rate

of speed in traveling, we dare not admit the principle—we wish to go as fast as we can."

Travel at 60 was not early, easy, or cheap. The British hit the mark sometime in the late 1830s or early 1840s, and soon after were running regularly at that clip. No one knows for certain when the first American opened the throttle far enough to test the limits of locomotive and track, but it must have been a wild ride.

A few express trains flirted with 60 before and after the Civil War. But as late as 1869 (the landmark opening of the railroad to the Pacific) most "fast" passenger trains managed a sincere average of 20 to 25 mph with sprints of probably twice that rate. Surely, passengers on the Pittsburgh, Fort Wayne & Chicago's *Western Express* were thrilled by the one of the fastest runs in the first *Official Guide*. It averaged 33 mph across the Indiana prairie from Fort Wayne to Chicago.

It took the full flower of America's industrial revolution to make 60 mph the benchmark of forward motion. Steel rails, knuckle couplers, and effective air brakes made it possible to double passenger train speeds between 1870 and 1890, from 30 or so miles per hour to the magic mile-per-minute. With breathtaking swiftness, express and passengers could travel in one hour a distance that previously might have taken days, or even a week. The continent shrank. New possibilities opened up.

Perhaps inevitably, Theodore Judah's 1857 predictions of 100 mph trains came true before the dawn of the 20th century. It was one of railroading's final barrier-breaking spectacles, before the airplane and science eclipsed the industry's power to astound. But 60 remained the Gold Standard.

Today, millions of Americans accelerate to, or through, 60 mph and regard the personal control of high velocity as a constitutional right. Without knowing it, they pay homage to a time when patrons of the Santa Fe Railway's *de Luxe* regarded 60 mph as an article of faith, just like the exquisite poached salmon on the Fred Harvey diner menu. Our idea of a day's travel was shaped by New York Central's *20th Century Limited*, which maintained a 16-hour schedule between the nation's two greatest cities because that is what it took, at an average speed of 60 mph, to make the 960-mile trip.

So what would B&O men like Sammy Wolfe or Charlie Rohlfing or Jesse Pilkerton have said if I tried to explain that 60 mph was a gloriously demented combination of Roman counting, Old English distance, and Babylonian astronomy which profoundly shaped American culture and society? After they stopped laughing, I doubt they would have cared, and for very good reasons.

They would have said that 60 per meant a good paycheck, and maybe the kind of swagger and limp that comes with too many years hunched over a throttle stand. They enjoyed the thrill of notching out a Q-4 Mike or a set of F7s past the 60 mark with a few thousand tons of urgent business in tow. But they knew better. I think now that they truly understood 60 mph as railroading's gift.

In their world—the railroading they tried to teach me—friction bearings and riveted cars rolled along at 60 mph because someone, somewhere, needed that freight. They pushed E units and aging Pullmans as fast as they dared go on B&O's punishing main line because there was a schedule to keep—a promise made to be at a station on time. It became a habit they chose to honor.

That is why 60 mph truly meant something. It wasn't just a limit, or a goal, or a thrill. It epitomized mankind's ability to transcend its inherent physical limitations. Sixty per became the frame of reference for a society constantly in motion.

We take for granted the mastery of distance, velocity, and space. Distance no longer represents a fundamental limitation. It is now more of an annoyance, or a mere cost factor. We casually travel about at speeds unimaginable to our great-great grandparents. The continental United States is the neighborhood, and the entire globe is our marketplace. Our space has become simultaneously vast and banal.

Babylonian kings, Julius Caesar, and Queen Elizabeth would have sacrificed empires to wield that kind of power. It would have given them the means to rule the world, or at least alter the fabric of history. As it turned out, brightly-painted 4-4-0s made high velocity—and its power—available to anyone with the equivalent of 2 cents per mile or a few pennies per ton.

A mile per minute for a pittance. Is there a better way to describe what the American railroad is all about?

December 2000

WE BROUGHT
THE NYC TO ITS KNEES

Joseph V. MacDonald

During the years 1932-36, I played in the Notre Dame University band, using a trombone I had bought with my earnings as a messenger in the offices of the Central Vermont Railway.

The band made two trips to away football games each year; these were medium-length trips, to Cleveland or Pittsburgh or Chicago. We wanted badly to go to New York for the Army game in Yankee Stadium, and in fall 1935, we finally accumulated enough money to go, provided we could get a low enough train fare. It was my senior year, and my last chance.

I was vice president of the band, and was delegated to negotiate for a reduced fare with the railroads serving South Bend, Ind. My first stop was the ticket window of the New York Central, where I asked to see a passenger agent. A haughty man came to the window: "What can I do for you, son?"

"I'd like to inquire about a special low fare for the Notre Dame band to go to New York City weekend after next."

"We have no special fares," he replied.

"But it's for the Notre Dame band," I said.

"I don't care who you are."

"But there are one hundred of us."

"I don't care how many of you there are," he said. "We have no special fares. The fare is twice the one-way fare less 10 percent, $64 round trip, coach. And if you want to go, you'd better tell us which train you want to go on, so we put a couple of extra coaches on for you."

"But why don't you have special fares?"

"Why should we?" he said. "We have the only railroad here."

"You *do not* have the only railroad here," I reminded him.

"Well, if you want to take the Pennsy's branch train down to Plymouth, and stand on the platform for a couple of hours, and crowd into their train, you're welcome to do so. And if you want to take the Grand Trunk Western here, and take a couple of days to get there, you're welcome to do that. But we have 17 trains a day to New York, and so far as we're concerned, we have the only service here."

I stepped next door to the GTW ticket window, and asked for a passenger agent. I told this man I wanted to inquire about a special low fare for the Notre Dame band to New York. He said, "Come on in."

Inside the office, he asked, "Now, what's this all about?" I told him, including what the New York Central had said about the GTW.

"Oh they did, did they?" he said. "We've always had trouble with the New York Central. We paid half the cost of the track elevation and of this station in South Bend. The name of the station is Union Station, but they persist in calling it New York Central Station. We've tried for years to offer group rates for students, but they've blocked us every time. Now you're looking for a special fare to New York; how would a cent a mile suit you, say, $18 round trip?"

We didn't have $6,400 for the NYC, but we did have $1,800. So I said, "That's just what we're looking for."

"Well," the GTW agent said, "that's what we would like to offer you. As far as the Grand Trunk Western is concerned, that's what we would be willing to take you to New York and back for. But I don't want to get your hopes up. In order to give an $18 fare, we would have to file a special tariff with the Interstate Commerce Commission. If nobody objects, it will go through. But, if anyone objects, like the New York Central, then the ICC will have a hearing sometime next spring. But to show you that we want to do it, we'll file and see what happens."

The next day, he called me and said that he had told the Pennsy and the NYC about the plan to file a special tariff. The Pennsy had said they didn't care one way or the other. The NYC said they would object. But the GTW went ahead and filed anyway, to show good intentions. But, he said, with the NYC objecting there was no hope of the rate going through.

Well, we in the band were mighty unhappy over the NYC's attitude. If they didn't want to carry us at a reduced rate, that was their business, but we resented having our New York trip prevented by the NYC interfering with the Grand Trunk's special rate.

So we went to the school's authorities, and obtained permission to put some pressure on the New York Central.

In those days, Notre Dame did not allow its students to go away on weekends without parental permission. But each year, one official trip was sponsored to an away football game, on which all students could go without needing special permission. This year, 1935, the trip was to Columbus, Ohio, for the Ohio State game.

For this official student trip to Columbus, a special train had been

arranged with the NYC, to load at the campus's powerhouse siding, running past St. Mary's College down to South Bend, then on to Columbus. At Columbus, NYC had trackage rights over Chesapeake & Ohio past the Ohio State stadium, so the Central could deliver us right to the stadium. One thousand students had signed up for the trip; New York Central's regular fare of about $10 was being charged.

I went down to the Pennsylvania Railroad ticket office in South Bend (the railroad had branchline service from South Bend to Plymouth and Logansport, on the old Vandalia route). I asked the agent how he would like to have 1,000 passengers for his Saturday morning train to Logansport, to change there to the Pennsy's Chicago-Columbus train.

"Well, we would sure like to have 1,000 passengers," he said, "But we would also like to have some notice, since we have only two coaches on that branch train."

I told him to make the arrangements, and that we would confirm the matter to him officially. We then notified the NYC that we were canceling the special train.

Now, the PRR didn't have tracks up to the Notre Dame campus. So we arranged for 20 streetcars to be at the campus at 6 a.m. Saturday. We piled on, and the streetcars went elephant-parade-style down to a point about a block from the PRR station. There, the Pennsy had a special train waiting for us, which they ran straight through to Columbus. Since the PRR didn't have trackage rights past the stadium at Columbus, we paraded 2 miles to the stadium.

⚒ ⚒

That was the year of the Big Game. Our team was completely baffled by Ohio State's razzle-dazzle offense, which resembled a basketball game on the field; Notre Dame tackled everyone but the player with the ball, and Ohio State was ahead 13-0 in a few minutes.

In the second half, Notre Dame came back, scoring a touchdown in the last minutes of the third quarter, but missing the extra point to keep it at 13-6. We got another touchdown with three minutes to play in the fourth quarter, but again missed the extra point—13-12. Then, with

30 seconds left to play, Bill Shakespeare threw a 45-yard pass to Wayne Miller in the end zone to make it 18-13. Ohio State's fans were stunned; not a person moved in the stands for 20 minutes.

Meanwhile, we collected the iron-pipe goal posts and paraded victoriously the 2 miles back to the station. En route, we stopped at a service station and had the goal posts cut into smaller pieces, and we put the pieces on the tender of the Pennsy's engines to transport them back to South Bend.

Monday, I got a call from the Grand Trunk Western passenger agent. He had just had a visit from the New York Central passenger agent, who had wanted to know if the GTW was still interested in the $18 tariff to New York. The NYC was going to join the tariff. "Now," the GTW man said to me, "we realize that if the NYC also gives you an $18 rate, you will likely go New York Central. But the Grand Trunk wants you to know that we want to take you."

Monday afternoon, at band practice, the same high-and-mighty NYC passenger agent visited us. "Boys," he said, "we didn't realize that you took this so seriously. We're sorry, and we want to make amends. We're going to give you a special $18 round-trip rate to New York City for next weekend. If you tell us which train you want to go on, we'll have a couple of extra cars for you." We thanked him, and said we would let him know.

Then we had a meeting. We decided that since the Grand Trunk was good enough to give us the special rate in the first place, we'd go via the Grand Trunk.

I went to see the GTW agent, and told him of our decision.

"That's what we've been waiting for," he said. "We're going to show you boys that the New York Central isn't the only railroad in South Bend. We're not going to put two coaches on the *Maple Leaf* for you; we're going to run a special train, and limit you to 20 passengers per coach, so you'll all have a four-seater. And the train crews will show you how to take the backs and cushions off, so you can make bunks out of them. We'll put a Pullman on, at regular fares, for anyone who wants to travel Pullman. We'll have specially

Grand Trunk Western 4-6-2 5611 and New York Central 4-6-4 5237 meet at South Bend Union Station in 1939. *Van-Zillmer collection*

low-priced meals in the diner, so you can stay within your budget: 25 cents for breakfast, 35 cents for lunch, and 50 cents for dinner, with special printed commemorative menus. We'll have a passenger agent go all the way with you, and he will meet you after the game to decide what time you wish to return.

"And," he added, "to show you that we can do anything the New York Central can, we'll match the running time of any New York Central train you wish, from the *20th Century Limited* on down, even though we'll have to go 50 miles farther to get there."

We selected a 1 p.m. departure on Friday; on the next track, the NYC's *Fifth Avenue Special* was loading for its 12:50 p.m. departure to New York City. Some students not in the band were taking the *Fifth Avenue.* They laughed at us. "You'll get lost in Canada somewhere. We'll tell you how the game came out."

We beat them to New York City by 2 hours.

We left South Bend behind a Pacific type locomotive with a sealed baggage car containing our instruments, five or six coaches for the 100-member band, a diner, and a Pullman. Aboard the train were a passenger agent and the district trainmaster. Helping the engineer (a favorite way of putting it among engineers in those days) were the traveling engineer and the traveling fireman. During one 5-mile stretch, we timed the train by the mileposts and the brakeman's watch: 200 seconds for the 5 miles, or 90 mph. We made the 234 miles from South Bend to Port Huron, Mich., in 233 minutes, despite changing engines at Battle Creek, Mich., and taking water twice. We passed the *Maple Leaf* in a siding somewhere in Michigan.

GTW parent Canadian National took us across Ontario to Suspension Bridge, N.Y. CN didn't set any speed records, apparently not having expected us so soon. But at Suspension Bridge, a real rhubarb arose. The GTW diner had been taken off, I suppose at Port Huron. Now a Lehigh Valley diner was to be put on the rear of our train; Lehigh Valley was CN's connection for New York-area through service. The LV diner was over in the United States, while the rear of our train was still on the Canadian side of the bridge. Railroads paid a fee each time they used this bridge. Whose switcher was going to incur the wheel charge in order to put the diner on our train? Not the Lehigh's, and just as positively, not the CN's.

Men from the two roads stood there arguing, and perhaps would be still be holding the train, except that the GTW passenger agent announced, "It's our train. We'll do the switching, and I'll take the responsibility." So the CN switcher ran over to the New York side, got the diner, brought it back, and tacked it onto the rear, and away we went.

We made the run from Suspension Bridge to Penn Station (LV's New York terminal, shared with PRR) in 8 hours flat. When we stopped on a curve in Mauch Chunk (now Jim Thorpe), Pa., the track was so superelevated that the dishes started to slide off the tables in the diner. Some years later, I told a Lehigh Valley conductor that we had made the run in 8 hours, and he flatly refused to believe me. But I was there.

Unfortunately, the football game was a tie.

Saturday afternoon, as promised, the GTW man met with us, and we decided on a 3 p.m. Sunday departure from Penn Station. As our train started climbing the hills of New York State, it got very cold. The first three cars were warm, but the rest of the train had no heat. The conductor repeatedly signaled the engineer for

A Grand Trunk Western charter train passes through Valparaiso, Ind., behind 4-8-4 steam locomotive No. 6323. *Jim Boyd*

more steam in the heating line. At every stop there were acrimonious exchanges between the conductor and the engineer. The engineer insisted that he was sending back so much steam that any more would burst the fittings. Yet the train, after the third car, was so cold that the water in the Pullman was beginning to freeze.

When we stopped at London, Ontario, the car-knockers found what was wrong. The GTW coaches had an unusual arrangement for the steam line shutoff valves: The handles were located in the vestibules of the cars. One of the band members had wondered what those handles were for, and he'd turned one of them, on the leading platform of the fourth car. The LV crew was not familiar with the GTW valve arrangement, and they never thought to check the position of the handles.

Some more excitement during the evening came with the emergency stop out in the middle of nowhere. The conductor went forward to ask the engineer the reason for the stop. The engineer asked why

he had been flagged down with a red lantern from the rear end. Again, it was a band member, who had picked up the flagman's red lantern on the rear platform, and waved the lantern from the side door to see what would happen.

Finally, early in the morning, we stopped at either Sarnia or Port Huron, where a lady from the depot's restaurant came out onto the platform ringing a handbell, calling all train passengers to breakfast inside.

One of the boys picked up the handbell, put it under his coat, and took it back to South Bend. Two days later, a half hour before the 6 a.m. gong that woke all of us in Sorin Hall each morning, this wretched band member ran through the corridors, ringing that handbell. That afternoon, Father Farley, the rector, summoned all the residents of the dormitory to a meeting. Father Farley told us—in the straightforward manner for which he was noted—that he would leave his office for 15 minutes. If that bell was not on his desk when he returned, no resident of Sorin Hall would be allowed to leave the campus until he graduated— *if* he graduated.

The bell was there when he returned, and the school returned it to the restaurant, with apologies.

From 1935 until 1942, when World War II ended such trips, the Notre Dame band went each year to New York City for the Army game, via the Grand Trunk Western and Lehigh Valley, for $18 round trip, each.

In 1956, when I returned to Notre Dame for my 20th reunion, I was talking with GTW's passenger agent in South Bend. He asked, "Do you know what you boys did with that trip? You broke the monopoly of the New York Central here. Ever since that trip, we have been able to give group rates to students, and they've gone along with us."

And that's the story of how a few college boys brought the mighty New York Central to its knees.

⚒ ⚒

A few years after graduation, I was in Chicago, and visited the GTW-CN office on Michigan Avenue. I asked how, since the regular fare was $64 round trip, could the GTW afford to give us the $18 fare. I was told that the $18 covered only the wages and fuel. "We didn't charge anything for maintenance or other charges, but we figured we neither made nor lost anything on the train. And we figured it was a good opportunity to show 100 Notre Dame boys that we had a first-class railroad. We figured that perhaps at some time in the future, one of you might have a car of freight to route, and you might send it our way."

As it happens, I was employed for several years at Continental Can Company's New York office, and I had to route many shipments of machinery from suppliers in the East to our plants in the Midwest and West. Whenever it was feasible, I short-hauled the poor Erie at Buffalo, and routed the shipment via CN-GTW to Chicago or (by GTW carferry) to Milwaukee. For a while, I kept a list of the cars that I sent via GTW; it was up to 85 cars when I stopped keeping track. I don't know whether any other Notre Dame band members were ever in a position to route a car, but I think I paid GTW back for the 1935 train!

January 2003

THANKS FOR HELPING ME SEE THE LIGHT, TED

Don Phillips

It's seldom that something as simple as a postcard grabs me in such an emotional way.

But there it was, mixed with the usual bills and junk mail—one of those occasional postcards from painter Ted Rose.

The painting on the face of the card gave me a chill and a tear at the same time. It was a typical overcast winter scene along the Illinois Central in the 1940s and 1950s when I was going to visit relatives on the IC main line in Carbondale, Ill. Big 4-8-2 No. 2604 was blasting along on double track, a cold wind roiling the smoke toward the photographer—er, painter—and obliterating everything from the tender back. In the scene, about to be covered by smoke, was a green block signal. Ted called the painting *Mainline Green*.

I went straight to the phone and called him. The conversation went like this:

"Ted, has that painting *Mainline Green* been sold?"

"No."

"How much do you want?"

"$2,800."

"Sold!"

"Great!"

That was my last conversation with Ted Rose. A few weeks later, he died of a fast-moving form of cancer that he thought he had licked. His wife Polly told me later several other calls came in right after mine, and another nine callers expressed interest over the next week. But this painting was mine. In fact, I think it was mine from the day Ted put a brush to that canvas.

I'll tell you a strange but true story about my conversation with Ted. Keep in mind the scene could be anywhere along the IC main in Illinois. But I knew exactly where it was.

"Is that near Carbondale?" I asked Ted. With hardly a pause, he said it was south of DuQuoin.

DuQuoin is just north of Carbondale. Since the prevailing wind is west-to-east out on the prairie, that means 2604 was pounding south toward Carbondale, just a few miles away. My goosebumps had goosebumps.

And now I'll spend a lot of time imagining what's behind the smoke. The 2600s were mostly freight hogs, but they also could handle passenger trains at speed. In fact, I have an IC timetable from the early 1950s that allows them 90 mph on

Ted Rose's painting, *Mainline Green*, depicts a winter scene along the Illinois Central commonly seen during the 1940 and '50s.

mainline passenger trains. Most likely, though, this is a freight that came off the St. Louis line at DuQuoin. It's not possible to say how fast it's going or how hard the wind is blowing, but the two are inexorably interconnected. I get a little cold just looking at it on my living room wall, where it has an honored place.

That was typical of a Ted Rose painting. He was technically accurate about locomotives, of course, but he was not an illustrator—he was a painter, and his job was to convey both the reality and the feeling of the moment. He succeeded so well.

I could go on and on about Ted, but thats been done in the many obituaries, as well as in bars and around living room

tables where we gather—especially those of us who are about his age at death of 61. But I just want to share one observation about Ted. He saw things that the rest of us didn't really see until we saw his paintings.

I gave Ted a ride to Cumberland, Md., a few years ago for a meeting of rail enthusiasts where he gave a talk. We drove to and from Cumberland along the old B&O main line through the Potomac Valley. But the weather didn't cooperate. It was overcast or drizzling rain, going and coming. It was a washout. At least it was a washout for me. Not Ted.

A few weeks later, a package arrived for me. It was a thank-you note—a small painting, about 12 inches square. The painter's view was down on the passenger platform at Cumberland, as if he was

laying on his stomach in a puddle of rain water. On the right, just entering the frame, was a CSX unit still in Chessie colors with the cat on the side of the unit dominating that part of the scene. In the distance was an approaching CSX freight, its glaring headlight reflecting off the rain puddle covering the platform. The sky was gray. Everything was wet.

He called it *Wet Cat*.

And one postscript: Take a look at the cover painting on the official Ted Rose 2003 calendar—a CSX freight just emerging from Randolph tunnel on a gray day.

That was a surprise grab shot on that same trip as we stood near the tunnel mouth.

Thanks, Ted. Bye.

Jim Boyd

CHICAGO: CITY OF RAILROADS

Mark W. Hemphill and Curt Richards

In 1830, no one was placing a finger on a map of the North American continent at Chicago, saying, "Here we will build the greatest railroad city on earth."

At that time, all Chicago consisted of was a surveyor's plat, a few crude cabins, and some trails scratched out of a swamp at the southwest corner of Lake Michigan.

Railroads were just beginning to think about crossing the Appalachian barrier. They were, in fact, still a wobbly technology; canals were the solid investment businessmen viewed as the future of transportation. But the interior of the continent was pregnant with possibilities, and Chicago, unknown to almost everyone, was a location unlike any other on earth.

A mere 26 years later, Chicago was without question the Rail Capital of the World, the focus of 10 trunk lines reaching from the Atlantic shore to the Mississippi River. "London, Paris, Berlin, Vienna, and Milan all developed important networks of lines, but none could compare with Chicago," wrote geographer James Vance.

In the end, almost no railroad bypassed Chicago, and as time has passed, it has become even more apparent that Chicago can hardly do anything but continue to soar in importance. Chicago established the entire railroad pattern of North America that is still in application today. Chicago defined and determined the history of railroads and railroading. Chicago has also become the central problem of North American railroads, which know that traffic will grow and the trains must go to Chicago, but no one is yet sure what Chicago will do to handle them!

⚓ ⚓

Three questions arise immediately: Why did railroads all go to Chicago? After all, they had a huge empty continent in which to build. They could have established this great nexus between East and West, North and South, almost anywhere they chose. Why did railroads stop at Chicago, and not simply continue through the city? There were no natural barriers—no mountains, no oceans, no rivers to arrest their progress; the prairie was just as flat on either side. And why—since all these railroads starting in or ending at Chicago create enormous congestion as they interchange trains with each other—do railroads continue sending their trains there, and not to some other junction?

The answer to the first question is that Chicago was a better location than all others. It drew railroads to it like iron filings. As soon as railroads first built there, other railroads could not avoid it. The answer to the second question is that railroads changed in function at Chicago, a pattern that persisted long enough to create a *fait accompli* that becomes the answer to the third question: Chicago is where the action is. Even now, Chicago cannot be undone without undoing the history of the entire North American continent.

What made Chicago's location superior to—choosing two examples—St. Louis or Sandusky, Ohio, was that it lay at the intersection of vast geographic realms. It is as far west as one can go on the Great Lakes and still remain within the temperate agricultural climates. It is as far east as one can go in the grain-growing belt before reaching the Great Lakes. It is within the same climate region as northern Europe, which meant that immigrants could pull up stakes one day in Prussia and put them down a few months later on raw

farmland in northern Illinois, with no requirement to change anything other than their currency. It is surrounded on three sides by flat, arable, fertile land, cheap for railroad construction, and on the fourth by the Great Lakes, which gave it cheap access to lumber from northern forests.

No other location had all these qualities. The chances of St. Louis, Chicago's arch-competitor, were diminished by geography. The Ozark Mountains to the southwest are neither arable nor suited to inexpensive railroad construction. The Mississippi River at the city's foot remained technologically unbridgeable until too late: St. Louis might as well have been on the edge of a cliff, from the point of view of a railroad.

Poor Sandusky! At the dawn of railroading, when the Baltimore & Ohio and others first crossed the Appalachians, and wondered where to go next, Sandusky was erroneously thought poised to become the western counterpart of New York City. But it was too far east and had no quality that made it unique among myriad possible ports on the Great Lakes. Today it is known only for its coal dock and to amusement-park fans.

⚓ ⚓

The growth of Chicago as a railroad capital was given its first impetus not by a railroad, but by the Erie Canal. Completed in 1825, the canal connected the Hudson River Valley and New York City with Lake Erie, and lowered the cost of transportation from the interior to Atlantic tidewater. Prior to its construction, the resources of the North American interior, all low-value bulk commodities—grain, meat, lumber—were barred from development by the cost of transportation. Their only opportunity to enter into world markets was through New Orleans, where the ocean voyage to European cities was excessively long and costly. An indication of the enormous change wrought by the canal is that in 1825, 95 percent of the export flow from states bordering the Ohio River went by way of New Orleans. By 1850, 69 percent went by way of the Erie Canal.

The key fact about the Erie Canal is that its effective terminus was Chicago, because of the Great Lakes. That made Chicago the logical place to concentrate,

grade, store, and market the commodities hauled in the canal. The canal set into motion a series of events that inevitably led to Chicago's ascendency. It increased the value of any commodity it hauled, relative to commodities that had to bear the cost of overland or Mississippi River transportation. That increased the value of farmland adjoining the Great Lakes, which increased the value of Chicago as a market point, which further made Chicago the logical destination for railroads.

Well before the Civil War, Chicago had been established as the clear choice for North America's central rail hub. Railroads around it fell into two patterns that dominated North American railroading. The pattern that first appeared was, surprisingly, west of Chicago, where railroads were conceived as low-cost, high-capacity replacements for wagon roads that would gather grain, carry it to the waterfront, and feed it to the Erie Canal.

While geography to the west of the city was conducive to canals, and the Illinois & Michigan Canal was completed from Chicago through to the Mississippi River system in 1848, canals were much too expensive to build throughout the grain-growing belt in any comprehensive way. Thus it was that Chicago's first railroad, the Galena & Chicago Union (a predecessor of Chicago & North Western), built west from the lake into farming country. It was soon joined by two similar lines, predecessors of Chicago, Burlington & Quincy and Chicago, Rock Island & Pacific.

These were the three original granger roads. Their primary function as gatherers of commodities, established in 1848, would persist until fairly recently. Note that just as the canal had created a need for these railroads by increasing the price of Chicago grain in the first place, the grangers again increased the price of Chicago grain, and thus accelerated Chicago's lead over competitor cities.

The second North American railroad pattern that Chicago established lay to the east. Here railroads were conceived as low-cost, high-speed, high-capacity replacements for canals, which would pipeline commodities concentrated in Chicago to the Atlantic Seaboard for consumption or export. The geography

Chicago's central business district in 1962 shows passenger stations abutting the core on the south and west sides, and coach yards and freight houses occupying swaths of valuable land. Only six streets skirted or penetrated the maze of tracks to the south. The warehouse-lined north and south branches of the Chicago River meet at lower right. *John Gruber collection*

was not conducive to canal construction, and Atlantic port cities blocked by the Appalachians from good canal routes to the west desired a piece of the action that New York City gained as the outlet of the Erie Canal. This led to multiple, competing rail lines to Chicago.

In 1852, Chicago was first connected by rail to the Atlantic coast by the Michigan Central, later part of the New York Central system. Eventually, every eastern railroad that aspired to importance found its way to Chicago, though four trunk lines would dominate: NYC, Pennsylvania, Baltimore & Ohio, and Erie. The superior speed and capacity of the trunk lines would render the Erie Canal superfluous. Their descendants, CSX and Norfolk Southern, act in almost identical function today, 178 years later!

By 1856, as railroads crested the Appalachian barrier and rapidly pushed westward, Chicago was the clear and preferred destination. Obviously, eastern railroads could not stop short—that would be like building a house complete except for the roof, unsatisfactory in every respect. But at Chicago, the eastern trunk lines stopped building. Why? Because they arrived second, after the grangers had already begun to establish their grain-gathering network.

While this seems counterintuitive—would it not accrue to the interest of an eastern carrier to control the transportation of a bushel of corn from Iowa farm to New York City dock?—it overlooks the fundamental difference between grangers and trunk lines. Consider the result had an eastern trunk line acquired a granger: Indeed, it would have controlled

that granger's traffic. But it also would set up as enemies every other granger, which then would find allies in the other trunk lines. From the point of view of any one trunk line, it was a gamble with high risk, for at best a low reward.

Moreover, the grangers, because of the unconcentrated nature of farming and stock-raising, were inherently weak. For a trunk line wondering what to do with its cash, it was simple and potentially more profitable to plow it back into its own line, thereby lowering its operating costs relative to the other trunks. To build past Chicago would have required building all the way to the Pacific Coast. Of the four great eastern trunk lines—NYC, PRR, B&O, and Erie—only the B&O tried to

Suburban train conductors at Illinois Central's Randolph Street Station count down the seconds to 5:35 p.m. on May 1, 1895. Today, the wood, iron, concrete, and faces have changed, but the drill is exactly the same at this commuter station: Leave on time!
C. W. Witbeck collection

go past Chicago through its acquisition of the Chicago & Alton, and it soon backed out of its mistake.

The opposite side of the coin was that grangers, as financially weak roads, never could afford to penetrate the eastern trunk-line territory in a meaningful way. Once past Chicago, they would have had to build all the way to the East Coast. The Milwaukee Road made an attempt, reaching Louisville as a condition of a 1970s merger, but the route was inferior and would not change the course of railroad history, only its own. The Wabash, an anomaly that had characteristics of both a trunk line and a granger, and spanned from Buffalo to Kansas City, sought an eastern outlet through Pittsburgh, but failed.

Thus was Chicago established as the epicenter of North American railroading, the hub around which all railroads must spoke. It remains so today.

I I

Three commodities came to dominate and define Chicago in the 19th century: grain, meat, and lumber. All three funneled through Chicago in amounts unprecedented in human history. Grain elevators began appearing on the Chicago

waterfront prior to the Civil War, lining the north and south branches of the Chicago River. As visitor James Parton noted of the grain trade in 1867, "it comes in bulk." Grain merchants established the Chicago Board of Trade in 1850 to create an orderly and enforceable market for grain. In turn, the grain created a market for food processing. Today, while grain movements through Chicago have greatly dwindled, Chicago retains a monstrous appetite for flour and sugars; it is the largest baking center in North America.

The second commodity, meat, defined Chicago to the world. Meat was a natural fit. Just as the granger railroads gathered the grain crop, they gathered the animals raised on the farms and concentrated them in Chicago for forwarding on the trunk lines to the East Coast. Introduction of the refrigerated boxcar in 1869 enabled relocation of slaughterhouses from the East to Chicago, for shipping chilled meat was cheaper and less troublesome than shipping live animals. Said one observer in the 1860s, "The corn crop is condensed and reduced in bulk by feeding it into an animal form, more portable. The hog eats the corn, and Europe eats the hog. Corn thus becomes incarnate; for what is a hog, but 15 or 20 bushels of corn on four legs?"

In the 1860s, Chicago's meat-packing industry outgrew its initial locations near downtown and moved 4 miles southwest of the city to the Chicago River's South Branch, where it established the Union Stock Yards in 1865. The Union Stock Yards & Transit Co. was created as a belt line to serve Chicago railroads. But after World War II, trucks enabled the meat-packing business to move even closer to the farm, to new slaughterhouses adjacent to feedlots in towns such as Dodge City, Kans., and Greeley, Colo. Chicago's role as "Meatpacker to the World" disappeared. But the economic power it gave to the city did not.

The third commodity, lumber, moved in the opposite direction to grain and cattle. Cut from forests surrounding the upper Great Lakes, it moved across the water to Chicago and westward onto the prairie, where it built barns, farmhouses, chicken coops, villages, and every other structure needed to occupy and develop the treeless prairies. Boxcars that came into Chicago laden with grain returned to farm villages laden with lumber. In the late 1860s, Chicago became the largest lumber distribution center in the world. The Chicago River was walled by storage and sales yards, and planing mills. As the northern forests were exhausted, southern lumber appeared in the market, delivered by Illinois Central, Chicago & Eastern Illinois, and others. Western lumber did not often penetrate the Chicago market until after World War II, except in certain grades that southern forests could furnish only with difficulty, such as clear quarter-sawn flooring stock, ceiling board, and window and door moldings. The availability and low price of lumber in Chicago encouraged furniture manufacturing and, notably, wagon manufacturing, which would by 1900 make Chicago the farm machinery capital of the world. Farm machinery needed iron and steel, which led to the establishment of steel mills.

I I

Once Chicago became the hub of North American railroading, it led to three results internal to the city: It became highly attractive to all types of industry, warehousing, and commerce; it developed a train-riding culture; and it created enormous congestion.

Industry gravitated to Chicago for the railroads. Cheap transportation lowered the price of raw materials that fed industry. Ready access to railroads running in all directions enhanced the value of manufactured goods and enabled Chicago factories and distributors to dominate the entire hinterland of the U.S., from Pittsburgh almost to the Pacific Coast, from the Canadian border almost to the Gulf Coast. Only the Deep South resisted Chicago, for lack of rail transportation, lack of consuming power, and a rate structure (the basing-point system) that protected indigenous manufacturers. The nation's first great mass-merchandisers, Sears and Montgomery Ward, chose Chicago for their headquarters and warehouses. While today Chicago is either a close second or third to New York City or Los Angeles in total manufacturing, it is a runaway first in the number of rail movements generated by manufacturing, according to the Chicago Area Transportation Study.

The first heavy industry to arise in Chicago was steel. Initially, it was driven by small manufacturers who wanted cheaper steel for their products than was furnished by Ohio and Pennsylvania mills—the Grand Crossing Tack Co., for instance, founded in 1883 to make carpet tacks, grew into Republic Steel. Chicago mills first focused on the products needed by railroads and farmers. The North Chicago Rolling Mills rolled the first steel rails in the U.S. in 1865; by 1875, Chicago was the rail-rolling capital of the U.S. Today, the Chicago District is the most concentrated steel-producing area in the U.S., with four integrated mills: U.S. Steel's Gary Works (largest in North America), Bethlehem's Burns Harbor Division; International Steel Group's Indiana Harbor Works (formerly LTV Steel and Acme Steel); and Ispat Inland's Indiana Harbor Works.

The advent of kerosene lamps and later the automobile led to a large petroleum refining presence at Whiting, Ind. Whiting was chosen by Standard Oil's John D. Rockefeller because it was close enough to Chicago, and the land was cheap. Successor BP Amoco's Whiting refinery is now third-largest in the United States.

This 1902 northward view makes it obvious where this busy rail intersection on Chicago's south side got its name. Six tracks of Illinois Central (two suburban, two passenger, two freight) cross the Pittsburgh, Fort Wayne & Chicago (PRR) and the Lake Shore & Michigan Southern (NYC). *Illinois Central*

The automobile industry also established a sizeable presence in Chicago. Ford's Torrence Avenue assembly plant dates to the 1920s, and Ford is developing a billion-dollar "parts campus" adjacent to Torrence for suppliers. GM's Janesville, Wis., assembly plant and Daimler-Chrysler's Belvidere, Ill., assembly plant are considered by the automakers and the railroads to be Chicago-area plants, as their transportation needs are met through Chicago intermodal ramps and freight yards.

The second great internal effect of Chicago's railroads was the development of a train-riding culture not seen in any other U.S. city. It is a culture different from New York's, because in New York, population tended to precede the railroad, whereas in Chicago, the railroads were generally there first. Chicago's population grew at a staggering rate: from 4,170 in 1837 to 26,000 in 1850, 300,000 in 1870, 1.1 million in 1890, and 3.3 million in 1930. But people could not live in the central city as in other great U.S. cities, for the downtown was choked into a small space by railroad yards, and industrial districts occupied the land immediately outside the yards. That forced residential development to the edge of the city. This, however, did not limit Chicago's growth, as

there were many rail lines coming into the city. It only made sense that workers would seek transportation on these lines and railroads would seek their dollars.

Because the rail lines did not arrive at one central downtown station but at six (or more, depending on how one counts them), Chicago workers tended to stratify into separate suburbs depending on where they worked. People who worked in the financial district, on the west side of the Loop, had the shortest walk to Union Station or La Salle Street, and tended to live in the western or southwest suburbs. People in the retail district, on the east side of the Loop, were closest to IC's Randolph Street Station, and tended to live in the south suburbs or adjacent northwestern Indiana. While other large cities with intensive railroad commuter systems lost them as business migrated to the suburbs, Chicago, with its Board of Trade, Mercantile Exchange, and Merchandise Mart—and their supporting casts of lawyers, accountants, bankers, and shoe repairmen—nurtured a downtown that could not fade.

The third internal effect was tremendous congestion. It took on three forms: a ring of passenger stations and freight houses around downtown that choked its

Illinois Central's 26th Street engine terminal on the lakefront just south of downtown in 1917 is recently enlarged. In the future are electrification of the innermost main tracks, in 1926, and built on fill in the lake, Soldier Field, Shedd Aquarium, the Field Museum, and Lake Shore Drive. *Illinois Central, David R. Phillips collection*

development and blocked city streets, a vast number of railroad lines crossing the grid of city streets in the residential neighborhoods that blocked street traffic, and a maze of railroad crossings that tied up the railroads themselves.

In 1909, architect Daniel Burnham proposed a single union station (as part of a grand Plan of Chicago) that would consolidate all the railroads into one terminal and make the city a more liveable place. It was expensive, controversial, and required the agreement of every railroad—and therefore was not adopted. Subsequent unified station proposals also failed. The union station problem was never solved, but went away, through the disappearance of long-distance passenger trains and the replacement of freight houses with intermodal terminals. That created new problems for Chicago—congested roads to the airports and truck traffic on city streets.

The second problem, railroad crossings with streets, was solved by city ordinances requiring the grade separation of railroads. Because Chicago is practically at lake level, this almost entirely took on the form of grade elevations. By 1909, ordinances required the elevation of 149 miles inside the city limits, about 75 percent of the lines within the city. Entire yards, such as NYC's Englewood, were elevated. Today, with the removal of extraneous tracks, they are quiet, bucolic, tree-lined, gravel-paved parkways, a world apart from the hubbub of the city just below.

Ⅰ　Ⅰ

The grade separations came about not from self-interest of the railroads, but from wounded civic pride. In the late 1800s, it was understood that Chicago was unabashedly all about capitalism. Everyone was there to make a buck, and everyone knew it. The greed came to an ugly denouement in 1886, when police suppressed a strike for the eight-hour workday at the McCormick factory, with the death of two workers. The following day, workers protested at Haymarket Square. Someone threw a bomb, shooting began, and seven policemen and four others were killed. "The world looked at Chicago with fear and wonder, and saw the future," said historian Donald Miller.

Chicago became self-conscious about its monomaniacal focus on greed, its filth and corruption. To change its image, it sought civic improvements: opera houses, parks, boulevards, the Chicago Art Institute. The ultimate expression of Chicago's new-found morality was the World's Columbian Exposition of 1893, a utopian fair constructed on the lakefront south of downtown. Clearly, grade crossings and smoky trains on the adjacent Illinois Central main line would not enhance this artifice, so it was the first to be elevated, in 1892. Others followed.

However, the grade-elevation mandate did not extend into most suburbs. This is apparent today at places such as Gresham, on Metra's Rock Island District, and Cicero, on BNSF, where elevated lines abruptly attain ground level immediately upon passing the Chicago city limits, and trains begin fighting for space with city streets and each other. Thus the third problem, the congestion that railroads inflict upon each other, still has not been solved.

So why are railroads not seeking to avoid Chicago today? The answer is that the geography that made Chicago superior in the 1850s remains superior today, except more so. You might as well ask a lobbyist to avoid meeting with congressmen as to ask a railroad to avoid Chicago. Of the four great east-west gateways—Chicago, St. Louis, Memphis, and New Orleans—Chicago's growth since 1970 has been nothing short of spectacular. What is driving Chicago today, of course, is transcontinental intermodal traffic, and it isn't going away.

If one were to start the development of North America all over again, and had ultimate power, the only change one might make in Chicago's location is to move it 20 miles south to the vicinity of Whiting, Ind., and avoid the hook that eastern railroads make around Lake Michigan to enter the city. So why not Whiting? Write it off to local geographic idiosyncrasy—that the Chicago River emptied into Lake Michigan at Chicago, and provided a watercourse that was easily made into a canal that crossed a low divide to the Mississippi.

But this is a minor quibble. The point is this: In this vast continent, with thousands of choices for the location of a great railroad city, Chicago's builders were accurate to within 20 miles.

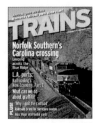

Jim Wrinn

THE LOOPS AT OLD FORT

Jim Wrinn

In the heart of western North Carolina is an overlooked mountain railroad grade, as demanding as it is mysterious: Norfolk Southern's loops at Old Fort, the spiral staircase of U.S. railroads.

It's well known locally—I knew about it because I grew up near the route—but few outside the region have heard of the daily battle that occurs between today's high-horsepower GEs and EMDs and the Old Fort grade.

Most railroaders and fans are familiar with two other mainline grades through this part of the Appalachians: the former Southern Railway's route via the infamous Saluda grade, and the impressively engineered loops of the former

Clinchfield Railroad on the eastern side of the Blue Ridge.

They are spectacular mountain crossings that have earned their place in history: Saluda for its in-your-face audacity, and Clinchfield for its graceful athleticism.

Saluda, of course, offered the greatest show of the three. The steepest mainline grade in the United States, Saluda put 2-10-2s, SD45s, and wide-nosed GEs all on their knees. It required trains running between Spartanburg, S.C., and

Asheville, N.C., to be hefted across in three and sometimes four cuts. It claimed runaways as late as 1971. All of this meant the continued use of a safety track until Norfolk Southern closed the route in December 2001. Saluda pitted brute strength against a short, tough 3-mile grade with portions as steep as 4.7 percent.

The Clinchfield put on a heavy-tonnage show in a more refined way. Built roughly 30 years after Saluda, Clinchfield's route benefited from better engineering, making its climb on a 1.2 percent grade, and using lots of track—19 miles of it—to keep things tolerable. Now part of CSX, it has been a coal conveyor between Appalachian mines and Southeastern power plants for better than 40 years, and it looks as if that role will continue for the foreseeable future.

And then there is the mountain railroad between these two extremes, the former Southern line between Old Fort and Ridgecrest, part of Norfolk Southern's busy Piedmont Division.

The mountain grade encompasses only 13 miles of the 141-mile Asheville district between Salisbury, N.C., and Asheville. Because Old Fort grade is situated between Saluda and the Clinchfield, I often think of it as if it were a middle child. It doesn't demand attention like the daredevil, and it's not graceful like the athlete. Old Fort is somewhere in between, doing what it does without drawing attention to itself—even though it should.

One of the expected outcomes of the 1982 merger of Southern and Norfolk & Western was to shift through freight traffic off Old Fort in favor of a routing via the more gentle N&W main through Lynchburg and Bristol, Va. But Old Fort has been a resilient mountain route, pumping unit coal trains into the Southeast and handling lots of local and regional traffic that couldn't go elsewhere.

At times it seems there is always a train ascending or descending Old Fort grade. Four daily merchandise trains (two each way) ply this east-west route, which lies between Norfolk Southern's busy north-south lanes in the Carolinas and

Tennessee. It also serves as an artery for unit coal, grain, and wood-chip trains in a growing region that constantly demands more electricity, food, and paper. Add in regular ballast trains from Inca on the former Murphy Branch, and it's not unusual in a 24-hour period to see 16 to 18 movements on the mountain.

From time to time, when Norfolk Southern's north-south mains to the east or to the west get real busy (especially the jam-packed Atlanta-Chattanooga line), or if the Atlanta terminal gets backed up, or there's a derailment on another main line in the region, their trains often detour through the mountains via Old Fort. As NS officials like to point out, their system is running at a high volume, but it's flexible, and running via Old Fort is one way to keep trains moving when trouble hits.

I   I

If you look at the dozen or so rail crossings of the Appalachians, from the Susquehanna River south to the Carolinas, the Old Fort crossing is among the most rugged. Westbound trains encounter a change in elevation of almost 1,000 feet from the start of the grade at Old Fort to the eastern continental divide at Ridgecrest, where the Southern Baptist meeting grounds and Interstate 40 are atop the 1,800-foot Swannanoa Tunnel, elevation 2,535 feet.

It's only 3 miles in a straight line between the restored 1890 wood depot (now a visitors' center) at Old Fort and the top of the mountain, but Old Fort's designers took the opposite approach to those who created Saluda.

Instead of going at the mountain straight on, they found a way to roll up a valley, grab a ridge, hoist the railroad up, and then grab another ridge, and keep riding it higher and higher. The tracks coil and roll like the copperhead snakes that inhabit this land.

And there's a life lesson here—the most direct path between two points may indeed be a straight line. But sometimes the best route is to meander until you get to your destination.

To keep the ruling grade at no more than 2.2 percent (the standard set by the Baltimore & Ohio's pioneering Appalachian crossing), the rails twist and turn in several loops—actually horseshoe curves

because they never completely close the gap. Because of this, the route has enough degrees of curvature to equal eight complete circles. In this area, trains—whether eastbound or westbound—travel in every direction of the compass, on curves ranging up to 14 degrees.

At one location, where the upper level is known as High Fill (because originally it was bridged, then filled in) and the lower level is known as Dendron, the tracks are only about 200 feet apart, but they're separated in elevation by more than 100 feet.

So challenging was this mountain that in summer 1981, EMD sent a test train to run up and down to evaluate its latest wheel-slip control gear for its 50 series locomotives.

This is a place where real railroading takes on a model-railroad-like feel. Above Andrews Geyser, it's not unusual at the neck of the Round Knob loop to see the head end of a 90-car train pass the end-of-train device on the last car, with 100 feet of elevation or more in between them.

Most railroaders know the area simply as *the loops*, and they have a great respect for what it takes to get up—and down—the mountain.

I   I

The struggle to surmount this grade takes place within the verdant mountainsides of the Pisgah National Forest.

The railroad follows the Mill Creek Valley westward to launch itself against the Blue Ridge, crossing the stream 11 times and passing through seven named tunnels. For short distances, the grade is actually 2.7 percent; factor in the curvature, and it's the equivalent of a 3 percent grade.

High above it all is an awesome backdrop: the Black Mountain chain, capped by Mount Mitchell, the highest peak east of the Mississippi at an elevation of 6,684 feet.

As you can imagine, building this route was difficult, dangerous, and deadly.

Construction on the Western North Carolina Railroad began in Salisbury in 1855, bogged down during the Civil War, and resumed at a slow pace in the 1870s.

The lack of urgency was attributed to a variety of factors, not the least of which was the steep terrain.

For many years, the railroad stopped at Old Fort—so named because in the late 1700s it was the farthest point of westward expansion into Cherokee Native American territory—and passengers for Asheville rode a stagecoach across the mountains.

In his 1967 novel *The Road*, author John Ehle wrote a fictionalized account of the building of a railroad across the Blue Ridge. He wrote clearly about the difficult work, yet the reality must have been sheer misery. The state of North Carolina provided convict labor to push the project along, at a great cost in human life.

Historian Matt Bumgarner notes that 3,644 convicts—nearly 50 percent of the state's inmate population—were put to work on the line between 1875 and 1892. Of that number, 461 died, most from disease, but many also from landslides and other accidents, not the least of which were premature explosions involving the nitroglycerine used to blast out tunnels.

Trains didn't reach Asheville until 1880—11 years after completion of the first transcontinental railroad.

From Asheville, builders pushed the line westward to Paint Rock, creating the route along the French Broad River to Knoxville, Tenn., and also westward to Murphy, N.C., a consolation prize for not reaching copper deposits in southeast Tennessee before another railroad did. Control of the Western North Carolina Railroad shifted with the 1894 consolidation of properties under the Richmond & Danville banner that resulted in the creation of the Southern Railway.

A summer downpour drenches No. 165 on a July 1990 evening as it hits the final stretch that leads into Swannanoa Tunnel. *Jim Wrinn*

With the line completed, others left the harsh conditions under which the grade was built to history and concentrated on the beauty of the route and the region. In the late 19th century, Asheville became a resort owing to its cool summer climate (and its historical role as a refuge for tuberculosis patients), and George Vanderbilt of New York Central fame located his family's summer estate, Biltmore, there. Commoners followed, as well, riding Pullmans on named trains into "the land of the sky." Early 20th century author Thomas Wolfe, an Asheville native, was so moved by a journey on the line that he wrote about it in his novel *Look Homeward Angel* and other books. Engineer, photographer, and frequent Trains contributor Frank Clodfelter made it a personal favorite, documenting both steam and diesel operations.

Passenger trains kept the route well traveled later than most. Southern decided to stay out of Amtrak in 1971 and kept running a regular train between Asheville and Salisbury, Nos. 3 and 4, until 1975. A railroad-sponsored excursion train between Asheville and Old Fort, the *Skyland Special*, that ran through 1977, and regular NS steam excursions put many riders in touch with the route for almost three decades. But in the past 10 years, the climb across the mountain between Old Fort and Ridgecrest has faded from public view. It's become just another line on the NS route map.

Still, the charm of this railroad was, and is, in its aloof personality—hidden in the forests, in the trees, and in the valleys. It is there. You just have to seek it out to find it. Almost a year after I left North Carolina for Wisconsin, I went back to

The kudzu on the eastern edge of High Fill has a great view of an eastbound Catawba unit coal train as it winds down the loops through Dendron in June 1998. The upper level, High Fill, is separated from Dendron in elevation by more than 100 feet, although the tracks are only about 200 feet apart. *Jim Wrinn*

make sure I understood the mystique of this railroad that taught me admiration and respect for mountain railroading.

ɪ   ɪ

It is a rainy and warm October 2005 Friday morning in Asheville. The yard is busy, and for good reason: This is the railroading hub for Norfolk Southern in western North Carolina, as it has been for more than a century.

Trains depart in four directions—west on the former Murphy Branch 46 miles to Sylva, where short line and tourist-hauler Great Smoky Mountains Railroad operates another 54 miles of the branch to Andrews (Andrews-Murphy is rail-banked by the state of North Carolina); north to Bulls Gap, Tenn., along the French Broad River, a water-level route through the mountains to Knoxville; south to Hendersonville on the now-closed Saluda line; and east to Salisbury via Old Fort, stepping down

from the mountains into the rolling Piedmont landscape.

The modern cinderblock yard office on Meadow Road is quiet, except for the banter between road foreman of engines Tony Johnson and trainmaster Mike Fields, who is lining up the day's work.

On this day, two six-axle GE C40-9Ws, Nos. 9869 in primer and 9175 in traditional NS "horsepower" black attire, leave the fuel rack at Asheville's 1924 roundhouse (still partly in use for running repairs and partly for warehousing) and pull up to the yard office. The two engines constitute today's P32—a helper job on the Piedmont Division.

Joining engineer Gilbert Joyce and conductor Boyd Wright, both with 33 years of service, are brakeman trainee Randy Quarterman, Fields, and me. Our mission is to run light to Greenlee siding, 35 rail miles to the east, and pick up a block of wood-chip cars that unit wood-chip train No. 66E has set off owing to engine trouble.

It sounds easy, but this day's constant downpour, caused by a stalled tropical depression, has complicated things. Loaded wood-chip cars, Wright points out, weigh 130 to 135 tons dry, but when they're wet, they get heavy. *Real heavy.* So much so that a pair of big 4,000-hp GEs—if they're lucky—can lug only 20 cars, about five fewer than normal, up the mountain. Back in F7 days, when Joyce and Wright started, it took five units to wrestle a train over the mountain. As the years went by and locomotives became more powerful, the standard became four GP30s, '35s, or '38s. For six-axles, it was three SD35s, '40s, or '45s. And now we have this pair. "The GEs can pull just as good if not better," Joyce says of his charge. "They just load a little slower."

ɪ   ɪ

On this day, the one thing in our favor is that fall is late—the trees are still green, for the most part, and there will be no

Shooting 60 to 80 feet in the air, Andrews Geyser is a man-made fountain that serves as an exclamation point to the magnificent piece of railroad engineering in the Old Fort loops. Stand at the geyser on a brisk fall day when the leaves have left the trees and the mist creates a rainbow; if the train is long enough, let it encircle you before it heads on its way. It is like magic. *Jim Wrinn*

leaves on the rails to make our return uphill climb even harder. All we have to worry about is wet rail and the sponge-like wood in the cars.

On a normal day, eastbound P32 would give a boost to a unit grain train bound for mills at either Statesville or Barber. Or it might push a 14,000-ton Catawba or Belmont coal train across Ridgecrest and help with braking on the descent into Old Fort, then take tonnage left by westbound merchandise trains at the base of the grade back to Asheville. But the grain is elsewhere today, and mines on CSX tracks have been more successful at winning contracts with Duke Energy to feed its Marshall Steam Station power plant at Catawba (Terrell on CSX).

So today, we have one goal: move the chips. We leave the yard limits, run 17 miles to Ridgecrest through mostly rolling hills, and slow as we enter Swannanoa Tunnel and begin the descent through the loops.

The key to coming down the mountain is control, right from the top, says Johnson, the road foreman. In fact, many engineers consider running down Old Fort more challenging than Saluda, since operations on the latter meant tying down the brakes and dragging down the hill, while Old Fort is much longer with more time for things to go wrong. An engineer must use skill and all the resources available to keep the train under control. Entering the tunnel at no more than 15 mph is imperative; making good use of the dynamic brakes is critical, and not making a large brake-pipe reduction too soon is a wise part of restraint. With light engines, we have little to worry about, but if Joyce were running a train with a full consist, he would have to manage his air with great care. Too much air and you stall, and if you stall, you can't bail off the air and rebuild it in time before a runaway.

Dispatchers who work this line learn, early on, how they can work with train crews to keep eastbounds moving safely down the mountain. The operating

philosophy is opposite to that on most mountain railroads. To keep eastbounds from using too much air on the mountainside, upgrade trains stop at Coleman siding, about halfway between Old Fort and Ridgecrest, for meets. Eastbounds keep moving because recharging the brake system after a release is a luxury crews cannot often afford. "Stopping at Coleman is a good way to piddle away air," Joyce points out.

Holding at around 10 mph, we drop through the tunnels that mark the upper elevations of the line: Burgin, High Ridge, McElroy, Lick Log, and Jarretts. Exiting one, Wright vouches for his engineer and engineers of this area: "If you can run a train here on the mountain grades we have, you can run it anywhere."

Amen to that, especially halfway down the mountain when we meet the crippled 66E at Coleman. We slip into the siding while 66E's lead unit, C39-8 8620, and the dead C40-9W, 9791, hold the sharply curving main with nine soaked cars in tow. Behind him, also on the main, is the local; soon its GP38-2s, 5332 and 5029, will follow 66E, dragging seven chip cars and two boxcars with them. We slip out of the east end of Coleman, wind our way through the loops, and follow Mill Creek into Old Fort.

⊥ ⊥

These wood chips started out at a chipping operation at Conrad, S.C. They would've gone up and over Saluda in multiple cuts, but now they make a roundabout trip out of South Carolina, through Charlotte to Salisbury, where they head west to their final destination, Blue Ridge Paper's plant at Canton on the old Murphy Branch.

The paper plant needs lots of wood chips, and 66E has left P32 quite a set-off: 31 cars at Greenlee and 9 at Old Fort. From Old Fort, we head to the remote siding at Greenlee, pick up 20 of the 31 cars, and head west. The other 11 chip cars will have to wait a day. The crew is anxious to evaluate the potential for trouble on the mountain.

"We've got a good test between Greenlee and Old Fort," Wright says. "If we can make it over Ebenezer Hill with 20 cars, we can make it up Old Fort mountain." We plod across the hill, taking 20 minutes to run the 4.6 miles from Greenlee to Old Fort. We will make it to Ridgecrest, the crew assures me. Not by much, but we'll make it.

Leaving Old Fort, Joyce puts the throttle in Run 6 or 7, but as he blasts out of Point Tunnel, the only bore near the bottom of the grade and the first one westbound trains encounter, he goes to Run 8 and stays there. We should cruise up the grade at 20 mph, but on this day, we struggle to stay between 16 and 18. There's little slipping—just a lot of water coming down from the heavens to get between the wheels and the rails.

At Dendron, where the curvature and the grades really get tough, we slither up the mountainside like a snake, encircling Andrews Geyser. We see the geyser through the trees once from cab height, once from an engine's height plus 20 feet, and finally from 80 to 100 feet above it.

Our GEs are momentarily headed eastbound until they sail around High Fill, the valley below now being the one we just traversed, and we turn west again. From here, we hug the mountainside. We'll turn eastward twice again as we exit the Mill Creek Valley—once at Graphite, and again at Coleman.

"Coleman is a good place to stall," Joyce says as we dip into the coves that mark the climb. Indeed, the siding where we met the train responsible for our mission today is in such a tight curve that track crews double-spike the rails in the curve in an effort to keep them where they're supposed to be.

On this day, we avoid a stall, pierce the series of upper tunnels, and 40 minutes after leaving Old Fort, crest the grade, entering Swannanoa Tunnel at 15 mph. A Norfolk Southern train has won the battle for Old Fort Mountain once again. We return to Asheville, having moved 20 cars closer to their destination. Tomorrow, the same crew will retrieve the stragglers at Greenlee and Old Fort, and 66E will be vindicated.

⊥ ⊥

It's appropriate that I took this journey in the rain. Twice, in 1916 and again in 2004, heavy rains saturated the ground on this mountain so much that washouts and landslides closed the railroad. Both were caused by the remnants of hurricanes that resulted in widespread flooding, destruction, and death.

The infamous floods of July 1916 wiped out the Southern for weeks. The disaster was so devastating, but the recovery so efficient, that Southern President Fairfax Harrison commissioned a book, *The Floods of 1916*.

The storms of September 2004, while not as severe as those of 1916, did heavy damage to the railroad, closing the Old Fort line, as well as the former Murphy Branch, for several days.

Track Supervisor Don Robinson, whose territory includes Old Fort grade, has a connection to both disasters. His grandfather, Luther Rohm Ludie, was section foreman at Denton when the 1916 storms plagued the mountain. He was among 500 men who labored 45 days straight, working in shifts, 24 hours a day, to reopen the railroad. "He used to tell

me stories about it when I was a child," Robinson said.

In 2004, the remnants of hurricanes Frances and Ivan swept across the Carolinas, forcing streams out of their banks and causing widespread damage on Old Fort mountain. The one-two punch of the two back-to-back hurricanes caused washouts of 200 to 300 feet in the highest part of the loops. By one count, the railroad suffered 52 washouts between Ridgecrest and Old Fort.

"It took 400 air dump cars of rock," Robinson said. Today, thousands of laborers aren't needed—hi-rail trucks dumped rock where trains couldn't venture. Once trains could return, they shuttled rip-rap and ballast from places where trucks could stockpile it at Old Fort and at Ridgecrest to the washout areas.

By the time of my visit a year later, some of the ugly gashes the water had made were starting to heal, and it will only be a few years before the floods of 2004 are a memory. Still, I have to ask, when will the waters be back again? This fall? Next fall? Not for 10 years? Or 20? Will Don Robinson have to fight this battle again?

There is, of course, no way of knowing. But this is for sure: The grade at Old Fort is as remarkable as ever. It is a daily miracle that the Norfolk Southern undertakes to move tonnage up and down the mountain.

As I write these lines, I reflect on this railroad and the many mountain grades I've been fortunate to see, at Horseshoe Curve, Moss Run, Moffat, Donner, and many other locations. And then my mind wanders to T. S. Eliot and his passage [from *Four Quartets*: "Little Gidding"]:

And the end of all our exploring
Will be to arrive where we started
And know the place for the first time.

"Yes," I think to myself as I recite the lines, "I've been to that place."

It's back home in western North Carolina, between Old Fort and Ridgecrest, where the trains loop their way into the mountains … and into your heart.

Joel Jensen

WHERE CHRISTMAS
IS JUST ANOTHER DAY

Joel Jensen

An excerpt from a Class I railroad's website says that if you work for the railroad, the term *24-7-365* will take on a personal meaning.

Your commitment on Christmas and all other holidays is included. Get used to it. It's been this way for ages, and a fact that I reconfirmed in Montana.

East of Evanston, Wyo., slate gray skies defy the December 21, 2008, forecast: "Partly cloudy skies with occasional snow showers." My gut instinct tells me otherwise, as does a convoy of cars slowly traversing Interstate 80 with a Highway Patrol escort. Miles of creeping cars and

trucks expose what lies to the east: a high-plains, Cowboy State blizzard.

Wind and snow paint hypnotic trails across the white and icy concrete. A coyote gnaws on the remains of a flattened jackrabbit in front of my truck. I make eye contact with the coyote. He snarls defiantly and does not budge. At the last second, empathy prevails as I swerve to miss him, since he's suffering from Wyoming winter starvation and seems willing

"No matter the hour, no matter the day"—servicing diesels at Glendive. *Joel Jensen*

to play a game of "highway chicken" for a few more swallows of food. I glance in my rearview mirror and realize I witnessed the coyote's last supper. The trucker behind me stayed his course and ended the coyote's battle for food. I'm onto Montana, east of my home state of Nevada, but it feels farther west to me.

I   I

Howdy Hotel, Forsyth, Mont.: Worn out by two and a half days of driving, I walk into the Howdy Hotel, which was built in 1905. It offers stiff drinks, food prepared by women long out of high school, and smoking rooms big and drafty enough to fly a kite in. Beverly Lopez recognizes me from my last pass through her bar.

"You again," 74-year-old Lopez says. "Yeah, yeah, yeah. Jim Beam on the rocks. Train photographer, and you want a room up high, straight across from the depot. $3 for the Beam. $24 for Room 125."

She's right on all counts. It's not exactly service with a smile, but after 30-plus years of catering to oil-field roughnecks, coal miners, and railroaders, Lopez understands the bartending game: A good memory trumps a smile. She hands me my room key and says a Forsyth railroader called Room 125 home

for more than 30 years. "He lived simply," she says.

After requesting "one more drink" five or six times, stories about railroaders unfold for the next several hours. By the end of Lopez's shift, I begin to think that I know more about the Forsyth, Laurel, and Glendive, Mont., and Sheridan, Wyo., train crews than their girlfriends, wives, or families do. Since I'm on the verge of pouring my life's story out to "Mom," I pass on one more drink, and tell Lopez that I'm headed to my room.

"Good idea. You're halfway there in more ways than one. You have a merry Christmas," she says.

The clock strikes midnight as I photograph the ex-Burlington Northern Forsyth depot from the comfort of my 70-degree room. Christmas Eve is under way; however, through my camera lens, all I see is another night on the railroad. BNSF coal trains, railroaders, and shuttle drivers come and go in a business-as-usual manner.

Holiday loneliness sets in as I gravitate between my cameras and TV, where Jimmy Stewart and a more-beautiful-than-ever Donna Reed compete for my attention. The movie, *It's a Wonderful Life*, doesn't resonate as I watch and record railroaders' home away from home. Options are limited for a trainman with an eight-hour rest cycle. In small towns

like Forsyth, all that lies between the depot and a hotel bedroom is a diner or an all-night bar. On Christmas Eve, the bar calls to most railroaders, which makes it no different than any other night of the year.

I   I

Christmas Eve Day, BNSF depot, Glendive: Keith Clingingsmith, BNSF conductor and United Transportation Union conductor training coordinator, briefs me about trainmaster Troy Brewer. Brewer will be my host while I photograph the railroad. "Troy's a good guy," Clingingsmith says, "but I think he's worked more than 20 days in a row."

Great. I'm just what an overworked railroader needs: a potential problem with a camera. As Brewer and I drive to the diesel servicing facility, he says he used to work in Gillette, Wyo. Railroad life in Glendive must be "a walk in the park" compared to the heart and soul of BNSF coal train operations, I say.

"Not really," Brewer says. "We had five of me in Gillette. I'm the only one here."

At that point, I remove my cleated, steel-toed boot from my mouth. I can't say that Clingingsmith didn't warn me.

I   I

Diesel servicing facility, Glendive: Day shift foreman Kent White greets me and gives me a head-to-toe safety equipment inspection. "You're ready to go off to combat, soldier, but you'll need earplugs and an escort." After an introduction to hostler John Morgan, I'm off and shooting.

Work at the terminal is feast or famine. The two-track diesel servicing facility in Glendive is the locomotive equivalent to an automobile's Jiffy Lube, as no major work is performed. Between here and the roundhouse or rebuild center, preventive maintenance reigns supreme.

The list of duties here is endless: top off fluids and sand, inspect brakes and wheels, make sure the cabs are stocked, clean toilets, and so on. Glendive diesel crews keep the freight and the coal pipeline flowing.

At times when no locomotives await service, rereading yesterday's newspaper makes a "foreigner" with a camera mildly interesting.

Then, out of nowhere, stress levels rise as eight power sets and 30-plus locomotives line up for inspection, servicing, and stocking—no matter the hour, no matter the day. More evidence that railroading knows no holidays.

Here's a good time for me, without an escort, to make coffee and clean up the break room.

⚰ ⚰

Glendive roundhouse, Christmas Day: I thought at some point I'd come across symbols of Christmas on the railroad. At the Glendive roundhouse I expected to see a terminal office Christmas tree or two, baskets filled with holiday treats, maybe even a blow-up Santa Claus atop the depot. No such luck. Other than last night's grade crossing photo, featuring a streaking coal train reflecting the red and green colors, nothing much resembling Christmas appeared on the railroad.

Getting desperate, I contemplate snapping a shot of a photo card taped to a brick wall. A railroader dressed up as Santa smiles at the terrified child standing next to him. This could have been a worthwhile image, provided a fellow co-worker hadn't pressed red thumbtacks through "Santa's" eyes and scrawled, "Look what the railroad has done to you, fat ass! Merry Christmas!"

With little mechanical activity at the roundhouse, Christmas Day isn't business as usual, which results in not much to photograph. This is not a bad thing. After all, it is Christmas "for Christ's sake." So, I take advantage of an early lunch and enjoy the traditional Christmas roundhouse dinner. Escort John Morgan hands me a stale box of Triscuits and points me to a meat-and-cheese platter provided by BNSF. "Dig in. What kind of soda do you want? I'm buying," Morgan says.

Coming from a hostler who is making double-time-and-a-half, I'm truly touched. "Thanks, John, I'll have one of those employee-discounted, 50-cent Cokes."

Meanwhile, workers file into the break room, checking out the orange,

"The colors of Christmas." *Joel Jensen*

Scotchlite-adorned "pumpkin" man with cameras. My squeaky clean, head-to-toe safety attire provides a source for good-natured ribbing. "Dude, you don't have to wear your hard hat, safety glasses, or hearing protection in the break room—though you might want to keep your earplugs in around this crowd! Merry Christmas, bud!"

Every circus needs a clown. Today, I'm him.

⚰ ⚰

West of Glendive, Christmas Day afternoon: Being away from the round-house workers feels strange as I sit alone in my truck near Marsh siding, 19 miles west of Glendive. I'm waiting to take a photo of a backlit train, and my thoughts turn to the eastbound coal load and its crew in the siding. I recall the Glendive trainmen's never-ending, profanity-laced tirades about four- to six-hour delays at Marsh and Colgate sidings (7 miles west of Glendive). It might be just another day on the railroad to the crew parked at Marsh, but I doubt it. With some luck and favorable dispatching, the railroaders could hope that a Christmas family get-together would be possible. But if the Glendive yard is plugged up, the crew will endure the dreaded four- to six-hour wait. Their location is not close enough to home to smell the turkey, or whatever else

is cooking, though frustratingly close enough to imagine it.

Driving east to Wibaux, Mont., a Christmas Day "must" photo is on my agenda. Built in 1895, the historic St. Peter's Catholic Church offers the opportunity to capture and combine the elusive connection between the railroad and Christmas. All that's missing is a church that's actually open for business and a former Northern Pacific Railway Q-4 Pacific-powered *North Coast Limited* passenger train.

⚰ ⚰

Sully Springs, N.D., New Year's Eve Day: Just another day on the railroad unfolds on the main line east of Glendive, forcing on-call section workers, welders, maintenance crews, and machine operators from Glendive and Baker, Mont., and Beach, Dickinson, Glen Ullin, and Mandan, N.D., into holiday action. A derailment of a single boxcar the night before has forced a 24-plus-hour closure of the near-capacity, single-track line. Holiday headaches occur across the entire Montana Division. To further complicate matters, a derailment on the former Great Northern Hi-Line has resulted in the rerouting of a number of time-sensitive container trains over the former Northern Pacific "Main Street of the Northwest"

"All that's missing is a church that's open for business." *Joel Jensen*

route. While I was photographing a crew replacing concrete tie clips, Troy Brewer came to mind. He must have figured a holiday derailment was in the works with one set of defective air brakes, wheels locking up (9- to 12-inch flat spots), and 2.5 miles of torn-up concrete ties, clips, and rail damage. Happy New Year, Troy.

Later that afternoon, with slow orders in place at Sully Springs, the tracks reopen. The opportunity to photograph train after train presents itself as the weather takes a North Dakota wintertime turn. Out of nowhere, mostly clear skies give way to a Great Plains blizzard. I guess I should have been more careful about what I wished for.

As I work my way back to Glendive, showcasing wintertime North Dakota railroading becomes more challenging. A gravel road south of Sentinel Butte offers more snowdrift than my truck can handle. Do I have a shovel? A cell phone? Of course not.

An hour or so passes before a couple of 70-something local gentlemen stop to help. It's just another day to them. They're more interested in my Nevada plates than my predicament.

"Las Vegas?" one of them says. "What the hell brings you way out yonder?"

"No, Ely," I reply.

Oblivious to the snow and 40 mph winds, the other man says, "My son moved to Vegas for drywall work. He's

been real disappointed about everything there, including the lack of work."

Knowing that my salvation is dependent on back-road conversation and the chain in the back of their pickup, I go with the flow. I patiently answer questions like, "Did you get to see that tiger tear up that magician?"

A half hour later, I'm back on Interstate 94, regretting that the best shot of the trip wasn't recorded: two old men, probably homesteader descendants, attaching a chain from their beat-up Chevy to mine, unmindful of the blizzard and completely absorbed in the work at hand, gloves not included.

West of Beach, I test side roads one more time, hoping to atone for photographs lost due to my truck's Sentinel Butte "derailment." I position my truck on a main line paralleling the BNSF service road. The view down the tracks portrays little other than windswept snow, diffusing Great Plains nothingness. Eventually, ditch lights and not much else appear to the east. Bad light, no scenery, and a world without color: There's no beautiful railroad calendar photo here. Perfect. North Dakota railroading for what it is on New Year's Eve or any other winter day.

⚲ ⚲

Utility job, Glendive yard: Due to a scheduling conflict, my ride-along with the afternoon Glendive utility crew won't

occur on New Year's Day as planned. Although I am disappointed, utility engineer Barry Green laughs as he reminds me of the point of my trip. "Joel, January 1 or 3, it's just another day on the railroad, right?" Right.

Former Burlington Northern and now BNSF 32-year veteran Green and second-year utility man, Heath Werner, are in charge of powering up trains. The two do other switch-related work, but tonight their work revolves around transferring locomotive sets from the diesel shop's ready tracks to their respective trains. Green is quiet and all business as he's surrounded by claustrophobic caverns of unit coal car consists. Green's time in a locomotive, throttle in hand, borders on a religious experience. Werner and I discuss quietly Werner's recent purchase of a long abandoned, Homestead-era, one-room schoolhouse. We said nothing about General Electric vs. EMD, BNSF paint schemes, or AC vs. DC Like most railroaders in Glendive, or anywhere else, it's just a job.

By 7 p.m. break time, crews completed several transfer moves, resulting in three westbound empty coal trains being powered up and ready to go. Carry-all driver Greg Dolch returns us to the depot.

Werner eats his brown-bag dinner and chats with fellow railroaders, while Green retreats to an office computer. No break for Green (there never is); he has off-the-clock railroad work to do, above and beyond the call of duty. Down south in Fort Worth, Texas, management is either frowning, scratching their heads, or smiling. Railroading to Green isn't just a job. It is a way of life.

⚲ ⚲

Last night, Glendive: Sacked out on Clingingsmith's La-Z-Boy recliner, I finally enjoy my holiday. I'm relaxing in front of his wall-to-wall flat screen TV, featuring the Oklahoma Sooners vs. Miami Hurricanes college championship football game. "What in the hell do you see in Glendive?" Keith asks.

Realizing that my feet are cold, I reply, "I don't really know, Keith. Hey, while you're up, can you kick the thermostat up a notch or two, and grab me another beer?"

"Sure. No problem."